Security Intelligence in the Age of AI

Security Intelligence in the Age of AI: Navigating Legal and Ethical Frameworks

EDITED BY

PUSHAN KUMAR DUTTA
Amity University, India

BHUPINDER SINGH
Sharda University, India

CHRISTIAN KAUNERT
Dublin City University, Ireland
University of South Wales, UK

AND

ANNITA LARISSA SCIACOVELLI
University of Bari Aldo Moro, Italy

emerald PUBLISHING

United Kingdom – North America – Japan – India – Malaysia – China

About the Book

Security Intelligence in the Age of AI: Navigating Legal and Ethical Frameworks is an edited volume exploring how artificial intelligence (AI) may be increasingly integrated into security intelligence practices, as well as the new, unforeseen problems this presents. With the ever-evolving AI technologies, hackers are finding new opportunities through this technology to engage in clever ways of breaching networks. But this rapid advancement also highlights substantial legal and ethical considerations that need to be managed cautiously in order to achieve responsible use. In this book, leading academics, practitioners and policy experts provide valuable insight across a range of AI security matters for building fairer and stronger future societies. These include the need for transparency in AI systems, bias reduction strategies and fairness analysis in algorithmic decision-making. Thematic Focus: Methodologies of surveillance and data processing in the framework for longitudinal research with an interdisciplinary perspective experience AI processes that are predictive rather than prescriptive. The broader review roundtable finally discusses AI and its implications on human rights and national securities balancing between security measures and civil liberties.

The volume also examines the policy environment that impacts AI and national security, canvassing existing authorities and where those gaps might work. The contributors offer timely perspectives on various challenges of international governance, with a focus on military AI and dual-use technologies. This text includes number of important teachings for practitioners that are drawn from several legal and ethical conundrums affecting current AI security ventures by utilising case studies. Developed to provide security managers, policymakers and academics with an authoritative but practical manual on AI in the best tradition of informative handbooks. The array of viewpoints provided by these chapters allow the reader to gain a more complete view of how best to approach these inter connections between technology, law and ethics in the field of security intelligence. In the end, *Security Intelligence in the Age of AI* stands as an important asset for anyone looking to utilise AI in a way that respects security frameworks. The necessity of working together on behalf of all stakeholders to develop a strong do no harm for the future age relying more heavily on legal mores to set out an ethics-based guideline book in this ever-more-digital world. Tackling these pressing challenges, this volume will extend our understanding of how society can reap the benefits from technological advances without compromising the basic rights and values.

Chapter 1

Can the Red Cross Redefine the Battlefield? Examining the ICRC's Influence on Autonomous Weapon Systems in International Humanitarian Law

Akash Bag[a], *Anwesha Ghosh*[b] *and Tejaswini Tripathy*[c]

[a]Adamas University, India
[b]Amity University, India
[c]National Law University Odisha, India

Abstract

Evaluating the ethical recommendations on artificial intelligence (AI) adopted by UNESCO member states during the 2021 general conference reveals significant insights into integrating historically disadvantaged groups within human rights and AI governance. The paper utilises a dual methodological approach: This analysis describes the aims and objectives of the UNESCO recommendations and examines their practical consequences and accessibility. At the heart of this examination lies the belief that the recommendations support an open universalism based on the inherent ethic of human rights. This method reflects postcolonial theories that emphasise enduring differences in representation and authority among global groups. The study examines how AI participants shape a system often favouring Eurocentric standards and values while affecting AI technology direction and growth. The research shows that even if the proposals endorse universal rights frameworks in AI technology, they clearly emphasise aiding the least developed countries with education and technology. Facilitating this educational outreach is the responsibility of the most advanced countries. Analysis showcases major deficiencies within the recommendations that do not address the needs and desires of communities that reject AI implementation. In addition, the previous supremacy of 'whiteness' in AI technology creates a constant barrier to genuine inclusion in AI governance and moral standards.

Security Intelligence in the Age of AI, 1–21

doi:10.1108/978-1-83608-156-220251001

Keywords: Artificial intelligence ethics; UNESCO recommendations; post-colonial theory; human rights; technological equity; critical idea analysis

Introduction

Autonomous weapon systems (AWSs) have become essential in discussions concerning international humanitarian law (IHL) because they can decide in combat without human oversight. Many issues centre on whether these systems follow essential principles of IHL regarding human control and responsibility in decisions leading to human loss (Asaro, 2012). Ethical discussions point out the dangers of violating human dignity and ethical values during conflicts, resulting in some pushing for a total prohibition on AWS (Sparrow, 2007). Regulatory discussions receive great support from the International Committee of the Red Cross (ICRC) as it examines ways to restrict the use of AWS from coinciding with IHL standards (Ivanov et al., 2021). The conversations investigate how AWS could restructure global regulations and challenge its credibility (Bode & Huelss, 2018). The focus is on the principle of distinction as a critical element of IHL that ranks combatants and civilians sharply apart (ICRC, 2023). This principle highlights the necessity to protect ethical norms in designing and implementing AWS (Rosert & Sauer, 2019). Furthermore, the term 'meaningful human control' about AWS has taken centre stage to forestall the occurrence of IHL violations through appropriate governance structures (Bode, 2023). Current laws are being reshaped to meet the unique challenges introduced by AWS, and they are being transformed into valuable suggestions for engineers and policymakers (Letendre, 2016).

The legal dialogue assesses how current IHL applies to conflicts, including advanced artificial intelligence (AI) technologies in AWS (Belikova & Akhmadova, 2021). The quick progress and future deployment of AWS by significant powers create a pressing need for defined international regulations and pacts to manage its implementation (Wyatt, 2020). The complex relationship among technology growth, ethics and existing laws urges the need for firm regulations to enforce the development and use of these systems in line with global humanitarian principles. The use of AWS in military strategies signals an essential change in current combat methods. To uphold humanitarian principles, these systems require adherence to the rules established by IHL (Szpak, 2020). Illustrating ongoing legal discussions and worldwide forums intends to confront likely difficulties with critical ideas such as distinction and proportionality that could lead some AWS applications to conflict with international regulations. It analyses the importance of establishing the latest legal instruments to oversee fully self-governing weapons (Maskun & Ramli, 2018) and the developing connection between troops and these modernly autonomous platforms (McFarland, 2015). This signals an essential challenge for a complete analysis and monitoring to verify that AWS aligns with recognised legal structures and observes the norms of IHL.

In ongoing debates about AWS legality, worldwide stakeholders, including the United Nations and the EU, express considerable worry. A key topic in these talks involves settling the conflicts surrounding AWS and their consequence for IHL (Shaw, 2003). In these discussions, the ICRC holds a key position influenced by the Geneva Conventions. The ICRC's perspective on AWS, particularly outlined in their May 2021 position, accentuates their critical role as a steward of IHL. The ICRC's historical responsibility to oversee the implementation of the Geneva Conventions emphasises the significance of their input and positions their recommendations as the cornerstone for ongoing discussion. The ICRC's position on AWS is used as the basic framework for analysis in this piece, which acknowledges that although IHL is still the major emphasis, other humanitarian laws and the laws of war initiation (*jus ad bellum*) will not be covered. The discourse will also exclude a detailed examination of the impacts of specific customary rules and treaty laws.

Furthermore, the discussion on AWS will be considered relevant across various forms of conflicts, both international and non-international, as governed by customary law. However, the application of AWS in specific types of conflicts, such as naval engagements, will not be addressed. Throughout the paper, the term 'IHL' will be consistently used to denote what may also be referred to as the Law of Armed Conflict or *jus in Bello*, while the use of the term 'AWS' will be prevalent, with 'Lethal Autonomous Weapon Systems' (LAWSs) used interchangeably where necessary. This approach ensures clarity and maintains the focus on the legal dimensions and implications of AWS deployment in contemporary conflict scenarios (Gunawan et al., 2022). In IHL, there needs to be an agreed methodical framework. Unlike national legal systems that operate within a hierarchical structure, international law functions horizontally, where no single source holds absolute authority, except for *jus cogens* norms, which are peremptory and overriding (Cassese, 2005). Further, this approach reflects the nature of international law, where court decisions and scholarly opinions serve primarily as interpretive aids rather than direct sources of law, contrasting with their often more substantive role in national legal contexts (Zimmermann et al., 2019, Article 38).

Therefore, the interpretation and application of international law rely heavily on the Vienna Convention on the Law of Treaties (1969), which mandates that treaties be interpreted in 'good faith'. In this landscape, the International Court of Justice (ICJ) statutes stand out as a recognised source that introduces a hierarchy within IHL. However, the significance of customary international law must be balanced. Customary law emerges from consistent state practice accompanied by a belief in its legal obligation (*opinio juris*) (Sinclair, 1984, Article 31–32). A key issue in addressing AWS within the framework of IHL arises from the absence of direct regulation by either treaty or established customary law (Henckaerts, 2005). This lack of clear legal guidance poses significant methodological challenges in defining AWS legally and weighing diverse scholarly opinions across multiple academic disciplines. The paucity of publicly available information and restriction to accessible data on military technology further complicates this analysis by imposing an inherent limit on the depth of analysis and the scope of conclusions significantly between nations (Taddeo & Blanchard, 2022). This lack of uniform understanding accentuates the need for more straightforward guidelines, suggesting that the ICRC's call for more stringent control measures is relevant and justified.

Current State of IHL

General Laws of Prohibition and Targeting Law

Within IHL, certain rules explicitly prohibit or regulate the use of specific weapons (Turns, 2006). While it's clear that some types of AWS and LAWS might fall under these regulated categories, applying these rules is not uniformly applicable to all AWS. This ambiguity underscores the necessity for a deeper understanding and clarification of existing IHL norms, particularly because no specific prohibitions are tailored to AWS and LAWS. The reliance on general provisions, such as those banning weapons that cannot distinguish between combatants and civilians, becomes essential (International Committee of the Red Cross, 1949; Bassiouni, 2001, Article 51 (4)). Such indiscriminate weapons are prohibited, alongside those causing superfluous injury or unnecessary suffering (Horvitz & Nehs, 2011). The applicability of AWS varies by context; for example, in naval warfare, the requirement for distinction may pose less of a challenge. Naval AWS needs to identify valid military targets from a distance, a task complicated by the potential for misidentifying the signatures of ships, which could result in targeting protected vessels (McFarland, 2020). This issue of misidentification is not exclusive to AWS; human operators are equally prone to such errors. However, the legal framework for addressing these mistakes by AWS remains unsettled, complicating their use and likely prompting future legal clarifications as these technologies are increasingly implemented (Doswald-Beck, 1995).

The laws of targeting, a core section of IHL, govern the conduct of attacks, specifying who or what may be legally targeted. This section is founded on four basic principles: military necessity, distinction, proportionality and humanity, all of which have a well-established history within IHL and apply to all conflict parties, regardless of their role as aggressors or defenders (Boothby, 2016). While these rules are universally binding, individual states may be subject to additional treaty obligations that further restrict the types of weapons and methods of warfare they can lawfully employ (Army, 1956; International Committee of the Red Cross, 1949). Historically, the concept of military necessity was defined as early as 1861 in the Lieber Code, which allowed only those measures 'lawful according to the modern law and usages of war (Lieber, 1863)' (Yale Law School, 1863, Article 15).

Distinction and Proportionality in Armed Conflict-Distinction

As military technologies have evolved and battlefields have expanded beyond well-defined zones to broader, more indeterminate areas, clear rules of distinction have become paramount (Boothby, 2016). The most definitive codification of these rules is encapsulated in Additional Protocol I (API) to the Geneva Conventions, mainly Article 48 can be found under the section for 'Basic Rules', which underlines the obligation of parties to a conflict to always differentiate between civilians and combatants, and between civilian objects and military objectives, directing operations solely against the latter (Kalshoven, 1978). Despite not being universally ratified, significant portions of API are recognised as customary law, thus binding all conflict participants (Boothby, 2016). The ICJ has reinforced that the principles of distinction are 'fundamental and intransgressible principles of law (ICJ, 1996)'. The ICJ clarifies that lacking the immediate means to comply with these principles does not justify indiscriminate attacks; rather, it obliges states to abstain from such actions. The application of this principle will necessarily vary depending on the available weaponry, intelligence and other pertinent information that could influence the decision-making process regarding an attack.

To give effect to the principles of IHL, particularly those concerning civilian protection, a clear definition of 'civilian' is essential. The API provides this definition in a way that broadly includes any person not classified under specific categories of combatants detailed in Articles 4A and 43 of the Geneva Conventions and the API itself (International Committee of the Red Cross, 1949; Bassiouni, 2001, Article 50(1)). This negative definition, which essentially categorises individuals as civilians unless proven otherwise, aims to minimise civilian casualties in conflict – a fundamental goal of IHL (Boothby, 2016). The distinction between combatants and civilians is further elaborated in Articles 43 and 44 of the API. Article 43 states that 'The armed forces of a party to a conflict consist of all organised armed forces, groups, and units which are under a command responsible to that party for the conduct of its subordinates, even if that party is represented by a government or an authority not recognised by an adverse party. Such armed forces shall be subject to an internal disciplinary system which, among other things, shall enforce compliance with the rules of international law applicable in armed conflict (International Committee of the Red Cross, 1949)' (Bassiouni, 2001, Article 43). The protocol modifies previous narrower definitions, like those in the Hague Regulations, by emphasising the need for armed forces to display a 'distinctive sign and to carry arms openly', adding a layer of transparency to combat operations (Boothby, 2016).

Moreover, the API commentary notes the flexibility in the term 'organised', suggesting that it encompasses groups collaborating under established command and rules rather than mere ad hoc cooperation (Boothby, 2016). Article 44 (3) addresses the obligations of combatants to distinguish themselves from civilians during attacks or preparations for attacks. This provision reflects a practical recognition of the complexities of modern armed conflicts, where traditional norms of combat visibility are not always possible but where the necessity for some form of distinction remains critical. The distinction between civilians and combatants, as elaborated in Articles 43 and 44 of the API, is crucial for enhancing civilian protection in conflict zones. These articles require combatants to carry arms openly to be recognised as such, a measure that significantly contributes to safeguarding civilians residing in or near war zones. Despite their value as interpretive tools for understanding the rules of distinction, these parts of the API are contentious and subject to reservations by some ratifying states, affecting the application of these rules and their recognition as customary law. Notably, the UK has reservations about Article 44(3), and the US has not ratified the API, explicitly rejecting Articles 43 and 44, citing concerns over the expanded definitions of prisoners of war and combatants as major obstacles (Boothby, 2016).

These objections, however, do not detract from the utility of these articles as guidelines for this analysis. Under API Article 50, the protocol clearly states that individuals should be considered civilians in cases of doubt, reinforcing the principle of protection (Bassiouni, 2001, Article 50; Bothe, 2013; International Committee of the Red Cross, 1949). This approach contrasts with earlier IHL frameworks, which, due to the more straightforward nature of traditional warfare, found it easier to distinguish between combatants and civilians (Boothby, 2016). The complexities of modern conflict, where the lines between combatant and civilian statuses are increasingly blurred, stress the importance of adhering to strict rules against indiscriminate attacks (Boothby, 2016). These challenges highlight the necessity for rigorous adherence to IHL in contemporary armed conflicts, ensuring that the principles of distinction and protection of civilians remain a priority.

Proportionality

The principle of IHL insists that a fine line between military strength and civilian suffering must stay unchanged. The idea that underlies IHL influences how force is applied and insists that attacks take premeditated measures rather than respond afterwards to their effects (Saul & Akande, 2020). Understanding this principle divides the discussion into the need for a prior evaluation of anticipated outcomes and the frequent confusion that regards proportionality as a simple ratio of harm to advantage (Dinstein, 2004; Saul & Akande, 2020). Explaining proportionality in military applications works better when the idea is organised into two distinct parts. Proportionality must be assessed through the expected outcomes of an attack, consisting of military advancement and the risk to civilians (Parks, 1990). Second, the actual outcome of the attack, whether it results in more or less damage than anticipated, should not influence this initial judgement. Essentially, the legality of an attack is evaluated based on the information available before it takes place, not the results that follow.

Critically, proportionality must be evaluated with the information available during decision-making, prioritising the attacker's judgement on potential military gains against expected civilian losses, the necessity of the military action and other related factors (Boothby, 2016). When the outcome diverges significantly from expectations, causing unforeseen civilian harm with minimal military benefit, subsequent evaluations must revert to the original anticipatory understanding (Saul & Akande, 2020).

Underlining the Issues of Unnecessary Suffering as a Part of the Proportionality of Harm

Central to these considerations is the prohibition of unnecessary suffering and superfluous injury, a doctrine extending from combatants to civilians, underscoring the principle that it is typically sufficient to incapacitate rather than annihilate the adversary (Dinstein, 2004; International Committee of the Red Cross, 1949). The evolution of this principle is further illustrated in the variance between the original and modified translations of the Hague Regulation 23 (e), highlighting the linguistic and interpretative shifts that influence the application of these rules (Dinstein, 2004; McFarland, 2020) (US Government, 1999, Article 23 (e)). The broader implications of these linguistic nuances for AWS reveal the ongoing relevance and challenges of translating historical humanitarian principles into guidelines that govern modern technological warfare (Boothby, 2016). The continuous dialogue between historical tenets and contemporary interpretations within IHL underscores a dynamic legal framework striving to reconcile the exigencies of military tactics with the imperatives of human dignity.

Military Necessity and the Martens Clause

Initially intended as a preamble to the Hague Convention of 1899, the Martens Clause now crucially shapes IHL beyond its initial meaning (Mero, 2000). By being part of later international pacts like the Hague Convention of 1907 and the Geneva Conventions of 1949, the clause reveals its lasting relevance and the same manner of its enforcement across diverse laws (Pustogarov, 1999). In situations not mentioned in the protocol or other agreements, under API Article 1(2), individuals receive protection thanks to the customs of humanity and conscience (International Committee of the Red Cross, 1949; McFarland, 2020). Due to its widespread and flexible wording, the clause is especially suited for novel technologies like AWSs. It creates a malleable legal structure to fit changing military advancements and techniques. Although recognised as traditional law, the application of the Martens Clause is diverse and subject to interpretation, especially regarding new technological developments in warfare such as AWS (Mero, 2000). The changeability of the clause is highlighted by its incorporation into several pacts that demonstrate our current perspectives on 'the tenets of humanity' tied to the particular setting and moment. Due to the vague wording and expansive nature of the clause's ideas, it brings forth analysis hurdles in diverse legal and educational systems.

Legal Status and Interpretations of AWS

While entrenched in customary international law, the Martens Clause presents two distinct interpretative approaches that significantly influence its application within IHL (Ticehurst, 1997). The narrow interpretation construes the clause as an extension of customary international law that remains applicable post-treaty

guidance shows a thoughtful but forward-thinking framework for incorporating AWS into military activities. It supports the design of a model that confirms these systems can uphold essential IHL guidelines such as distinction and proportionality. This research highlights a crucial joint between technology, ethical considerations and legal frameworks, demanding persistent assessment to harmonise military progress and humanitarian needs (Mizokami, 2020; Pandya, 2019).

Military Necessities, Challenges and Responsibility Conundrum

The intertwining of humanitarian considerations with the intrinsic military objectives within IHL elucidates a profound commitment to moderating the harsh realities of armed conflict. Informed notably by historical precedents such as the St. Petersburg Declaration of 1868, which asserts the necessity for warfare to accommodate the imperatives of humanity UNHRC (1869), the dual forces of military necessity and humanitarian concerns coalesce to frame the legal and ethical landscape of contemporary warfare as described by Dinstein (Dinstein, 2004). This duality is manifest in the foundational principles of IHL, aiming not only to dictate the conduct of war but also to alleviate its calamities (UNHRC, 1869). The concept of military necessity and its application to AWS under IHL is a vital yet complex area of contemporary legal discourse. Military necessity requires that force employment must be essential for achieving a legitimate military objective, balanced against the overarching principles of proportionality and distinction. The absence of explicit guidance within ICRC recommendations regarding military necessity raises essential considerations concerning AWS deployment's lawfulness and ethical implications.

However, the counterpoint is also noted, where the significant military advantage provided by AWS might justify their use, akin to the debated status of nuclear weapons under customary international law for states, not a party to specific treaties banning their use (Burroughs, 1998). The discussion extends to the nature of AWS and its operational characteristics. Contrary to concerns that AWS may inherently tend towards indiscriminate effects, current deployment primarily enhances combatant capabilities and precision in missile systems, suggesting a non-indiscriminate nature. Thus, each AWS must be evaluated on a case-by-case basis, considering specific system capabilities and the context of use to ensure compliance with the principles of military necessity, proportionality and distinction mandated by IHL (Boothby, 2016).

Discussion

The evolving concept of machine autonomy in AWS is fundamentally intertwined with the advancements in processing power and computer technology over recent decades. This progress has enabled AWS to perform tasks and operations independently, without human intervention post-activation, which is central to their definition of autonomy (McFarland, 2015). This capability allows AWS to operate in real-world environments for extended periods without human supervision, raising critical questions about the necessary degree of human involvement to ensure lawful and ethical use (McFarland, 2015). The ICRC has emphasised the importance of adequate human supervision, timely intervention and deactivation of AWS to maintain control and compliance with IHL (International Committee of the Red Cross, 1949). However, there is no specific guidance on what constitutes 'effective' human oversight, leading to varied interpretations and implementations by different states and military organisations (Ticehurst, 1997). Despite the absence of explicit requirements in the current IHL for human involvement, there is a consensus among nation-states and major military and non-governmental organisations that some level of human interaction is essential. This consensus has emerged as a customary norm, shaping the interpretation and application of IHL in the context of AWS.

The interplay between human omission and the autonomy of weapon systems is portrayed by incidents such as the Patriot missile system malfunction, where, despite manual control, a fatal error occurred due to the system's misidentification of a friendly aircraft as a hostile target (McFarland, 2015). This incident underscores that human involvement does not inherently guarantee the safety of AWS. In contrast, situations exist where the delay caused by human decision-making could compromise the effectiveness of military responses, indicating a nuanced balance must be struck between machine autonomy and human oversight. The debate on the definition and classification of AWS is further complicated by examples such as landmines, which, under a strict interpretation, might be considered autonomous due to their ability to engage targets without ongoing human intervention. The classification of landmines as AWS and the broader implications of their use underscores the complexities of autonomous systems in warfare, where the ability to differentiate between combatants and civilians is crucial.

The shift of the debate about AWS distils military interaction from a warfare perspective, displacing old conceptions of military involvement and the relationship between human supervision and mechanised action during the current IHL. The extension of AWS to landmines suggests the dynamics of the minimum amount of independence required for a weapon system to be considered as such under IHL, even though there is general non-acceptance of such categorisation. This example demonstrates why it is crucial to identify the degree of 'meaningful control' required before instantiation and underlines the 'unknowable' nature and the legal implications of such systems (Micheli, 2020). The matter continued to concrete concerns of targeting processes and contrast human soldiers and AWS. Human combatants are experienced combatants who are programmed within the legal and ethical standards of ROE/IHL; their reaction patterns within those standards can, therefore, be considered generally predictable. Compared to AWS, SAP HANA uses algorithms where complicated decisions are made in straightforward and clear choices in black and white by programming and sampling. Since systems that do not incorporate human fluidity cannot adapt to situations they have not been trained for, their behaviour, when in operation, may vary (BBC, 2023; Kallenborn, 2021; Richemond-Barak & Feinberg, 2015). Also, a relative comparison of highly developed systems like Israel's Iron Dome underlines the AWS benefits in those applications where an instantaneous response and overshooting accuracy are crucial, like in missile defence applications (Richemond-Barak & Feinberg, 2015). As with the earlier examples, these systems prove that AWS can perform beyond human skills in a particular setting with a well-defined task and few uncontrolled variables like those found in naval battles (Bistron & Piotrowski, 2021). While it provides more of the technical and operational aspects of AWS, it also covers the ethical and juridical questions concerning the usage of AWS.

When IHL is adopted, the outlooks regarding the regulation of AWS trigger crucial questions linked to the foreseeability and morality of such technologies. The ICRC has also recommended the complete prohibition of any AWS that functions unpredictably, as IHL already bans weapons with non-distinctive impact (International Committee of the Red Cross, 1949). This proposal highlights the need to provide sufficient capacity to understand, predict and explain the effects when applying AWS to meet the principles of distinction and the requirement to do everything possible to assess the lawfulness of an attack (International Committee of the Red Cross, 1949 Article 57 (2)). Furthermore, the ICRC underlines ethical reasons to ban the use of AWS to target human beings, pointing at the prohibition that is not reflected in current IHL rules but might be compared with the Biological Weapons Convention (International Committee of the Red Cross, 1949). This convention clearly demonstrates how AWS used to deliver or use prohibited weapons would violate IHL, further supporting the finding that AWS should abide by the existing legal instruments regarding weapon prohibitions. The discussions on how AWS should be regulated within IHL are laden with many factors regarding the need for and the extent to which potential legal frameworks are needed. CCW discussions, the EU and nations such as France, Germany and Sweden demonstrate the general but split concern with strict regulation and even prohibition of AWS and LAWS. However, these discussions have not yet coalesced into support for initiating negotiations towards a legally binding framework, as evidenced by the ongoing deliberations and the European Commission's recent AI Act proposal, which notably exempts military applications of AI from its scope (Dahlmann, 2019; Warehem, 2023). The ICRC has proposed several specific regulatory measures, including limiting AWS to engage only military objectives by nature. Current IHL does not explicitly restrict AWS to such targets, indicating a gap between ICRC recommendations and existing legal obligations (International Committee of the Red Cross, 1949).

Moreover, although US Navy officials express cautious reliance on automated systems, no comprehensive legal restriction aligns with the ICRC's vision, suggesting that any existing limitations are more a product of operational prudence rather than regulatory mandates (Larter, 2022). Regarding the operational use of AWS, including drones, limitations often relate to technological constraints rather than explicit legal prohibitions. These include range, duration and geographical scope of operations, which indirectly enforce a degree of human oversight by necessity (International Committee of the Red Cross, 1949; McFarland, 2015; Pilkington, 2015). The ICRC's suggestion to formally incorporate human judgement and control for specific attacks highlights a consensus among nations on maintaining some level of human oversight over AWS. This approach aligns with a general understanding within IHL that weapon systems should involve 'broader human involvement'. However, it stops short of demanding direct human control for each operation (Pilkington, 2015).

The current discussion on AWS pivots on stringent constraints proposed to mitigate their operational contexts, specifically excluding scenarios where civilians or civilian objects might be present. This reflects a deliberate progression beyond existing IHL, which traditionally permits military actions where proportional advantages justify operational risks. The ICRC advocates for a restrictive application of AWS, emphasising a zero-tolerance approach to civilian endangerment, which, although aligned with humanitarian principles, may render AWS operationally ineffectual in conventional warfare contexts. Similarly, emerging consensuses underscore the indispensability of human oversight in AWS deployment. Despite not being mandated by IHL, the trajectory of state practices and declarations might herald the evolution of these norms into customary law, reinforcing the call for human-machine interaction to ensure control and accountability in utilising AWS. This analysis scrutinises the implications of such restrictions and the realistic intersection of ethical imperatives with practical warfare strategy (International Committee of the Red Cross, 1949).

Conclusion

The evolution of autonomous weaponry traces its roots to early experiments with pilotless aircraft during World War I, signalling the commencement of a century-long journey towards increasingly sophisticated unmanned systems (BBC, 2022). With the Vietnam War, the deployment of unmanned drones extended beyond combat roles, encapsulating propaganda dissemination (Axe, 2021). The turn of the 21st century marked a significant proliferation in drone usage, particularly highlighted by their operational roles in Middle East conflicts, drawing both extensive media coverage and public scrutiny (Johnston & Sarbahi, 2016). Criticism from human rights organisations such as Human Rights Watch has emphasised autonomous drones' ethical and legal implications (Rudolf, 2014). Nonetheless, the trajectory of drone development continues towards greater autonomy, especially within naval operations where autonomous systems are extensively integrated (Dinstein, 2004).

The accelerated adoption of AWS technology has prompted a definitive and strongly worded recommendation from the ICRC, marking a significant shift in their discourse on autonomous weapons (Copeland et al., 2022). The potential for drone swarms as a formidable military asset underscores this discourse, positing such technology as a cost-effective yet strategically advantageous tool (Kallenborn, 2020). Although the exact extent of development in autonomous drone technology remains ambiguous, civilian applications have already demonstrated the operational viability of drone swarms (Kallenborn, 2020). The economic appeal of drones is highlighted by their low operational costs relative to their potential military utility, exemplified by scenarios where inexpensive drone swarms could potentially neutralise high-value targets such as battleships at a fraction of the cost (Crane, 2014). Additionally, drones' compact size and radar evasion capabilities accentuate their strategic appeal (Coluccia et al., 2020). Recent conflicts, notably in Ukraine, have evidenced the effective use of modified civilian drones with inherent autonomous features for combat purposes, challenging the enforceability of bans in conflict zones and raising issues concerning dual-use technology and predictability (Axe, 2023; Borger, 2022; Corrigan, 2020). In response to such developments and the lessons drawn from contemporary warfare, Taiwan is reportedly intensifying its investment in drone capabilities, further reflecting a global trend towards integrating advanced autonomous technologies into military strategies (Al Jazeera, 2020; Chung, 2022).

AWS appears destined to become a fixture on future battlefields, with existing efforts to prohibit their use unlikely to achieve widespread support or success. Notwithstanding, there is an acknowledgement within the international community that AWS is already subject to certain restrictions under existing IHL, with consensus among military leaders and nations regarding the necessity of maintaining some human oversight in the deployment of such technologies (Larter, 2022). The ICRC has issued recommendations that might not alter AWS's legal landscape significantly within the framework of IHL. Yet, these recommendations could catalyse further discourse and potentially guide a gradual shift in customary law towards greater alignment with the ICRC's positions. While the immediate impact of the ICRC's suggestions may be limited, there is notable support among some nations for extending existing IHL constraints on the development and utilisation of AWS. Consequently, the ICRC's input will likely influence ongoing discussions and shape forthcoming regulatory efforts concerning autonomous military technologies.

References

Al Jazeera. (2020, November 4). United States approves $600m sale of armed drones to Taiwan. https://www.aljazeera.com/news/2020/11/4/united-states-approves-600m-sale-of-armed-drones-to-taiwan

Army, D. (1956). *The law of land warfare (FM 27-10)*. CreateSpace Independent Publishing Platform. https://irp.fas.org/doddir/army/fm27-10.pdf

Asaro, P. (2012). On banning autonomous weapon systems: Human rights, automation, and the dehumanization of lethal decision-making. *International Review of the Red Cross*, *94*(886), 687–709. https://doi.org/10.1017/s1816383112000768

Axe, D. (2021). *Drone war vietnam*. Pen and Sword Military.

Axe, D. (2022, March 18). The Russian army is running out of trucks for its war in Ukraine. *Forbes*. https://www.forbes.com/sites/davidaxe/2022/03/18/as-predicted-the-russian-army-is-running-out-of-trucks-for-its-war-in-ukraine/

Axe, D. (2023, July 10). Ukraine's $10,000 drones are dropping tiny bombs on Russian troops. *Forbes*. https://www.forbes.com/sites/davidaxe/2022/04/13/ukraines-10000-drones-are-dropping-tiny-cheap-bombs-on-russian-troops/

Bassiouni, M. C. (2001). Protocol additional to the Geneva Conventions of 12 August 1949, and relating to the protection of victims of non-international armed conflicts

D., Liivoja, R., & Sanders, L. (2022). The utility of weapons reviews in ng concerns raised by autonomous weapon systems. *Journal of Conflict and Law*, *28*(2), 285–316. https://doi.org/10.1093/jcsl/krac035

T. (2020, June 18). Africa's ICT infrastructure: Its present and prospects. *Commons*. https://policycommons.net/artifacts/1451480/africas-ict-icture/2083288/

(2014). Cultural globalization: 2001–10. *Semantic Scholar*. https://www.cscholar.org/paper/Cultural-globalization-:-2001-%E2%80%93-10-Crane/7650c9ed61025e081ad044f5c532f297d

, A. (2019). Towards a regulation of autonomous weapons – A task for the *ropean Leadership Network*. https://www.europeanleadershipnetwork.org/ntary/towards-a-regulation-of-autonomous-weapons-a-task-for-the-eu/

Y. (2004). *The conduct of hostilities under the law of international armed* Cambridge University Press.

B. (2023, March 28). Mind the gap. *Human Rights Watch*. https://www.g/report/2015/04/09/mind-gap/lack-accountability-killer-robots

Beck, L. (1995). The San Remo Manual on international law applicable to conflicts at sea. *American Journal of International Law*, *89*(1), 192–208. doi.org/10.2307/2203907

O., Durant, F. C., & Guilmartin, J. F. (2024, January 9). Rocket and system. *Encyclopædia Britannica*. https://www.britannica.com/technology/and-missile-system

Y., Aulawi, M. H., Anggriawan, R., & Putro, T. A. (2022). Command ibility of autonomous weapons under international humanitarian law. *Social Sciences*, *8*(1). https://doi.org/10.1080/23311886.2022.2139906

s, J.-M. (2005, March 5). ICRC study on customary rules of international tarian law. *ICRC*. https://www.icrc.org/en/doc/resources/documents/misc/.htm

. A., & Nehs, R. M. (2011). Proportionality and international humanitarian n economic analysis. *Global Change, Peace & Security*, *23*(2), 195–206. doi.org/10.1080/14781158.2011.580960

Rights Watch. (2023, February 16). Review of the 2023 US policy on my in weapons systems. https://www.hrw.org/news/2023/02/14/review-2023-cy-autonomy-weapons-systems

). Legality of the threat or use of nuclear weapons. *International Court of* . https://www.icj-cij.org/case/95

23, March). The principle of distinction. *International Committee of the Red* https://www.icrc.org/sites/default/files/wysiwyg/war-and-law/03_distinction-

nal Committee of the Red Cross. (1949). Protocols additional to the Geneva tions of 12 .... https://www.icrc.org/en/doc/assets/files/other/icrc_002_0321.

nal Committee of the Red Cross. (2021, February 26). ICRC position on mous weapon systems. https://www.icrc.org/en/document/icrc-position-mous-weapon-systems

(2022, April 6). New Russian land mine poses special risk in Ukraine. *The York Times*. https://www.nytimes.com/2022/04/06/us/politics/russia-ukraine-ines.html

(Protocol II), 16 I.L.M. 1442 (8 June 1977). In
conventions (1937-2001) (pp. 585–587). Bril
9789004478428_088
BBC, B. (2022, April 7). The inquiry, are drones
Service. https://www.bbc.co.uk/programmes/w3
BBC, B. (2023, November 6). What is Israel's iron
it work? *BBC News*. https://www.bbc.com/news
Belikova, K., & Akhmadova, M. (2021). Develop
legal regulation of the use of lethal autonomo
artificial intelligence. *Laplage em Revista*, 7(3C),
s2446-6220202173c
Bell, J. (2021). Toyota and the Taliban: How the
favorite | al arabiya English. *Alarabia News*.
world/2021/08/17/Toyota-and-the-Taliban-H
terrorist-favorite
Bistron, M., & Piotrowski, Z. (2021). Artificial in
systems and their influence on sense of security
https://doi.org/10.3390/electronics10070871
Bode, I. (2023). Practice-based and public-deliberat
control over the use of force. *European Journal o*
Bode, I., & Huelss, H. (2018). Autonomous weapo
international relations. *Review of International S*
Boothby, W. H. (2016). *Weapons and the law of*
Press.
Bothe, M. (2013). New rules for victims of armed c
1977 protocols additional to the Geneva Conver
Michael Bothe. In *New rules for victims of arme*
https://brill.com/display/title/60615
Borger, J. (2022, March 28). The drone operators w
for Kyiv. *The Guardian*. https://www.theguard
drone-operators-who-halted-the-russian-armoure
Burroughs, J. (1998). *The legality of threat or use o*
historic opinion of the International Court of Just
Casey-Maslen, S. (2015). *Weapons under internatio*
University Press.
Cassese, A. (2005). *International law*. Oxford Univ
Christie, E. H., Ertan, A., Adomaitis, L., & Klau
autonomous weapon systems: Exploring the c
traceability. *AI and Ethics*, 1–17. https://doi.org/1
Chung, L. (2022, April 3). Taiwan looks to develop
Ukraine lessons. *South China Morning Post*. ht
military/article/3172808/taiwan-looks-develop-mi
lessons
Coluccia, A., Parisi, G., & Fascista, A. (2020). Det
tirotor drones in radar sensor networks: A review
doi.org/10.3390/s20154172

Copeland
addres
Securi
Corrigan,
Policy
infrast
Crane, D
seman
d6dee
Dahlman
EU?
comm
Dinstein,
conflic
Docherty
hrw.o
Doswald-
armed
https:/
Fought,
missil
rocket
Gunawa
respo
Coge
Henckae
huma
5mxla
Horvitz,
law:
https:
Human
auton
us-po
ICJ. (19
Justic
ICRC. (
Cross
0.pdf
Internati
conv
pdf
Internati
auto
auto
Ismay, J
New
land-

Ivanov, D. V., Korzhenyak, A. M., & Lapikhina, E. S. (2021). Lethal autonomous weapons systems and international law. *Moscow Journal of International Law*, (3), Article 3. https://doi.org/10.24833/0869-0049-2021-3-6-19

Johnston, P. B., & Sarbahi, A. K. (2016). The impact of US drone strikes on terrorism in Pakistan. *International Studies Quarterly*, *60*(2), 203–219. https://doi.org/10.1093/isq/sqv004

Kallenborn, Z. (2020, October 14). A partial ban on autonomous weapons would make everyone safer. *Foreign Policy*. https://foreignpolicy.com/2020/10/14/ai-drones-swarms-killer-robots-partial-ban-on-autonomous-weapons-would-make-everyone-safer/

Kallenborn, Z. (2021, October 5). Applying arms-control frameworks to autonomous weapons. *Policy Commons*. https://policycommons.net/artifacts/4142898/applying-arms-control-frameworks-to-autonomous-weapons/4952115/

Kalshoven, F. (1978). Reaffirmation and development of international humanitarian law applicable in armed conflicts: The diplomatic conference, Geneva, 1974–1977. *Netherlands Yearbook of International Law*, *9*, 107. https://doi.org/10.1017/s0167676800003792

Khan, F. A., Li, G., Khan, A. N., Khan, Q. W., Hadjouni, M., & Elmannai, H. (2023). AI-driven counter-terrorism: Enhancing global security through advanced predictive analytics. *IEEE Access*, *11*, 135864–135879. https://doi.org/10.1109/access.2023.3336811

Klare, M. T. (2019). Autonomous weapons systems and the laws of war. *Autonomous Weapons Systems and the Laws of War | Arms Control Association*. https://www.armscontrol.org/act/2019-03/features/autonomous-weapons-systems-laws-war

Larter, D. (2022, August 19). The US Navy says it's doing its best to avoid a "Terminator" scenario in quest for autonomous weapons. *Defense News*. https://www.defensenews.com/digital-show-dailies/dsei/2019/09/12/the-us-navy-says-its-doing-its-best-to-avoid-a-terminator-scenario-in-its-quest-for-autonomous-weapons/

Letendre, L. (2016). Lethal autonomous weapon systems: Translating legal jargon for engineers. In *2016 International conference on unmanned aircraft systems (ICUAS)* (pp. 795–800). IEEE.

Lieber, F. (1863). Instructions for the government of armies of The United States in the Field. *Avalon Project - General Orders No. 100: The lieber code*. https://avalon.law.yale.edu/19th_century/lieber.asp#art15

Losey, S. (2021, July 14). Austin: AI is crucial for military, but commanders will pull the plug on misbehaving systems. *Military.com*. https://www.military.com/daily-news/2021/07/14/austin-ai-crucial-military-commanders-will-pull-plug-misbehaving-systems.html

Maskun, M., & Ramli, R. N. (2018). A new treaty for fully autonomous weapons: A need or a want? *Hasanuddin Law Review*, *4*(1), 54. https://doi.org/10.20956/halrev.v4i1.1300

McFarland, T. (2015). Factors shaping the legal implications of increasingly autonomous military systems. *International Review of the Red Cross*, *97*(900), 1313–1339. https://doi.org/10.1017/s1816383116000023

McFarland, T. (2020). Autonomous weapon systems and the law of armed conflict. *Cambridge Core*. https://www.cambridge.org/core/books/autonomous-weapon-systems-and-the-law-of-armed-conflict/09BFF6BB5B88E34935678B5A0606A8A7

Mero, T. (2000). The Martens Clause, principles of humanity, and dictates of public conscience. *American Journal of International Law*, *94*(1), 78–89. https://doi.org/10.2307/2555232

Micheli, V. (2020, December 23). Deep learning has (almost) all the answers: Yes/no question answering with Transformers. *Medium*. https://medium.com/illuin/deep-learning-has-almost-all-the-answers-yes-no-question-answering-with-transformers-223bebb70189

Mizokami, K. (2020). AI vs human fighter pilot dogfight: Simulated F-16 dogfight video. *Popular Mechanics*. https://www.popularmechanics.com/military/aviation/a33765952/ai-vs-human-fighter-pilot-simulated-dogfight-results/

Pandya, J. (2019, March 13). The dual-use dilemma of Artificial Intelligence. *Forbes*. https://www.forbes.com/sites/cognitiveworld/2019/01/07/the-dual-use-dilemma-of-artificial-intelligence/

Parks, W. H. (1990). Air war and the law of war. *The Air Force Law Review*, *32*, 171–174.

Pfanner, T. (2005). Asymmetrical warfare from the perspective of humanitarian law and humanitarian action. *International Review of the Red Cross*, *87*, 149–174.

Pilkington, E. (2015, November 19). Life as a drone operator: "Ever step on ants and never give it another thought?". *The Guardian*. https://www.theguardian.com/world/2015/nov/18/life-as-a-drone-pilot-creech-air-force-base-nevada

Pustogarov, V. (1999). The Martens Clause in international law. *Journal of the History of International Law*, *1*, 128–129.

Richemond-Barak, D., & Feinberg, A. (2015, November 4). The irony of the iron dome: Intelligent defense systems, law, and security. *SSRN*. https://papers.ssrn.com/abstract=2685858

Rosert, E., & Sauer, F. (2019). Prohibiting autonomous weapons: Put human dignity first. *Global Policy*, *10*, 373.

Rudolf, P. (2014). Killing by drones - The problematic practice of U.S. *German Institute for International and Security Affairs*. https://www.swp-berlin.org/assets/swp/Killing_by_Drones_-_The_Problematic_Practice_of_U.S._Drone_Warfare_-_Peter_Rudolf.pdf

Saul, B., & Akande, D. (2020). *The Oxford Guide to international humanitarian law*. Oxford University Press.

Schwarz, E. (2021). Autonomous weapons systems, artificial intelligence, and the problem of meaningful human control. *Philosophical Journal of Conflict and Violence*, *5*(1), 53–72. https://doi.org/10.22618/tp.pjcv.20215.1.139004

Seixas-Nunes, A. (2022). AWS and the IHL requirements (chapter 4) - The legality and accountability of autonomous weapon systems. *Cambridge Core*. https://www.cambridge.org/core/books/legality-and-accountability-of-autonomous-weapon-systems/aws-and-the-ihl-requirements/B0AA54BFB67711F7D178CE33D8589EB2

Sharkey, A. (2018). Autonomous weapons systems, killer robots and human dignity. *Ethics and Information Technology*, *21*(2), 75–87. https://doi.org/10.1007/s10676-018-9494-0

Shaw, M. N. (2003). *International law* (5th ed.). Cambridge University Press.

Sinclair, S. I. M. (1984). *The Vienna Convention on the Law of Treaties*. Manchester University Press.

Solis, G. D. (2010). The law of armed conflict. *Cambridge Core*. https://www.cambridge.org/core/books/law-of-armed-conflict/286ED6AD4C4164B473DF03E339F64A86

Sparrow, R. (2007). Killer robots. *Journal of Applied Philosophy*, *24*(1), 62–77. https://doi.org/10.1111/j.1468-5930.2007.00346.x

Staff, T. (2022, April 11). Russian tank blows up civilian car, kills elderly couple. https://www.tmz.com/2022/03/08/russian-tank-blows-up-civilian-car-kills-elderly-couple-ukraine/

Szpak, A. (2020). Legality of use and challenges of new technologies in warfare – The use of autonomous weapons in contemporary or future wars. *European Review*, *28*(1), 3.

Taddeo, M., & Blanchard, A. (2022). A comparative analysis of the definitions of autonomous weapons systems. *Science and Engineering Ethics*, *28*. https://doi.org/10.1007/s11948-022-00392-3

Ticehurst, R. (1997). The Martens Clause and the laws of armed conflict. *International Review of the Red Cross*, *37*(317), 125–134. https://doi.org/10.1017/s002086040008503x

Turns, D. (2006). Weapons in the ICRC study on customary international humanitarian law. *Journal of Conflict and Security Law*, *11*(2), 201–237. https://doi.org/10.1093/jcsl/krl010

UNHRC. (1869). *Saint Petersburg Declaration - Declaration Renouncing the Use, in Time of War, of Explosive Projectiles Under 400 Grammes Weight*. University of London Press.

UNHRC. (1997). *Convention on the prohibition of the use, stockpiling, production and transfer of anti-personnel mines and on their destruction*. UN.

Wareham, M. (2023, March 28). Stopping killer robots. *Human Rights Watch*. https://www.hrw.org/report/2020/08/10/stopping-killer-robots/country-positions-banning-fully-autonomous-weapons-and

Warehem, M. (2023, March 6). Statement to convention on conventional weapons GGE meeting on lethal autonomous weapons system. *Human Rights Watch*. https://www.hrw.org/news/2023/03/06/statement-convention-conventional-weapons-gge-meeting-lethal-autonomous-weapons

Wyatt, A. (2020). Charting great power progress toward a lethal autonomous weapon system demonstration point. *Defence Studies*, *20*(1), 1–20. https://doi.org/10.1080/14702436.2019.1698956

Zimmermann, A., Tams, C. J., Oellers-Frahm, K., Tomuschat, C., Zimmermann, A., Tams, C. J., Oellers-Frahm, K., & Tomuschat, C. (Eds.). (2019). *The Statute of the International Court of Justice: A commentary* (3rd ed.). Oxford University Press.

Artificial Intelligence (AI) has a lot of impact on human life. From the last 5 years, the use of AI has exploded across many different fields including finance, transportation, retail and content creation, healthcare and many more. Now, AI knocks the doors of courts. Several Artificial Intelligence researches are going on in Judiciary System. Individuals in India want their claims to be resolved as quickly as possible because the number of legal cases in the country is growing in number. There's a growing need for quick and efficient resolution of legal issues because more and more cases are being filed every day. Consequently, an intelligent system of judgement prediction based on previous judgements is required. With the support of AI and ML, such a system can help judges, lawyers and people with the ability to predict future events, empowering them to make well-informed and strategically advantageous decisions.

Process to Create Legal judgement prediction (LJP) Model

LJP, commonly referred to as case outcome prediction or legal outcome prediction, is the use of ML to forecast court decisions based on past performance information. The idea is to employ computational models to help lawyers determine how likely a case is to turn out, given a set of input variables. This is how it typically operates:

Gathering of Data

Gather a dataset of previous court cases, including case facts, arguments made in court, earlier decisions and any other related information. Every case in the dataset needs to have its ultimate verdict or result labelled.

Feature Extraction

Determine and extract features pertinent to the prediction task from the gathered data. These characteristics might include the nature of the legal issues at hand, the relevant jurisdiction, prior legal decisions, the participating lawyers and more.

Pre-processing of Data

To handle missing values, standardise formats and prepare the data for ML model input, clean and pre-process it.

Training Model

Select an appropriate ML algorithm, like decision trees (DTs), logistic regression or more sophisticated models like support vector machines (SVMs) or neural networks.

Utilising the previous instances to identify patterns and correlations between the attributes and the legal outcomes and use the labelled dataset to train the model.

Assessment and Validation

To evaluate the trained model's performance, validate it using a different dataset that wasn't utilised for training.

Assess the model's prediction abilities by analysing its accuracy, precision, recall and other pertinent measures.

Implementation

The model can help legal experts forecast the outcome of fresh cases once it has been trained and validated. It is noteworthy that predicting judicial judgements is a difficult undertaking because of the ambiguity that accompanies legal proceedings and the wide range of variables that might affect the resolution of cases. Furthermore, when putting such systems into place, ethical and legal issues need to be taken into mind, as judgements made by ML models can have significant consequences.

In addition, human judgement should always play a major role in legal decision-making because these technologies are designed to support, not to replace, legal practitioners.

A branch of AI referred to as ML is able to learn from data without explicit programming.

ML allows for the gradual improvement of a computer's performance on a task through experience. Three primary classifications exist for ML which are shown in the Fig. 2.1.

ML Categories

Supervised Learning

Supervised learning involves training the algorithm using a labelled dataset, which consists of paired input data and output labels. In order for the algorithm to be capable to classify or predict fresh, unknown data, it is essential to first learn a mapping from input to output. Usually for it to categorise or predict new, unseen data, two common supervised learning problems are regression and classification.

Unsupervised Learning

Unsupervised learning involves handling unlabelled data and requires the algorithm to look for patterns or structures on its own without direct supervision. The learning of association rules, dimensionality reduction and grouping are examples of common unsupervised learning problems.

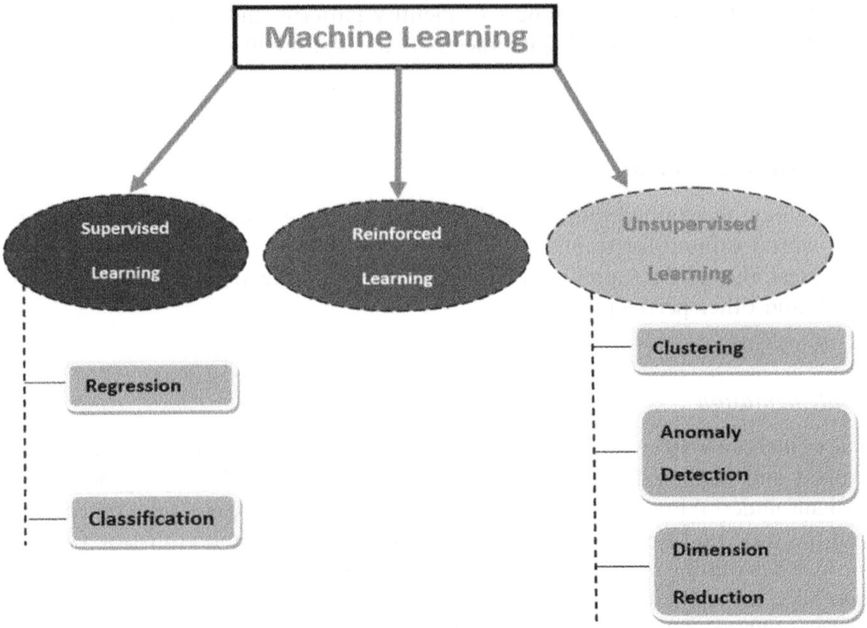

Fig. 2.1. Machine Learning Classifications.

Reinforcement Learning

Reinforcement learning is carried out by an agent through contact with the environment and feedback in the form of rewards or punishments. The agent seeks to acquire knowledge of a policy or strategy that optimises the cumulative payoff in the long run. It is frequently employed in situations where an agent must choose a series of actions, and trial and error is utilised to determine the best course of action. These classifications are not exclusive of one another, and there are also hybrid strategies. Semi-supervised learning, for instance, makes use of both labelled and unlabelled data, while transfer learning makes use of information from one task to enhance performance on another. Other specialised categories exist as well, such as meta-learning and self-supervised learning, which illustrate the field's diversity and ongoing evolution.

Literature Survey

Throughout the rest of the paper, there will be a brief survey of relevant publications on an analysis of LJP in various cases, as well as a discussion of related issues.

Legal Judgement Prediction models on various cases across different countries are listed below.

LJP Model on Occupational Accidents Cases

Sarkar et al. (2016) proposed a model that focused on the prediction of occupational events; it also included guidelines for explaining accident scenarios such as near-misses, property damage and injury instances. For the intent of prediction, Grid Based Classification and Regression Trees (GB-CART), genetic algorithms (GA-CART) and pruning-CART were employed. The experimental findings demonstrated that the GA-CART outperforms other methods in terms of accuracy. Furthermore, the optimal rules derived from GA optimised CART are examined to enhance workplace safety protocols.

According to the results, GA-CART performs better than the others in terms of recall values, precision and accuracy.

LJP Model on Dowry Death Cases

Sil and Roy (2020) proposed a method that focused on 'Dowry Death' cases; a Supervised ML Algorithm, SVM, was made use of as part of a prediction system to support judicial decisions by determining a person's guilt or innocence. The performance of the model accuracy achieved was 93%.

LJP Model on Outcomes of Accident Cases

Aissa et al. (2020) focused on accident cases. Linear regression (LR), DT, SVM and random forest (RF) were applied to the dataset, and, on the performances, general inferences were made. Data collecting and updating, data pre-processing, document representation, feature extraction, training pertinent classifiers, and system evaluation were all completed. The RF was outperformed than others.

LJP Model for Car Accident Cases With Mental Suffering Damages

Hsieh et al. (2021) proposed a model with only one victim and one defendant cases. The optimal predictive model was built using RF, classification tree (CART) and k-nearest neighbour (KNN) algorithms. Results from the experiment showed that the RF model performed better than the other models. One hot encoding Technique was used for data pre-processing. For CART and KNN, the feature selection algorithms sequential backward selection (SBS) and sequential forward selection (SFS) and recursive feature elimination with cross-validation (RFECV) for RF were used. The dataset was made by legal experts.

LJP Model on Outcomes of Divorce Cases

Goel et al. (2019) proposed a model Augur Justice, which is a classification technique and deals with divorce cases. It assists the user in figuring out the likelihood that their case will win or lose. A variety of functions of the natural

suggested model were uplifting, with a 93% F1-score, 93% precision, 92.05% accuracy and 94% recall. One hundred twenty thousand five hundred six cases of US rulings from the Supreme Court judicial repository were collected. The shortcomings of the suggested model are a small dataset of a particular domain was used. There was no effective noise reduction technique, instead of a pre-trained CNN model, embedding was used. The only statistical method used to identify the significant features (predictor variables) in the input data was the recursive feature elimination (RFE) measure, and it would be preferable if the model functioned steadily over a period of time, in various situations and cases, even with diverse judges.

Findings and Discussions

Training and Testing ratio for most of the above prediction models taken as 70: 30 and few taken as 60:40 and 80:20 or 75:25. The datasets in the legal system, AI is being studied and used more in China and less in Saudi Arabia. Furthermore, the majority of the evaluated research offers experimental data and conclusions about the use of AI in the worldwide legal system. Only a small number of nations have completely adopted AI approaches in their legal systems. These results show that, unlike other industries like healthcare and agriculture, the deployment of AI in the legal system is still in its infancy and has not yet reached maturity. Even though there hasn't been much research done on the subject, the examined literature offers information that the current study found useful.

Numerous studies used hybrid deep learning models, ML, and deep learning to anticipate and classify judgements in various cases.

Insufficient datasets were used for ML training and testing. The sources from where datasets are collected, its size and how they extracted features are listed in Table 2.1.

Metrics like mean square error (MSE), root mean square error (RMSE) R^2 in the case of regression and Accuracy, Precision and Recall in the case of classification were used to gauge performance but produced acceptable accuracy and performance. The details of the researches, algorithms, metrics used and limitations, its future scope are listed in Table 2.2. In future, an accuracy and performance of the LJP models will be improved.

Unbalanced data collection led to overfitting and underfitting issues. Apart from Chinese researchers, many researchers manually built their datasets. CAIL2018 dataset was used by Chinese.

Neural networks are becoming a major force in the legal field. It is possible to develop and contrast a deep learning and AI models algorithms with empirical models.

Table 2.1. Dataset Details of Literature Survey.

Reference	Type of Case	Dataset Collection	Period	Number of Records	Drawback
Sarkar et al. (2016)	Occupational accident cases	steel plant	2010–2013	4,744	The study used limited data points (features)
Sil and Roy (2020)	Dowry cases	judgements from trail courts of west Bengal manually processed dataset	Unspecified	Unspecified	Insufficient data points
Aissa et al. (2020)	Accident cases	Errachidia court judgements in Morocco manually processed datasets for injury and death cases	2017–2019	514	Small datasets
Hsieh et al. (2021)	Accident cases	judgements from Taiwan Taichung District Court own dataset created and is available in Zenodo.org	2006–2020	483	Limited datasets
Goel et al. (2019)	Divorce cases	Indiankanoon.com and also from wikipedia	Unspecified	39 (26 Hindu, and 7 Christian, 6 Muslim cases)	Tiny datasets
Chen et al. (2019)	Preliminary cases	CAIL 2018 data set	Unspecified	Unspecified	Small sample size
Park and Chai (2021)	Online privacy invasion cases	Westlaw database	January 2000 to December 2018	1,098	Not large dataset

(*Continued*)

Table 2.1. *(Continued)*

Reference	Type of Case	Dataset Collection	Period	Number of Records	Drawback
Aletras et al. (2016)	Human rights cases	European court	Unspecified	Unspecified	Poor features
Shang (2022)	Criminal cases	China supreme court CAIL 2018 small, Large and CAIL 2019 small, large datasets. The website https://github.com/thunlp/CAIL can be used to access the original data	2018–2019	CAIL 2018 small – 196,000 CAIL 2018 large -1,500,000. CAIL 2019 – not specified	CAIL2018 consists of criminal cases of 2.6+ million but it retain the cases with a single defendant
Alghazzawi et al. (2022)	Court rulings	United States rulings of court from the Supreme judicial repository	Unspecified	120,506	Used a dataset with a specific domain

Table 2.2. The Literature Survey Findings, Limitations and Future Scope.

Reference	Algorithm/Technique Used	Performance Metrics	Limitation(S)	Future Scope
Sarkar et al. (2016)	GB-CART, GA-CART and pruning-CART	Accuracy, Precision, Recall	There was no experimentation with alternative methods that could address the missing value issue.	Could include the use of additional ensemble techniques, support vector machines (SVMs), k-nearest neighbour, or other predictive models, or the collection and analysis of more data points to improve prediction power and the extraction of higher quality rules that could guarantee a decline in accidents.
Sil and Roy (2020)	SVM	Accuracy	Less accuracy Binary classification	To get greater accuracy, the extra parameters will be added in the future.
Aissa et al. (2020)	Linear regression, SVMs, Random Forest (RF) and decision trees (DTs)	The actual performance of applied models was not mentioned. This paper contains the general conclusion that RF was outperformed than DT.	Features are extracted manually.	In future, apply other learning and evaluating classifiers and draw the performance conclusions and prepare the datasets using NLP techniques instead of manual processing.

(Continued)

Table 2.2. *(Continued)*

Reference	Algorithm/Technique Used	Performance Metrics	Limitation(S)	Future Scope
Hsieh et al. (2021)	Optimal KNN, Optimal CART and Optimal RF, the feature selection algorithms sequential backward selection (SBS) and sequential forward selection (SFS)	10-fold cross-validation and performance of the model with RMSE, R^2 and MSE	Only one victim and one defendant cases taken	In order to create a new dataset and determine whether or not the outcomes will be improved, it would be beneficial to extract the characteristics from the original documents of judgements using natural language processing techniques. Use the same regression models to get optimal results.
Goel et al. (2019)	Augur justice, Supervised ML algorithms Naive-Bayes, RF and DT	Accuracy	For Christian dataset, the Augur Justice algorithm performance accuracy is low.	In future, with new justice algorithms, accuracy will be improved.
Chen et al. (2019)	FastText and TextCNN and compared with MLKNN and MLLOC models	Accuracy, Precision, Recall, F1 score	Accusation prediction model performance showed is low. Precision, Recall, F1 score for this model are low.	Keep working to increase the model's prediction accuracy in the future and explore more facets in order to build deep learning-based models for judicial decision-making.

Park and Chai (2021)	NNET, LDA, CART, RF and SVM	Accuracy	Handles only Adware, Cyberattack, Malware, Spam, Spyware, Vandalism, Virus	In future can handle more privacy invasion cases.
Aletras et al. (2016)	SVM	Accuracy	Failed to deal with the feature that reduces performance. Binary classification	Examine the variables that most closely predict the outcome to get the increased accuracy of above 79%.
Shang (2022)	Proposed LJP, PS-LJP PCA-PS-LJP models and compared with baseline existing models CNN HLSTM TOPJUDGE PCA-PS-LJP, proposed model on four data sets which are open, CAIL2018_Large, CAIL2018_Small, CAIL2019_Large and CAIL2019_Small, achieved the best results compared to all the benchmark prediction models.	Macro average precision (MP), Accuracy (Acc), F1 (macro average F1 value) and macro average recall rate (MR)	Only PCA-PS-LJP model has improved performance. But remaining two proposed models LJP, PS-LJP have almost same performance with benchmark models.	Pre-trained models can be applied to improve performance.

(Continued)

Table 2.2. *(Continued)*

Reference	Algorithm/Technique Used	Performance Metrics	Limitation(S)	Future Scope
Alghazzawi et al. (2022)	Hybrid model of neural networks was a combination of long short-term memory (LSTM) + CNN and the proposed model performance compared with classifiers, DL models. LSTM + CNN model outperforms than other compared models.	10-fold cross-validation Precision Accuracy *f*-Score Recall	There was no effective noise reduction technique. An embedding was employed instead of the CNN pre-trained model. The only statistical method used to identify the significant features (predictor variables) in the input set of data was the RFE measure.	Future studies could look into models which are pre-trained such as word2Vec, Glove or fastText, using feature selection techniques other than the RFE, using datasets of judiciary from various domains (court data from various jurisdictions), and researching cutting-edge noise reduction techniques.

Conclusion

This chapter provides an overview of the several legal prediction studies currently in existence. Numerous industries have already seen changes due to automation and ML. It is necessary to make quantitative and quantitative legal predictions. This survey provides information on algorithms, measurements, datasets, performance, constraints, conclusions and potential future developments. The RF algorithm produces the greatest results out of all of these legal prediction methods. When used for binary prediction, SVM yields superior results. Deep learning models also yields efficient results. Still, there is potential to increase the accuracy of the predictions regarding the different kinds of legal decisions that may be made using the existing ML techniques, deep learning techniques that make use of natural language processing. Future legal forecasts are probably going to be more prevalent in the legal field.

References

Aissa, H., Tarik, A., Zeroual, I., & Yousef, F. (2020). Using machine learning to predict outcomes of accident cases in Moroccan courts. *Procedia Computer Science*, *184*, 829–834. https://doi.org/10.1016/j.procs.2021.03.103

Aletras, N., Tsarapatsanis, D., Preoţiuc-Pietro, D., & Lampos, V. (2016). Predicting judicial decisions of the European court of human rights: A natural language processing perspective. *PeerJ Computer Science*, *2*, e93.

Alghazzawi, D., Bamasag, O., Albeshri, A., Sana, I., Ullah, H., & Asghar, M. Z. (2022). Efficient prediction of court judgments using an LSTM+ CNN neural network model with an optimal feature set. *Mathematics*, *10*(5), 683.

Chen, B., Li, Y., Zhang, S., Lian, H., & He, T. (2019). A deep learning method for judicial decision support. In *IEEE 19th International Conference on Software Quality, Reliability and Security Companion (QRS-C), Sofia, Bulgaria* (pp. 145–149). https://doi.org/10.1109/QRS-C.2019.00040

Goel, S., Roshan, S., Tyagi, R., & Agarwal, S. (2019). Augur justice: A supervised machine learning technique to predict outcomes of divorce court cases. In *Fifth International Conference on Image Information Processing (ICIIP), Shimla, India* (pp. 280–285). https://doi.org/10.1109/ICIIP47207.2019.8985764

Hsieh, D., Chen, L., & Sun, T. (2021). Legal judgment prediction based on machine learning: Predicting the discretionary damages of mental suffering in fatal car accident cases. *Applied Sciences*, *11*(21), 10361. https://doi.org/10.3390/app112110361

Park, M., & Chai, S. (2021). AI model for predicting legal judgments to improve accuracy and explainability of online privacy invasion cases. *Applied Sciences*, *11*(23), 11080. https://doi.org/10.3390/app112311080

Sarkar, S., Patel, A., Madaan, S., & Maiti, J. (2016). Prediction of occupational accidents using decision tree approach. In *IEEE Annual India Conference (INDICON), Bangalore, India* (pp. 1–6). https://doi.org/10.1109/INDICON.2016.7838969

Shang, X. (2022, June 24). A computational intelligence model for legal prediction and decision support. *Computational Intelligence and Neuroscience*, 5795189. https://doi.org/10.1155/2022/5795189

Sil, R., & Roy, A. (2020). A novel approach on argument based legal prediction model using machine learning. In *International Conference on Smart Electronics and Communication (ICOSEC), Trichy, India* (pp. 487–490). https://doi.org/10.1109/ICOSEC49089.2020.9215310

Sivaranjani, N., Jayabharathy, J., & Safa, M. (2019). A broad view of automation in legal prediction technology. In *3rd International conference on Electronics, Communication and Aerospace Technology (ICECA), Coimbatore, India* (pp. 180–185). https://doi.org/10.1109/ICECA.2019.8822019

Chapter 3

Customer Churn Prediction for Retention Analysis

Rajesh Saturi, Siripothula Rahul, Zuha Siddiqui and Rachamalla Nikhitha

Vignana Bharathi Institute of Technology, India

Abstract

This abstract provides a comprehensive overview of the research on Customer Churn Prediction for Retention Analysis. In today's corporate context, understanding and mitigating customer churn has become critical for long-term success. This study focusses on the building and testing of predictive churn models aimed at forecasting customer attrition behaviour. Using advanced deep learning methods such as artificial neural networks (ANNs), the study examines past customer data to uncover trends and indications linked with attrition. It also investigates the integration of diverse information including customer involvement, contentment and transactional history to improve forecast accuracy. The proposed approach comprehends the heterogeneity of client bases and employs customer segmentation using the *K*-means algorithm to personalise retention strategies to distinct customer groups, detecting and addressing varied requirements and preferences. The project's unique feature is the inclusion of duration prediction for churn, which allows organisations to prioritise retention efforts based on the projected duration of churn for individual customers. In essence, the project aims to enhance the field of customer churn prediction and retention analysis by combining cutting-edge methodologies to apply targeted and timely retention measures, eventually nurturing customer loyalty and increasing the lifetime value of their customer base.

Keywords: Customer churn; deep learning; customer segmentation; customer retention; churn prediction; artificial neural networks (ANNs)

Security Intelligence in the Age of AI, 39–53

doi:10.1108/978-1-83608-156-220251003

predicting land-line client migration and conducted comparison studies using seven modelling methodologies. The suggested feature set outperforms existing feature sets in terms of prediction accuracy and it concluded that to improve the feature set, additional attributes should be added in the future (Sandhya Rani et al., 2021).

Hyeon Ahn, Sang-Pil Han and Yung-Seop Lee explored the factors influencing customer attrition in the Korean mobile service industry. The influence of a consumer's partial abandonment on the association between attrition predictors and total abandonment was investigated and addressed that churn determinants have an impact on customer churn in either a direct or indirect manner a customer's status change.

K. Sandhya Rani, Shaik Thaslima, N. G. L. Prasanna, R. Vindhya and P. Srilakshmi suggested a technique for churn prediction using Logistic Regression to determine the company's churn factor based on past data. This system saves the organisation time and effort by analysing past data to respond to the circumstances. Amal M. Almana, Mehmet Sabih Aksoy and Rasheed Alzahran demonstrated standard data mining strategies for identifying customer churn tendencies. C5.0 and CART ended up performing better than regression in terms of efficiency. Finally, suggested that employing RULES family approaches to datasets can produce the finest patterns.

Proposed System

The proposed system aims to revolutionise customer retention strategies through the integration of advanced predictive modelling, customer segmentation and duration estimation within a unified framework. At its core, our system leverages deep learning algorithms such as artificial neural network (ANN) and decision tree to accurately predict customer churn and estimate the potential duration of churn for individual customers. This predictive capability is essential for businesses looking to not only identify potential churners but also proactively develop timely and targeted retention strategies. An important feature of our system is the incorporation of duration estimation, allowing businesses to prioritise retention efforts based on the urgency of each customer case.

A key advancement in our proposed system is the focus on customer segmentation using the K-means clustering algorithm. Instead of treating the entire customer base uniformly, our system employs sophisticated clustering techniques to group customers with similar characteristics and behaviours analysed through exploratory data analysis of customer data. This segmentation provides a more detailed understanding of the diverse factors influencing churn, facilitating the extraction of meaningful insights from various customer segments (Ahmad et al., 2019). By acknowledging and addressing the distinct requirements and inclinations of every group, companies may customise their retention tactics for greater effectiveness and personalisation. This approach not only helps in reducing customer attrition but also enhances retention efforts on high-risk segments, ultimately improving the company's ability to proactively retain customers and mitigate churn.

In short, the major objectives of the proposed system include (see Fig. 3.1):

- The primary goal is to build a predictive churn model and utilise its results to generate a target list.
- Identifying the characteristics of churners and obtaining insights through exploratory data analysis.
- Segmenting the model output for targeted retention campaigns or strategies.

Methodology

The project mainly comprises four consecutive tasks to be performed. These four tasks are as follows:

(1) Data Exploration and Analysis
(2) Predictive Model Building
(3) Customer Segmentation
(4) Integration and User Interface

Data Exploration and Analysis

The initial step for constructing any machine learning model is data modelling and data exploration. The dataset used for implementing the proposed system is downloaded from Kaggle. It consists of customer churn data of a telco organisation that provided mobile and internet services to consumers. The dataset contains approximately 7,043 customers' data and 21 attributes that describe the various features of customers like gender, tenure, partner, dependants, monthly charges, total charges, payment method (see Fig. 3.5), contract type, internet service, streaming services provided and so on. Currently, the system is implemented using this telco customer data, but the architecture is outlined in a way that it can be used by any sort of business organisation to understand their customers and retain them.

Initially, data preprocessing is performed which involved handling missing values in the dataset, followed by transforming categorical variables into numeric using one-hot encoding and feature scaling methods. Then, exploratory data analysis such as univariate and bivariate analysis is performed on each attribute of the customer data to recognise the characteristics that influence the customer attrition and resulted in the following conclusions.

- Greater churn is observed in the case of month-to-month contracts, no online security, no tech support or customer support, early years of subscription, fibre optics internet and lower total charges as seen in Figs. 3.3 and 3.4.

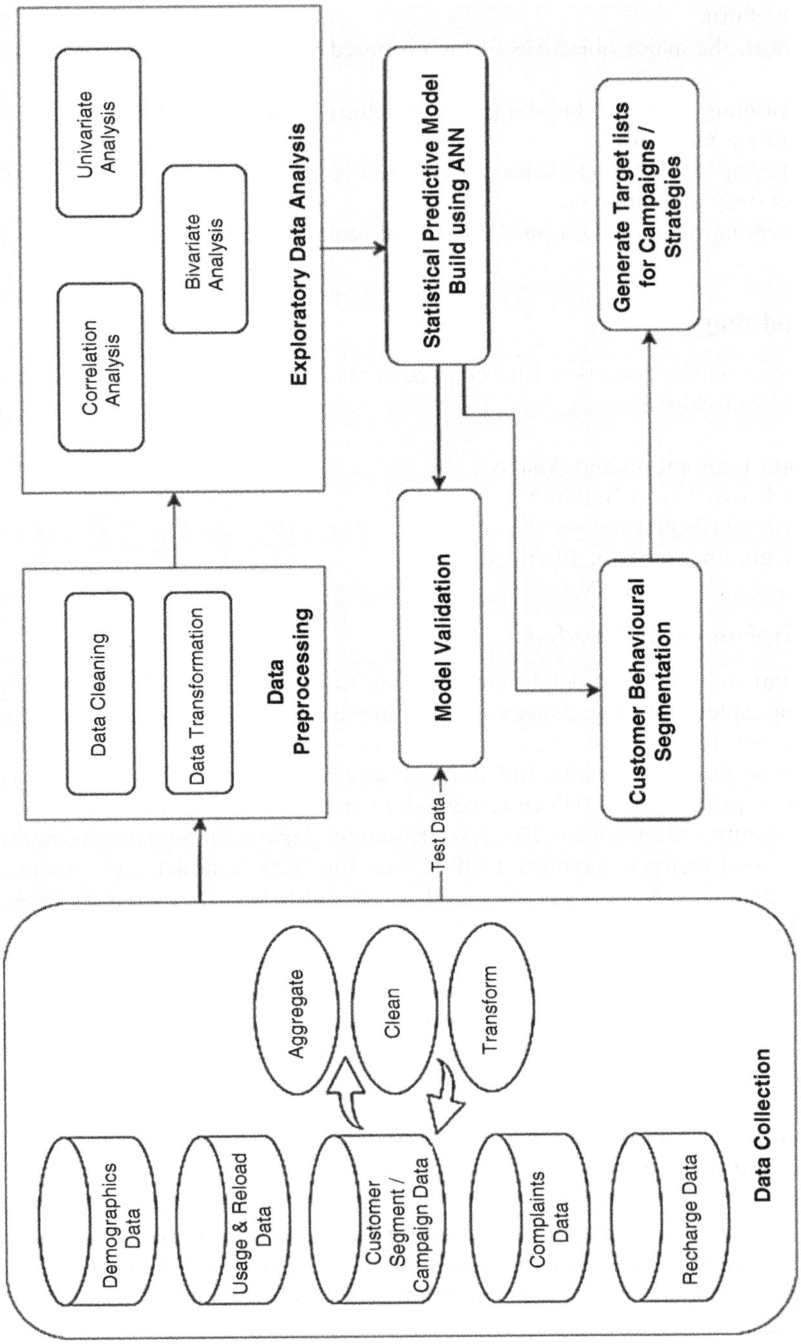

Fig. 3.1. Customer Churn Prediction for Retention Analysis System Architecture.

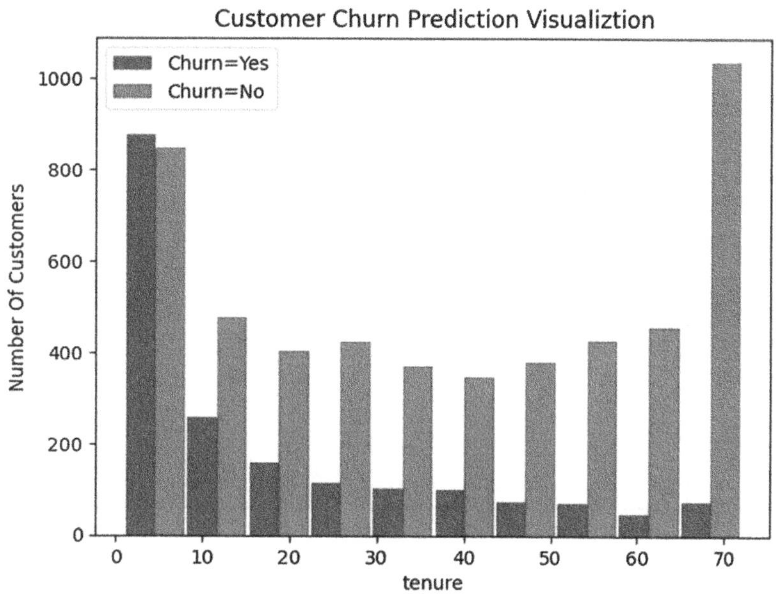

Fig. 3.2. Churn by Tenure Visualisation.

- Long-term agreements, subscriptions without internet access and clients who have been with a company for more than five years all show lower churn rates as seen in Fig. 3.2.
- There is very little effect of variables like gender, numerous lines and phone service availability on attrition.
- Electronic check mediums are the highest churners as seen in Fig. 3.5.
- Contract Type – Since monthly clients have no set of terms and are essentially pay-as-you-go, they are more likely to discontinue service (Dahiya & Bhatia, 2015).
- The categories with no tech support and no online security are major turners.
- Non-senior citizens have a high turnover rate.

Predictive Model Building

The preprocessed data are now used to train the ANN model to build a robust and accurate customer churn prediction model.

ANN models are ideal for churn prediction because they can capture complex, non-linear correlations in data. Churn prediction requires understanding nuanced patterns and correlations in consumer behaviour that standard linear models may be difficult to detect (Ammar & Ahmed, 2017). These complicated patterns may

We have used the *K*-means algorithm here for customer segmentation as it can detect unique groups within a dataset efficiently and divide clients into clusters based on common qualities, actions or preferences. *K*-Means is a realistic and scalable approach for customer segmentation, allowing businesses to easily assess and respond to the different preferences and behaviours demonstrated by their client base, thus improving consumer satisfaction and delivering targeted business strategies.

The output data of the predictive churn model is provided as input to the segmentation model. These data are initially scaled using StandardScaler to normalise its features. The dimensionality of the scaled data is then reduced to two main components using principal component analysis (PCA). The new data frame contains the principal components that are obtained. The Elbow Method is then used to calculate the ideal number of clusters for K-means by plotting the inertia (within-cluster sum of squares) versus different values of '*k*'. The point of the elbow in the plot indicates an optimal number of clusters as shown in Fig. 3.6. Finally, *K*-Means clustering is performed with a chosen '*k*' value (in this case, 4), and the resulting cluster labels are added to the data frame, which includes the principal components along with the assigned cluster labels for each data point. This resulting dataset is further used for the segmentation of any new customer (Almana et al., 2014). Thus, the customers are categorised into four segments

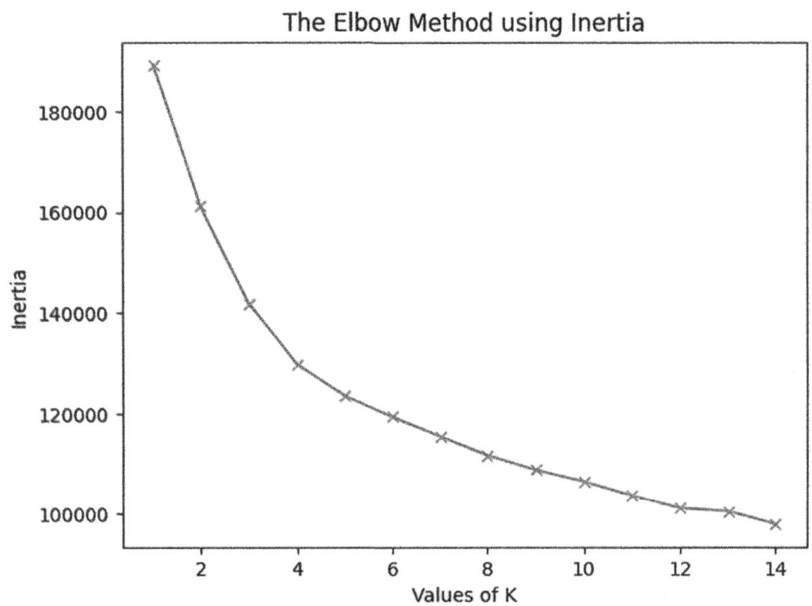

Fig. 3.6. Graph Representing Optimal No. of Clusters Using the Elbow Method.

namely conditionally loyal subscribers, conditional churners, lifestyle migrators and unsatisfied customers. Finally, effective targeted retention strategies are designed by considering the characteristics of each customer segment.

Integration and User Interface

A web interface is developed for deploying and integrating the predictive and segmentation models using Flask, a web framework of Python (Huang et al., 2012). The user interface comprises input fields for the various attributes describing customer features and buttons to initiate analysis. Users can input those features, and the system processes and predicts whether the customer is likely to churn or not. On the other hand, the segment type of the user is identified by considering churn prediction results. If the customer is likely to churn, then the system provides the period of churn by comparing the tenure of the user with its corresponding segment's average tenure and provides the customer characteristic distribution graphs as well as appropriate retention strategies as an output in an intuitive manner (Ahn et al., 2006).

Results

An efficient and accurate predictive model that anticipates customer churn along with the duration of churn is developed using the ANN algorithm with an accuracy of 81.74% and customer behaviour segmentation is performed using the *K*-means clustering algorithm, and decision tree algorithm is employed for customer segment classification with an accuracy of 96.576% as shown in Table 3.1. Characteristics and behaviour patterns of each customer segment are extracted and displayed to the user as shown in Figs. 3.8–3.10, which leveraged in tailoring targeted customer retention strategies.

Here (in Fig. 3.7) cluster 0 represents unsatisfied customers, cluster 1 represents conditional churners, cluster 2 represents conditionally loyal subscribers and cluster 3 represents lifestyle migrators.

Table 3.1. Classification Report of Customer Segmentation.

	Precision	Recall	f_1-Score	Support
Cluster 0	1.00	1.00	1.00	465
Cluster 1	0.93	0.94	0.93	512
Cluster 2	0.97	0.97	0.97	511
Cluster 3	0.97	0.96	0.97	615
Accuracy			0.97	2,103
Macro avg	0.97	0.97	0.97	2,103
Weighted avg	0.97	0.97	0.97	2,103

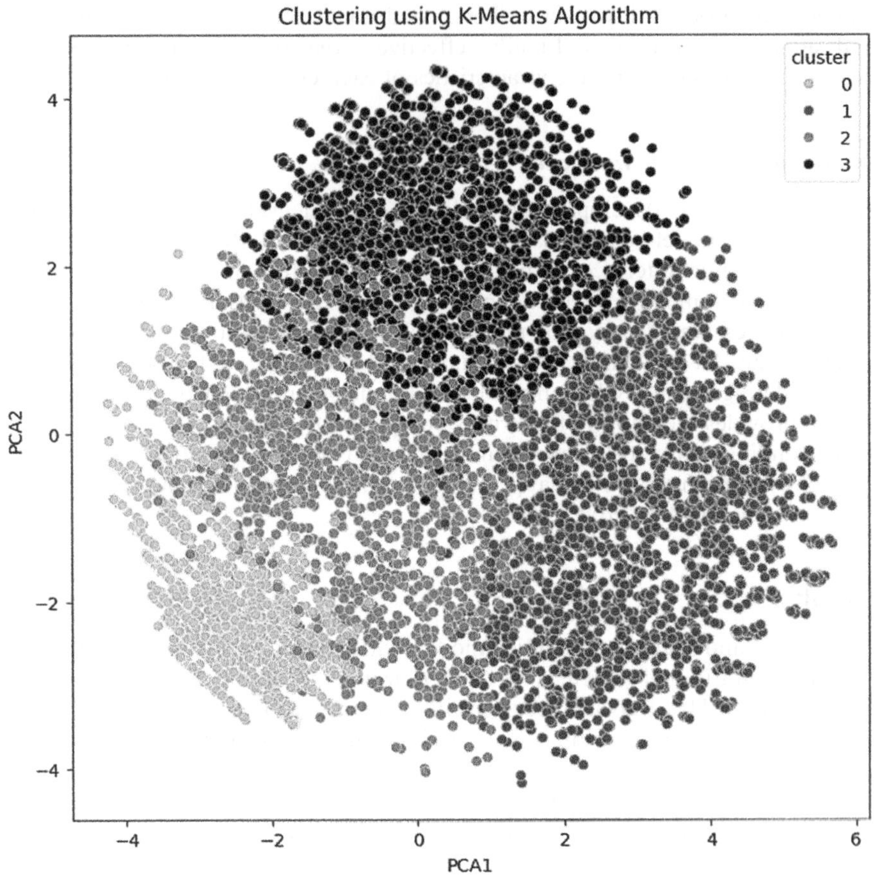

Fig. 3.7. Customer Segments Scatter Plot.

Conclusion

As a result, this paper offers a very reliable 'Customer Churn Prediction for Retention Analysis' system that has effectively used ANN algorithms to forecast customer attrition, offering a thorough comprehension of possible churners, their anticipated duration of churn and segmentation based on distinct customer attributes. The study has successfully identified intricate, non-linear patterns in customer behaviour by utilising ANN models, which has led to a more accurate and nuanced churn forecast. The inclusion of a crucial dimension, time prediction allows retention efforts to be prioritised according to the urgency of individual client cases. By addressing the varied demands and preferences of distinct client groups, customer segmentation further improves the effectiveness of the system by customising retention strategies. The outcome is a powerful tool for businesses to

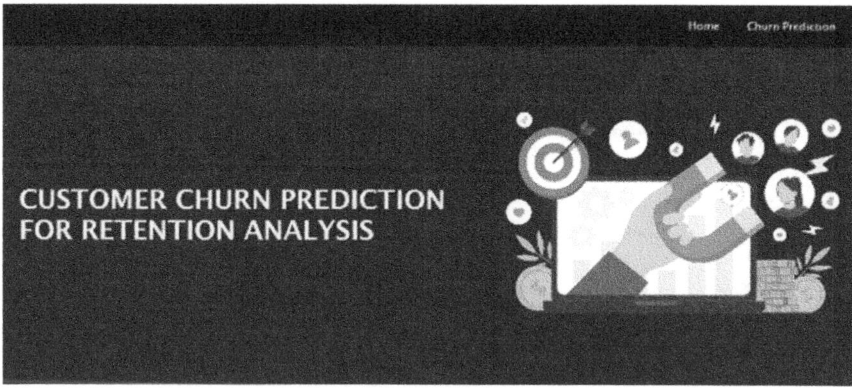

Fig. 3.8. Customer Churn Prediction for Retention Analysis Home Page.

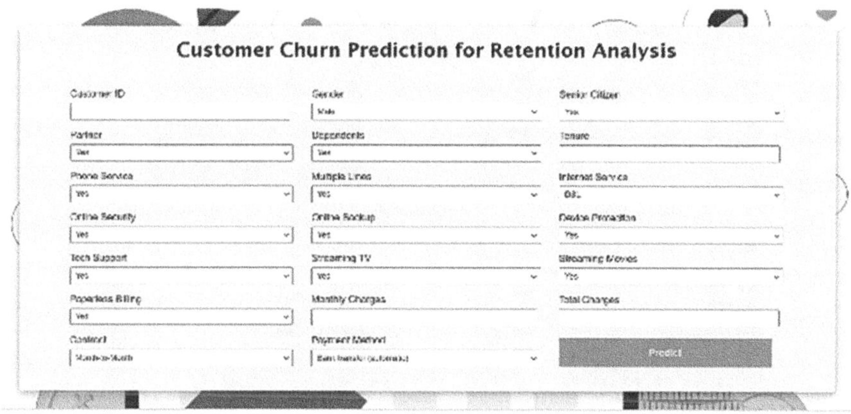

Fig. 3.9. Churn Prediction Page.

proactively manage customer churn, formulate targeted retention plans and ultimately strengthen customer relationships, fostering sustainable growth and long-term success. However, further research can concentrate on developing KPIs for tracking and monitoring customer usage behaviour, providing a list of churn drivers and recommending cross-selling and upselling strategies can assist in reducing customer attrition rate and enhance business profitability even further.

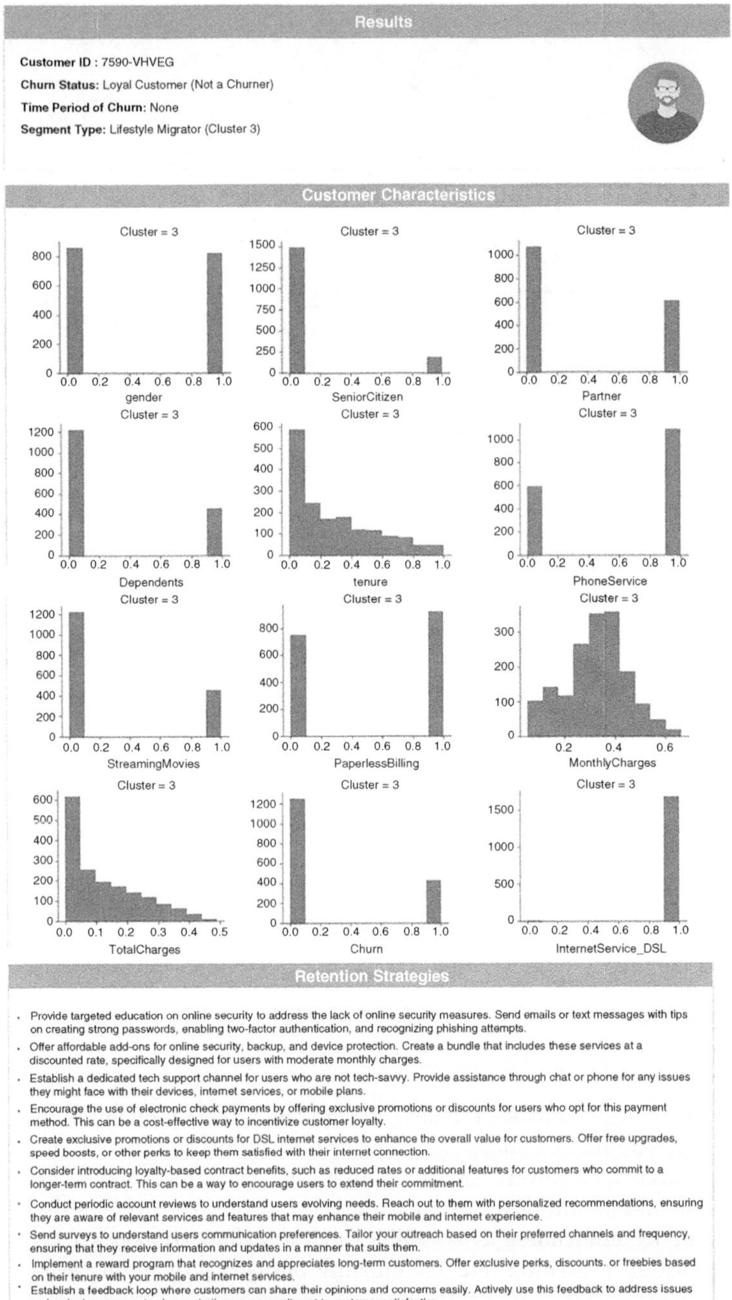

Fig. 3.10. Customer Characteristics and Retention Strategies.

References

Ahmad, A. K., Jafar, A., & Aljoumaa, K. (2019). Customer churn prediction in telecom using machine learning in big data platform. *Journal of Big Data*, *7*(11). https://doi.org/10.31838/jcr.07.11.308

Ahn, J.-H., Han, S.-P., & Lee, Y.-S. (2006). Customer churn analysis: Churn determinants and mediation effects of partial defection in the Korean mobile telecommunications service industry. *Telecommunications Policy*, *30*, 552–568.

Almana, A. M., Sabih Aksoy, M., & Alzahran, R. (2014, May). A survey on data mining techniques in customer churn analysis for telecom industry. *International Journal of Engineering Research and Applications*, *4*(5), 165–171.

Ammar, A., & Ahmed, D. (2017, January). Maheswari Linen, A review and analysis of churn prediction methods for customer retention in telecom industries. In *International conference on advanced computing and communication systems*. IEEE.

Dahiya, K., & Bhatia, S. (2015). *Customer churn analysis in telecom industry*. IEEE.

Huang, B., Kechadi, M. T., & Buckley, B. (2012). Customer churn prediction in telecommunications. *Expert Systems with Applications*, *39*, 1414–1425.

Lalwani, P., Kumar Mishra, M., Singh Chadha, J., & Sethi, P. (2021, February). *Customer churn prediction system: A machine learning approach*. Springer.

Prabadevi, B., Shalini, R., & Kavitha, B. R. (2023, June). Customer churning analysis using machine learning algorithms. *International Journal of Intelligent Networks*, *4*, 145–154.

Saleh, S., & Saha, S. (2023, June). Customer retention and churn prediction in the telecommunication industry: A case study on a Danish university. *SN Applied Sciences*, *5*, 173.

Sandhya Rani, K., Thaslima, S., Prasanna, N. G. L., Vindhya, R., & Srilakshmi, P. (2021, July). Analysis of customer churn prediction in telecom industry using logistic regression. *International Journal of Innovative Research in Computer Science & Technology*, *9*(4), 101–112.

Chapter 4

Elevating Project Manager Responsibilities in Construction Projects Through Augmented and Virtual Reality Integration: A Review

Khush Attarde and Javed Sayyad

Symbiosis Institute of Technology, Pune Campus, Symbiosis International (Deemed University), Pune, India

Abstract

Construction project management (PM) is a complex undertaking that requires various skills and knowledge. Managing quality, assets, finances, supply chains, labour and progress are all critical to the success of a project. Any delays in project completion can result in significant financial losses and unsustainability. However, the emergence of augmented reality (AR) and virtual reality (VR) technologies is revolutionising the construction industry. These technologies enable visualisation, interaction and integration of the real world and three-dimensional components. Through AR/VR, controlling and interacting with a construction project virtually while visualising it is possible. This paper reviews and discusses integrating AR/VR technologies for construction PM, focussing on increasing cost-effectiveness, sustainability, productivity and effectiveness. Integrating AR/VR technologies leads to more effective communication between two parties, and these techniques can also be useful for enhancing customer relations and sales. The project manager is responsible for overseeing every task related to the project, managing these tasks using immersive technologies beneficial.

Keywords: Project management; augmented reality; virtual reality; construction sector; immersive technology; project manager; sustainability

Security Intelligence in the Age of AI, 55–75

doi:10.1108/978-1-83608-156-220251004

Introduction

Augmented reality (AR) and virtual reality (VR) are constantly evolving technologies that have recently gained popularity. Researchers are actively working to make these technologies more user-friendly and increase their applicability. Although AR/VR are used to create immersive experiences, they are fundamentally different. In AR, the user's environment is the real world, while in VR, the environment is entirely virtual (Suh & Prophet, 2018). These technologies can potentially revolutionise how businesses operate by giving customers realistic product visualisation. AR integrates digital information with a user's physical environment. The 3D components seamlessly blend with the real world, providing an immersive experience. AR relies on various hardware components such as sensors, displays, processors and input devices, including cameras, GPS, accelerometers and solid-state compasses. The compass is used to orient the system or device, while GPS is used to determine its location (Suh & Prophet, 2018). AR requires a high computational power device and can be accessed using mobile devices, glasses, and contact lenses.

VR creates a simulated 3D environment that allows users to interact with a virtual world (Anthes et al., 2016). The level of realism depends on the skills of the 3D graphic artist. VR environments are created using modelling software. Users deep inside the virtual and detach from the real environment. VR can be classified as non-immersive, semi-immersive and fully immersive. Non-immersive VR is accessed from a computer system, and controlled using peripherals. In semi-immersive VR, users can access it using different glasses and headsets, but control is still done using a console. Fully immersive VR allows the user to fully immerse in a 3D world and interact using different devices, not necessarily consoles (Anthes et al., 2016).

Table 4.1 shows the differences between AR/VR technologies. Mixed reality (MR) is an advanced version of AR/VR that integrates both real and virtual

Table 4.1. Comparative Analysis of AR and VR Technology With Respect to Different Parameters.

Parameters	**AR**	**VR**
Environment	Combination of the present scenario in real world and virtual.	Simulator or virtual world
Immersive ability	It is not fully immersive technique	It is fully immersive technique
Cost	Less cost compared to VR	High cost than AR
Quality	Quality is compromised in AR	High quality can be seen in VR
Focus	Not able to provide a focus	It is a very focused system
User location	Users need to be present in the required location	It is okay if the user is not present in the location

environments to make location and visualisation of updates related to the construction site easier. MR combines the benefits of both technologies to minimise their limitations. The MR setup has no limitation of boundaries, making it a valuable tool for construction management. AR/VR technologies are increasingly utilised in various sectors, including healthcare, education and construction. In particular, these emerging technologies are proving to be highly effective in various sectors; here we will discuss the construction industry. However, these systems can be expensive to implement. The construction industry involves huge investments and requires a large team comprising engineers, labourers, accountants, construction managers, financial managers and supervisors. Effective management of materials and resources is crucial for successful project completion. However, the cost of the entire setup may increase due to the advanced system requirements. Collaborative management at each level is essential to complete the project effectively and produce a profitable output.

The project manager plays a critical role in ensuring the successful completion of a project by managing various resources such as finance, planning, logistics, human resources, quality and sales management. They oversee the team and adjust job processes to deliver profitable outcomes. The sub-department of the project manager to supervise can be seen in Fig. 4.1 which here collaborates using AR/VR devices to make decisions. The construction industry has become increasingly concerned with sustainability due to global concerns regarding

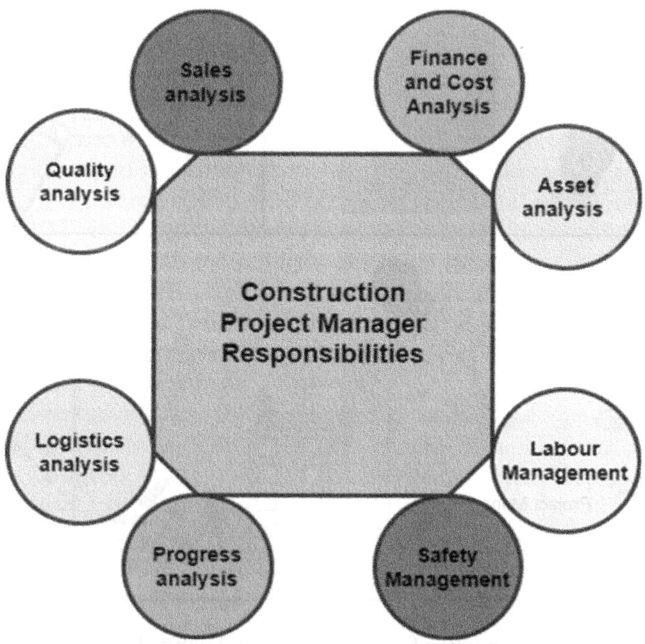

Fig. 4.1. Key Responsibilities of a Project Manager in Decision-Making for Effective Project Supervision.

papers was subsequently assessed. This rigorous quality assessment focussed on evaluating the research methodology, the credibility of the sources and the relevance of the findings to the overarching objectives of the literature review. I want you to know that ensuring the reliability and validity of the information included in the review was paramount. Throughout the review process, ethical considerations were followed, including proper citation and acknowledgement of original authors and the critical assessment and disclosure of potential conflicts of interest. The comprehensive methodology in this literature review provides valuable insights for academia and industry practitioners.

Literature Analysis

Evolution of the Literature

This section provides an analysis of AR/VR, which has been collected from various sources and quantitatively analysed for data collection. The SCOPUS and Dimensions AI databases were searched, filtered and restricted to Engineering, Management and Technology to conduct a graphical analysis of resources. Searching for the string 'AR/VR' filtering to Engineering and Management in the Dimension AI and SCOPUS database produced 3,864 and 26,341 publications, respectively. Searching for the string 'AR/VR' filtering to only the Management field in the Dimension AI and SCOPUS databases produced 984 and 2,325 publications, respectively. The research in AR/VR technologies has been increasing in the last five years, focussing on their application in management.

The search includes research papers, magazines and books. AR/VR technology in construction management is becoming more prevalent due to its cost effectiveness and high productivity. The number of research paper publications on this topic will increase in the coming years. This technology is crucial for maintaining quality, cost, sales and sustainability in construction projects, and therefore, research in this area is expected to proliferate. In Table 4.2, you can find the number of research papers published in various journals. These papers cover different topics, including engineering, technology, PM, business and decision studies. Some of these papers also focus on sustainability in the construction sector by embedding AR/VR.

Content Analysis of Project Management

The available literature on AR/VR in construction PM is diverse. Various studies have explored the applications and implications of these technologies. Behzadi (2016) study examines how AR/VR can improve communication, work scheduling and labour management within the construction industry. Kirchbach and Runde (2012) explore the potential of AR for construction control, emphasising its utility in site management and productivity enhancement. Rodrigues (2021) focusses on civil construction planning, highlighting the role of AR in real-time modification and visualisation for efficient planning. Raziapov (2022) research delves into the application of AR methods in construction, emphasising the

Table 4.2. Analysis of Publishers and Publication in 'AR/VR for Construction PM' Filtering It to Management.

Name of Publication	**No. of Paper Published**
Automation in Construction	74
Technological Forecasting and Social Change	69
Procedia Computer Science	52
Journal of Cleaner Production	35
Procedia CIRP	30
Computers in Industry	26
Procedia Manufacturing	23
Futures	19
Cities	13
Sustainable Cities and Society	13
Journal of Building Engineering	13
Organization Technology and Management in Construction: an International Journal	3
Procedia Engineering	1

cost-effectiveness and productivity gains achieved through AR technology. Khan and Panuwatwanich (2021) presents the applicability of building information modelling (BIM) integrated with AR in building facility management, showcasing its potential for timely asset management and increased efficiency. Kharisov et al. (2022) article compares AR/VR with BIM, underscoring the extensive future scope of AR/VR in construction. Yu et al. (2018) study focusses on more competent construction site management by implementing innovative, intelligent site models, leading to productivity and efficiency gains. Korkmaz et al. (2018) paper emphasises the role of AR technology in highway construction project delivery, leading to improved management and cost reduction. Although dated, the 2013 study by Kim et al. (2013) discusses the application of AR in construction design and planning.

Table 4.3 provides tabular analyses of the selected research or review literature, outlining the research methodology and respective inferences. Additionally, a column is included to highlight the various job processes of a project manager, such as facility, human resource, logistics, delay, safety, sales, health and sustainability management. This highlights the critical role that project managers play in completing productive construction projects. Further, the following sections examine the importance of AR/VR for specific tasks or jobs of project managers in construction PM, aligning it to cost-effectiveness, productivity, safety and sustainability.

Table 4.3. Selected Papers for Literature Table for AR/VR in Construction PM.

Ref.	Year	Topic Name	Responsibilities	Research Methodology	Inferences
Ahmed (2018)	2019	A review on using opportunities of AR/VR in construction PM	Delay, quality, safety and resource management	Review done for progress tracking and training, time, cost and safety management.	Review on technologies was done here very well
Albahbah et al. (2021)	2021	Application areas of AR/VR in construction PM: A scoping review	Quality management	Review done for defect and quality management.	The US focusses on AR/VR technologies for quality management and progress tracking, impacting sales and cost-effectiveness.
Rodrigues (2021)	2021	Civil construction planning using AR	Planning	Shows strategic construction planning focussing on foundation laying and localising tools.	Tool enhances planning efficiency virtual real-time modifications and can be utilised for various steps.
Raziapov (2022)	2021	Application of AR methods in construction	Designing and planning	BIM with AR technology enables real-time object visualisation, enabling immediate action.	It explores AR and BIM for maintenance and management, highlighting cost-effectiveness, productivity, and quality.

Khan and Panuwatwanich (2021)	2021	Applicability of BIM integrated AR in building facility management	Resource management	BIMAR, a software combining BIM for design and various functions, is utilised in facility management and mobile device handling.	BIMAR enhances facility management productivity by timely asset and improved supply chain management.
Kharisov et al. (2022)	2022	Management of the implementation of a construction project based on integrated digital models	Planning and decision making	Explores challenges of utilising integrated digital modelling, including VR/AR/MR, for operations and decision-making.	The study compares AR/VR with BIM for construction using modern integrated digital models, revealing its high future scope.
Yu et al. (2018)	2018	Smarter construction site management using the latest information technology	Resource management and safety maintenance	3D scanning, BIM, AR, and VR integration for construction site management is crucial for managing jobs.	It proposes an innovative, intelligent site model using BIM for improved decision-making and efficiency.
Tarek and Marzouk (2022)	2022	Integrated AR and cloud computing approach for infrastructure utilities maintenance	Resource and facility management	Software designed to enhance visualisation of infrastructure networks, enhancing operation efficiency and workflow.	It suggests facility and operation management can enhance efficiency, and labour work can be efficiently managed using cloud services with AR.

Babalola et al. (2023) and Bao et al. (2022), emerges as an effective strategy in significantly reducing injuries and damage. Trending technologies, including the Internet of Things (IoT), blockchain (Nanayakkara et al., 2019), artificial intelligence (AI) and robotics, when integrated with AR, VR and MR demonstrate the potential to not only enhance productivity but also elevate safety standards. The conceptual framework presented in Harichandran et al. (2021), integrating Digital Twin with VR, provides a holistic solution for maintaining safety and updating the environment.

Impact of COVID-19 for Health and Safety in Construction Sector

The COVID-19 pandemic has significantly impacted health monitoring, and technology is increasingly important in construction projects. According to research analysing the impact of COVID-19 on Jordanian construction workers, delays in the construction industry have resulted in economic losses (Nykänen et al., 2020). Despite these challenges, the implementation of VR technology for safety training has effectively improved safety and health measures by providing a realistic and immersive environment for training (Nykänen et al., 2020). The construction industry can use unmanned aerial vehicles (UAVs), AI and AR/VR technologies for betterment. Still, their adoption is expected to increase in the coming years, indicating a positive trend towards technology integration for safety and health, as revealed by Nnaji et al. (2020).

Sustainability for Health and Safety in Construction Sector

Sustainability has become a core responsibility of project managers, requiring them to reduce resource wastage and adopt technologies that promote a sustainable environment. This study (Schiavi et al., 2022) suggests that IoT, Digital Twin and other technologies play an instrumental role in achieving sustainability goals while reducing energy consumption. Integrating BIM with VR/AR technologies can reduce energy consumption by remotely monitoring and modifying various PM aspects, such as safety and health monitoring, progress tracking, financial tracking and resource management. Researchers in Fathalizadeh et al. (2021) emphasise the importance of sustainable and environment-friendly PM based on their research conducted in Iran. Integrating BIM and VR/AR technologies facilitates data flow and improves communication, significantly creating a sustainable PM ecosystem.

Resource Management

This section will discuss resource management in the construction sector as it plays a crucial role. In Section 'Recruitment and Employment Engagement', recruitment and management of human resources is discussed. In Section 'Workforce Training and Development' discussion on the need for training and development in the last section, that is, Section 'Logistics Management' reviews analyses on logistics management.

Recruitment and Employment Engagement

The adoption of AR/VR technologies is revolutionising recruitment processes in the construction sector. By combining AI's analytical capabilities with these immersive technologies, organisations can streamline recruitment efforts by evaluating past experiences and aligning them with the demands of construction projects (Ahmed et al., 2017). This approach ensures the recruited workforce is skilled and adaptable to the evolving needs of modern construction projects. The industry's integration of AR/VR in recruitment and talent management underscores its forward-thinking approach, acknowledging the transformative potential of these technologies in shaping a workforce that can meet the demands of the contemporary construction landscape. AR/VR technologies are beneficial for training and development for enhancing employee engagement and optimising operations management in the construction industry. Creating a conducive work environment requires understanding and addressing employees' needs and limitations (Abioye et al., 2021).

Workforce Training and Development

In the construction industry, where the skill set and proficiency of the workforce play a pivotal role, the immersive capabilities of VR present a transformative approach to training and development. The industry's dynamic nature, often characterised by day or week-based contractual engagements (Townsend et al., 2012), necessitates an agile and adaptive approach to workforce training. The industry's dynamic nature requires an agile and adaptive approach to workforce training, and VR's ability to simulate real-world scenarios offers a unique advantage. It facilitates a nuanced analysis of a worker's training needs and aligns their skills with the specific requirements of construction projects (Hou et al., 2017). This expedites onboarding and contributes to the workforce's ongoing development, enhancing task-specific proficiency and overall project efficiency. AR/VR technologies are transforming internship programs, vital for nurturing the next generation of engineers. AI manages recruitment, analysing previous experiences and seamlessly transitioning interns into engineering roles within AR/VR frameworks (Ahmed et al., 2017). These immersive environments provide interns with hands-on experience, actively participating in the design and validation of construction projects under the guidance of seasoned engineers. The result is a more efficient learning curve for interns and a workforce adapt to leveraging AR/VR technologies for effective PM (Adami et al., 2023).

Logistics Management

Using AR/VR in logistics management is a transformative approach that uses AI or human knowledge to enhance visual perception. According to Ciuffini et al. (2016), AR/VR have a positive impact on managing materials for construction projects. By employing these technologies, facility management becomes more productive and reduces excess operational costs. Connectivity with vendors is streamlined through AR/VR, enabling dynamic adjustments based on project requirements. Mobile AR facilitates real-time vendor comparisons, ensuring optimal quality and cost-effectiveness in material procurement. The technologies enable decision-making with precision and efficiency, leading to a reduction in unnecessary costs. Delays in construction projects, often attributed to vendor and logistics delays, are mitigated through effective logistics management with AR/VR. This resonates with the concept of Construction 4.0, which aligns with the ongoing revolution in the construction industry, similar to Industry 4.0. AR/VR technologies are transforming the need for effective facility and logistics management, especially in the context of Construction 4.0 (Alaloul et al., 2020).

Quality and Sales Management

Quality Management

Ensuring high-quality construction projects is paramount; detecting defects and irregularities is key. According to Noghabaei et al. (2020), immersive technologies like AR/VR have proven effective in enhancing defect detection and improving project quality. Identifying the reasons for defects and holding project managers responsible for taking corrective actions are equally important. Recruitment and selection of highly experienced experts are crucial for maintaining quality. AR/VR technologies can aid in training and analysing the workforce's quality, ensuring the necessary skills are developed for project success. In addition, finance plays a critical role in quality maintenance tasks, and immersive technologies can be used to predict financial needs and minimise defects. As per Alaloul et al. (2022), incorporating Industry 4.0 in construction can significantly enhance quality and productivity. Skilled professionals can remotely contribute to improving the quality of architecture and aligning project goals with customer requirements, thereby ensuring project success.

Sales Management

Effective sales management is essential for project managers to ensure appropriate ROI. Immersive technologies like AR/VR can facilitate proper budget planning, optimising profits and ROI (Walasek & Barszcz, 2017). Immersive technologies can streamline the often time-consuming sales processes, resulting in enhanced consumer investment (Potseluyko et al., 2023). Efficient financial management can cultivate investor interest and prevent delays due to a lack of financial resources. AR technologies can enable investors to track construction progress and validate financial aspects efficiently, while vendors can be seamlessly connected for streamlined finance and sales management. Integrating immersive technologies like AR/VR with Industry 4.0 technologies like smart robotics, cloud computing and IoT can transform sales and revenue management (Srivastava et al., 2022). Immersive technology aids in the effective project presentation, attracting investor interest, and ensuring proper financial management. Finance validation becomes easily trackable, and vendors are seamlessly connected for streamlined financial operations, leading to efficient sales and revenue management.

Discussion, Challenges and Opportunities

Based on the information provided, it seems that there are two tables (Table 4.4) that outline the challenges and opportunities related to a specific topic.

The review paper appears to be aligned with these tables, and the discussion and summary have been critically analysed to obtain the findings from the paper. It would be helpful to know what the specific topic is and what the findings were. Integrating AR/VR technologies in the construction sector is a game-changer. These technologies enable project managers to analyse and rectify potential delays

Table 4.4. Impact of AR/VR for Project Manager in Construction Sector (A) Challenges (B) Opportunities.

Challenge	**Impact**
Part A	
Technological Integration Complexity	Adopting AR/VR technologies requires seamless integration into existing PM systems, posing challenges in compatibility and interoperability with diverse software and hardware. Complexity in technological integration may hinder the widespread adoption of immersive technologies, especially for construction firms with diverse legacy systems.
Cost Implications	Implementing AR/VR technologies involves significant upfront hardware, software development and training costs. Small and medium-sized construction firms may face financial constraints, limiting their ability to invest in immersive technologies and hindering widespread adoption.
Skill Gaps and Training	The proficient use of AR/VR technologies requires specialised skills that may be lacking in the current workforce. Inadequate training programs can underutilise the technologies, limiting their potential benefits in improving PM processes.

(Continued)

Conclusion

The construction sector has a high budget, and different parameters incur losses. A project manager is in charge of the project overall to make it successful. This review paper thoroughly discusses and finds that immersive technologies can be implemented to reduce losses and increase productivity by enhancing sales. This integration approach makes the project cost-effective and safer. It also improves the quality of the construction product. The qualitative analysis of the studies performed related to the roles and responsibilities of project managers is briefly discussed in this paper. A project manager is an important person who can affect the project effectively. It makes projects and processes sustainable and environment-friendly. It also enhances the communication between people and stakeholders related to the project. The immersive technology framework can be enhanced in the future, and few works on the construction site can be modified remotely. Devices for AR/VR/MR technology can be developed to gain more advantages.

References

Abioye, S. O., Oyedele, L. O., Akanbi, L., Ajayi, A., Delgado, J. M. D., Bilal, M., Akinade, O. O., & Ahmed, A. (2021). Artificial intelligence in the construction industry: A review of present status, opportunities and future challenges. *Journal of Building Engineering*, *44*, 103299.

Adami, P., Singh, R., Rodrigues, P. B., Becerik-Gerber, B., Soibelman, L., Copur-Gencturk, Y., & Lucas, G. (2023). Participants matter: Effectiveness of VR-based training on the knowledge, trust in the robot, and self-efficacy of construction workers and university students. *Advanced Engineering Informatics*, *55*, 101837.

Afzal, M., Li, R. Y. M., Ayyub, M. F., Shoaib, M., & Bilal, M. (2023). Towards BIM-based sustainable structural design optimization: A systematic review and industry perspective. *Sustainability*, *15*(20), 15117.

Ahmed, S. (2018). A review on using opportunities of augmented reality and virtual reality in construction project management. *Organization, Technology & Management in Construction: An International Journal*, *10*(1), 1839–1852.

Ahmed, S., Hossain, M. M., & Hoque, M. I. (2017). A brief discussion on augmented reality and virtual reality in construction industry. *Journal of System and Management Sciences*, *7*(3), 1–33.

Alaloul, W. S., Liew, M., Zawawi, N. A. W. A., & Kennedy, I. B. (2020). Industrial revolution 4.0 in the construction industry: Challenges and opportunities for stakeholders. *Ain Shams Engineering Journal*, *11*(1), 225–230.

Alaloul, W. S., Saad, S., & Qureshi, A. H. (2022). Construction sector: Ir 4.0 applications. In C. M. Hussain & P. Di Sia (Eds.), *Handbook of smart materials, technologies, and devices: Applications of Industry 4.0* (pp. 1341–1390). Springer.

Albahbah, M., Kıvrak, S., & Arslan, G. (2021). Application areas of augmented reality and virtual reality in construction project management: A scoping review. *Journal of Construction Engineering*, *14*, 151–172.

Anthes, C., García-Hernandez, R. J., Wiedemann, M., & Kranzlmüller, D. (2016). State of the art of virtual reality technology. In *2016 IEEE aerospace conference* (pp. 1–19). IEEE.

Babalola, A., Manu, P., Cheung, C., Yunusa-Kaltungo, A., & Bartolo, P. (2023). A systematic review of the application of immersive technologies for safety and health management in the construction sector. *Journal of Safety Research*, *85*, 66–85.

Bao, L., Tran, S. V. T., Nguyen, T. L., Pham, H. C., Lee, D., & Park, C. (2022). Cross-platform virtual reality for real-time construction safety training using immersive web and industry foundation classes. *Automation in Construction*, *143*, 104565.

Behzadi, A. (2016). Using augmented and virtual reality technology in the construction industry. *American Journal of Engineering Research*, *5*(12), 350–353.

Ciuffini, A. F., Di Cecca, C., Ferrise, F., Mapelli, C., & Barella, S. (2016). Application of virtual/augmented reality in steelmaking plants layout planning and logistics. *Metallurgia Italiana*, *7*, 5–10.

Conlin, J., & Retik, A. (1997). The applicability of project management software and advanced it techniques in construction delays mitigation. *International Journal of Project Management*, *15*(2), 107–120.

Fathalizadeh, A., Hosseini, M. R., Silvius, A. G., Rahimian, A., Martek, I., & Edwards, D. J. (2021). Barriers impeding sustainable project management: A social network analysis of the Iranian construction sector. *Journal of Cleaner Production*, *318*, 128405.

Gao, Y., Gonzalez, V. A., & Yiu, T. W. (2019). The effectiveness of traditional tools and computer-aided technologies for health and safety training in the construction sector: A systematic review. *Computers & Education*, *138*, 101–115.

Harichandran, A., Johansen, K. W., Jacobsen, E. L., & Teizer, J. (2021). A conceptual framework for construction safety training using dynamic virtual reality games and digital twins. In *ISARC. Proceedings of the international symposium on automation and robotics in construction* (Vol. 38, pp. 621–628). IAARC Publications.

Hou, L., Chi, H. L., Tarng, W., Chai, J., Panuwatwanich, K., & Wang, X. (2017). A framework of innovative learning for skill development in complex operational tasks. *Automation in Construction*, *83*, 29–40.

Huang, Y., Shakya, S., & Odeleye, T. (2019). Comparing the functionality between virtual reality and mixed reality for architecture and construction uses. *Journal of Civil Engineering and Architecture*, *13*(1), 409–414.

Khan, S., & Panuwatwanich, K. (2021). Applicability of building information modeling integrated augmented reality in building facility management. In *EASEC16: Proceedings of the 16th East Asian-Pacific conference on structural engineering and construction* (pp. 2139–2148). Springer.

Kharisov, I., Artamonova, I., Bilenko, P., & Sborshikov, S. (2022). Management of the implementation of a construction project based on integrated digital models. In A. Ginzburg & K. Galina (Eds.), *Building life-cycle management. Information systems and technologies. Lecture notes in civil engineering* (Vol. 231). Springer. https://doi.org/10.1007/978-3-030-96206-7_12

Kim, H. S., Kim, C. H., Moon, H. S., Moon, S. Y., Kim, Y. H., & Kang, L. S. (2013). Application of augmented reality object in construction project. In *2013 third world congress on information and communication technologies (WICT 2013)* (pp. 117–120). IEEE.

Kirchbach, K., & Runde, C. (2012). Augmented reality for construction control. In *2012 16th international conference on information visualisation* (pp. 440–444). IEEE.

Korkmaz, K. A., & Tanbour, E. Y. (2018). Augmented reality technology for highway construction project delivery. In *Proceedings of the 2018 10th international conference on computer and automation engineering* (pp. 31–35).

Lappalainen, E. M., Seppänen, O., Peltokorpi, A., & Singh, V. (2021). Transformation of construction project management toward situational awareness. *Engineering Construction and Architectural Management*, *28*(8), 2199–2221.

Nanayakkara, S., Perera, S., Bandara, D., Weerasuriya, G. T., & Ayoub, J. (2019). Blockchain technology and its potential for the construction industry. In *Proceedings of the 43rd Australasian universities building education association (AUBEA) conference: Built to thrive: Creating buildings and cities that support individual wellbeing and community prosperity* (pp. 662–672).

Nnaji, C., & Karakhan, A. A. (2020). Technologies for safety and health management in construction: Current use, implementation benefits and limitations, and adoption barriers. *Journal of Building Engineering*, *29*, 101212.

Noghabaei, M., Heydarian, A., Balali, V., & Han, K. (2020). Trend analysis on adoption of virtual and augmented reality in the architecture, engineering, and construction industry. *Data*, *5*(1), 26.

Nykänen, M., Puro, V., Tiikkaja, M., Kannisto, H., Lantto, E., Simpura, F., Uusitalo, J., Lukander, K., Räsänen, T., Heikkilä, T., & Teperi, A.-M. (2020). Implementing and evaluating novel safety training methods for construction sector workers: Results of a randomized controlled trial. *Journal of Safety Research*, *75*, 205–221.

Okpala, I., Nnaji, C., & Karakhan, A. A. (2020). Utilizing emerging technologies for construction safety risk mitigation. *Practice Periodical on Structural Design and Construction*, *25*(2), 04020002.

Omar, H., & Mahdjoubi, L. (2023). Practical solutions for improving the suboptimal performance of construction projects using dubai construction projects as an example. *Engineering Construction and Architectural Management*, *30*(6), 2185–2205.

Pamidimukkala, A., & Kermanshachi, S. (2021). Impact of Covid-19 on field and office workforce in construction industry. *Project Leadership and Society*, *2*, 100018.

Pan, Y., & Zhang, L. (2021). Roles of artificial intelligence in construction engineering and management: A critical review and future trends. *Automation in Construction*, *122*, 103517.

Potseluyko, L., Pour Rahimian, F., Dawood, N., & Elghaish, F. (2023). Application of immersive technologies in the self-building sector. In L. Potseluyko, F. P. Rahimian, N. Dawood, & F. Elghaish (Eds.), *Platform based design and immersive technologies for manufacturing and assembly in offsite construction: Applying extended reality and game applications to PDfMA* (pp. 49–66). Springer.

Rane, N. (2023, September 16). Integrating building information modelling (BIM) and artificial intelligence (AI) for smart construction schedule, cost, quality, and safety management: Challenges and opportunities. *SSRN*. https://doi.org/10.2139/ssrn.4616055

Raziapov, R. V. (2022). Application of ar technologies in the building industry. In *AIP conference proceedings* (Vol. 2559). AIP Publishing.
Rodrigues, M. (2021). Civil construction planning using augmented reality. In *Sustainability and automation in smart constructions: Proceedings of the international conference on automation innovation in construction (CIAC-2019), Leiria, Portugal* (pp. 211–217). Springer.
Safikhani, S., Keller, S., Schweiger, G., & Pirker, J. (2022). Immersive virtual reality for extending the potential of building information modeling in architecture, engineering, and construction sector: Systematic review. *International Journal of Digital Earth*, *15*(1), 503–526.
Schiavi, B., Havard, V., Beddiar, K., & Baudry, D. (2022). Bim data flow architecture with AR/VR technologies: Use cases in architecture, engineering and construction. *Automation in Construction*, *134*, 104054.
Sikarwar, R. S., & Shelake, A. G. (2022). Delay analysis of residential construction by using augmented reality and virtual reality. In *National conference on advances in construction materials and management* (pp. 41–53). Springer.
Srivastava, A., Jawaid, S., Singh, R., Gehlot, A., Akram, S. V., Priyadarshi, N., & Khan, B. (2022). Imperative role of technology intervention and implementation for automation in the construction industry. *Advances in Civil Engineering*, *2022*, 1–9.
Suh, A., & Prophet, J. (2018). The state of immersive technology research: A literature analysis. *Computers in Human Behavior*, *86*, 77–90.
Tarek, H., & Marzouk, M. (2022). Integrated augmented reality and cloud computing approach for infrastructure utilities maintenance. *Journal of Pipeline Systems Engineering and Practice*, *13*(1), 04021064.
Townsend, K., Lingard, H., Bradley, L., & Brown, K. (2012). Complicated working time arrangements: Construction industry case study. *Journal of Construction Engineering and Management*, *138*(3), 443–448.
Walasek, D., & Barszcz, A. (2017). Analysis of the adoption rate of building information modeling [BIM] and its return on investment [ROI]. *Procedia Engineering*, *172*, 1227–1234.
Wang, Q., & Kim, M. K. (2019). Applications of 3d point cloud data in the construction industry: A fifteen-year review from 2004 to 2018. *Advanced Engineering Informatics*, *39*, 306–319.
Yu, Z., Peng, H., Zeng, X., Sofi, M., Xing, H., & Zhou, Z. (2018). Smarter construction site management using the latest information technology. In *Proceedings of the institution of civil engineers-civil engineering* (Vol. 172, pp. 89–95). Thomas Telford Ltd.

performance management, posing numerous challenges, and provides guidance for organisations looking to implement these technologies. This paper highlights recent efforts related to emotional AI and how it can be applied within an updated performance management context.

Keywords: Emotional AI; performance evaluation; performance management; sentiment analysis; emotion recognition

Introduction

In the modern era, the fast-paced business world means organisations constantly seek new ways to improve performance evaluation and management. However, since this performance evaluation is predicated on subjective assessments and a very small scale of data collection, it can bring about irregularities and prejudices (Cherniss & Goleman, 2019). The issue although seems to underscore the precision and objectivity with which enterprises evaluate employee performance that supposedly Emotional AI (Emotional Artificial Intelligence) aims to address (Gupta et al., 2023). This helps in a more accurate, objective and empathetic way of performance appraisal and management form the Human Resource perspective using Emotional AI. But the more human centric aspect of Emotional AI means that it cares about employee welfare and then assesses the rest as part of a bigger picture (Li et al., 2021). It provides companies with the necessary data for growing beyond traditional performance measurement, which fails to capture most of the emotional and mental work crucial to a successful future of work and employee satisfaction. Emotional AI serves a critical role in distilling the emotional and psychological features which drastically affect long-term efficacy and worker contentment (Patel & Sharma, 2022). A productive employee can still burn out, become extremely stressed or disengage, and these issues may not always show up in the context of traditional evaluations. Early intervention could prevent the drop in performance or morale by identifying trends like this before they even begin and emotional AI can do just that (Singh et al., 2024).

And another impressive use-case: removing bias and subjectivity from performance reviews (Emotional AI). These can sometimes impact traditional assessments due to unusually relative bias, occasional prevalence of favouritism, cultural misunderstanding or unconscious bias (Zhang et al., 2020). In contrast, data-driven emotional AI can objectively identify discrete emotional cues itself rather than through the filter of possibly corrupt human impressions. So, those performance reviews are even more of a level playing field to benefit all employees equally (Zhang & Liu, 2021).

It is also worth noting that emotional AI, a type of artificial intelligence that discerns overall characteristics of human emotional reflection, expression and experiencing joy or sadness, etc., Goleman and Cherniss (2019) could have huge implications on how conducive performance management systems are achieved in the future. It is a more advanced form of data analysis that utilises machine learning and natural language processing as well as affective computing.

Understanding emotions that can be extracted from speech, facial expression or body reactions provides a better way to perform performance analysis of employees (Brown & Lee, 2022).

Using emotional AI to evaluate employees within an organisation enables managers to measure beyond mundane numbers and other mechanical standards and reach the more personal level of a team member's emotional signature amongst peers (Kim & Lee, 2023). It aids in more effective job performance evaluation, enhanced point-to-point feedback and an exemplary management approach. Real-time sentiment analysis might show a manager how employees react to feedback and potential issues before they become serious (Berkovsky et al., 2019). These emotion recognition tools can tell how employees interact with their coworkers or allow you to monitor workplace stress among individuals to streamline development and support. The use of emotional AI in management has some obvious benefits but also creates many challenges (Bhardwaj & Kumar, 2021). In order to guarantee the effective and responsible use of this technology, some other significant concerns, like data privacy, ethical considerations and the validation process that AI models undergo, must be tackled (Bianchi-Berthouze, 2019).

Emotional AI Be Integrated Into Traditional Performance

By doing so, integrating Emotional AI with old performance review processes boosts the efficacy and rationality of evaluations. Also, find out how businesses can implement this technology successfully into the current situations (Boehm & Lyubomirsky, 2018). Likewise, emotional AI can dissect the emotional conditions of employees using different data sets from communication patterns to facial expressions. By connecting this feedback back to performance reviews, organisations are able to leverage insights into the broader view of employee performance (Calvo & Peters, 2019). So that means if an employee is consistently stressed or aggravated, managers may want to take the people-centred part of a job into consideration when assessing their work performance; mechanisms for frequently receiving feedback while traditional performance reviews are usually handled semi-annually (or even annually), the long lags where employees do not receive feedback become unnecessary squandered time. Unprecedented emotional AI provides dynamic test results approached by daily tracking of employee performance and happiness (Canli & Lesch, 2020). This way, managers are able to address issues right as they come up contributing towards an environment of constant learning and support rather than waiting for annual reviews, untapped potential simply by analysing human emotions and put together with performance data could point out the order of emotional sentiment in an individual identifying strengths or lack of those may accomplishment (Carter & Lee, 2020). Enter this information when developing a development plan that is personalised to your employees. For example, if an employee is excellent at working in a group but fails when it comes to talking with the audience, they can suggest special courses on these topics. Emotional AI can give managers data-driven insights on how employees feel and perform to facilitate better decision-making (Clarke & Watson, 2022). AI can help reveal patterns that are harder to spot in real time say a downward trend in engagement or motivation for instance, giving managers the ability to address these sooner than later. These data could supplement human judgement making sure that evaluations are fair and complete (Crutchfield & Richards, 2021).

Additionally, ethical concern that organisations will be grappling with about as we start to integrate Emotional AI in our day-to-day lives. Therefore, decision-makers for performance evaluations need to have very clear policies on how they collect and analyse emotional data. Discretion with the employees in terms of these processes will help ensure that trust is built and technology used wisely (D'Mello & Graesser, 2020). While Emotional AI provides more benefits than a simple modal or numerical review, the human aspect of reviews is not replaceable. Human-centric AI should reinforce human judgement rather than supersede it (Danson & Roe, 2021). AI-generated insights should be leveraged as a facilitator for managers to improve their assessments, making sure that human interactions continue playing centre stage in the reviews. This balance will help retain the employee engagement and morale that can come from getting personal feedback or support (De Graaf & Allouch, 2022).

Understanding Emotional AI: Emotional AI is a colloquial name for affective computing and can be defined as systems or devices that can sense, interpret and theoretically respond to human emotions (Di Domenico & Ryan, 2019). These systems analyse a variety of inputs, such as facial expressions, voice tonality and intonation patterns, body movements/posture or physiological signals, to estimate the emotional state. This technology draws from psychology and computer science and is born from machine learning and neural network growth (Duffy & Gross, 2020).

Applications of Emotional AI in Different Sectors: Although the technology is still nascent, its applications can be seen across healthcare, education, customer service and human resources (Ekman & Keltner, 2018). Emotion recognition technology allows a deep understanding of behavioural patterns that can be utilised in therapy, customer service and assessing employee well-being and performance. This paper investigates Emotional AI's role in Performance Appraisal and Management. I will review the latest developments in Emotional AI and its organisational applications and assess it as a new force for performance management. Through case studies and empirical evidence, this study aims to analyse how Emotional AI can aid in bettering performance evaluation processes, leading to superior management strategies (Elfenbein & Ambady, 2021).

Emotional AI is a game changer in improving performance evaluation and management for different sectors, as such systems can identify the emotions of users. Implementing this method in performance management systems can help reduce personal bias and subjectivity from reviews and drive better employee engagement, which corollaries in more robust organisational outcomes (Fernandez & Chapman, 2021).

Significance of Emotional AI Matter in the Context of Performance Evaluation

Traditional performance evaluations are rife with human biases that yield outcomes and influence spirits. Emotional AI, however, is another way humans make decisions without human biases using data. Human emotions are intricate and therefore it is subject to variability. Using any experience of human beings who give subjective response – Objective models designed in the Biometric field which usually utilises specific algorithm known since machines do not get partial all responses seen could be into adjustable unique operation but standardised across untold human interaction dry run reveal based on predictive multimodal biometrics: voice tone/facial recognition analysis combined – espressivo (Fischer & Manstead, 2022). The AI systems could generate a more accurate level of an employee's performance, based off the cues they find from emotions and behaviour that would be difficult to measure without AI and unbiased as to whether or not said employee deserves promotion/reward. Yet, Emotional AI facilitates ongoing tracking – not just an era of episodic encounters (Frijda & Mesquita, 2020).

It enables businesses to collect live data about the performance of employees which will help them in delivering feedback and coaching at the right time (Goleman & Boyatzis, 2022). This kind of immediacy enables employees correct performance more rapidly, and contributes to an environment focused on daily improvement and development (Grandey et al., 2020).

Also, Emotional AI in performance management will increase employee engagement. Intelligent surveys and personalised insights conducted by AI systems give employees the opportunity to be more engaged in their evaluations (Gross & John, 2021). This in turn results to improved job satisfaction and higher retention rates since employees are likely to feel appreciated, heard and understood. Consequently, Emotional AI is able to determine which skills are causing a person to fail and prescribe personalised training programs. Based on performance data, AI can guide the best-suited development paths tailored to employees' career aspirations and organisational needs (Hallowell & Li, 2021). This data-driven approach not just helps employees to build their skill set, it also results in improving the overall performance of any organisation (Humphrey & Ashforth, 2020). Thus, it delivers end-to-end performance feedback of employees to the managers for making informed decisions. Use strategic talent management to provide feedback with more data led approach so that it is accurate and justified (Ickes & Simpson, 2019).

Literature Review

One example of this is Emotional AI. In fact, its application to management evaluation as well as performance evaluation has been discussed at length for several years. In this literature review, we have examined this state-of-the-art research on Emotional AI in performance evaluation, technological advancements and

Data Analysis and Discussion

The descriptive statistics of the survey data provide a detailed overview of the HR professionals and managers' demographics (Table 5.1), their experience with Emotional AI and their perceptions of its effectiveness. The respondents have an average age of 39.2 and a standard deviation of 10.5, showing a good range in age among them. These professionals have an average of 12.3 years of experience in HR or management; this points to a high level of expertise within their respective fields.

On the other hand, the mean of 2.8 years about their experience using emotional AI indicates that although the majority of the respondents are acquainted with this technology to an extent, its integration into their practices is somewhat recent. One to seven years of experience suggests a wide range and may affect the level of familiarity with Emotional AI tools in-depth. Perceived accuracy of emotional AI is rated high, with an average score of 4.1 and a standard deviation of 0.8, which is an overall positive score for the tech being able to deliver precise evaluations. With a mean of 4.3 and SD = 0.7, this suggests that respondents thought Emotional AI also makes performance assessment more objective. It is clear from these scores that there are some differences across the different members in the perception of when we should use air power (along with it ranging from 2 to 5), overall satisfaction with Emotional AI, scored at a mean of 3.9 (SD = 0.9), highlights a general positive, but slightly ambiguous perspective regarding the effect – or better lack thereof – of the technology. Respondents rated their satisfaction with Emotional AI on a scale of 2–5, and overall the results show high levels of satisfaction from customers, but also points to areas for improvement with addressing adverse concerns and increasing (end-user) experiences (Velagaleti et al., 2024). To sum up, these findings suggest that emotional

Table 5.1. Descriptive Statistics of HR Professionals and Managers.

Variable	Mean	Standard Deviation	Minimum	Maximum
Age	39.2	10.5	25	58
Years in HR/Management	12.3	8.4	3	30
Experience with emotional AI (years)	2.8	1.9	0.5	7
Perceived accuracy of emotional AI	4.1	0.8	2	5
Perceived objectivity of evaluations	4.3	0.7	2.5	5
Overall satisfaction with emotional AI	3.9	0.9	2	5

Source: Original work.

AI is seen as a valuable technology in terms of performance evaluation but also outshines human judgement in terms of precision and objectivity (Vistorte et al., 2024b). However, the inconsistent pleasure and efficacy experienced means that more specific Emotional AI system development is needed to meet user needs and organisational constraints (Varma et al., 2024).

Hypothesis Testing

Paired Sample *T*-Test results (Table 5.2) show that performance appraisals made with emotional AI are more accurate and objective than traditional appraisals. However, in terms of evaluations, the mean score for traditional methods is 3.8, whereas Emotional AI evaluations show higher with a mean score of 4.2 T (Sharma & Mishra, 2024).

The mean difference of −0.4 indicates that Emotional AI technologies are associated with improved accuracy. The test statistic (*t*-value) of −3.50 and the *p*-value of 0.001 confirm that this difference is statistically significant, suggesting that Emotional AI significantly enhances the accuracy of performance evaluations. The mean score indicates that traditional evaluations scored 3.9 for objectivity, while Emotional AI scored a +0.4 higher on average (objectively). In other words, Emotional AI likely makes your assessments more objective per se; this is also supported by the mean difference of −0.4 and a *t*-value of −4.10 ($p < 0.001$). Having both *p*-values below 0.05 is pretty strong evidence to invalidate the null hypothesis and, as a result, prove that Emotional AI technologies do better in accuracy and objectivity than traditional ones. These results reinforce the potential of this type of technology to improve performance reviews.

Discussion

The results of this study provide insights into the significant effects Emotional AI technologies can have on facilitating more accurate and unbiased performance appraisals (Mantello & Ho, 2024). Paired Sample *T*-test results corroborated this

Table 5.2. Paired Sample *T*-Test Results.

Metric	Mean (Traditional)	Mean (Emotional AI)	Mean Difference	Standard Deviation	*t*-Value	*p*-Value
Accuracy of evaluations	3.8	4.2	−0.4	0.9	−3.50	0.001
Objectivity of evaluations	3.9	4.3	−0.4	0.8	−4.10	<0.001

Source: Original work.

hypothesis, showing that Emotional AI significantly outperforms traditional evaluations (Better Accuracy and Precision) (Subhadarshini et al., 2024).

Evaluations: While their emotions are measured so accurately with Emotional AI technologies, the increased degrees of accuracy imply these tools better evaluate employee positioning (Magni et al., 2024). Traditional evaluation processes are typically subjective, leading to inaccuracies and often reflecting assessment biases. Emotional AI uses algorithms and data analytics to provide an objective perspective of different components involved in the performance measurement process, making it more reliable in evaluating employees (Zhang, Antwi-Afari, et al., 2024). There is the opportunity for increased precision in decision-making, promotion of non-discriminatory performance evaluations and a return to appropriateness within morals (Guo et al., 2024).

The objectivity of assessments: As Emotional AI technologies come to the fore, we see increased objectivity and a decrease in bias or subjectivity from performance evaluations (Zhang, Chen, et al., 2024). Those traditional methods can be susceptible to personal biases that might jeopardise the fairness and consistency of evaluations (Chang et al., 2024). The Emotional AI solutions provide data-driven insights that use science to remove human biases and add a more objective layer (Zhou et al., 2024). It could well be argued that we should come as close to perfective or imperfection as we can when appraising employee performance (Sharma & Tiwari, 2024). This increased objectivity is vital to ensure a fair and more standardised performance management system that avoids evaluations based solely on one's own subjective buying in, or not buying into an individual (Singh & Chouhan, 2023).

Organisational implications: The practice implications for organisations of similarly improving evaluation power with Emotional AI. If emotional AI is integrated into the organisation's performance management system, doing so can make performance reviews more accurate and objective (Zhao et al., 2024). Implementing these technologies can help organisations improve feedback mechanisms, personalised growth programs and talent development efforts. However, organisations need to be mindful of risks. How can we responsibly deploy Emotional AI so that it is ethical and provides the desired outcomes?

Challenges and Limitations of Traditional Performance Evaluation

Subjectivity and Bias: Traditional performance evaluation systems are fraught with bias, which may be conscious or unconscious. Despite their best intentions, managers can let personal biases, anecdotal experiences and cultural misunderstandings taint how they perceive employees (Venkateswaran et al., 2024). This subjectiveness may result in biased assessments that are not a fair measure of morale and career advancement.

Lack of Comprehensive Behavioural Understanding: Traditional appraisals often only measure productivity results, like sales stats, project completion records/attendance, etc. However, these metrics cannot take into account intangibles such as motivation, team spirit, creativity and stress levels. It is, after all, a bad idea to be mindful of how stressful work becomes long-term sustainable (Jia et al., 2024).

Feedback Mechanisms and Employee Development Performance reviews happen once or twice a year, which means employees will only get feedback in 6–12 months (Yin et al., 2024). This can also make process improvements more difficult by widening the gap between current behaviours and previous assessments. Enter Emotional AI can solve these limitations by assessing each situation in real time (Lai et al., 2024).

Bioethical, Moral Aspects of Emotional AI Privacy and Consent Collection of emotional data wreaks havoc with privacy requirements for apparent reasons (Warrier et al., 2024), thereby breaching existing laws regulating the invasion of a person's rights as the algorithm or organisation may have argued that if every smile is equivalent to understanding exact sentiment, then what could be considered proprietary? (Al Naqbi et al., 2024). Data can only be collected to the extent that employees have been adequately informed, and this must include why it is being done. Clear policies must be established around the ethical and transparent use of employee emotional data (Barile et al., 2022).

Increasing over-surveillance risk: Although AI brings abundant opportunities (Chaturvedi et al., 2023), it also enhances the threat of increased emotional intelligence derived from data captured during a regular conversational flow (over-surveillance) (Edwards & Steers, 2021). Their constant display of their emotions can make them feel like they are being 'watched' and undermine trust in the employee/manager relationship (Gagné et al., 2021). Finding an equilibrium between checking and setting against privacy is essential for a good relationship between employees and AI systems (Matson & Shiga, 2022).

Bias in Emotional AI Systems: Like all AI systems, those based on emotional interpretation are subject to bias relating to their training data (Norman & Hogan, 2021). For example, it is known that if the emotional recognition system is taught to a very limited demographic, then understanding transfers poorly between cultures (or personality types) (Sanchez-Burks & Huy, 2022). Creating fair and unbiased Emotional AI systems involves using diverse and representative training data (Wilk & Groth, 2023).

Future Research Directions: Although this study contributes to our understanding of Emotional AI's efficacy, more research is required to identify its possible long-term effects and drawbacks (Liu & Wang, 2023). Further research is needed to evaluate the practical use of Emotional AI in diverse industry-specific contexts and its implications for employees' satisfaction and development, including mechanisms tailored specifically towards ensuring integration with existing performance management tools (Zheng & Wu, 2022). Furthermore, research efforts should overcome the threats posed by emotional AI technologies at an ethical level and ensure their proper deployment (Kumar & Muralidharan, 2022). In short, it confirms the game-changing value of Emotional AI in performance evaluation and management. Emotional AI technologies can help to make performance management less biased and more effective by improving the quality of manager evaluations (Reddy & Thompson, 2021). The potential for Emotional

D'Mello, S. K., & Graesser, A. C. (2020). Analyzing affective states during human-computer interaction using facial emotion recognition. *International Journal of Human-Computer Studies*, *140*, 102434. https://doi.org/10.1016/j.ijhcs.2020.102434
Danson, A., & Roe, R. A. (2021). AI-enhanced employee evaluations: The role of emotional intelligence. *Journal of Organizational Behavior*, *42*(2), 205–224. https://doi.org/10.1002/job.2525
De Graaf, M. M. A., & Allouch, S. B. (2022). Emotional AI and trust in the workplace. *Computers in Human Behavior*, *133*, 107287. https://doi.org/10.1016/j.chb.2022.107287
Di Domenico, M., & Ryan, R. M. (2019). AI-driven emotion recognition and its impact on employee motivation. *Journal of Business Research*, *105*, 160–170.
Du, Y., Crespo, R. G., & Martínez, O. S. (2023). Human emotion recognition for enhanced performance evaluation in e-learning. *Progress in Artificial Intelligence*, *12*(2), 199–211.
Duffy, M. K., & Gross, J. J. (2020). Emotional AI in conflict management and its role in promoting workplace harmony. *Academy of Management Review*, *45*(3), 687–707.
Dutta, A., & Singh, A. (2022). Emotional AI applications in performance management: Innovations and challenges. *Journal of Organizational Psychology*, *22*(4), 45–59.
Edwards, G., & Steers, J. (2021). Emotional AI in the workplace: Integrating technology for effective performance evaluation. *International Journal of Human-Computer Interaction*, *37*(10), 902–919.
Ekman, P., & Keltner, D. (2018). Emotion AI: Challenges in detecting and interpreting human emotions. *Annual Review of Psychology*, *69*, 625–647.
Elfenbein, H. A., & Ambady, N. (2021). Leveraging emotional AI to enhance performance feedback. *Psychological Bulletin*, *147*(5), 500–521. https://doi.org/10.1037/bul0000343
Fernandez, R. S., & Chapman, K. (2021). Emotional AI: Enhancing employee well-being through adaptive feedback. *Human Resource Management Review*, *31*(4), 100746. https://doi.org/10.1016/j.hrmr.2020.100746
Fischer, A. H., & Manstead, A. S. R. (2022). Emotion recognition in AI and its applications in workplace settings. *Cognition & Emotion*, *36*(2), 192–211.
Frijda, N. H., & Mesquita, B. (2020). Emotional AI and its role in organisational decision-making. *Journal of Business Ethics*, *167*(3), 497–512.
Gagné, M., Deci, E. L., & Ryan, R. M. (2021). The role of emotions in motivation and performance management: Implications for the workplace. *Industrial and Organizational Psychology*, *14*(4), 671–689. https://doi.org/10.1017/iop.2021.56
Goleman, D., & Boyatzis, R. E. (2022). Emotional intelligence and AI-driven management systems: Implications for leadership. *Frontiers in Psychology*, *13*, 820393.
Goleman, D., & Cherniss, C. (2019). The impact of emotional intelligence on workplace performance: A comprehensive review. *Academy of Management Perspectives*, *33*(1), 1–16. https://doi.org/10.5465/amp.2018.0086
Grandey, A. A., & Gabriel, A. S. (2020). The dark side of emotional labour in AI-mediated performance evaluation. *Journal of Occupational Health Psychology*, *25*(4), 231–245.

Gray, P., & Finney, J. (2022). Enhancing performance reviews with emotional AI: Benefits and risks. *Human Resource Development Quarterly*, *33*(3), 311–327. https://doi.org/10.1002/hrdq.21402

Gross, J. J., & John, O. P. (2021). Emotional AI and its potential to transform performance management. *Organizational Behavior and Human Decision Processes, 161*, 1–10. https://doi.org/10.1016/j.obhdp.2020.12.002

Guo, Y., Li, Y., Liu, D., & Xu, S. X. (2024). Measuring service quality based on customer emotion: An explainable AI approach. *Decision Support Systems, 176*, 114051.

Gupta, R., Sharma, S., & Patel, N. (2023). AI-enhanced performance evaluation and employee development: A review. *Human Resource Management Review*, *33*(2), 100–112.

Hallowell, N., & Li, C. (2021). The role of AI in enhancing emotional intelligence: A review of empirical studies. *AI & Society*, *36*(4), 933–944.

Harrington, A., & Lee, S. (2023). Evaluating the effectiveness of emotional AI in employee performance assessments. *International Journal of Management Reviews*, *25*(2), 272–290. https://doi.org/10.1111/ijmr.12345

Hernandez, J., & Li, W. (2021). Emotional intelligence and AI-driven performance metrics: A new paradigm for employee evaluation. *Technology in Society*, *67*, 101723. https://doi.org/10.1016/j.techsoc.2021.101723

Humphrey, R. H., & Ashforth, B. E. (2020). How emotional AI is changing leadership styles in the digital age. *Leadership Quarterly*, *31*(4), 101315. https://doi.org/10.1016/j.leaqua.2019.101315

Ickes, W., & Simpson, J. A. (2019). Emotion recognition in AI systems: New directions for research and applications. *Emotion Review*, *11*(3), 219–232.

Isen, A. M., & Gopal, A. (2021). The impact of emotional AI on productivity and well-being in organizations. *Journal of Applied Psychology*, *106*(5), 787–801. https://doi.org/10.1037/apl0000847

Jain, A., & Fauvel, S. (2020). Emotion AI and organizational culture: Opportunities and challenges. *Information & Management*, *57*(4), 103244.

Jia, N., Luo, X., Fang, Z., & Liao, C. (2024). When and how artificial intelligence augments employee creativity. *Academy of Management Journal*, *67*(1), 5–32.

Joseph, D. L., & Newman, D. A. (2019). Emotional AI and employee development. A meta-analysis of outcomes. *Human Performance*, *32*(4), 275–290.

Keltner, D., & Ekman, P. (2021). Emotion AI and its implications for employee evaluations and workplace dynamics. *Social Cognitive and Affective Neuroscience*, *16*(5), 467–479. https://doi.org/10.1093/scan/nsab013

Kim, H., & Lee, J. (2023). Ethical considerations and data privacy in emotional AI applications. *Ethics and Information Technology*, *25*(3), 211–225.

Kleber, B. T., & DeChurch, L. A. (2020). Emotional AI in the workplace: Impacts on teamwork and collaboration. *Group & Organization Management*, *45*(2), 175–201.

Kumar, V., & Muralidharan, A. (2022). Leveraging emotional AI for enhanced employee engagement and performance evaluation. *Human Resource Management Journal*, *32*(4), 445–461. https://doi.org/10.1111/1748-8583.12345

Lai, T., Zeng, X., Xu, B., Xie, C., Liu, Y., Wang, Z., & Fu, S. (2024). The application of artificial intelligence technology in education influences Chinese adolescent's emotional perception. *Current Psychology*, *43*(6), 5309–5317.

Lazarus, R. S., & Folkman, S. (2020). AI-driven emotion recognition and its role in stress management. *Journal of Occupational Health Psychology*, *25*(3), 174–186.

Li, J., Chen, X., & Wang, L. (2021). Real-time sentiment analysis for employee feedback: Applications and implications. *International Journal of Human-Computer Studies*, *149*, 102621. https://doi.org/10.1016/j.ijhcs.2021.102621

Liu, Y., & Wang, L. (2023). Emotional AI in performance management: A review and future research agenda. *Journal of Organizational Behavior*, *44*(5), 634–655. https://doi.org/10.1002/job.2707

Magni, D., Del Gaudio, G., Papa, A., & Della Corte, V. (2024). Digital humanism and artificial intelligence: The role of emotions beyond the human-machine interaction in Society 5.0. *Journal of Management History*, *30*(2), 195–218.

Mantello, P., & Ho, M. T. (2024). Emotional AI and the future of wellbeing in the post-pandemic workplace. *AI & Society*, *39*(4), 1883–1889.

Matson, E., & Shiga, S. (2022). Enhancing employee performance through emotional AI: Ethical considerations and practical applications. *AI & Society*, *37*(3), 711–723.

Norman, J., & Hogan, R. (2021). Emotional intelligence and AI-driven performance assessment: A synergy for the future workforce. *Journal of Applied Psychology*, *106*(12), 1983–1996. https://doi.org/10.1037/apl0000906

Patel, N., & Bhatia, R. (2021). Emotional AI in organizational performance management: Theory and practice. *Business Horizons*, *64*(6), 761–772. https://doi.org/10.1016/j.bushor.2021.09.002

Patel, N., & Sharma, S. (2022). Enhancing feedback mechanisms with AI-driven emotion recognition tools. *Performance Improvement Quarterly*, *35*(1), 15–30. https://doi.org/10.1002/piq.21345

Prentice, C., Dominique Lopes, S., & Wang, X. (2020). Emotional intelligence or artificial intelligence–an employee perspective. *Journal of Hospitality Marketing & Management*, *29*(4), 377–403.

Ramamurthy, C., & Anitha, B. (2024). Moderating role of AI on the relationship between emotional intelligence and employee performance. *Educational Administration: Theory and Practice*, *30*(5), 14174–14180.

Reddy, S., & Thompson, D. (2021). The role of emotional intelligence and AI in modern performance management systems. *Journal of Strategic and International Studies*, *12*(2), 85–99.

Sanchez-Burks, J., & Huy, Q. (2022). Emotional AI and leadership: Enhancing performance management through empathy and data-driven insights. *The Leadership Quarterly*, *33*(1), 101597. https://doi.org/10.1016/j.leaqua.2021.101597

Saxena, P., Priyadarshini, I., Sharma, S., & Jora, R. B. (2022, March). Role of emotional and artificial intelligence on employee performance in service industry: A review of literature. In *2022 8th international conference on advanced computing and communication systems (ICACCS)* (Vol. 1, pp. 1564–1567). IEEE.

Sharma, A., & Mishra, A. (2024). Power of emotions in AI: Strengthening the bond of human-machine with heart. In *Artificial intelligence solutions for cyber-physical systems* (pp. 64–72). Auerbach Publications.

Sharma, S., & Saxena, P. (2024). Role of emotional and artificial intelligence in employee performance: A perspective from the Indian service industry. *Abhigyan*, *42*(1), 43–56.

Sharma, S., & Tiwari, V. (2024). Emotional intelligence in business and management: A bibliometric analysis of the last two decades. *Vision*, *28*(4), 419–435.

Singh, A., & Chouhan, T. (2023). Artificial intelligence in HRM: Role of emotional-social intelligence and future work skill. In *The adoption and effect of artificial intelligence on human resources management, part A* (pp. 175–196). Emerald Publishing Limited.

Singh, A., Kumar, R., & Das, S. (2024). Validation and reliability of AI models in performance management: Challenges and solutions. *Journal of Applied AI Research*, *40*(4), 187–205.

Subhadarshini, S., Nayak, A., & Sukanya Nisitgandha Biswal, D. S. C. (2024). The Future of performance management: Leveraging AI for better feedback and coaching. *Journal of Informatics Education and Research*, *4*(2).

Varma, A., Pereira, V., & Patel, P. (2024). Artificial intelligence and performance management. *Organizational Dynamics*, *53*(1), 101037.

Velagaleti, S. B., Choukaier, D., Nuthakki, R., Lamba, V., Sharma, V., & Rahul, S. (2024). Empathetic algorithms: The role of AI in understanding and enhancing human emotional intelligence. *Journal of Electrical Systems*, *20*(3s), 2051–2060.

Venkateswaran, P. S., Dominic, M. L., Agarwal, S., Oberai, H., Anand, I., & Rajest, S. S. (2024). The role of artificial intelligence (AI) in enhancing marketing and customer loyalty. In *Data-driven intelligent business sustainability* (pp. 32–47). IGI Global.

Vistorte, A. O. R., Deroncele-Acosta, A., Ayala, J. L. M., Barrasa, A., López-Granero, C., & Martí-González, M. (2024b). Integrating artificial intelligence to assess emotions in learning environments: A systematic literature review. *Frontiers in Psychology*, *15*, 1387089.

Vistorte, A. O. R., Deroncele-Acosta, A., Ayala, J. L. M., Barrasa, A., López-Granero, C., & Martí-González, M. (2024a). Integrating artificial intelligence to assess emotions in learning environments: A systematic literature review. *Frontiers in Psychology*, *15*, 1387089.

Warrier, U., Shankar, A., & Belal, H. M. (2024). Examining the role of emotional intelligence as a moderator for virtual communication and decision-making effectiveness during the COVID-19 crisis: Revisiting task technology fit theory. *Annals of Operations Research*, *335*(3), 1519–1535.

Wilk, S. L., & Groth, M. (2023). Integrating emotional AI into performance feedback systems: Opportunities and challenges. *Human Resource Management Review*, *33*(2), 100845.

Yellapantula, K., & Ayachit, M. (2019). Significance of emotional intelligence in the era of artificial intelligence: A study on the application of artificial intelligence in the financial and educational services sector. *Ushus Journal of Business Management*, *18*(1), 35–48.

Yin, M., Jiang, S., & Niu, X. (2024). Can AI help? The double-edged sword effect of AI assistant on employees' innovation behaviour. *Computers in Human Behavior*, *150*, 107987.

Zhang, X., Antwi-Afari, M. F., Zhang, Y., & Xing, X. (2024). The impact of artificial intelligence on organizational justice and project performance: A systematic literature and science mapping review. *Buildings*, *14*(1), 259.

Zhang, J., Chen, Q., Lu, J., Wang, X., Liu, L., & Feng, Y. (2024). Emotional expression by artificial intelligence chatbots to improve customer satisfaction: Underlying mechanism and boundary conditions. *Tourism Management*, *100*, 104835.

the threats and hindrances. It goes into the current legal area, views various laws and regulations for AI but also looks at where laws and regulations are lacking or have limits. This chapter thereafter discusses important legal aspects such as transparency, accountability, and liability of AI systems; privacy issues and data protection in relation to AI and machine learning; biases inherent in the data used by ML algorithms, or other algorithmic decision-making systems; and human rights dimensions of these. It delves into these issues in detail with recent research and case studies. It introduces a new legal framework to tackle these issues, through encouraging appropriate development and use of AI, providing human agency, oversight and control over AI that may affect individuals as well as protecting fundamental rights and freedoms. The plan includes significant aspects, such as compulsory impact assessments for AI applications at high risk, obligations to be certified and audited, accountability mechanisms and a reinforced transparency enabled by disclosure (Wright & Kreissl, 2018).

AI has gained momentous popularity among the security intelligence community with surveillance, data analysis and threat detection topping the list of numerous AI technologies that have been deployed (Zuboff, 2019). The advancements of AI, in this area can be understood by the fact that recently number of studies shows that it automates those processes which were operating under human intervention in traditional process and subsequently ensure more efficient way not only for identifying potential threats but also do it with much precise accuracy (Binns, 2018). For example, AI has the potential to revolutionise cybersecurity by automating threat detection and response, thus taking cyber defenses to a whole new level of readiness considering how much more vicious-driven and advanced threats are getting more often today (Cath, 2018). Yet the application of AI systems in security contexts raises issues about accountability, transparency, and ethical implications. One of the central challenges is that there is no single definition for what AI refers to and how it functions with security intelligence. Various stages of legislative frameworks are in place across different jurisdictions to deal with these (Dignum, 2019). For instance, a few countries have started to examine the legal facets of AI decision-making, most notably in terms of who or what should be held responsible when self-directed machines take actions (Gasser & Almeida, 2017). This ambiguity of whether AI is to be considered as an object or a Subject of Law, complicates the measures required for establishing accountability mechanisms. Second is uncertainty, this can also create the obstacle for regulating AI in security applications effectively (Jobin et al., 2019). Additionally, the lower down the chain intelligent systems come in relation to autonomy, the more legal questions are raised about their compliance with existing standards surrounding privacy, data protection and broader human rights. As AI can perform ever greater surveillance, the technology raises significant privacy concerns: its effectiveness frequently depends on such data being linked with vast quantities of personal information (Kahn & Kearns, 2020). The real challenge is combining the operational advantages of AI and fulfiling individuals' basic rights. More recent authors cite concerns for security dangers to democracy due to AI and say strict data protection and ethical policies governing AI use in security settings is essential as a measure against potential abuses which could protect citizens rights (Mittelstadt et al., 2016).

The law must also tackle bias and discrimination in the AI algorithms. Research has found that AI can also inherit human prejudices, and do so in a way that escapes them gone the system is allowed to operate without unwavering monitoring and regulation. And for good reason, as a lack of transparency in this field can often result in biased algorithms and unfair profiling of individuals or groups – particularly dangerous when dealing with security intelligence. That said, establishing principles of global standards as far as fairness and accountability are concerned will effectively ensure that AI technologies become an active player in the security projects while maintaining a level of ethics (Russell & Norvig, 2020). At the end of the day, with AI constantly getting better and being used across a wide range of industry sectors – from security intelligence to health data processing – we need thorough legal regulation in place that takes into account what might go wrong. This framework should include an agreed scope for AI, accountability mechanisms for autonomous systems, respect of privacy rights for individuals and guidelines on bias mitigation. Addressing these issues at an early stage might enable policy makers to take full advantage of the potential benefits of AI, and do so in a way that would respect fundamental rights while applying ethical governance to practices around security. Subsequent parts of this paper will explore these problems further and offer practical solutions for constructing a workable legal framework to govern the employment of AI in security intelligence (Russell & Norvig, 2020).

Background on the Use of AI in Security Intelligence

Security intelligence has become increasingly important with the growing volume of AI in recent years as it strengthens threat detection and response capabilities. Cyber threats are growing in quality and size, for which conventional security measures are usually inadequate, requiring the assistance of AI technologies. Covered in Part 2 of this series, Background section on AI/ML applications in Security Intelligence, outlining AI capabilities with benefits and challenges. AI is the capability of a machine to imitate intelligent human behaviour such as learning, reasoning, and problem-solving. From a security intelligence perspective, AI is used in many ways including machine learning, deep learning and natural language processing. This includes being able to process massive amounts of information quickly and identify trends that could suggest threats in security systems. For example, AI algorithms can parse through the millions of events and find anomalies that could mean a possible cyberattack or security vulnerability – which allows organisations to respond as things happen instead of reacting after it has already happened. Security intelligence AI is used widely in security intelligence, with one major application of it is cybersecurity (Smith et al., 2014). AI has been shown to automate threat detection, which enables organisations to detect and counterbalance risks quicker than ever before in the traditional methods.

Security systems benefit tremendously from machine learning because they allow such systems to adapt to new threats by analysing historical data, constantly refining the way in which they operate (Solove, 2021). Now more years down the track, with today's evolved threats and adversaries running rampant employment of sophisticated tactics to remain under the radar, this has become a critical capability. According to one systematic review, organisations that employed AI cybersecurity saw 30% better threat detection and response times (Taddeo & Floridi, 2018).

AI being used in the Physical Security Domain A common example is an AI integrated surveillance system that can alert to unusual activities during real-time video feed analysis and determine unauthorised access attempts. Facial recognition and behaviour analysis technology systems help security personnel to ensure improved situational awareness (Thierer, 2016). Combining AI with physical security enhances operational efficiency, whilst allowing for better allocation of resources through enhanced threat based alert notification (United Nations Educational Scientific and Cultural Organization (UNESCO), 2021). While AI automation has several advantages to security intelligence, there are roadblocks that must be discovered and dealt with. Arguably the biggest issue around AI algorithms is bias, of which if not correctly managed can cause alienation and discrimination (Vinuesa et al., 2020). Research has shown that biased training data can lead to unequal outcomes, which can be heavily skewed against some demographic groups. For instance, it is crucial for AI systems to be fair and accountable so that they remain reliable and trustworthy for the public, while upholding ethical principles. But the rollout of AI technology also has serious implications for privacy and data security concerns. Massive quantities of personal data need to be collected and analysed for an AI system to work at peak power, but this can sometimes impede on the rights of individual privacy (Weller, 2019). As AI is increasingly used by organisations for surveillance and monitoring, the necessity for each of the jurisdictions to establish clear legal frameworks that will govern usages whilst ensuring fundamental rights and liberties has arrived. The context in which AI is being used for security intelligence is a fluid and fast one, as the history made manifest ex post facto without benefit of hindsight will attest. As companies further integrate AI algorithms to supplement their security toolbox, it becomes ever more essential that organisations negotiate the beneficial integration of these capabilities and the accompanying ethical and legal risks. Going forward, research should help to create an extensive legal framework that tackles the problem of these issues and at the same time allows for a responsible use of AI in matters related to security. It allows stakeholders to make the best use of AI technologies without sacrificing accountability or individual rights.

Importance of Establishing a Legal Framework

As with many aspects of AI that will be developed and implemented in numerous industry verticals, it is important to set up a legal framework for the use of AI within security intelligence (AI Act, 2023). The widespread use of AI systems in security domains (e.g. surveillance, threat detection) has introduced new complexities but the current legal framework does not address those already established IA solutions often executed under cover deployment as expected from defendant AI systems without raising any suspicion. A robust legal framework can clarify and steer the ethical employment of AI, so that they are applied to guarantee human rights and integrity. Chief among these issues is the human bias and discrimination that can be encoded into AI algorithms. Some machine learning models can result in biased decisions unless closely monitored and regulated; proven by a lot of research. For example: biased dataset will end up with unfair profiling in law enforcement, unfairly exploiting the marginalised sections. A strong regulatory framework can set standards for the ethical design and implementation of AI systems to make sure that they function in a way that is safe, transparent, and accountable while mitigating the risks of discrimination (Binns, 2018).

In addition, the absence of a common AI-specific legal definition creates challenges for regulation. The result of this is that, having each jurisdiction on a different path to constituting legal frameworks the inconsistency has created obstruction for good governance. The European Union is working on its proposed Artificial Intelligence Act, seeking to level AI systems by risk and introduce a systemic hosting framework in regulation. Nevertheless, the impact of such regulations may be attenuated without a shared set of legal definitions and standards internationally (Brundage et al., 2020). Ultimately, a common legal framework could improve international cooperation and reconciliation of norms between countries in facing the problems raised by AI technologies. Furthermore, in debates over AI in the security intelligence sector, but there are huge concerns about privacy and data protection. All that extensive data collection is a serious privacy issue to make AI functionality effective. By providing guidelines for how data can be used and abused, it becomes possible to define clear rights granted to the individual while still permitting an organisation to use AI in these domains. This is essential to ensure that the public has trust in AI technologies and that their use remains responsible. Finally, an emphasis must be placed by the government on legislation with respect to AI in security intelligence (Cath & Taddeo, 2018). Provision of such a framework also will enable assessments and transparency about the implications of ethical considerations and risks associated with bias/discrimination, as well as privacy protections that are subject to differing interpretations amongst Countries both individually and in collaboration. This is why we urgently need proactive legal rules to make sure that the deployment of these technologies empower security while remaining fully compatible with our core freedoms and values as AI continues to evolve.

Current Legal Landscape

AI in Security intelligence has a dynamic evolving landscape in terms of the legal sector. With the converging of security practices and AI technologies, an

traditional cases may potentially bypass it altogether. Most current laws do not deal adequately some fairly new and emergent technologies – such as repercussions to privacy and civil liberties as a result of AI-based technologies. For example, Europe's General Data Protection Regulation (GDPR) comprises stringent data protection measures, however the accountability when AI systems harms or infringes upon an individual's right is questionable. We also need clear standards around the liability implications of decisions made by autonomous systems that have negative outcomes (Kahn & Kearns, 2020).

In summary, notwithstanding promising developments in active laws and regulations pertaining to AI in security intelligence, the challenges remain. Considering the rapid evolution of AI technologies, cohesive frameworks that cater to accountability, transparency and ethical considerations must take centre stage. Comprehensive legal criteria could serve as a method of linking the rights framework to technology and ensure that we fulfil the benefits AI can bring while protecting individual interests and enhancing public trust.

Gaps and Limitations in the Current Framework

Moreover, the theoretical framework of security intelligence regarding AI also indicates some deep gaps and weaknesses which suggest to hamper supportive governance and responsibility. However, some legislation is not keeping up with the pace of this evolution, which can cause regulatory uncertainty and misuse. A key limitation within the current framework is the apparent absence of a common understanding of what constitutes AI. To make things more complicated, the identification of standards for consistent regulation may also be difficult since different jurisdictions tend to give their own interpretations about them. The proposed Artificial Intelligence Act in Europe, on the other hand, is trying to divide AI systems between risk levels – a classification system that has already come under fire for its lack of robust definitions and ambiguity concerning what these are supposed to cover. This inconsistency poses challenges for the facilitation of international cooperation and compliance, as stakeholders may understand different sets of legal obligations across borders.

Further, the current laws often are not designed for AI, and they may struggle to address it as such. Whilst modern privacy regulations implement strong safeguards for personal data, they are not specifically designed to address the intricacies of AI-driven decision processes. Transparency and Accountability The opacity of a lot of AI algorithms raises many questions about what happens to data, when it is used or how decisions that impacts themselves are made. The dearth of transparency can be harmful in situations such as those related to law enforcement or surveillance, where interest in these concerns are likely high and would likely have a significant impact on public understanding. A further major constraint is who should be held liable when AI systems cause detriment. Moreover, current legal frameworks struggle to grapple with how the decision making of an autonomous system should be broken out among developers, users and also the AI itself. This ambiguity deters many organisations from innovating and adopting the use of AI, as they are at risk of legal recourse if their technology is determined to have bias or discrimination. As identified by recent research on liability issues are rooted more in the complex causality and agency at play within AI systems which is something many legislative approaches are not dealing with when it comes to this technology.

This results in another big gap, the ethics of AI showing that bias and discrimination play too great a part in decision-making mechanisms via AI. Indeed, research has shown that using biased training data in security applications can cause discriminatory results, only deepening the inequalities in our current society. The current regulations do not require that these AI systems be continually monitored or audited, and to address these risks more closely. Ultimately, the processes to create an AI security intelligence regulatory framework are taking shape, but plenty of gaps and limitations remain. This is a challenging legal landscape with no single definition of what AI entails, inadequate privacy protections, unresolved questions on liability and international conflicts in how this area is governed – to say nothing of the ethical concerns (also linked by MSU College) as well. Overcoming these challenges is key to building public confidence in AI technologies and when appropriately employed, securing their use responsibly within the security domain. A key element to controlling the new frontier in AI will be through forward-thinking legal regulation (Lee & Yoon, 2020).

Key Legal Considerations

There are a number of important legal considerations the integration of AI into security intelligence needs to take into account when deploying in a way that is both responsible and ethical. Chief among them has been the risk for AI algorithms to become biased, and therefore lead to results that reflect such prejudice in an unfair manner. Recent research has shed light on the role that strong bias testing and continual bias diagnostics play in detecting and removing or at least extinguishing biases in security AI systems. Algorithmic bias can reinforce existing inequities and decrease public faith in the fairness of security mechanisms.

A big one is whether you understand the decisions your AI are making in other words, how transparent and explainable those processes appear. Moreover, due to the automation of AI systems, it is also more non-trivial for humans to exactly decipher how an AI system reached a particular decision – which then opens up questions about accountability and due process (the right of being heard). It is vital to guarantee the transparency and interpretability of AI-related final decisions made in security intelligence so that the rule-of-law principle, as well as rights at an individual level, remains intact. Another important aspect to consider when deploying AI is privacy and data protection. The large-scale data collection and analysis required for AI to be effective may infringe on people's rights to privacy, especially in the absence of defined policies or permission mechanisms. Policy makers and legal practitioners need to strike the balance between benefiting from the operation of AI while upholding civil liberties, a matter as sensitive as it is essential. Security Intelligence with AI, Legal Considerations – Last but not least!

Indeed, more robust legal frameworks and ethical guidelines are necessary to address these challenges in order to properly exploit AI capabilities without compromising fundamental rights and confidence of those we seek to protect.

Transparency and Explainability of AI Systems

Transparency and Explainability: In the context of security intelligence, trust becomes critical and transparency/explainability into AI systems will determine accountability. Given the rising percentage of AI in decision-making, it is important that individuals comprehend how these systems work to arrive at conclusions that have significant ramifications, both on an individual and societal level. Transparency the behaviour of clarity in how decision-making is happening, which algorithms are being used and what data is being used for AI systems: Explainability the act of explaining the rationale behind certain output or decision taken by these system. Transparency: Given the 'black box' nature of many AI models, transparency is a significant challenge. One of the biggest problems in AI today is the difficulty users have to understand how these algorithms come up with their answers, leading frequently accusations such as bias and unfair treatment. Recent research has similarly pointed out that the lack of transparency in AI systems makes it difficult to recognise and correct biased behaviour built into algorithms, which can then result in biased outcomes affecting our security. An example is if an AI used to detect threats produces biased alerts it can lead to a greater harm on more disadvantaged communities, making worse social inequalities than we currently suffer.

In addition, regulatory frameworks like the General Data Protection Regulation (GDPR) have emphasised transparency as a key requirement within AI systems. These policies would require organisations to explain how they are using personal data in the processing with AI algorithms. A requirement that not only promotes responsibility but helps the citizen to comprehend and object decisions individuals believe are prejudiced against them. Support for explainability (conjecture with academic source from literature) – greater transparency through methods such as XAI can lead to improved communication between AI systems and operators, thus inherently encouraging ethical treatment of security intelligence. Keeping trust as the centre of this modernisation effort ensures a good foundation for stakeholders, and this is important because it will help in the responsible deployment of AI technologies in sensitive domains such as security intelligence.

Accountability and Liability for AI-Driven Decisions

A fundamental construct in the legal framework for applying AI to security intelligence will be one of accountability and liability for decisions driven by AI. This becomes particularly significant as AI systems start making automated decisions that have the potential to affect individuals and the societies at large. The complexity of AI technologies challenges traditional accountability notions and a myriad of different stakeholders like developers, users, organisations using the use cases. The current literature confirms the point that clear accountability for AI needs to be agreed upon in order for everyone involved to know where the buck stops. Responsibly, developers are on the hook for creating AI systems that reduce bias and are used ethically and users must take notice and see to it that these technologies apply appropriately in security contexts embarrassed by these practices. This type of shared responsibility is necessary for building trust, and thus preventing some AI risks from ever occurring (Mittelstadt et al., 2016).

Furthermore, there has always been an argument about liability: fault-based versus strict. Because AI decision-making can be different than the more material and easily conceptualised harms of classical product liability or corporate liability, the currently existing legal frameworks often do not have an easy handle on how to address this. For instance, in the case of predictive policing using an AI system that causes false alarms, who is responsible can be confusing. Clear liability rules are a critical component of protecting the rights and interests of individuals, as well as facilitating responsible use of AI. For policymakers grappling with how to regulate a more authentic set of the motivations behind AI governance while managing expectations and anticipations, accountability within AI governance is critical. This might be for a review of the audit and verification cycle to be compliant with ethical and legal necessities. Dealing with issues of accountability and liability improve the ways to deal with AI in security intelligence and build public confidence towards these technologies.

Proposed Legal Framework

A new legal framework for the use of AI in security intelligence would help to cope with the challenges AI technologies present in regard to a complex approach providing that such kind of thinking is intelligent, ethical and has elements of responsibility. This framework is necessary to avoid trade off innovation for accountability, transparency and individual rights protection.

An important line in the proposed framework would demarcate finer definitions and classifications of AI systems according to risks they pose. The EU's AI Act also takes this approach by differentiating between tiers of risk in the different kinds of applications of AI and applying stronger regulation to 'high-risk' systems where they are applied for security purposes. This classification is designed to make sure that developers and users understand what obligations and responsibilities they have when deploying AI technologies in high stakes areas, such as law enforcement and national security. It also underscores the need for those decision-making processes to be transparent and explainable when they involve AI. New research suggests that: Users need to understand the process by which AI systems arrive at their decisions, especially in high-stakes scenarios where resolution could make a difference in people's lives. Such a framework can force organisations to explain the decisions of their models, therefore holding them accountable and building trust amongst all stakeholders.

Furthermore, the legislation needs audit and regular monitoring of AI models to be included in the legal framework to handle bias and discrimination. And as emphasised in new studies, performing periodic tests can be used to detect and correct algorithmic biases, aiming for fair and equal AI. To sum up, a different legal framework is essential for the use of AI in security intelligence and for dealing with their ethical consequences. This model can help ensure responsible AI deployment that respects individual rights and public trust by defining standards, encouraging transparency, and ensuring accountability.

Implementation and Enforcement

Lastly, it is crucial to establish a regulatory framework that legalises and reinforces the use of security intelligence technologies powered by AI, ensuring they are implemented responsibly and ethically. With all the other stakeholders in line, governmental bodies, private sector organisations, and civil society would be there to address it further as an integrated approach that deals with the AI technologies complexities. A crucial part of the process for putting AI into practice is to create guidelines and norms on how AI would be built, implemented. For example, laws like the proposed AI Act by the European Union will classify AI systems depending on how risky they are and will have stricter requirements for high-risk usages in particular security contexts. In practice, these are supported by the specific compliance mechanisms that an organisation can follow to ensure adherence to legal standards. New research even states that the adoption of industry-standard security protocols ISO/IEC 27001 as critical for systematic developing and maintaining secure AI applications. These standards help reduce risks associated with AI technologies which, in turn helps in establishing and enhancing trust by public organisations. AI systems are technically complex, which make enforcement especially challenging. The fast pace of progress in AI research and development can make it hard for regulators to keep up, leading to laws that quickly become obsolete. Consequently, it is important for regulators to engage in dialogue with industry stakeholders, as the legal frameworks need to be flexible and responsive to new threats and technologies. Finally, AI itself is the focus of many different areas including computer science, mathematics and cognitive science, so interdisciplinary work in training students to (1) develop expertise aligning with some aspect of AI; (2) gain computational skills; or (3) solve a problem using machine learning will provide an exciting work place powering future growth. Accountability: A critical consideration that must not get left out of the legal formulation, is a comprehensive framework for accountability. The most important thing is that the organisations are responsible for the decisions of their respective AI, especially when those decisions have a negative impact (OECD, 2021). These studies underscore the need for explicit liability norms to allocate accountability between developers, users and deployers of AI-based security technologies. This kind of transparency is critical in order to avoid problems associated with AI systems and protect victims from any misuse or failure. However, the AI must be continuously monitored and audited to meet ethical standards as well as legal requirements. By conducting frequent assessments, potential biases can be captured and AI studies would be able to function impartially. Recent literature has emphasised that organisations adopt a proactive risk management strategy by including auditing processes as part of their ongoing operational frameworks (OpenAI, 2023).

Finally, a legal framework for AI in security intelligence has to be formulated and enforced collaboratively by all the stakeholders implementing strict guidelines for compliance; vigorous mechanisms of accountability must thwart those that breach these standards, and regular monitoring should track the implementation. Through a proactive examination of these issues, policymakers can create guiding principles that enable effective regulation to promote accountability on AI while respecting rights of individuals and public trust in privacy protection (Pasquale et al., 2014).

Conclusion

This integration with security intelligence opens up both an opportunity and a challenge unique to AI: that of requiring a thorough legal framework. As AI continues to improve and its use becomes more prevalent, we need guidelines for how the technology can lawfully be used in areas like national security or law enforcement. These have to include transparency – letting you understand when and how your data was used for a decision; accountability – making sure that (de) dikoten know that the system takes decisions based on data; bias mitigation – making sure that systems are not unfair, especially with respect to Article 15 GDPR; securing rights of individuals and many more. This is one of the most important goals a framework like this should be created to address the transparency in terms of how decisions made by AI are reached. These days, research suggests it is important for users to understand the rationale behind decisions being made by AI systems – especially if they have substantial implications on human lives. The law can enforce a requirement that companies explain AI-aided decisions in plain language and thus foster accountability and acceptance of these new technologies by the public. Lastly, the framework also needs to deal with continuous monitoring and auditing of AI systems to minimise risks such as biases and discrimination. Attestation also provides the means to become aware of whether there are any biases hiding inside artefacts, and it enables to overcome those hidden biases when we strive for AI algorithms that function impartially and consistently as outlined in recent research. This is particularly crucial in security situations, as biased decision-making can result in unfair conclusions and compound the societal disparities.

While AI is revolutionising the landscape of security intelligence, it is equally important for never static legal frameworks to evolve with these technological advances while ensuring bedrock principles of justice and fairness remain unchanged. Stakeholders in this field can therefore exploit the security-enhancing possibilities promised by AI, while maintaining the protection of human rights and protecting against unintended consequences – provided we tackle legal liability, explainability and guaranteeing human control over these technologies. By taking a holistic, interdisciplinary approach that builds on the existing legal basis and challenges traditional siloed ideas of how AI will interact with people in society, policy makers can create an environment where AI will flourish in a responsible manner, while contributing towards the security wellbeing of nations and their citizens.

References

AI Act. (2023). European commission. https://digital-strategy.ec.europa.eu/en/policies/regulatory-framework-ai

Binns, R. (2018). Fairness in machine learning: Lessons from political philosophy. In *Proceedings of the 2018 conference on fairness, accountability, and transparency* (pp. 149–158). https://doi.org/10.1145/3287560.3287598

Brundage, V., Avin, S., Wang, J., Belfield, H., Krueger, G., Hadfield, G., Khlaaf, H., Yang, J., Toner, H., Fong, R., Maharaj, T., Koh, P. W., Hooker, S., Leung, J., Trask, A., Bluemke, E., Lebensold, J., O'Keefe, C., Koren, M., Théo, R., …, Markus, A. (2020). Toward trustworthy AI development: Mechanisms for supporting verifiable claims. *AI & Society*, *35*(4), 1–12.

Cath, C. (2018). Governing artificial intelligence: Ethical, legal, and technical opportunities and challenges. In *Proceedings of the international conference on artificial intelligence* (pp. 123–134).

Cath, C., & Taddeo, M. (2018). The ethics of artificial intelligence: A survey of the literature. *Journal of Artificial Intelligence Research*, *61*, 1–36.

Dignum, V. (2019). Responsible artificial intelligence: Designing AI for human values. *ITU Journal: ICT Discover*, *1*(1), 1–12.

European Commission. (2020). White paper on artificial intelligence: A European approach to excellence and trust. https://ec.europa.eu/info/sites/default/files/commission-white-paper-ai-2020.pdf

European Union Agency for Fundamental Rights (FRA). (2020). *Facial recognition technology: Fundamental rights considerations in the context of law enforcement*. FRA.

Gasser, U., & Almeida, V. (2017). *A layered model for AI governance*. Harvard Kennedy School.

Ghosh, S., & Kaur, H. (2021). Ethical implications of artificial intelligence in healthcare: A systematic review of the literature. *Artificial Intelligence in Medicine*, *113*, 101036.

Jobin, A., Ienca, M., & Andorno, R. (2019). The global landscape of AI ethics guidelines. *Nature Machine Intelligence*, *1*(9), 389–399.

Kahn, S., & Kearns, M. (2020). The ethical implications of AI in decision-making processes: A review of current research and future directions. *AI & Society*, *35*(2), 345–357.

Lee, K.-F., & Yoon, S.-J. (2020). The role of transparency in AI systems: Implications for user trust and ethical considerations in design and deployment practices. *AI & Society*, *35*(4), 733–744.

Mittelstadt, B. D., Allo, P., Taddeo, M., Wachter, S., & Floridi, L. (2016). The ethics of algorithms: Mapping the debate. *Big Data & Society*, *3*(2). https://doi.org/10.1177/2053951716679679

OECD. (2021). Recommendation on artificial intelligence: OECD principles on AI. https://www.oecd.org/going-digital/ai/principles/

OpenAI. (2023). ChatGPT [large language model]. https://chat.openai.com/chat

Pasquale, F., & Citron, D. K. (2014). Introduction: The law of algorithms: A new frontier in legal scholarship and practice. *Harvard Law Review Forum*, *127*(2), 1–16.

Russell, S., & Norvig, P. (2020). *Artificial intelligence: A modern approach* (4th ed.). Pearson.

Smith, B., & Anderson, J. Q. (2014). *AI and the future of work: How artificial intelligence will impact jobs and employment*. Pew Research Center.

Solove, D. J. (2021). Privacy self-management and the consent dilemma. *Harvard Law Review*, *126*(7), 1880–1903.

Taddeo, M., & Floridi, L. (2018). How AI can be designed to be ethical. *Nature Machine Intelligence*, *1*(2), 90–92.

Thierer, A. (2016). *The ethics of artificial intelligence and robotics*. The Independent Institute.

United Nations Educational Scientific and Cultural Organization (UNESCO). (2021). Recommendations on the ethics of artificial intelligence. https://unesdoc.unesco.org/ark:/48223/pf0000379987

Vinuesa, R., Azizpour, H., Leite, I., Balaam, M., Dignum, V., Domisch, S., Felländer, A., Langhans, S. D., Tegmark, M., & Nerini, F. F. (2020). The role of artificial intelligence in achieving the sustainable development goals. *Nature Communications*, *11*(1), 233.

Weller, A. (2019). Transparency: Mitigating bias in algorithmic decision-making systems through transparency. In *Proceedings of the AAAI/ACM conference on AI ethics and society* (pp. 20–26).

Wright, D., & Kreissl, R. (2018). Data protection by design: A new approach to privacy regulation. *International Data Privacy Law*, *8*(3), 213–224.

Zuboff, S. (2019). *The age of surveillance capitalism: The fight for a human future at the new frontier of power*. Public Affairs.

Chapter 7

Strategising Algorithm: The Prospects and Perils of Artificial Intelligence (AI) in Criminal Justice Reformation

Sofia Khatun and Sivananda Kumar K.

Christ University, India

> No one truly knows a nation until one has been inside its jails. A nation should not be judged by how it treats its highest citizens but its lowest ones. – Nelson Mandela

Abstract

The criminal justice system relies significantly on human decision-making, with the parole system primarily responsible for addressing convicted criminals' rehabilitation. A paradigm change in prisoner rehabilitation and reintegration is underway with the introduction of artificial intelligence (AI) into correctional institutions. A specific approach to alleviate the effects of human error is by utilising artificial intelligence to enhance human decision-making. Algorithms are being utilised in several jurisdictions to offer judges guidance on the appropriate type and level of punishment that should be imposed on convicted criminals. While human judgement has long played a crucial part in criminal justice systems, technological advancements are progressively augmenting the ability to make decisions. This paper examines the necessity of establishing broad restrictions on the application of algorithms in sentencing determinations. Critique plays a vital role in criminal sentencing; however, the implementation of algorithms in advisory capacities may compromise this significance. To uphold condemnatory sentencing, it is essential to recognise a principle of 'meaningful public control', which necessitates ethical accountability from representatives of the wider political community. This principle does not prohibit the use of algorithms; still it does impose restrictions on their implementation. The review posits that AI has the potential to improve fairness and efficiency in pretrial and jail systems within the criminal justice framework

Security Intelligence in the Age of AI, 111–133

Published under exclusive licence by Emerald Publishing Limited
doi:10.1108/978-1-83608-156-220251007

integration of AI, predictive policing analytics, computer-aided response, and live public safety video businesses, law enforcement will enhance their ability to promptly respond to situations, proactively avoid threats, strategically allocate resources, and thoroughly investigate and evaluate criminal activities. AI has been applied in a variety of ways to overcome these challenges (Engelke, 2020).

- The ability to file cases electronically and pay court fees from anywhere has greatly enhanced convenience for lawyers. They can now access comprehensive case information from any location. Furthermore, data transfer between various criminal justice system components including the court, police and prison is made easier by the interoperable criminal justice system (ICJS). This promotes a smoother and more efficient process. ICJS provides convenient access to documents such as FIR, Case diary, and charge sheet, all in one platform (Caplan et al., 2018).
- The handling of situations has changed dramatically since AI was introduced. NSTEP is a comprehensive process service tracking application with a user-friendly web application and a complementary mobile app. Its purpose is to simplify and streamline serving summons and notices (Silva & Kenney, 2018).
- District Court, Subordinate Court and the High Court orders, rulings and case information are stored in the National Judicial Data Grid (NJDG), an expensive database. The court's Project has developed an effective web platform that allows users to obtain this important data. The Taluka courts and the associated District courts update the data continuously providing access to all of the nation's computerised district and subordinate courts' judicial records and rulings. Through web services high courts, throughout the nation have also joined the National Judicial Data Grid (NJDG), providing easy access for members of the public engaged in judicial procedures. NJDG is a tool for monitoring cases in order to manage, identify and shorten their duration by giving prompt feedback on policy choices can significantly cut down on case disposition delays and pendency (Rodriguez, 2020).
- In India, AI is heavily used in law enforcement. The start-up company Staqu unveiled JARVIS, a platform for video analytics, in November 2019. It can assist law enforcement in monitoring any violent incidents that occur inside a certain region. Police are able to efficiently deploy personnel to stop the situation from betting worse and to protect both people and property by using real-time event identification. Our programme uses AI and computer vision to provide succinct, real-time, notifications, therefore producing meaningful data lengthy CCTV video footage (McGill, 2008). This cuts down on amount of time needed to find relevant information greatly. In addition to Punjab, Haryana, Rajasthan, Bihar, and Telangana, Staqu serves eight states and union territories. A similar initiative, the Police Artificial Intelligence System (PAIS), created by Staqu, was put into place by Punjab Police in 2018. With the use of this programme, users may access an extensive database that contains more than one lakh records of offenders who are presently serving prison sentences throughout Punjab. To improve user

experience, it provides practical capabilities like face and text searches. The UP Police have also benefited from Trinetra, a different product with comparable capabilities (Haugh et al., 2018a).

- AI is used in many different fields, including digital forensics, image processing, crime scene reconstruction, pattern recognition, DNA evidence, and psycho/narcoanalysis (Noor & Manantan, 2022).
- AI has several uses in various disciplines consisting of DNA analysis, picture processing, pattern recognition, psycho/micro analysis, digital forensics and crime scene reconstruction (Dakalbab et al., 2022). AI is a useful tool for forensic professionals and investigators because it can generate logical evidence, rebuild crime scenes in three dimensions, handle evidence skilfully and analyse it to make logical conclusions. By evaluating vast volumes of data and spotting possible threats, AI algorithms are frequently employed to discover, stop and forecast future criminal activities (Pauwels, 2020).
- Artificial intelligence has significant contributions to make in the administration of correctional facilities that can be utilised to allocate cells based on several factors, such as the offender's age, criminal record, family background, and the nature of offence (Brennan-Marquez & Henderson, 2019). AI-based monitoring provides practical answers to a number of problems, such as reducing violence in correctional institutions, identifying security concerns, carrying out crowd research, finding security weaknesses or illegal access to prisoners. AI is often used in database construction and legal research. Well-known resources for thorough legal research tools include Westlaw, Lexis Nexis, Google Scholar, Fast Case and Ross Intelligence (Chauhan, 2024).

In response to a question about whether AI could be used to shorten case pending time, the law minister, Kiren Rijiju, stated that, when the e-courts projects was being implemented, phase two that started in the year 2015, it was realised that integrating cutting-edge machine learning and AI technologies was essential to improving the effectiveness of justice delivery system. He stated,

> The Supreme Court of India has established an Artificial Intelligence Committee to investigate the use of AI in the judicial domain (Puolakka & Van De Steene, 2021). The committee has identified the translation of judicial documents, legal research assistance, and process automation as the primary applications of AI technology (Bawa, 2000).

Several law firms are enthusiastic about evaluating novel technologies that provide immediate access to judicial precedents and pronouncements concerning cases involving pertinent legal matters. Cyril Amarchand Mangaldas established the inaugural law office in India to interface artificial intelligence into its legal research, analysis, and documentation processes (Gabriel, 2022). To enhance and modernise their legal services to increase their efficacy and precision, the organisation entered into a partnership agreement with Kira Systems, a technology start up based in Canada, in 2017. Mumbai-based organisation ML software developed by the 'legal technology' firm Riverus can read through immense quantities of cases, 'understand' them, and parse instances with similar content in a fraction of the time (Marda, 2018).

- According to Honourable Chief Justice Bobde, SUPACE, a hybrid of artificial and human intelligence previously described in the article, would not be utilised in the decision-making process. Data collection and processing will be the sole responsibility of artificial intelligence. Using this gateway, the Supreme Court intends to manage the volume of data it receives from case filings using machine learning (Ünver, 2018).
- Utilising SCI-Interact software, the Supreme Court eliminated paper from all 17 chambers in 2020. This computer programme allows judges to access documents, annotate petitions, and append annexures (Berk, 2021).
- Previously, the Department of Legal Affairs (DoLA) of the Ministry of Law and Justice introduced LIMBS, a web-based application, or the Legal Information Management & Briefing System. The software could monitor cases uploaded by the relevant Commission rates from high courts and tribunals. The objective was to monitor the complete life cycle of a case effectively (Johnson, 2020).
- The Supreme Court began using SUVAAS, a locally built neural translation technology, in November 2019 to improve the accuracy and efficiency of translating court orders and judgements from English into regional tongues (Tyson & Zysman, 2022).

The Pretrial and Jail Systems, Current Trends, and Failures

The prospect of applying AI to the criminal justice system is promising due to the frequent inadequacy of our existing protocols and decision-making procedures. In the past two decades, there has been an exceptional increase in the number of people being imprisoned, which has raised questions regarding the fairness of the legal system (Leys, 2018). In order to examine the present shortcomings of the justice system and the possible uses of AI (Table 7.1), it is beneficial to grasp the differentiation between the pretrial/jail systems and the broader criminal justice system. Pursuant to the requirements of due process, a defendant must undergo a trial (or enter a guilty plea after being fully informed of their rights) prior to being sentenced. Nevertheless, as a result of the accumulation of cases and the duration required to prepare the prosecution and defence, several months will pass before the trial commences. During this period, determinations need to be made regarding the defendant's lodging arrangements (Sheikhzadeh et al., 2024). Usually, a pretrial hearing takes place where a judge determines whether to grant the defendant release and establish certain measures to ensure the defendant's presence at trial (such as cash bail or community surveillance), or to deny release and keep the defendant in custody until the trial. Setting aside the Constitution, the existing functioning of the pretrial prison system violates basic conceptions of justice and fairness. The system's failure can largely be ascribed to the fact that our judges are human, and hence vulnerable to the inherent imperfections and constraints of the human

Table 7.1. AI-Related Concepts and Concerns.

Serial No.	Application	Description	Concerns
01	Surveillance and Security (Tappan, 1954)	Drone patrols, video analytics driven by AI for activity tracking, and facial recognition	Invasion of privacy, can amount to misuse
02	Risk Assessment (Tappan, 1954)	AI systems to evaluate the likelihood of recidivism and direct treatment initiatives	Algorithmic prejudice predicated on past data, absence of human discretion
03	Case Management (Murphy, 2007)	AI-assisted analysis of prisoner data to expedite release processes and parole hearings	Overuse of artificial intelligence, impartiality, and openness in decision-making
04	Education and Rehabilitation (Kaminski & Urban, 2021)	Personalised learning initiatives using AI and virtual reality therapy for psychological conditions	Technology availability and manipulation potential

condition. Two major constraints in the judicial system are judicial bias and the predominantly internal character of judicial decision-making (Caton, 2015).

More precisely, racial bias has played a substantial role in the choices made by human judges inside the pretrial system. A notable study discovered that the white defendant who was released before trial had a nearly 20% higher likelihood of being rearrested compared to the black defendant in similar circumstances (Zafar, 2024). The study concluded that there is compelling evidence indicating that racial bias is influenced by bail judges relying on inaccurate stereotypes that overstate the perceived risk of releasing black defendants (Deeks, 2019). In addition to the legal implications, the rapidly increasing rate of pretrial imprisonment is also worrisome from an economic perspective, as taxpayers bear the financial burden of jail expenses (Schrempf-Stirling & Wettstein, 2017).

The Utilisation of AI to Enhance the Effectiveness of Correctional Facilities and Services

Reintegrating condemned people into society and assisting in their reformation are critical tasks performed by correctional facilities. At the same time, nevertheless, it has been seen that jails are increasingly becoming into hubs where

Kleinberg pertained to the potential of the algorithm to decrease imprisonment populations by as much as 42% while crime rates remained unchanged, or decrease crime by as much as 24.8%, without any corresponding increase in incarceration rates. Furthermore, the data indicated that it is possible to achieve these improvements while concurrently diminishing the ethnic disparity in detention (Uggen & Manza, n.d.). By providing more precise predictions concerning the minority of defendants who truly present a substantial risk of evading trial or endangering the community, the implementation of this algorithm has the potential to reduce criminal activity, diminish incarcerated individuals, conserve financial resources for taxpayers, and foster a more just system of justice (Van De Steene & Knight, 2017).

Legal Backdrop and Governance Framework

Due Process

The fundamental basis of the criminal justice system is the principle of due process: the constitutional assurance of a just and impartial legal action. To guarantee defendants' right to due process, the legal system must have safety measures or, as Justice Antonin Scalia aptly described in the case of *Blakely v. Washington*, 'circuit-breakers' that act as a barrier between the individual and the machinery of justice controlled by the state. There have been instances where automated systems have either implicated or disregarded the principles of due process of law (Puolakka & Suomela, 2023). According to the Brady doctrine and its descendants, the government is required to provide whatever material it has that could prove the defendant's innocence or be used to challenge the credibility of a witness. Multiple appellate courts have ruled that disclosure of material pertaining to a computer code is necessary if an explanation of the code could potentially benefit the defendant more than the explanation provided by the government (Butt, 2023). Therefore, algorithms seem to be identifiable in specific situations and definitely prior to a trial. If a code provided evidence of true innocence, the government would probably be required to disclose it (Tidball, 2024). Although certain pre-trial investigations may occur prior to a bail hearing, it is important to note that there is no entitlement to pre-trial investigations before the determination of release. Therefore, it is improbable that the defendant's legal basis for obtaining access to material that determines his bail will be derived from the Brady concept (Pluff & Nair, 2023).

Equal Protection

The principles of equity and fairness are important as the Fifth and Fourteenth Amendments to the United States Constitution guarantees that 'denying to any person within its jurisdiction the equal protection of the laws' is not an authorised action by either the federal government or any state (Singh, 2024). When it comes to classifications that discriminate based on gender, race, or any other questionable class, the Supreme Court has set strict criteria of scrutiny under the Equal

Protection Clauses. There might be a flood of equal protection lawsuits if risk assessment tools factor on such categories while making their determinations (Katzenstein et al., 2010).

Unbiased Decision-Making

Beyond these particular legal doctrines, the issue of making rational, impartial decisions is more fundamental. While achieving complete objectivity is highly improbable for both humans and algorithms, any concrete strides in that direction ought to be regarded positively. Alas, it is indisputable that the criminal justice system continues to function under the weight of enormous racial disparities and other forms of prejudice (Vacca, 2004). An examination of the extent to which judges' decisions may be swayed by extraneous factors is revealed through statistical analysis. Unquestionably, a human judge possesses certain details that are not accessible to existing algorithms. For instance, the defendant's demeanour or emotional state during the hearing may be absent (Weiner, 1975). The utilisation of AI risk assessment algorithms may mitigate bias and produce more equitable outcomes compared to the existing judge-based system. Crime could be substantially reduced without an increase in the prison population, or the jail population could be diminished without an increase in crime rates, according to the Kleinberg simulation, due to the enhanced precision of algorithmic predictions (Sakhalkar & Magar, 2023). Notwithstanding this, AI is not devoid of bias. All of these benefits are contingent on artificial intelligence optimising unambiguous variables that were determined and imputed by a programmer, an imperfect human. Numerous studies demonstrate that ML or AI systems that have received inadequate training will behave unsatisfactorily; furthermore, if the training data contains unfairness, the resulting algorithm may also contain or exacerbate that bias (Manning, 2020).

In this regard, however, one benefit of risk assessment algorithms is that errors are consistent, rectifiable, and identifiable. After identifying and rectifying a bias in the pertinent datasets or source code, subsequent iterations of the software will have acquired knowledge of and rectified that error. In contrast, human bias is renowned for being challenging to eradicate, and individual human judges experience unique learning curves (McLeod, 2010).

Role of Supreme Court Portal for Assistance in Court's Efficiency (SUPACE)

President S. A. Bobde of India stated, 'They will not permit AI to infiltrate the decision-making process'. It is essential to observe that in every circumstance that makes en-route to a high court or the Supreme Court, many documents are produced, such as charge sheets, orders, judgements from lower courts, and more (Whitt, 2017). Re-examining each of these documents to locate crucial information requires a significant investment of time. This complete process contributes to the judiciary's sluggishness and inefficiency. SUPACE will prove beneficial in this circumstance. AI will analyse the data to identify the most significant features and concerns raised by the parties and furnish the judges with pertinent information to facilitate their decision-making process (Khan, 2023). It will facilitate legal investigation and monitoring of the development of a lawsuit. However, it will not engage in the process of decision-making. The SUPACE portal, initially introduced as a pilot initiative, has been utilised in the high courts of Bombay and Delhi to handle criminal cases. Additionally, a committee is investigating the potential application of artificial intelligence in the context of motor accident claims tribunals (Davis, 2019).

Criticisms

The elevated utilisation of AI and other algorithms in the criminal justice system has sparked considerable controversy on account of the numerous legal, political, and ethical goals they attempt to achieve. This dispute has been largely fuelled by fundamental inquiries regarding the constraints of algorithms and the essence of individual justice (Williams et al., 2018). Although it is unfeasible to address every potential criticism due to the dynamic nature of algorithmic integration into the prison system, this section shall endeavour to tackle the most persistent and critical issues: algorithmic bias, inadequate transparency, utilisation of sensitive variables, and human–machine interface error (Cataleta, 2020).

Algorithmic Bias and Fairness

Critics have investigated the possibility that the development and application of the algorithms contain systematic bias. The fundamental argument posits that algorithms are not infallibly impartial and objective instruments; rather, they are susceptible to bias due to inadequate data curation and the choice of variables that the algorithms aim to optimise (Durai, 1929). While acknowledging that human judgement is not devoid of bias, the existence of human-like biases in computer algorithms has been a significant source of concern due to the fact that one of the promises of algorithms is the elimination of the defects that define human biases. An illustrative instance of this criticism concerning pretrial and sentencing algorithms is presented in a 2016 ProPublica investigation that sought to quantify the extent of racial partiality in the risk assessment application COMPAS. Based on outcomes in Broward County, Florida, the analysis concluded that black defendants 'were significantly more likely to be erroneously judged to have a higher rate of recidivism than white defendants'. The ProPublica analysts identified a statistically significant discrepancy in the false-positive rate based on race. Numerically speaking, it is entirely plausible that both ProPublica and COMPAS are accurate. In fact, it is mathematically demonstrable that under the definitions of both ProPublica and COMPAS, no algorithm can be 'fair' when comparing two groups with varying baseline rates of recidivism (Spariosu, 2018). Supplementary fairness criteria have been proposed by other scholars, each of which possesses distinct advantages and disadvantages (Epps, 2015). Nevertheless, whichever criterion is selected, it will inevitably clash with alternative potential definitions of equity. Conceptual occurrences of algorithmic bias may result from these distinctions; however, upon closer inspection, they are merely mathematical inevitability resulting from the pursuit of a specific conception of fairness. In conclusion, algorithmic bias is unquestionably possible, and formal mathematical enshrinement does not render an algorithm impartial (Ruttkamp-Bloem, 2023). Nevertheless, not all discrepancies arise from inherent bias; certain inequities might arise as mathematical repercussions of an underlying fairness definition.

Lack of Transparency

One major criticism of using AI in the justice system is the absence of public accountability and openness regarding the algorithms, particularly those that influence judicial rulings. This argument often intersects with the prior issue of algorithmic bias, as increased openness could expedite the identification and correction of algorithmic prejudice (Simburg et al., 2007).

The Concept of Interpretability in the Field of Machine Learning

The aforementioned transparency concerns become increasingly significant as algorithms transition into the domain of machine learning (ML) and artificial intelligence (AI). Some machine learning approaches, such as deep learning, allow algorithms to learn from fresh data. However, this might lead to a lack of interpretability in certain aspects of the programmable decision-making process (Chothani & Agarwal, 2012). By employing a straightforward algorithm, such as a formula for score computation, a programmer can readily trace the computing process to comprehend the derivation of a specific score. However, machine learning algorithms might be exceedingly intricate to the point where it becomes impossible for any individual to comprehend the process by which the algorithm has reached its outcome (Hallevy, 2024). The phenomenon referred to as the 'black box' in machine learning can result in a compromise between the accuracy and transparency of these tools. Several recent technology advancements have the potential to alleviate these issues or reduce the extent of the trade-off (Weiss, 2000). Significant advancements have been achieved in enhancing the interpretability and transparency of widely used black box machine learning (ML) techniques, while maintaining their high accuracy. Furthermore, significant advancements have been made in developing rigorous validation and auditing techniques for fully opaque machine learning algorithms (Dressel & Farid, 2018). By understanding the training procedures employed and having access to the algorithm's outputs, researchers can generate a proxy model that can be evaluated for bias. This technique can be enhanced even more when there is access to the actual training data for analysis. The issue of interpretability in machine learning is directly associated with concerns around private techniques and data. Providing defendants with access to the precise variables being analysed does not guarantee that they will be able to comprehend the relationship between these factors.

Understanding this relationship may require access to the fundamental training data as advanced machine learning can only provide assistance if the models are built with externally valid data (Vo & Plachkinova, 2023).

Use of Sensitive Variables

There are numerous risk assessment tools that jurisdictions might utilise, and the elements included in each evaluation vary significantly. Other systems, such as COMPAS, incorporate specific demographic elements such as gender, along with broader socio-economic considerations (Çaylak, 2023). Like any other type of prejudice, the utilisation of sensitive factors in risk assessment algorithms should not be assessed in isolation, but rather in relation to the current system of human decision-makers. Concerns pertaining to the application of unsuitable variables in pretrial decision-making are, in fact, not unique to artificial intelligence. At the moment, judges already take into consideration socioeconomic and demographic criteria, probably without even being aware of it. Algorithms offer a distinct possibility to eliminate or restrict the usage of protected classifications (Lettieri et al., 2023). This is because the input variables are well-defined and there are numerous additional variables that can equally or more accurately forecast a defendant's peril. The accuracy of an algorithm can vary based on the type and level of detail of the data it is permitted to analyse. However, the algorithm can still function effectively even if it is simply allowed to assess non-sensitive factors such as past criminal records and previous instances of missing court appearances (Warren & Hillas, 2018).

Human–Machine Interface Error

A further concern regarding AI's implementation in the penal system is the possibility of negative or reckless interactions between human judges and artificial intelligence. The fact that judges can completely dismiss suggestions and insights generated by risk assessment tools or only accepting proposals made for detention while this regarding the recommendations for release could potentially create bigger issues for concern (Wallach and Asaro, 2017).

Recommendations

Forming a forum to discuss possible legal and reformatory solutions is necessary given the conflicts such as criticism and challenges of risk assessment algorithms and the need to address the growing jailed population. Some focus on intellectual property limitations that imped transparency while others propose measures to make judges more accountable for the conclusions of risk assessment (Bonavita et al., 2021). This segment provides a thorough analysis of the merits of the previously mentioned suggestion and advocates in favour of adopting open source software, allowing the utilisation of these tools while preserving the procedure established by law (Bagaric et al., 2018).

Exceptions to Intellectual Property Law

Since transparency is essential to detect possible algorithmic bias, reformers frequently criticise the intellectual property structure that permits algorithms to be kept confidential. According to the records documented by Amanda Levendowski, there are several ways in which ambiguous copyright laws might serve as a barrier to impartial security researchers and journalist's efforts in this domain. As a result, she has pushed for board exclusions to the copyright, fair use doctrine for AI research. By doing this, the legal ramifications of reverse engineering opaque methods will be lessened and increase in data sets will be available for machine learning training. Expert witnesses, sometimes known as analysts, would need to offer specialised analysis of algorithmic tools (Gul, 2018). As a result, pretrial hearings could become significantly more costly, perhaps causing defendants without financial resources to be deprived of a plausible defence. Trade secret law has a broad scope that extends beyond algorithms used for pretrial risk assessment. Modifying the legislation to address this particular requirement may unintentionally result in the establishment of more exceptions and amplify the intricacy of trade secret regulations in other areas of the economy (Haugh et al., 2018b). This strategy has the potential to be an improvement compared to the current situation, despite the new obstacles it presents. However, there might be alternate approaches that might effectively deal with the same transparency challenges while minimising potential downsides (Peters et al., 2015).

Open-Source Procurements

An effective approach would involve mandating, as part of the tendering procedure, that any algorithms directly used for guiding judicial decision making must be developed on a 'open-source' platform. Making all the fundamental data sets, variable weights, and training methods accessible to the public would allow not only a specific defendant but also civil society groups to examine them closely (Khan, 2023). This examination would safeguard the rights of individuals while ensuring that algorithms are not unintentionally worsening problems of racial inequality. The government possesses the jurisdiction to establish the conditions under which it engages in contracts with private corporations responsible for developing these algorithms, which encompasses determining the extent of transparency required. If it is financially advantageous, contractors are likely to modify their products to comply with the new criteria. Government purchasers have a substantial amount of influence in determining the terms of procurement to promote greater openness (Farley, 2017). Instead of introducing additional exceptions in intellectual property legislation that could lead to unforeseen outcomes, this approach would merely necessitate a clause in the initial procurement agreement that transfers ownership of the algorithm and all related datasets to the government, rather than permitting the private company to maintain ownership after the project's completion (Wykstra, 2018). In order to achieve complete openness, the government would need to provide the source code and variable selection for public scrutiny. In addition, procurement officers would require access to the underlying data used to train machine learning algorithms in order to comprehend their functionality and assess their reliability (Etzioni & Etzioni, 2017). Fortunately, a significant portion of the pertinent data is currently accessible to the public. However, there is still potential for enhancing the availability of this data by providing it in a comprehensive manner that can be easily processed by machines. Procurement officers must possess the ability to identify the specific training set utilised to duplicate the machine learning system design and to identify any shortcomings in the selection of training data. This lawyers the degree of technical expertise required for courts to evaluate risk assessment results and for defendants to challenge them (Booth, 2019). The government would need to improve its own technical abilities to oversee algorithm, modifications in response to new data, growing technological complexity, or the identification flaws or biases. It is proposed to establish a council formed by the central government to advise and scrutinise artificial intelligence's application in the legal system thoroughly (Song, 2018). This group will be entitled to make suggestion for legislation that would enable the reasonable employment of AI. This organisation might be set up as a government advisory council made up of experts around the nation or as a presidential commission. The Supreme Court has the authority to impose a requirement for the use of open-source algorithms if it can be demonstrated that the absence of such algorithms poses a substantial risk to the fair administration of justice (Bagaric et al., 2021). Alternatively, each state has the option to independently choose to utilise risk assessment tools that already possess publicly available algorithms, such as the PSA tool, or to incorporate open-source specifications into their procurement contracts. This idea would require government purchasers to incur higher initial expenses, as they would essentially be purchasing, rather than leasing, the algorithm from private producers. There is a possibility of diminishing the motivation for private sector innovation in the ongoing advancement of these algorithms (Vogelman, 1968).

Human Interactions and Training

However, even open-source data and code fail to mitigate the consequences of human–machine error. The outcomes of the risk assessment are improbable to be utilised favourably if judges disregard them entirely or apply them asymmetrically. Nevertheless, these implementation barriers might be partially surmountable if methods of involving justices in the decision-making process or holding them accountable when they systemically disregard recommendations are discovered (Nishi, 2019). Researchers presented judges with data pertaining to judicial disparity in release decisions, variations in the rates of failures to appear and re-arrest among defendants released by each judge, and the disparate consequences of the predominant reliance on cash bond, all through the use of a collaborative approach. Upon receiving this information, the judges recognised the practicality of adopting a novel release strategy and reached a consensus regarding the necessity for increased consistency in release determinations. The presentation of algorithmic guidelines to judges 'in an explicit and understandable framework to increase the transparency of the decision-making process' was of equal significance in the collaborative approach (Robinson, 2001). Numerous individuals, according to research, suffer from 'algorithmic aversion', or mistrust of algorithms. However, this aversion can be surmounted by educating individuals on the inner workings of algorithmic systems (Ahmed & Akl, 2024). Likewise, despite the fact that actuarial data has demonstrated greater dependability than human prognostication across a broad spectrum of domains, judges often opt to rely on factors that have diminished associations with risk, including prosecutorial advice, the specific characteristics of the current charge, and community connections. Judges' adherence to an actuarially generated release recommendation can be enhanced by two things: firstly, providing them with the knowledge that the tool's validity is substantiated by an extensive body of research; and secondly, elucidating the reasons why statistical inference frequently surpasses human judgement in terms of accuracy (Lemley & Casey, 2019). In fact, a technologically advanced, more precise algorithm for risk assessment might be able to mitigate this issue. In situations where a judge grants bail to a defendant on the basis of a risk assessment generated by an AI algorithm but the assessment proves to be inaccurate, the judge may more easily assign blame to the algorithm if the algorithm is consistently dependable and the judge consistently adheres to its verdict (Caplan et al., 2011).

Insights gained from this methodology can be applied to the implementation of artificial intelligence in pretrial justice. For instance, involving release officers and judges in the development of novel tools, elucidating the effectiveness of said tools, and exposing problematic realities such as release discrepancies and human error in decision-making could foster increased collaboration and facilitate the integration of AI in the pretrial environment (Margetts, 2022).

It is critical to not only ensure that the algorithms used for risk assessment operate in a transparent manner but also to strengthen public support for the continued integration of these technologies into society as a whole. As the sophistication, algorithms advances via novel forms of machine learning, both the general public and judges will inherently develop a greater scepticism towards techniques that are more complex to comprehend or elucidate diminishing the probability of encountering significant political opposition to 'unaccountable' AI (Trang et al., 2024).

Conclusion

Artificial intelligence (AI) has many potential uses in correctional facilities, but there are also certain obstacles to overcome. Concerns around privacy, consent, and prejudice must be carefully considered from an ethical standpoint (Table 7.1). To guarantee the ethical and responsible use of convicts' data, AI systems must be built with their privacy rights in mind. Furthermore, AI runs the danger of leading to biased treatment of particular groups of prisoners if it is not properly controlled and audited on a regular basis, therefore reinforcing pre-existing prejudices in the criminal justice system. The increased implementation of algorithms appears to be particularly well-suited for the prison system, and pretrial risk assessment in particular. Implementing and integrating algorithms successfully within the correctional system may serve as a valuable pilot programme for subsequent implementations throughout the criminal justice system. It is important to bear that errors are probable even in algorithms that are transparent and meticulously executed. The applicable standard, however, should not be perfection. Instead, it should conduct a thorough comparison between the artificial intelligence and human error baseline and the potential partnerships between the two that can be formed in the real world. Over the course of human history, progressively discovered improved and novel instruments that facilitate more precise judgements regarding matters of justice and yield superior results for society as a whole. The existing justice system continues to be profoundly defective, and while it will be difficult to strike a balance between the contributions of software and human intuition, doing so is necessary in order to establish a more equitable society. AI signifies an uncharted domain of potential in the realm of corrections, holding the capacity to augment the efficacy of rehabilitation endeavours while also aiding in the overarching objectives of diminishing recidivism rates and bolstering public safety.

References

Aggarwal, A. (2023). The Indian prison and apathy of prisoners in 21st century: A reformative approach. *CPJ Law Journal*, *14*, 174.

Ahmed, A., & Akl, M. (2024). Scout TB: An AI robot for the screening of tuberculosis among prisoners – A novel technique. https://doi.org/10.32388/MPQ2R4

Amirthalingam, K. (2017). The importance of criminal law. *Singapore Journal of Legal Studies*, 318–328.

Arowosegbe, J. (2023). Data bias, intelligent systems and criminal justice outcomes. *International Journal of Law and Information Technology*, *31*. https://doi.org/10.1093/ijlit/eaad017

Asaro, P. M. (2019). AI ethics in predictive policing: From models of threat to an ethics of care. *IEEE Technology and Society Magazine*, *38*(2), 40–53. https://doi.org/10.1109/MTS.2019.2915154

Bagaric, M., Hunter, D., & Wolf, G. (2018). Technological incarceration and the end of the prison crisis. *Journal of Criminal Law and Criminology*, *108*(1), 73–135.

Bagaric, M., Hunter, D., & Svilar, J. (2021). Prison abolition: From naïve idealism to technological pragmatism. *Journal of Criminal Law and Criminology*, *111*(2), 351–406.

Bawa, P. S. (2000). Towards prison reforms. *India International Centre Quarterly*, *27*(2), 155–162.

Benneh Mensah, G. (2023). AI in the legal system, transparency, interpretability and the right to a fair trial: The challenges and implications for the Ghanaian civil and criminal justice systems. https://doi.org/10.13140/RG.2.2.14854.96324/1

Berk, R. A. (2021). Artificial intelligence, predictive policing, and risk assessment for law enforcement. *Annual Review of Criminology*, *4*(4), 209–237. https://doi.org/10.1146/annurev-criminol-051520-012342

Bonavita, M., Arcucci, R., Carrassi, A., Dueben, P., Geer, A. J., Le Saux, B., Longépé, N., Mathieu, P.-P., & Raynaud, L. (2021). Machine learning for Earth system observation and prediction. *Bulletin of the American Meteorological Society*, *102*(4), E710–E716.

Booth, R. (2019, July 3). Police face calls to end use of facial recognition software. *The Guardian*. https://www.theguardian.com/technology/2019/jul/03/police-face-calls-to-end-use-of-facial-recognition-software

Brennan-Marquez, K., & Henderson, S. E. (2019). Artificial intelligence and role-reversible judgment. *Journal of Criminal Law and Criminology*, *109*(2), 137–164.

Brown, B., Carlucci, R. G., DeGrange, W., & Stewart, S. (2021). Building teams and processes for equitable AI. *Phalanx*, *54*(4), 32–37.

Butt, J. (2023). The impact of artificial intelligence (AI) on the efficiency of administrative decision making including ethical & legal considerations and comparative study about countries already incorporated AI for administrative decisions. *Acta Universitatis Danubius - Juridica*, *19*, 7–25.

Caplan, J. M., Kennedy, L. W., & Miller, J. (2011). Risk terrain modeling: Brokering criminological theory and GIS methods for crime forecasting. *Justice Quarterly*, *28*(2), 360–381. https://doi.org/10.1080/07418825.2010.486037

Caplan, R., Donovan, J., Hanson, L., & Matthews, J. (2018, April 18). Algorithmic accountability: A primer. *Data & Society; Data & Society Research Institute*. https://datasociety.net/library/algorithmic-accountability-a-primer/

Cataleta, M. S. (2020). Humane artificial intelligence: The fragility of human rights facing AI. *East-West Center*. https://www.jstor.org/stable/resrep25514

Caton, J. L. (2015). *Autonomous weapon systems: A brief survey of developmental, operational, legal, and ethical issues*. Strategic Studies Institute. US Army War College. https://www.jstor.org/stable/resrep11227

Çaylak, B. (2023). Issues that may arise from usage of AI technologies in criminal justice and law enforcement. In *Algorithmic discrimination and ethical perspective of artificial intelligence* (pp. 119–132). https://doi.org/10.1007/978-981-99-6327-0_8

Chauhan, D. (2024, April). *Artificial intelligence in criminal justice system ensuring protection of human rights, fairness and final*. CLS. https://www.researchgate.net/publication/379994914_Artificial_Intelligence_in_Criminal_Justice_System_Ensuring_protection_of_Human_Rights_Fairness_andfinal

Chothani, P., & Agarwal, V. (2012). International law: Intellectual property and outsourcing to India. *GPSolo*, *29*(4), 68–69.

Crawford, K., & Schultz, J. (2019). AI Systems as state actors. *Columbia Law Review*, *119*(7), 1941–1972.

Dakalbab, F., Abu Talib, M., Abu Waraga, O., Bou Nassif, A., Abbas, S., & Nasir, Q. (2022). Artificial intelligence & crime prediction: A systematic literature review. *Social Sciences & Humanities Open*, *6*(1), 100342. https://doi.org/10.1016/j.ssaho.2022.100342

Davis, L. M. (2019). *Higher education programs in prison: What we know now and what we should focus on going forward*. RAND Corporation. https://www.jstor.org/stable/resrep19903

De Spiegeleire, S., Maas, M., & Sweijs, T. (2017). *Ai – Today and tomorrow* (pp. 43–59). Artificial intelligence and the future of defense. Hague Centre for Strategic Studies. https://www.jstor.org/stable/resrep12564.8

Deeks, A. (2019). The judicial demand for explainable artificial intelligence. *Columbia Law Review*, *119*(7), 1829–1850.

Dressel, J., & Farid, H. (2018). The accuracy, fairness, and limits of predicting recidivism. *Science Advances*, *4*(1), eaao5580. https://doi.org/10.1126/sciadv.aao5580

Durai, J. C. (1929). Indian prisons. *Journal of Comparative Legislation and International Law*, *11*(4), 245–249.

Engelke, P. (2020). *AI, society, and governance: An introduction*. Atlantic Council. https://www.jstor.org/stable/resrep29327
Epps, D. (2015). The consequences of error in criminal justice. *Harvard Law Review*, *128*(4), 1065–1151.
Etzioni, A., & Etzioni, O. (2017). Should artificial intelligence Be regulated? *Issues in Science and Technology*, *33*(4), 32–36.
Farley, H. S. (2017). Introducing digital technologies into prisons: Issues and challenges. https://www.researchgate.net/publication/319182655_Introducing_digital_technologies_into_prisons_Issues_and_challenges?_tp=eyJjb250ZXh0Ijp7ImZpcnN0UGFnZSI6Il9kaXJlY3QiLCJwYWdlIjoicHVibGljYXRpb24iLCJwcmV2aW91c1BhZ2UiOiJwdWJsaWNhdGlvbiJ9fQ. Accessed on April 24, 2024.
Gabriel, I. (2022). Toward a theory of justice for artificial intelligence. *Dædalus*, *151*(2), 218–231.
Gamo, M. D. (2013). Voices behind prison walls: Rehabilitation from the perspective of inmates. *Philippine Sociological Review*, *61*(1), 205–227.
Gerber, A. S., Huber, G. A., Meredith, M., Biggers, D. R., & Hendry, D. J. (2015). Can incarcerated Felons Be (Re)integrated into the political system? Results from a field experiment. *American Journal of Political Science*, *59*(4), 912–926.
Gillis, T. B., & Spiess, J. L. (2019). Big data and discrimination. *The University of Chicago Law Review*, *86*(2), 459–488.
Gul, R. (2018). Our prisons punitive or rehabilitative? An analysis of theory and practice. *Policy Perspectives*, *35*, 97–122.
Hallevy, G. (2024). *The basic models of criminal liability of AI systems and outer circles* (pp. 69–82). http://doi.org/10.2139/ssrn.3402527
Haugh, B. A., Kaminski, N. J., Madhavan, P., McDaniel, E. A., Pavlak, C. R., Sparrow, D. A., Tate, D. M., & Williams, B. L. (2018a). *Appendix B.: The national artificial intelligence research and development strategic plan* (pp. 15–64). RFI Response. Institute for Defense Analyses. https://www.jstor.org/stable/resrep22865.11
Haugh, B. A., Kaminski, N. J., Madhavan, P., McDaniel, E. A., Pavlak, C. R., Sparrow, D. A., Tate, D. M., & Williams, B. L. (2018b). *Strategy 7 proposed changes* (pp. 8–10). RFI Response. Institute for Defense Analyses. https://www.jstor.org/stable/resrep22865.8
Jain, E. (2018). Capitalizing on criminal justice. *Duke Law Journal*, *67*(7), 1381–1431.
Johnson, J. S. (2020). Artificial intelligence: A threat to strategic stability. *Strategic Studies Quarterly*, *14*(1), 16–39.
Kaminski, M. E., & Urban, J. M. (2021). The right to contest AI. *Columbia Law Review*, *121*(7), 1957–2048.
Katzenstein, M. F., Ibrahim, L. M., & Rubin, K. D. (2010). The dark side of American liberalism and Felony disenfranchisement. *Perspectives on Politics*, *8*(4), 1035–1054.
Khan, J. (2023). Guarding the scales of justice: Assessing the human rights implications of AI technologies in criminal justice systems in India. *International Journal of Advanced Legal Research*, *4*. https://www.researchgate.net/publication/372914201_Guarding_the_Scales_of_Justice_Assessing_the_Human_Rights_Implications_of_AI_Technologies_in_Criminal_Justice_Systems_in_India?_sg=r2jgsjCrp1ToSW9DOTro_YY9gqPh7iaFlcJunrLDoNjUmpxMZcJyyC2MBXF_BEXAMQ2hwtrtIMFkAMc&_tp=eyJjb250ZXh0Ijp7ImZpcnN0UGFnZSI6Il9kaXJlY3QiLCJwYWdlIjoiX2RpcmVjdCJ9fQ

Lea, G. R. (2020). Constructivism and its risks in artificial intelligence. *Prometheus, 36*(4), 322–346.

Lemley, M. A., & Casey, B. (2019). Remedies for robots. *The University of Chicago Law Review, 86*(5), 1311–1396.

Lettieri, N., Guarino, A., Zaccagnino, R., & Malandrino, D. (2023). Keeping judges in the loop: A human–machine collaboration strategy against the blind spots of AI in criminal justice. *Soft Computing, 27*, 1–19. https://doi.org/10.1007/s00500-023-08604-z

Leys, N. (2018). Autonomous weapon systems and international crises. *Strategic Studies Quarterly, 12*(1), 48–73.

Manning, R. A. (2020). *Emerging technologies: New challenges to global stability*. Atlantic Council. https://www.jstor.org/stable/resrep26000

Marda, V. (2018). Artificial intelligence policy in India: A framework for engaging the limits of data-driven decision-making. *Philosophical Transactions: Mathematical, Physical and Engineering Sciences, 376*(2133), 1–19.

Margetts, H. (2022). Rethinking AI for good governance. *Dædalus, 151*(2), 360–371.

McGill, J. (2008). An institutional suicide machine: Discrimination against federally sentenced aboriginal women in Canada. *Race/Ethnicity: Multidisciplinary Global Contexts, 2*(1), 89–119.

McLeod, A. M. (2010). Exporting U.S. Criminal justice. *Yale Law & Policy Review, 29*(1), 83–164.

Meena, M., & Joshi, A. (2023). AI policing in criminal justice: Methods & concerns in crime detection and prevention in India. *NFSU Journal of Law and Artificial Intelligence, 2*, 7–15.

Murphy, E. (2007). The new forensics: Criminal justice, false certainty, and the second generation of scientific evidence. *California Law Review, 95*(3), 721–797.

Nishi, A. (2019). Privatizing sentencing: A delegation framework for recidivism risk assessment. *Columbia Law Review, 119*(6), 1671–1710.

Noor, E., & Manantan, M. B. (2022). *Artificial intelligence* (pp. 87–136). Raising standards. Asia Society. https://www.jstor.org/stable/resrep48536.10

Pauwels, E. (2020). *Artificial intelligence and data capture technologies in violence and conflict prevention: Opportunities and challenges for the international community*. Global Center on Cooperative Security. https://www.jstor.org/stable/resrep27551

Peters, D. J., Hochstetler, A., DeLisi, M., & Kuo, H.-J. (2015). Parolee recidivism and successful treatment completion: Comparing hazard models across propensity methods. *Journal of Quantitative Criminology, 31*(1), 149–181.

Pluff, A., & Nair, S. (2023). "Don't blame the robots" – Artificial intelligence bias & implications for nuclear security. *Stimson Center*. https://www.jstor.org/stable/resrep51827

Puolakka, P., & Suomela, M. (2023). Digitalization supports human rights in Finnish prisons. *Advancing Corrections Journal, 16*, 50–61.

Puolakka, P., & Van De Steene, S. (2021). Artificial intelligence in prisons in 2030: An exploration on the future of AI in prisons. *Advancing Corrections Journal, 11*, 126–136.

Robinson, P. H. (2001). Punishing dangerousness: Cloaking preventive detention as criminal justice. *Harvard Law Review, 114*(5), 1429–1456. https://doi.org/10.2307/1342684

Rodriguez, L. (2020). All data is not credit data: Closing the gap between the fair housing act and algorithmic decisionmaking in the lending industry. *Columbia Law Review*, *120*(7), 1843–1884.

Rozell, D. J. (2020). Values in risk assessment. In *Dangerous science* (pp. 29–56). Ubiquity Press. https://www.jstor.org/stable/j.ctv11cvx39.6

Ruttkamp-Bloem, E. (2023). Intergenerational justice as driver for responsible AI. In *Artificial intelligence research* (pp. 18–30). https://doi.org/10.1007/978-3-031-49002-6_2

Sakhalkar, U., & Magar, S. (2023). Emergence of artificial intelligence in Indian criminal justice system. *Shodhasamhita*, *10*, 483–488.

Santiago, T. (2019). Combating AI bias through responsible leadership. *National Defense*, *103*(787), 19–20.

Sarcevic, A. (2018, May 29). Can sentencing be enhanced with artificial intelligence? *Informa Connect Australia*. https://www.informa.com.au/insight/can-sentencing-enhanced-artificial-intelligence/

Schoonmaker, S. V. (2017). Withstanding disruptive innovation: How attorneys will adapt and survive impending challenges from automation and nontraditional legal services providers. *Family Law Quarterly*, *51*(2/3), 133–192.

Schrempf-Stirling, J., & Wettstein, F. (2017). Beyond guilty verdicts: Human rights litigation and its impact on corporations' human rights policies. *Journal of Business Ethics*, *145*(3), 545–562.

Sheikhzadeh, M., Amirmohammad-Bakhtiari, M., & Nourmandipour, P. (2024). The vague future of AI: The theory of AI perfection. *American Journal of Computer Science and Technology*, *7*, 24–28. https://doi.org/10.11648/j.ajcst.20240701.14

Shen, O. (2020). AI dreams and authoritarian nightmares. In J. Golley, L. Jaivin, B. Hillman, & S. Strange (Eds.), *China dreams* (pp. 142–156). ANU Press. https://www.jstor.org/stable/j.ctv12sdxmk.17

Silva, S., & Kenney, M. (2018). Algorithms, platforms, and ethnic bias: An integrative essay. *Phylon (1960-)*, *55*(1 & 2), 9–37.

Simburg, M. J., Haver, P., Brushaber, S., Bain, S., Nguyen, S., Nash, D. D., Liao, Y. R., White, H. B., McDonald, B., Kops, A., Lindeboom, B., Pandya, B. H., & Karim, N. (2007). International intellectual property law. *The International Lawyer*, *41*(2), 379–394.

Singh, S. (2024, March 30). e-Justice in India: The role of AI in advancing constitutional values. In *Two-day international seminar on impact of artificial intelligence on constitutionalism and rule of law*. Panjab University.

Skeem, J. L., & Monahan, J. (2011). Current directions in violence risk assessment. *Current Directions in Psychological Science*, *20*(1), 38–42.

Song, S. (2018). Preventing a Butlerian Jihad: Articulating a global vision for the future of artificial intelligence. *Journal of International Affairs*, *72*(1), 135–142.

Spariosu, M. I. (2018). Information and communication technology for human development: An intercultural perspective. In *Remapping knowledge* (pp. 95–142). Berghahn Books. https://doi.org/10.2307/j.ctv3znztw.6

Tappan, P. W. (1954). The legal rights of prisoners. *The Annals of the American Academy of Political and Social Science*, *293*, 99–111.

Tidball, M. (2024). *Disabling criminal justice: The governance of autistic adult defendants in the English criminal justice system*. Bloomsbury Academic.

Tiwana, D. K., & Singh, P. (2022). A study on concept of prisons and their importance in modern society: With reference to prison reform system. *International Journal for Legal Research and Analysis, 1*, 268–279.

Trang, N., Linh, N., Hoang, N., Kiet, P., Loan, L., & Phuc, N. (2024). Right to a fair-trial when applying artificial intelligence in criminal justice – Lessons and experiences for Vietnam. *Journal of Law and Sustainable Development, 12*, e601. https://doi.org/10.55908/sdgs.v12i3.601

Tyson, L. D., & Zysman, J. (2022). Automation, AI & work. *Dædalus, 151*(2), 256–271.

Uggen, C., & Manza, J. (n.d.). Democratic contraction? Political consequences of Felon disenfranchisement in the United States. *American Sociological Review, 67*, 777–803.

Ünver, H. A. (2018). *Artificial intelligence, authoritarianism and the future of political systems*. Centre for Economics and Foreign Policy Studies. https://www.jstor.org/stable/resrep26084

Vacca, J. S. (2004). Educated prisoners are less likely to return to prison. *Journal of Correctional Education, 55*(4), 297–305.

Van De Steene, S., & Knight, V. (2017). Digital transformation for prisons: Developing a needs-based strategy. *Probation Journal, 64*. https://doi.org/10.1177/0264550517723722

Vo, A., & Plachkinova, M. (2023). Investigating the role of artificial intelligence in the US criminal justice system. *Journal of Information, Communication and Ethics in Society, 21*, 550–567. https://doi.org/10.1108/JICES-11-2022-0101

Vogelman, R. P. (1968). Prison restrictions. Prisoner rights. *The Journal of Criminal Law, Criminology, and Police Science, 59*(3), 386–396. https://doi.org/10.2307/1141762

Wallach, W., & Asaro, P. (Eds.). (2017). *Machine ethics and robot ethics*. Routledge is an imprint of the Taylor & Francis Group.

Warren, A., & Hillas, A. (2018). Lethal autonomous robotics: Rethinking the dehumanization of warfare. *UCLA Journal of International Law and Foreign Affairs, 22*(2), 218–249.

Weiner, R. I. (1975). The criminal justice system at the breaking point. *Social Work, 20*(6), 436–441.

Weiss, R. P. (2000). Introduction to "Criminal Justice and globalization at the New millennium". *Social Justice, 27*(2(80)), 1–15.

Whitt, M. S. (2017). Felon disenfranchisement and democratic legitimacy. *Social Theory and Practice, 43*(2), 283–311.

Williams, B. A., Brooks, C. F., & Shmargad, Y. (2018). How algorithms discriminate based on data they lack: Challenges, solutions, and policy implications. *Journal of Information Policy, 8*, 78. https://doi.org/10.5325/jinfopoli.8.2018.0078

Wykstra, S. (2018). Philosopher1s corner: What is "Fair"? Algorithms in criminal justice. *Issues in Science and Technology, 34*(3), 21–23.

Zafar, A. (2024). Balancing the scale: Navigating ethical and practical challenges of artificial intelligence (AI) integration in legal practices. *Discover Artificial Intelligence, 4*. https://doi.org/10.1007/s44163-024-00121-8

Završnik, A. (2020). Criminal justice, artificial intelligence systems, and human rights. *ERA Forum, 20*(4), 567–583. https://doi.org/10.1007/s12027-020-00602-0

Chapter 8

Recommendations for Lawmakers Towards Building a Trustworthy AI Ecosystem

Anjali Raghav, Sahil Lal, Manmeet Kaur Arora and Bhupinder Singh

Sharda University, India

Abstract

With the continual progress of artificial intelligence (AI) technologies and their integration into different parts of society, it is important for policymakers to put in place comprehensive governance frameworks that will foster responsible development. This chapter presents the most significant recommendations that policymakers would find useful to keep in mind when crafting legislation and regulations around AI. The chapter discusses new research and leading practices from across the computer science, ethics, law and public policy fields. It points to stories of successes and ways in which governments elsewhere are grappling with challenges posed by AI technologies. These recommendations have been developed to be flexible and open system that can be fit in different local political, economic, social and cultural circumstances.

Keywords: Artificial intelligence; stakeholder engagement; AI infrastructure; risk assessment; international cooperation

Introduction

The rapid development of artificial intelligence (AI) has ushered in a new era for multiple sectors, ranging from the healthcare industry to the banking and finance sector. These recommendations focus on defining AI principles, engaging with diverse population, investing in AI infrastructure, promoting AI literacy and skills for the workforce society, ensuring the data governance including personal right to privacy consideration, conducting risk assessment whatsoever prior-launch or implementation (prevention-based policy), and fostering international cooperation.

Security Intelligence in the Age of AI, 135–151

doi:10.1108/978-1-83608-156-220251008

Through following these recommendations, policymakers can foster a context that draws the best from AI while addressing pitfalls and respecting privacy, civil and societal rights (AI Act, 2023). But these developments also bring with them considerable ethical and governance concerns, requiring the building of an AI ecosystem that is deemed trustworthy (Binns). Transparent AI, Robust and privacy respectful: Comprehensive documentation that allows complete traceability of the systems should they be implemented in unsafe environments, ensuring responsible and ethical operation (Brundage et al., 2020). The chapter on the idea of trustworthy AI is about the significance of legislature structures to support a basis which permit for a trustworthy advance and engine, and deployment in reckless mode.

Overview of Trustworthy AI

In principle, reliable AI includes some of the essential principles for ensuring ethical deployment of an AI system (Cath & Taddeo, 2018). Transparency, Accountability, Fairness and Dependability: these are the pillars which guide our actions. Transparency means making AI process understandable to its users and stakeholders, while accountability ensures that the appropriate mechanisms are exercised when the outcomes or biases of AI decisions go wrong. However, system robustness refers to the ability of a system to work properly under different circumstances and its resistance against malicious attacks (Dignum, 2019). Human oversight, technical robustness, privacy and data governance, transparency, diversity, non-discrimination and societal and environmental well-being are the seven key requirements for trustworthy AI identified by the European Commission. These requirements are to standardise the development of AI systems so they not only achieve this baseline, but the values and ethical norms in the society. Hence, putting it in a collective way, Trustworthy AI development is not just a technical challenge but rather a socio-technical endeavour that requires the active communing of all stakeholders from law-makers to technologists to ethicists to civil society (European Commission, 2020).

Power of Legislative Framework

Transparency: Legislative frameworks provide the underpinning sets of rules and standard that are customary for accountability trustworthy AI practices. The dynamic nature of the AI technologies is such that existing laws are likely to lag behind at least some of these innovations. Failure to close this gap can result in ethical quandaries and unintended effects unless addressed through a complex set of rules (Gasser & Almeida, 2017). A well-drafted legislative framework at the outset can substantially reduce the risks associated with AI by giving a clear definition on data usage, algorithmic accountability, and user privacy (Ghosh & Kaur, 2021). For example, the approach of some regulations, like the forthcoming EU Artificial Intelligence Act, is to establish a risk-based AI governance. The legislation classifies AI uses by their perceived risks to individual or societal rights, placing more stringent requirements on high-risk uses and fewer restrictions on low-risk scenarios. In addition, legal frameworks can help alleviate trust that AI technologies are built with ethics in mind (Jobin et al., 2019). Lawmakers can also use legal tools to demystify AI systems for both users as well as stakeholders by enforcing transparency in algorithms and decision-making process. This transparency is key to establishing public trust that AI will be used responsibly and ethically (Kahn & Kearns, 2020).

In addition, legal frameworks also make certain those technologies built in AI do so with consideration for ethics thus creating public trust over tech such. Legislating the transparency of algorithms and decision-making processes would also contribute to unmasking AI systems for both their operators and end users. This openness is crucial in establishing public trust that AI systems will be used responsibly and ethically. Beyond simply acting in the best interests of the public, clear and effective legislative frameworks will also help to foster innovation by demonstrating a set of rules that entrepreneurs or businesses can follow. Knowing the law surrounding AI means your companies or organisation are able to work within this framework of rights and responsibilities instead of fearfully avoiding innovating with any fear of being brought into legal dissemination (Lee & Yoon, 2020). Ultimately, as we struggle to navigate the nuances of including AI in our lives, it is crucial to develop a robust AI ecosystem. This translation from moral/ethical imperatives to solid legislative foundations really matters with regards to the design and deployment of these technologies. National and international legislation for securing the trustworthiness in AI systems will help us to use the full potential of AI by protecting our individual rights and societal values (Mittelstadt et al., 2016).

Applying Principles of Trustworthy AI helps to clearly define and understand what challenges in designing/composing the responsible development nature of AI are – using those principles also as an ethical compass. As AI systems are integrated into society, it is important that they behave in an ethical, transparent and accountable manner.

Key Principles of Trustworthy AI

The principles based on which a Trustworthy AI is built to be used for developing and operating an AI system are:

- Equity – AI systems must be free of bias and prejudice (OECD, 2021). This means training with multiple datasets in order to prevent reinforcing the current societal environments. Ensures AI applications do not unfairly disadvantage groups based on race, gender or similar characteristics – especially in critical areas like hiring or law enforcement (OpenAI, 2023).
- Transparency: the decision-making process, and its relationship to user interfaces in AI systems should be visible (Pasquale & Citron, 2014). Transparent decision-making allows stakeholders to understand how decisions are taken,

creating trust and keeping things accountable. This even include information about the data used for training and algorithms used (Russell & Norvig, 2020).
- Accountability – The scheme postulates that there should be clear-outs lines of responsibility for the outcomes AI produces. The responsibility for decisions made by harm causing AI systems is crucial, and it should fall either completely on the shoulders of developers, somewhere between developers and organisations, or finally de jure over the shoulder of AI (Smith & Anderson, 2014). This principle means that there should be some channels for restitution and remedies (Solove, 2021).
- Robustness: AI systems should be both secure and resilient to adversarial attacks (Taddeo & Floridi, 2018). The algorithms should generalise well over different conditions and remain robust against adversarial attacks or failures. A workshop participant engaged in Policy: one of the most significant aspects, not entirely captured by FMEA workflows or tools that deals with ethical robustness as well – safe and reliable systems satisfy ethical standards from conception to decommissioning (Thierer, 2016).
- Human-Centred Design: AI should be developed to support the well-being of all human beings. This principle focuses on the role of human primacy in AI operations, guarantees that technology is used to augment, not replace human skills.

Ethical Issues of AI Creation

The ethical dimension of AI development is multifaceted and intricate. Key considerations include:

- Some Where There Is Bias and Fairness – as we mentioned earlier, training data with bias in it. Developers need to be intentionally vigilant about discovering and addressing these biases, by selecting data with caution and designing algorithms. Second, continuous monitoring and auditing is required to uphold fairness in the long run.
- Privacy and Data Protection: AI systems typically process large amounts of personally identifiable information and, as such, concerns regarding the lack of privacy are heightened. Developers should adopt concrete data protection strategies to protect consumers' sensitive information and at the same time they need to respect individual privacy rights as well, but when it comes to make an effective that will help developers safeguard their users' data throughout (United Nations Educational Scientific and Cultural Organization (UNESCO), 2021).
- Opacity: The black box nature of many AI models makes it difficult to foster transparency efforts. Therefore, understanding of decision making and the components of those decisions should be at strive with algorithms for developer solution. This transparency is critical to trust users.
- Having Accountability: Introducing AI decision making to have some accountabilities from AI. It requires us to create a new framework which sets

out who is accountable when an AI system does cause harm or take the wrong decision. It could be through mandates to ensure that organisations are accountable for their AI use (Vinuesa et al., 2020).

- AI for Social Good: Human-Centric AI and Ethical Use of AI. That includes judging how well AI applications adhere to ethical norms and are advancing the broader societal good, rather than reinforcing or creating new divisions (Weller, 2019).

Stakeholder Engagement Identifying Key Stakeholders Strategies for Effective Collaboration

Long-term success with your AI projects depends on strong stakeholder engagement. It entails locating, listening and working with individuals or groups who have an investment in or are impacted by the AI efforts being done. By doing this, various perspectives will be considered and trust and collaboration will built in the project from beginning to end due well implementation of stakeholder engagement at each stage (Wright & Kreissl, 2018).

Identifying Key Stakeholders

What are the key steps in stakeholder engagement? Step 1: Identify key stakeholders. This procedure typically starts with a full layout of any groups that may come into contact or influence the AI project. Stakeholder categories can be classified to:

- Regulatory Bodies: Governments who will establish norms over AI technologies through their agencies or by informing existing regulatory bodies. It's essential they have a seat at the table to enforce legal and ethical standards (Zuboff, 2019).
- AI Developers and Practitioners – Data scientists, software engineers, project managers who design and implement AI systems. Without it we're not going to know what this machine can and cannot do.
- End Users: These are potential individuals who use the AI, like employees or customers and to ensure that it is fit for their intended uses and meets their expectations. And you can get their feedback for a user-friendly design and functionalities (Binns, 2018).

Part of the answer is that this group of stakeholders consists of ethical advisors and advocacy groups, which are primarily concerned with ensuring fairness, transparency and accountability in AI systems. How they view the work narrative helps account for possible biases and social implications (Cath, 2018).

- Investors and Financial Stakeholders: People, especially investors, who fund AI projects are among the individuals most interested in seeing the success of this project. Get them involved so that there is alignment in the project goals and at least one leg on financial expectations (Dignum, 2019).

Effective Collaboration Techniques

Having identified our 'tribe' of key stakeholders, the development of relevant strategies to engage these groups is paramount. Below you will find four successful strategies:

- Stakeholder engagement at the beginning of the work so that there is trust and the project can be shaped according to their feedback from day one (Jobin et al., 2019). Discussions: Talking about your project or service can help you ground assumptions, work through differences of opinion upfront, and get stakeholders more invested from the get-go (Kahn & Kearns, 2020).
- Contextualise: Making sure that communication is two-way between an incident response manager and stakeholders requires having open lines of communication. By arranging meetings, newsletters or even setting up a public digital platform – you make sure that stakeholders remain updated regarding the progress of tasks and can provide immediate back (Mittelstadt et al., 2016).
- Customised Engagement Plans: Each stakeholder has different interests and issues; hence, the mechanism of engagement should be tailored to take reasonable measures to consider these differences. For example, developers may love a technical update but other quarters might be more interested in the ethical implications of certain choices (Russell & Norvig, 2020).
- Implementing Feedback Mechanisms: Others will have differing perspectives, giving them an opportunity to express how they feel throughout the life of a project. To help with this, you can perform surveys, host focus groups, or carry out workshops mobilising all voices (European Commission, 2023).
- Creating Relationships: Positive relationships with stakeholders, increasing collaboration and backing throughout implementation process. These connections can be strengthened through informal interactions or networking opportunities, which nurtures a collaborative atmosphere.

Stakeholder preferences can also change over time which is why it is crucial to track sentiment, and adapt engagement strategies accordingly. Continuous evaluation can reveal evolving issues or changes in stakeholder priorities.

The development of AI systems has become so rapid that strong policy recommendations are now needed to govern them properly. With AI systems growing to be foundational in many industries, legislation becomes more and more important for ensuring accountability and transparency. This chapter sets forth core policy measures to establish a more holistic AI governance regulatory framework.

Regulatory Frameworks for AI Governance

AI in governance comprehensive legislative strategy to ensure responsible use of AI. The things to be focused by the policymakers are:

- Create a Cohesive Regulation: Governments needed to formulate detailed regulations that describe how any AI technology can be used in an ethical way. Such this involvement in stimulus should include, laying down of acceptable practices and measures to maintain human rights standards with strict sanctions for wrongdoers. Despite their constantly changing nature, AI regulations must be flexible while providing clear guidance to both developers and end-users (Information Technology Alliance for Public Sector (ITAPS), 2023).
- Establish Oversight Bodies: Mechanisms – such as independent regulators – should be employed to oversee the integration of AI and adherence to responsible practices. These bodies are empowered to carry out audits, conduct risk–based assessments, and investigate complaints with respect to AI systems. Particularly in ensuring that AI applications do not violate individual rights or lead to discriminatory practices (UNESCO, 2021).
- Foster International Collaboration: Since AI is a global technology, it is necessary to ensure international cooperation so that regulations can be established among borders. Policymakers must engage other countries in a dialogue to share best practices and agree on global guidelines for AI governance. However, by looking at it from a collaborative standpoint, we may not only enable the management of risks attached to cross-border data flows but also ensure that ethical considerations can be universally implemented (Department of Legal Affairs, Government of India, n.d.).
- Seeking Public Engagement: This involves reaching out to the public for a greater understanding, conversation and ultimately trust around the governance of AI and its transparency (European Parliament, 2022). There must be platforms for the public to convey their worries and contribute to AI policies. A participatory approach also could increase accountability by taking different points of view into account when making choices.
- Perform Impact Assessments: Conduct sweeping impact assessments to check potential risks and ethical concerns, before rolling out AI systems (Zuboff, 2019). These evaluations should encompass privacy and security considerations as well as a social impact assessment to verify that AI applications comply with societal values, avoid doing harm.

Accountability and Transparency in the Process

Trusted AI requires tools to provide accountability and transparency at all stages of the lifecycle of an AI system.

- Algorithms Are More Transparent: Organisations must be honest regarding the operational details of their AI systems, and need to bear clarity while defining how these operate (Binns, 2018). This goes from configuration for

notifications on data sources to train algorithms through methodologies getting the decision making until the bias itself within the system. It enables users and stakeholders to understand how decisions are made and builds trust.
- Accountability – Everyone and No one: Clearly defined lines of accountability are necessary to address any adverse consequences that may arise from AI decisions. The authors recommend that policies define lines of accountability for AI systems and how responsibility should be assigned when AI systems make wrong decisions or produce biased outputs. This accountability mechanism could entail holding clauses liable and providing relief for victims.

Continuous monitoring of AI systems through regular audits means should be sought so as to maintain compliance with the ethical standards. Companies need to have internal practices and procedures for examining how well their AI applications are working, where they might be biased.

- Protection of User Rights – Legislation should protect users by enabling them to learn how their information is used by an AI system. People should be able to call into question any decision made by automated systems and claim remedies in case they feel aggrieved.
- Training and Awareness Programs for the Evolution: To foster ethical AI development, organisations must spend time investing in training developers, policymakers and users. There are efforts underway to educate people on the ethics of AI technologies and raise awareness within organisations, like by using these platforms (Dignum, 2019).

Investment in AI Infrastructure Funding Mechanisms for AI Development Public–Private Partnerships (PPPs)

To drive breakthrough – and the increasing influx of AI applications – a foundational investment in AI infrastructure is critical. We can see that in the age of AI technologies when things are getting more and more automated, we need a solid infrastructure to ease its development, deployment and scalability. This chapter examines the mechanisms through which AI is funded, and underscores the necessity of PPPs to upgrade AI infrastructure.

Funding Mechanisms for AI Development

The second, investing in AI infrastructure may stimulate economic growth and innovation through various funding mechanisms: public funding, private investment and hybrid mechanisms.

- Public Finance: Public resources in the form of grants, subsidies or direct investment by governments are an essential component for building AI infrastructure. Encouragement in this domain could be supported via public funding initiatives targeting research institutions and universities with a focus on AI technologies for innovation and talent development. For example, national governments could earmark AI research within their own budgets or set up innovation hubs as PPPs in a 'collaboration-for-innovation' model (Gasser & Almeida, 2017).

- Venture Capital: Venture capital (VC) has become the primary funding source for AI startups and innovators. Since then, many VC firms are starting to see they the potential of AI across a wide range of industries and have made massive investments in companies who focus on AI technologies (Jobin et al., 2019). Global VC investments in AI have picked up over the last couple of years, signalling a mounting belief that this technology can help push economic expansion.
- Corporate Investments: Large corporations are spending huge amounts on AI infrastructure as well to improve upon their operational capabilities and stay ahead. Typically, companies divert resources to build in-house AI technologies or purchase startups that solve a specific problem. A trend that is not only driving the growth of the AI ecosystem but also allows companies to utilise more advanced technology to enhance efficiency and productivity (Mittelstadt et al., 2016).
- Crowd Funding: One more way how to raise some of the capital for an AI project is through crowdfunding platforms. This will further benefit the ecosystem by helping entrepreneurs to reach a broader audience pool and allow more people to invest in the promising startups or initiatives. It democratises funding so that a greater variety of projects can be built, which will add to the growing pool of AI techniques.
- PPPs: Any partnerships between government entities and private sector organisations can greatly increase the availability of funding for infrastructure development in AI. PPPs enable the sharing of resources, knowledge and reduce the risks by utilising the best from both sectors. These arrangements serve to enable major projects that may be difficult for either sector to take on solo (Russell & Norvig, 2020).

Education and Skill Development Promoting AI Literacy Training Programs for Policymakers and Practitioners

To handle the complexities of AI in the modern world, you need education and skill development. AI literacy along with specialised training courses for policymakers and practitioners are fundamental to deliver AI technologies gradually being built into different sectors in a responsible and effective manner (Smith & Anderson, 2014).

Promoting AI Literacy

AI literacy is the learning of knowledge and skills required to understand, evaluate, and effectively use AI systems. It helps individuals interface with AI technologies in safe, ethical ways and builds a society able to understand abuses of AI in daily life. It is typically the task of school and university settings to include AI in their curricula by broadening educational strategies. This integration could be started from the school level itself, in K-12 education and subjects such as mathematics, science and computer studies can incorporate basic AI knowledge. We need to transition in our school programs from just teaching kids how to use AI tools, into educating the about how they work and the ethical implications of their use. An example would be project-based learning which works to engage students in real-world AI issues and develop this way of critical thinking. To help prepare students to become well-informed citizens for whom the societal impacts of AI – such as bias and privacy – are discussed openly and widely, teachers should engage students in those very discussions. Additionally, community engagement is important. Educational centres could add workshops for families and communities that would explain what Ai is and how it really works, in person formats. The University takes this outreach seriously because it helps to develop a recognition and awareness of AI in society more generally but also the need for responsible usage by all ages (Taddeo & Floridi, 2018).

Educator and Practitioner Training

Though training of the public in AI literacy is critical, specialised training programs for policymakers and those on the frontlines are equally indispensable. These programs need to home in on the skills that decision-makers will then use to draft the regulations and policies that govern AI technologies well. Policy makers must be educated on the technical details of AI systems – what they can and cannot do. They are able to do so because they understand this in a comprehensive perspective, which allows them to develop more insight-led, balance-policies that walk the line between innovation and ethics (Vinuesa et al., 2020). For example, workshops by AI experts could explain concepts of machine learning, data privacy, algorithmic bias and societal impacts of deploying AI. Domain-specific training on how AI tools could be integrated within their workflows for practitioners in healthcare, finance, education and other fields. They need the type of training programs that produce skilled and practical applications of AI, as well an awareness to how it impacts in line with productivity versus just excellent standards. One is, for instance, training healthcare professionals to use diagnostic tools driven by AI while also educating them about the criticality of patient data privacy. Equally, teachers could be taught to use AI powered teaching assistants to improve the students experience without losing educational integrity (Weller, 2019).

Collaborative Efforts

Therefore, for conducting such training it is necessary to have collaboration between educational institutions, government organisations and private companies. PPPs can help to reduce and share costs for resources, and design cutting-edge training solutions that are adaptable to industry-specific needs.

There is also an increasing need to regularly assess these educational interventions, as existing schemes become outdated in the fast-moving technology sector. Identifying a need for more systematic evaluation, this work presents the Macedonia methodology that is designed to generate feedback from participants in order to improve both training content and delivery methods, thus better equipping both policymakers and practitioners to face new challenges from AI technologies (OECD, 2021). To conclude, the prioritisation on AI literacy and setting up specialised courses can play a major role in establishing a responsible society with enough knowledge to manage AI. With a long-term strategic commitment to education and inter-stakeholder collaboration at all levels, we can prepare citizens to interact with AI in a way that is ethical and productive for the individual as well as enable policymakers to serve as informed governors of these new tools. An approach that is multi-pronged in nature will create 'intelligent citizens' with a sharpened public will to seize the opportunities ushered by AI, while also dealing with its threats carefully.

AI synthesis makes by now available or its direct combination into various divisions, resulting from which it can lead to great opportunities and risks. Effective Strategies to Mitigate Risks and Harness AI Potential The language of the industry has evolved substantially in recent years, from worrying about how AI is going to show up and destroy jobs leading by Harold Innis or dubbing Artificial General Intelligence just around the corner. An important step here is to build evaluation frameworks for AI risks and attaining potential solutions (Kahn & Kearns, 2020).

A Framework for Assessing the Risks of AI

Envision, for instance, a strong risk assessment framework is critical to identifying, analysing and managing the risks associated with AI technologies. These norms usually include a few pillars such as:

- Risk Identification: Identifying Potential Risks of AI systems is the first step in any Risk Assessment. This includes an assessment of a number of risk factors such as data quality, algorithmic bias and human rights risks associated with deployment of AI technologies. All companies that depend on AI must audit their systems to expose weaknesses that might end up having negative consequences.
- Risk Analysis: After identifying the risks, companies need to analyse how likely these risks are and what impact they can have. This analysis can be qualitative or quantitative and may range from a simple visual assessment to the determination of exact concentrations. Quantitative risk assessment may use numeric characterisation or quantitative probability analysis to identify how likely a factor is to contribute to risks, while Qualitative risk assessments are based on the person judgement or by expert discussion aggregating the list of all potential risk factors.

- Risk Prioritisation – Not all risks are critical, it is important that we prioritise them based on the significance. Risk matrices can be used to group risks based on their probability and impact, enabling organisations to address the most severe risks upfront.
- Lifelong Risk Assessment: AI technologies are highly dynamic and ongoing monitoring at all stages of the lifecycle is necessary to identify new or change risks. Organisations should entail thoroughly monitoring in real time which refers to the early warning indicators which contain anomalies or changes in a performance where the risks will originate consistently.
- Involvement of Stakeholders: Bringing stakeholders into the risk assessment process is important for identifying various perspectives and views. Such stakeholders can be developers or users, and public policymakers/ethicists who would be able to contribute their own understanding of potential risks and ethical concerns.

Risk Assessment and Mitigation Frameworks for Evaluating AI Risks Strategies for Addressing Potential Harms

After you have created a risk assessment framework that is as inclusive as possible, your organisation must make sure to take action to mitigate the most significant risks identified:

- Introduce Strong Governance: Organisations should establish strong governance mechanisms which define AI risk manage roles and responsibilities. This includes tasking oversight committees to review AI projects for ethical standards and strict compliance with regulations.
- Data Management: Eradication of Bias or low-quality data exposure is essential. The usage of strict data governance policies to secure the integrity, privacy and security of data at each phase of the data lifecycle within a company.
- To Achieve Fairness in AI Systems: Fairness is only one of several ethical blind spots that AI has, but perhaps the most crucial. Preventing Algorithmic Bias These biases can be detected and corrected during model-built stage using methods like algorithm audit, data augmentation through diverse datasets, bias detection tools, etc. by organisations prior to deployment of an AI model.
- Openness and Accountability: This is important to make AI used clearly traceable back to those affected by it. Businesses must work towards implementing explainable AI, which means they can see through the model to understand how decisions are made, and what is driving their outcomes.
- Training and Awareness Programs – Keeping employees informed about the ethical aspects of AI technologies is key to developing a responsible culture inside organisations. A good place to start is in-house training programs that raise awareness around the dangers of AI and develop effective strategies for detecting and dealing with these problems ahead of time.

- Disaster Recovery Plans: Companies should develop emergency response plans for addressing AI-based outcomes that are at risk of harm or unintended consequences. To this end, incident response plans should detail the steps for incident notification, investigation and mitigation so that action can quickly be taken if problems emerge.

Data Governance and Privacy Best Practices for Data Management Ensuring User Privacy and Security

In the age of data driven decision-making, organisations depend heavily on reliable, secure and compliant datasets which has made data governance and privacy crucial aspects in managing data. Data governance is how organisations handle their data: it must be accurate, available to the right people and protected from unauthorised eyes – all while respecting user privacy. This section goes over some dos and don'ts of data management as well as how to help maintain a secure and private user experience (Kahn & Kearns, 2020).

Data Management Best Practices

Create a Data Governance Framework: To manage data well, you need an excellent data governance framework. This framework must define policies, procedures and roles based on data management. It also should clearly spell out which party will undertake the data quality management, security and compliance with relevant regulations. In this way, organisations are able to provide clear guidelines around how data is managed across different departments.

Good Quality Data Makes Good Decisions: They should have a way to measure and maintain the quality of data by creating consistency in accuracy, completeness and standardisation. Regular audits can allow for the early detection of problems and the preservation of data integrity.

Data Lifecycle Management: As a business owner, you have to understand the stages through which data moves such as creation, storage, use, archiving and removal. Organisations need a strategy to determine the duration they must keep live datasets and when they should be archived or discarded. This will ensure compliance with legal regulations and in addition, it will reduce not only the storage costs but also lowers risks because outdated or irrelevant data does not linger around.

Use Metadata Management

Provides Context on the Data: where does it come from, what is its purpose and how to structure it. And the use of rich metadata allows users to understand the context within which they are interacting with data and it aids in more effective data discovery. Good namespace management even enables tracking of data lineage which is very important when it comes to auditing and compliance.

Real and Regular Compliance Checks: Organisations that must are continuously and always evolving to meet newer regulations such as GDPR or HIPAA. Compliance checks by law are a routine to make sure your data practices all meet the legal requirements. These checks play a vital role in assessing areas where improvement is required and help to avoid any legal risk due to non-compliance.

Protecting User Privacy – And Security

Data Categorisation: A strong data categorisation build is necessary when we are dealing with the protection of classified information. Next, organisations ought to identify data sensitivity levels (e.g., public, internal, confidential) in order to apply the correct security measures. The classification is especially useful in determining who should have access to what type of data and in what context.

Access control policies to ensure only necessary personnel can access sensitive information. Access can be limited based on specific roles in the industry using role-based access controls (RBAC). Access permissions for different datasets are audited regularly, ensuring that only people who need access to any particular data can access it.

Data Encryption: Data should be encrypted at rest and in transit, providing an extra level of security against unauthorised access or breaches. That means if data is intercepted in transit, or accessed between the storage and retrieval points without authorisation, it is still encrypted and cryptographically unreadable without the necessary decryption keys.

Incident Response Plans – Have a well-prepared incident response plan for a fast and effective security breach or data breach resolution process. The regulations say that companies should have policies to detect breaches, provide notice to individuals whose data has been breached and mitigate any damages, within the procedures of the law.

User Education and Awareness – educating employees on how to properly handle sensitive information is key to safeguarding privacy and security standards. With the help of regular training sessions, employees can identify possible threats which may come as a phishing attack or the other social engineering tactics to violate rights and privacy.

Routine Security Audits: Companies can stay ahead of the curve and block weaknesses within their systems before these lead to any complexity by performing security audits from time to time. These audits should not only evaluate technical controls (e.g., firewalls, intrusion detection systems), but also procedural controls (unique policies concerning data access).

Conclusion

The landscape of AI legislation is changing fast as the dust settles on both the positive and adverse impacts of AI. To provide an elementary insight as countries pass regulations for AI across the globe, here we attempt to summarise some of the overarching recommendations and shed light on where AI legislation needs to go.

Create robust regulatory systems: Governments need to build a broad regulatory framework that sets the rules of the road for AI systems, where such technologies pose unique challenges. They would help to define what is acceptable use of AI, how accountability should be managed and compliance with ethical standards.

Advance International Cooperation: International collaboration is crucial because AI is a global technology. In order to achieve borderless AI while protecting the rights of human, countries need to cooperate in regulatory harmonisation and exchange best practices together with development of common standards.

Stakeholder Engagement: Policymakers should involve a wide range of stakeholders more proactively throughout the legislative process. This varied coalition of relevant parties – from technologists, ethicists, civil society organisations, and industry stakeholders – would ensure that the mode of regulation adopted is inclusive and accounts for a wide-range (covering societal) concern.

Transparency and Accountability: Legislation should ensure transparency in the operations and decision-making processes related to AI systems. An AI application runs on a policy framework that clearly defines the accountable organisation for the product.

AI-specific Education and Training: The educational system, as well as training programs for policymakers, practitioners, and the public will be important to implement future regulations regarding AI. These programs must improve AI technologies, ethical considerations, and regulatory compliance.

Create adaptive regulatory approach: Regulatory mechanisms are not rigid or lack the power to change through fast-paced AI development. This could include developing regulatory sandboxes that permit the testing of new technologies for safety and compliance.

References

AI Act. (2023). European commission. https://digital-strategy.ec.europa.eu/en/policies/regulatory-framework-ai

Binns, R. (2018). Fairness in machine learning: Lessons from political philosophy. In *Proceedings of the 2018 conference on fairness, accountability, and transparency* (pp. 149–158). https://doi.org/10.1145/3287560.3287598

Brundage, V., Avin, S., Wang, J., Belfield, H., Krueger, G., Hadfield, G., Khlaaf, H., Yang, J., Toner, H., Fong, R., Maharaj, T., Koh, P. W., Hooker, S., Leung, J., Trask, A., Bluemke, E., Lebensold, J., O'Keefe, C., Koren, M., Théo, R., … Markus, A. (2020). Toward trustworthy AI development: Mechanisms for supporting verifiable claims. *AI & Society*, *35*(4), 1–12.

Cath, C. (2018). Governing artificial intelligence : Ethical, legal, and technical opportunities and challenges. In *Proceedings of the international conference on artificial intelligence* (pp. 123–134).

Cath, C., & Taddeo, M. (2018). The ethics of artificial intelligence: A survey of the literature. *Journal of Artificial Intelligence Research*, *61*, 1–36.

Department of Legal Affairs, Government of India. (n.d.). Summary of recommendations. https://legalaffairs.gov.in/sites/default/files/chapter%2011.pdf

Dignum, V. (2019). Responsible artificial intelligence: Designing AI for human values. *ITU Journal: ICT Discover*, *1*(1), 1–12.

European Commission. (2020). White paper on artificial intelligence: A European approach to excellence and trust. https://ec.europa.eu/info/sites/default/files/commission-white-paper-ai-2020.pdf

European Commission. (2023). Artificial intelligence act. https://digital-strategy.ec.europa.eu/en/policies/regulatory-framework-ai

European Parliament. (2022). Citizens discuss recommendations with institutions, lawmakers, and NGOs. https://multimedia.europarl.europa.eu/en/video/citizens-discuss-recommendations-with-institutions-lawmakers-and-ngos_N01_AFPS_220124_CFP2

Gasser, U., & Almeida, V. (2017). *A layered model for AI governance*. Harvard Kennedy School. https://doi.org/10.2139/ssrn.3041703

Ghosh, S., & Kaur, H. (2021). Ethical implications of artificial intelligence in healthcare: A systematic review of the literature. *Artificial Intelligence in Medicine*, *113*, 101036.

Information Technology Alliance for Public Sector (ITAPS). (2023). ITAPS offers lawmakers key recommendations to reform government IT acquisition. https://www.itic.org/news-events/news-releases/itaps-offers-lawmakers-key-recommendations-to-reform-government-it-acquisition

Jobin, A., Ienca, M., & Andorno, R. (2019). The global landscape of AI ethics guidelines. *Nature Machine Intelligence*, *1*(9), 389–399.

Kahn, S., & Kearns, M. (2020). The ethical implications of AI in decision-making processes: A review of current research and future directions. *AI & Society*, *35*(2), 345–357.

Lee, K.-F., & Yoon, S.-J. (2020). The role of transparency in AI systems: Implications for user trust and ethical considerations in design and deployment practices. *AI & Society*, *35*(4), 733–744.

Mittelstadt, B. D., Allo, P., Taddeo, M., Wachter, S., & Floridi, L. (2016). The ethics of algorithms: Mapping the debate. *Big Data & Society*, *3*(2). https://doi.org/10.1177/2053951716679679

OECD. (2021). Recommendation on artificial intelligence: OECD principles on AI. https://www.oecd.org/going-digital/ai/principles/

OpenAI. (2023). ChatGPT [large language model]. https://chat.openai.com/chat

Pasquale, F., & Citron, D. K. (2014). Introduction: The law of algorithms: A new frontier in legal scholarship and practice. *Harvard Law Review Forum*, *127*(2), 1–16.

Russell, S., & Norvig, P. (2020). *Artificial intelligence: A modern approach* (4th ed.). Pearson.

Smith, B., & Anderson, J. Q. (2014). *AI and the future of work: How artificial intelligence will impact jobs and employment*. Pew Research Center.

Solove, D. J. (2021). Privacy self-management and the consent dilemma. *Harvard Law Review*, *126*(7), 1880–1903.

Taddeo, M., & Floridi, L. (2018). How AI can be designed to be ethical. *Nature Machine Intelligence*, *1*(2), 90–92.

Thierer, A. (2016). *The ethics of artificial intelligence and robotics*. The Independent Institute.

United Nations Educational Scientific and Cultural Organization (UNESCO). (2021). Recommendations on the ethics of artificial intelligence. https://unesdoc.unesco.org/ark:/48223/pf0000379987

Vinuesa, R., Azizpour, H., Leite, I., Balaam, M., Dignum, V., Domisch, S., Felländer, A., Langhans, S. D., Tegmark, M., & Nerini, F. F. (2020). The role of artificial intelligence in achieving the Sustainable Development Goals. *Nature Communications*, *11*(1), 233.

Weller, A. (2019). Transparency: Mitigating bias in algorithmic decision-making systems through transparency. In *Proceedings of the AAAI/ACM conference on AI ethics and society* (pp. 20–26).

Wright, D., & Kreissl, R. (2018). Data protection by design : A new approach to privacy regulation. *International Data Privacy Law*, *8*(3), 213–224.

Zuboff, S. (2019). *The age of surveillance capitalism : The fight for a human future at the new frontier of power*. PublicAffairs.

Chapter 9

Price of Security: Balancing Security With Civil Liberties and Risks in AI-Driven Surveillance

Manmeet Kaur Arora, Sahil Lal, Bhupinder Singh and Anjali Raghav

Sharda University, India

Abstract

The growing usage of artificial intelligence (AI) in surveillance systems also poses important questions regarding the trade-offs between security, civil liberties and associated risks. *The Price of Security: Balancing Security with Civil Liberties and Risks in AI-Driven Surveillance* covers the various nuances of impact of AI-infused surveillance on how society operates as well as individual rights. The research starts by providing a background on how surveillance technologies have evolved, taking into consideration that AI has made traditional methods of surveillance turn into advanced and real-time systems with capacity to make decisions. While these developments ostensibly provide better security, they also represent grave dangers to privacy and civil liberties. We provide several case studies where AI surveillance has been pushed way beyond ethical limits and subsequently evoked public outcry and often legal charges at the same time. This in turn is part of an ongoing dialogue about the larger question of how to address security and privacy issues effectively in a networked culture.

Keywords: AI; balancing security; civil liberties; risks; AI-driven surveillance

Introduction

The impact of artificial intelligence (AI) is profound, and this has also been noticed in the surveillance world as well where it has transformed itself fundamentally making human works much more accurate than ever. The chapter also

Security Intelligence in the Age of AI, 153–169

Published under exclusive licence by Emerald Publishing Limited
doi:10.1108/978-1-83608-156-220251009

looks at the development of AI surveillance and how this was a concept that many governments and companies alike, failed to recognise how important it is and what to do about such a fundamental morning civil liberties/security dichotomy. It also examines the AI-powered surveillance regulation in the proposed research regime and highlight areas of weakness when existing legislation is not sufficient to safeguard human rights. It analyses the role of policymakers in setting up frameworks that guarantee transparency and accountability in the use of these technologies. The paper supports compromise that balances public safety against individual rights. The researchers said that these results indicate that negotiations between technologists, ethicists and lawmakers will have to arrive at some middle ground on where AI in surveillance is permitted and where it is prohibited. If constructive-theoretics on those are developed, then the beneficial capabilities of AI can be combined with minimal impact to civil liberties as a by-product (Wright & Kreissl, 2018).

AI in Surveillance: A Review

Traditional surveillance is revolutionised by AI with it embracing modern technologies like machine learning, computer vision and predictive analytics. This enables high-performance real-time monitoring and analysis that gives the surveillance system unparalleled precision in identifying objects, tracking movement and reporting anomalies (Zuboff, 2019). AI enhanced cameras can for example distinguish humans, animals and non-living objects from each other greatly reducing false alarms related to irrelevant movements. Facial recognition technology is a case in point of AI creating an indelible impression by quickly identifying people at airports or corporate offices (Binns, 2018).

Background of Surveillance Technologies

Surveillance started small through older techniques like watchtowers and surveillance on foot (Cath, 2018). The introduction of closed-circuit television (CCTV) in the mid-20th century represented a major improvement for keeping an eye on various public places. Though, previous systems simply acted re-actively storing escalations without necessarily integrating real-time analytics. Revolutions in AI are having us move from a system of recording (reacting) to proactively monitoring and real-time responding to vulnerabilities (Dignum, 2019).

Over time, the various AI technologies were integrated into other sectors beyond public safety. Retailers use AI to detect theft by checking the patterns of behaviour that customers are exhibiting, and heath care facilities will be able to monitor the health status of their patients all using AI. The wider trend of tech-enabled security Sean Bush with Secure works discusses how his company leverages threat intelligence for better insight into attackers and its customers (Gasser & Almeida, 2017).

Security and Civil Liberties Must Be in Balance

On the other hand, as AI-powered surveillance becomes more prevalent and sophisticated in scope, it prompts widespread issues over privacy and civil liberties. The spectre of mass surveillance and misuse of data necessitates ethical considerations. Unlike more dangerous possibilities, like facial recognition technology that allows people to be tracked without their agreement and is a potential violation of privacy (Jobin et al., 2019).

The answer to this is that we must develop strong legal frameworks, which ensure rights and security go hand in hand. When developing and implementing surveillance technologies, policymakers must weigh the ways in which such tools would compromise the fabric of society and ensure that their policies will temper rather than further their effect. Such a balance is crucial not only for public trust, but also to prevent security measures from superseding basic civil freedoms (Kahn & Kearns, 2020).

All in all, the inclusion of AI into surveillance systems is a great leap forward for security technology. But it requires thoughtful reflection about moral consequences and willingness to protect our civil rights. The imperative for ensuring a security and privacy coexistence will be crucial to our future societal health as we inextricably adopt these technologies (Mittelstadt et al., 2016).

The Evolution of Surveillance Technologies

Surveillance technology has undergone a huge transformation over the last decade from old style methods to new AI based tech. In this episode, we caught up with Joe who gave us a primer on the historical origins of surveillance, its transmutation into AI and some of the significant advances that cropped in branch of privacy.

Surveillance Methods Out of Scale

Historically, surveillance was based almost entirely on direct observation and primitive recording devices. Methods like these were used by human monitors based on strategic points, looking at footage through tools such as binoculars or cameras to be reviewed later on. In public health for example, data collection consisted of hospital or clinic reports (sometimes compiled via surveys and direct observations). Despite adoption of a system like the National Notifiable Disease Surveillance System (NNDSS) at the federal level by centres like the Centres for Disease Control and Prevention (CDC), which can find disease trends, assessing past illnesses manually on paper forms such as vaccination cards could be a slow process to identify emerging infectious diseases after 2006 (Russell & Norvig, 2020). But these methods were largely reactive in nature, addressing issues retroactively instead of pre-emptively stopping them.

The Pathway Into AI-Powered Systems

The dichotomy in surveillance has been turned on its head with the rise of AI. AI based on machine learning or AI, systems makes it possible to analyse sets of data in real time that are so massive that they can be pooled and threat detection can take place. Whereas traditional systems needed a human to watch hours of footage and pick out anomalies, AI can detect patterns and identify unexpected happenings immediately in virtually any kind of video feed. In particular, this transition is very useful in environments where speed of response is essential one example might be an airport or busy public area (Russell & Norvig, 2020). Further, the surveillance set-up is aided by advanced technologies and AI integration with other technologies like IoT has enabled surveillance to magnify its capabilities. And since smart cameras have AI onboard – they can speak to each other and other devices, receiving and sending signals – an all-encompassing security solution is achieved that grows more flexible over time, adapting to transformed circumstances (Russell & Norvig, 2020).

Some of the Critical Advanced Technologies in the AI Surveillance

The use of AI in surveillance has resulted in a number of important advancements including:

- Facial Recognition Technology: Its application is in quick identification of individuals by matching live footage with databases of known faces. Real-time tracking of suspects in security settings has now become a critical tool, thanks to this technology.

By examining the existing data – or rather existing data – AI could also anticipate a strike and propaganda even before it occurs. By doing so businesses are able to be proactive, efficiently using their time and eliminating risk (Smith et al., 2014).

- Better Object Identification: This means that the cameras can make out between different kinds of objects and behaviours. This feature helps to minimise false alarms from movements that do not pose a security hazard while making sure the actual threats are taken care of swiftly (Solove, , 2021).
- Immediate Alerts: AI systems will instantly notify you if a there is suspicious activities taking place, so that security professionals can respond to a possible threat-like activity.
- Data Integration: As a way to more widely expand the information available, modern surveillance systems can share data from different databases, sources and across entities such as social media feeds or public records (Taddeo & Floridi, 2018).

Finally, the transition from classic surveillance techniques to AI-powered systems is evidently a big leap in public safety and security management.

Although the traditional approaches set the stage for the monitoring of practices, AI developments have transformed surveillance to focus more on preventative measures to add safety and better cope with modern threats (Thierer, 2016).

Ethical Considerations in AI Surveillance

The move to inject surveillance with AI has ignited a deep ethical conversation around the moral fabric of these tools, privacy-centric implications and the power of consent in such practices. This chapter explores these crucial dimensions to assess the wider implications of AI-assisted surveillance over society (United Nations Educational Scientific and Cultural Organization (UNESCO), 2021).

Ethical Issues in Surveillance Technology

This raises complicated ethical questions about the use of AI for surveillance. There are already concerns about bias in AI algorithms, such as those underlying facial recognition technologies. The technology has been proven to be error prone, misidentifying the face of individuals (via NIST) and particularly in the case of marginalised communities – often tributing wrongful accusations or worsening societal divides which disadvantages those groups. Biases in law enforcement are harmful not only because they make law enforcement more inefficient but also because these biases lead to discrimination which leads to further injustice. Second, concerns exist about the ethical implications of deploying AI surveillance by authoritarian states (Weller, 2019). There is nothing to stop Governments using them to repress dissent, covertly surveil citizens or trample on basic human rights. Fair uses and moral implications of quick access go well beyond the merely privacy at the individual level to broader societal values such as freedom, justice and equality.

Moral Implications of Surveillance Technologies

The foundational principle of privacy in a democratic society is at great risk from AI surveillance. Because AI systems are developed to collect and process huge quantities of personal data, it provides an ideal ground for individuals who can be monitored continuously without their permission. This kind of widespread surveillance may create a climate of fear and self-censorship whereby people change what they write or do knowing that scrutiny is constant. Another key issue is data protection. Vulnerabilities in surveillance systems enable collection of sensitive information, hence the concerns data leaks and unauthorised access. With cyber threats on the rise, the extension of personal data is so much unwanted. It is obligatory to have a strong data protection in place to prevent the misuse or theft of individuals data (AI Act, 2023).

Privacy Concerns and Data Protection

Authentic consent is a foundational element to surveillance ethics. People have the right to know when they are being watched and give their consent for the collection and application of their data. Such permission rarely is the case – many surveillance systems look in on people who never asked to be watched. The absence of this information creates mistrust between citizens and institutions. Instituting well defined protocols in order to promote informed consent and avoid all these issues is what organisations need. It will require informing people in detail on what data is collected from them and how that data is used, stored/protected. In addition, creating processes to allow people to opt-out of or challenge surveillance actions can help society and foster responsibility. To sum up, ethical reflections on AI-based surveillance even go beyond this already complex issue. So in the course of evolving technology for essential human need, how can various stakeholders such as policy makers, technologists and civil society work together to build frameworks which are ethical on one hand yet unlock AI's real potential in areas of security and public safety? It is a delicate balance of whether we become secure states at the expense of our rights or if we foster societies that aspire to rever our security and individual needs in an interconnected world (Binns, 2018).

Security Risks Associated With AI Surveillance

The adoption of AI in modern surveillance systems has greatly increased the various risks related to security that should not be taken lightly. This chapter analyzes Threats related to AI surveillance, Weak spots within these systems and provides some Case Study where AI miscreantzation was observed (Brundage et al., 2020).

AI-Related Dangers: The Way Matters Stand

These AI surveillance systems, despite improving the security functionality also pose some potential risks. Among the key worries are adversarial attacks – when malevolent actors trick AI algorithms into incorrect answers. For example, adversaries could use methods to elude their identity in front of face detection cameras or present doctored inputs that make AI categorise bad behaviour (Cath & Taddeo, 2018). Such security gaps can jeopardise the credibility of network video surveillance data and may limit the effectiveness of security deployment. Another concern is the level of data privacy such systems imperil. Having the function of using huge personal information which should be kept highly confidential raises constraints of potential unauthorised access and abuse. As cybercriminals start attacking the databases that store this information being collected by surveillance technologies, the risk of data breaches also grows (Dignum, 2019).

Vulnerabilities in AI Systems

They, with all their ability to score a perfect hit every time, are not secure in the sense that they cannot be breached. A key problem was the bias inherent to algorithms whose body of trained data essentially mirrors our societal prejudices. The same AI system may be trained to look for more instances of surveillance in certain leading to discrimination and civil rights infringements when the programme disproportionately targets (ie, gender, etc). Additionally, because AI algorithms are very complicated, there will also be operational vulnerabilities. These systems also require regular updates or monitoring, because their relevancy can diminish with age and thus may not be as accurately able to react to future threats or environmental changes. States stuck like this leave security holes that are any attacker dream (European Commission, 2020).

Examples of AI Abuse in Surveillance

Case studies This potential for a misuse of AI technology with respect to surveillance uses has been illustrated by varied case studies An example was in London, where trials of facial-recognition technology were met with outrage over privacy infringements. The lack of oversight over the use of facial recognition had critics raising it as a civil liberties issue and one that resulted in wrongful IDs. As citizens tried to defend their rights against what they felt were violation of privacy, legal challenges started erupting. Predictive policing programs in the United States have been criticised for inheriting and entrenching historical racial biases encoded in historical crime data. Often they are based on algorithms that use historical crime data to forecast future incidents. However, this strategy may serve to exacerbate existing inequalities and racial bias by further surveilling communities already over-policed, perpetuating a dynamic of mistrust between law enforcement and the citizenry. One example from China, in which the local government subjects citizens to constant surveillance with AI at any given moment. Report after report suggests the technology is actually not used to 'prevent crimes' but, instead, to stifle dissent and manipulate the public.§§ These applications lack transparency and accountability which has serious ethical questions about the trade off between national security and individual freedom. To sum things up, AI-driven surveillance technologies are providing more powerful security capabilities but at the cost of higher risks that need to be mitigated upfront (Gasser & Almeida, 2017). Recognising the threats specific to these systems, understanding their vulnerabilities and being informed from misuse case studies is required for creating ethical frameworks and regulatory measures that respect civil rights while delivering public safety. A thoughtful combination of these tools will be key to shaping the future practices around AI surveillance that both society, and those bodies responsible for them, can live with (Ghosh & Kaur, 2021).

Legal Framework and Regulations

The legislation of legally recognising AI-powered surveillance is complicated and always changing. This chapter will study the contemporary legal landscape concerning AI surveillance, as well as international standards and guidelines available on the subject that hope to tackle their ethical and technical concerns (Jobin et al., 2019).

Current Laws Governing AI Surveillance

For example, some countries have passed laws to control AI in surveillance applications. The General Data Protection Regulation (GDPR) of the European Union regulates the processing of personal data and, in particular, biometric data used by facial recognition. An important concept key to the GDPR is the privacy and rights of an individual in how businesses are collecting data. The legislation also acts as a model for privacy protection globally, shaping laws in other regions. Legal frameworks are incredibly different state-by-state here in the United States. One of the provisions in the amendment concerns citizens being protected from unreasonable searches and seizures and, therefore, by extension also from the AI surveillance methods used. But those traditional legal doctrines are still being interpreted for modern surveillance technologies by the courts. A few states even passed laws on facial recognition technology stating that law enforcement needs a warrant to deploy it. Moreover, there is a move to embed accountability mechanisms in order to make surveillance practices more respectful of individuals' rights. Such obligations include elements of notice and consent, oversight and redress for misuse (Kahn & Kearns, 2020).

Basic International Standards and Rules

There is a move on an international level towards increased regulation around AI surveillance. In fact, the United Nations, as well as the Council of Europe are taking steps to open dialogue about establishing human rights-oriented standards encouraging innovation in technological security. Transparency, accountability and fairness We rely on the OECD Principles on AI to help ensure that powerful AI systems work for people and are transparent, understandable and fair. The guidelines are designed to persuade AI member countries to apply policies related to ethical AI usage in the context of surveillance. In addition, the European Commission has introduced legislation to help guarantee that AI technology is designed and utilised in accordance with basic rights. But so far, no globally responsive framework has been put into place to govern the use of AI surveillance worldwide. Different legal environments in countries make it harder to define common international standards.

Future Legislative Trends

With the advancement of AI technologies still in progress, future legislation is also likely to improve privacy protection and address ethical concerns surrounding surveillance applications. One trend that has been anticipated is the additional regulation of biometric data use. It is entirely possible that the Governments would start enforcing severe limitations on the use of facial recognition (and indeed all biometric) systems in order to kerb abuse and safeguard their subjects. Premised on this main concept, another trend that is acting as a catalyst for chatbot growth within the financial industry is the demand for transparency in AI algorithms. And legislators may impose disclosure requirements on organisations, specifically as they relate to the decision-making processes that go along with surveillance using algorithms. This can provide unprecedented transparency for AI and reduce biases within these systems, which in turn could create trust with the public (Lee & Yoon, 2020). Additionally, there is likely to be a focus on the role of the public in that surveillance policy-making. Involving citizens in dialogues around the ethics of AI surveillance may be one way to shape more comprehensive regulations that resonate with shared societal priorities. Finally, the law relevant to AI surveillance is diverse and currently nascent. Laws in place differ considerably between regions, international norms are beginning to develop but they have not yet become universal. As our society contemplates the tough ethical questions that these technologies raise, we can also likely expect future legislative efforts to focus on strong safeguards for privacy rights, transparency and meaningful democratic oversight of any type of AI surveillance being capable of serving the public interests without grossly intruding on individual rights.

Balancing Security Needs With Civil Liberties

There is a tricky balance that needs to be found when one starts fitting AI into surveillance systems: where do security interests trump personal rights? Chapter 5: Ethical AI implementation strategies, the role public perception/integration and trust play in application, responsible surveillance best practices.

Approaches to Implementing Ethical AI

For a balance between security and civil liberties, organisations are required to implement ethical frameworks when deploying AI technologies. The most basic of these is the necessity and proportionality principle, meaning that surveillance measures should only be adopted when absolutely necessary and shall be proportional to the threat. Such scrutiny involves assessing actual risks and benefits associated with surveillance initiatives against individual rights of only the very minimum breaching (Mittelstadt et al., 2016). Transparency is another key element. Entities should clearly disclose information about their surveillance practices: what data they collect, the purposes for which data is obtained and used and who has access to it. Thus, this transparency builds trust among the public and to know how surveillance technologies affect their privacy. In addition, the institution of effective supervision is also very much required. They proposed the creation of independent oversight bodies to supervise AI surveillance projects that are legally and ethically appropriate. They can also offer mechanisms for reporting complaints or seeking recourse for breaches of privacy.

Public Opinion and Trust Concerns

AI-driven surveillance technologies heavily rely on public perception as a linchpin for general acceptance. Some worry that power could be abused and civil liberties eroded. The use of such an unproven technology for a practice as sensitive (and often racially charged) as the surveillance of people only serves to underscore why high-profile cases of wrongful identifications by similarly unreliable systems have understandably fostered public scepticism about the face recognition business. Cases in which individuals were mistakenly arrested based on incorrect AI evaluations, for example, have prompted demands for more control of surveillance and accountability. In order to build such confidence, we must involve our communities in conversation around the implications of surveillance technologies. Policymakers and organisations need to provide opportunities for engagement of various stakeholders, including civil rights groups, technical experts and the public at large. Including ordinary people in decision-making can deal with concerns and create a culture of surveillance ownership (OECD, 2021).

Best Practices for Responsible Surveillance

Navigating the fine line between security requirements and civil liberties, there are a number of best practices that can help guide ethical AI surveillance:

- Establish Clear Policies: Organisations need to establish comprehensive policies detailing what all the surveillance activities encompass and where these starts and stop. Individual rights must stand first, but a policy that combines them would also do well to look into security considerations.
- Engineer for Privacy: If we must have surveillance systems, they must be engineered to begin with a built-in set of privacy safeguards. These practices range from collecting the least amount of necessary data to securely storing and processing all data.
- Perform Regular Audits: Regular audits of AI surveillance systems could help to identify potential biases or inefficiencies. These should be audited for compliance with established ethical standards and requirements.
- Encourage Diversity: Conversing with varied communities about surveillance can help weed out biases in AI systems. Empowerment of marginalised voices can contribute to a more subjective digest of the output.
- Training Stakeholders: One of the primary requirements for having a mature public conversation about AI surveillance is being able to educate the public on

what it really means. Workshops, seminars and awareness campaigns could help people to know their rights and promote the practice of responsible journalism.

In other words, appropriately balancing security requirements against civil liberties in AI-driven surveillance depends on a multidimensional framework of ethical deployment strategies, public buy-in and best practices. Organisations that want to derive the benefits of AI in today's surveilled world but are sensitive about respecting individual rights can do so by placing widespread transparency, accountability and community involvement at the top of their priorities.

Technological Solutions for Risk Mitigation

This requires strong technological measures that it can implement to reduce the risks of AI in surveillance. These strategies comprise AI safety precautions, open algorithm protocols and ongoing vigilance and response framework will be discussed in this chapter (Pasquale et al., 2014).

Safety: Precautions and Protocols for AI

In an era where AI technologies continue to be integrated into surveillance practices, setting up safety measures and protocols becomes mandatory. We recommend that organisations classify AI-systems based on potential risks to individuals and society. This can be used to identify the level of oversight and regulation that an implementation should receive. For example, systems classified as 'high-risk' may justify more oversight than those labelled with the less risky descriptors 'limited risk', or 'minimal risk'. This protocol provides an important approach to data handling and validation in AI systems. Organisations need to validate data sources strictly and verify the datasets available for training AI are not biased or inaccurately representative. That way, data poisoning (in which nefarious or careless actors use biased data to create AI manipulation) can be averted. Moreover, using input sanitisation aids in defending against malicious and dangerous inputs which would otherwise threaten the overall performance of the system.

Strengthening Transparency Element for AI Algorithms

To ensure that the entire process remains invisible transparency is key to the acceptance of AI driven surveillance systems. It is critical that stakeholders know how these algorithms work and how they make their decisions. Organisations need to aim for Explainable AI or explainability-oriented processes that offer transparency into how algorithms make decisions. By providing selling points behind particular results, businesses increase transparency and improve the possibility for users to query or contest decisions governed by AI. In addition, audit trails can be created to ensure transparency in AI systems. These records should capture every interaction, and each decision that the system executes, so they can be reviewed comprehensively when it is necessary. Audits can find and amend biases or inefficiencies in algorithms to make them fairer and work better.

Strategies for Continuous Monitoring and Incident Response

Real-Time Detection: To be able to capture any deviation or security anomaly at real time, continuous monitoring of AI surveillance system is necessary. To identify threats This automated monitoring tool, use behaviour and patterns analysis of the system by applying machine learning on top of that. Adding a proactive enforcement component allows fast incident responses before they grow out of control. Therefore, it is equally important to prepare a complete incident response plan. The plan should detail how incidents of AI system detection, reporting and mitigation will be handled. Maintain responsibilities are prudential with the intentions to find out at each layer or section of the platform when a breach in security occurs or, for instance, if hardware starts malfunctioning. Testing and revising this plan will improve the capacity of emergency services to handle changing threats. Organisations should also place an emphasis on training and education for the human side of AI systems. Training to teach users how to operate these technologies safely and what scope of risks might be possible are both important. To sum up, any serious use of tech to kerb risks in AI-powered surveillance is a multi-step process that were just introduced here. Responsible AI surveillance is possible through establishing solid safety measures, improving transparency in algorithms and continued monitoring coupled with incident response strategies. This work is critical for defending civil liberties and building confidence in the tools that increasingly shape security nightstands.

The Future of AI in Security and Surveillance

AI Tech Trends The Road Ahead for Security and Surveillance These technologies are going to become ever more important in public safety and spark major conversations about how we keep that balance between our civil liberties (our freedoms) with the demand for safety.

Latest Trends and Innovations

AI has made such progress that its applications in security and surveillance have been nothing short of exciting. One of the biggest trends we see is predictive analytics, which can predict when and where crime might happen using history data. Predictive policing models that provide data-driven forecasts of crime patterns for law enforcement agencies, thereby increasing the ability to use resources more effectively so as to anticipate and prevent crimes before they occur. They can help to isolate hot areas and identify high-risk individuals, which enables a pre-active public safety effort. Another major innovation is combining advanced sensors with AI power drones and surveillance systems. The UAVs could be used to hover above and monitor large groups in situ, help maintain area security checkpoints as well as surveillance on the ground during live events or emergencies. Further, AI-based video analytics also improve situational awareness by automatically identifying abnormal behaviours or activities in real-time, thus sending an alert to authorities. In addition, the introduction of natural language processing (NLP) in the surveillance of platforms such as social media is also becoming an important tool to give advance indications of potential criminal hazards or unrest. The AI can identify pre-injury indicators by listening to online chatter and discerning patterns that suggest when things might turn violent,... (which will) allow time for preventive measures [...] to be put in place.

Future AI Applications for Public Safety

And we see that same potential in how AI technologies will be leveraged throughout public safety as they continue to mature. Law enforcement organisations will increasingly rely on AI to provide it with a deeper service offering which can allow them to be more successful and prolific in what they do, the potential of that is visible through the predictions that point out towards efficiency and effectiveness for law enforcement agencies. An example is the universe of data they will soon be operating over, with AI systems capable of analysing huge quantities from countless sources (surveillance cameras, social media or emergency calls) to few together an accurate live picture that could also lend itself to faster decision making. Further, improvements in facial recognition software can be expected to make identification processes more precise. This could be a boon to finding missing people or even suspects in criminal investigations. Yet, the progress has to be made very carefully as there is an ongoing concern about privacy breach possibilities and misuses.

Ongoing Debate: Security vs. Privacy

However, though some advances in AI for public safety are encouraging, the issue of security vs. privacy is sure to raise its contentious head again and again. The capacity for abuse of surveillance technologies raises important ethical considerations about fundamental civil liberties. But critics have said that racheting up surveillance could slacken the slope into Big Brother-like surveillance of its citizens. The difficulty is in establishing a regulatory framework that can balance the opportunity to leverage AI technology – increasing security as well as protecting civil liberties. Strict regulations governing the use of AI surveillance technologies should be balanced with flexibility that policymakers must take into account. That said, it will be important to make sure these systems are used ethically and responsibly, where attention is fully exerted on transparency and accountability. Also important is the role of public engagement in these challenges. They should be in a position to discuss where AI technologies are considered to be deployed within their communities. That engagement helps create trust between law enforcement and the communities they protect, so that even in times of security measures do not come at the cost of individual rights. To summarise, the future of AI in security and surveillance is mixed with the good side and bad side. As new trends develop with regard to the legal landscape, it becomes imperative that we create an environment wherein technological advancements can be maximised without sacrificing public safety or privacy rights. Getting the balance right, therefore, will potentially deliver a higher level of security overall without putting in jeopardy the freedoms that are at the heart of democratic values.

Conclusion

As we look deeper at the distinctions of surveillance tech in an ever-growing digital world, it is important to remember what we have gathered and where the stalwart hand takes us. AI is increasingly being integrated into surveillance systems and the application of these technologies has massive potential to improve public safety yet also raises alarming issues with respect to privacy and civil liberties. The conclusion extracts specific findings, provides policy advice and practical implications and suggests some directions for developing ethical AI. As we have been looking at AI-based surveillance, several important themes have jumped out. In the same way that AI capabilities are not always welcomed by human rights advocates, as AI increases the efficiency and effectiveness of surveillance systems, it brings with it thorny ethical and legal questions about bias, privacy violations and potential misuse. History suggests that the choices we make in surveillance technology follow a slippery slope to worse and more invasive technologies if they go unchecked, potentially eroding fundamental human liberties. Second, no attempt to balance between security needs and civil liberties is a reliable safeguard against using mass surveillance for political purposes. When organisations implement AI tools, they should keep in mind the ethical aspects and ensure that their surveillance practices do not violate core freedoms. Transparency, accountability to ensure public trust in these systems Last but not least, continual oversight and audit processes are crucial to the management of AI surveillance risks. And responsible conduct around these technologies is possible with the implementation of safety controls and protocols; more algorithmic transparency would also help and having incident response strategies in place certainly leads to more prepared organisations.

Policy and Practice Recommendations

Here are some specific recommendations to policymakers and practitioners interested in working towards a future that is more responsible in surveillance technology.

- Define Regulation at Scale: The regulation of AI in surveillance should be expanded to a point where enforcement can occur reliably and systematically. What we need are regulations that put privacy first and allow for practical security. It is necessary to try to find a balance that can suit all these interests in order to gain the confidence of the public.

- Enforce Ethical Guidelines: These guidelines shall not only serve as a basis to these organisations but also be adopted by them promoting the best practices in AI surveillance. These standards must remain transparent, accountable and inclusive in decision-making processes.
- Invest in Public Engagement: Engaging communities around practices of surveillance needs to happen, or communities and citizens will never trust! Regulations also need to be shaped to reflect societal values and shall involve diverse stakeholders as much as possible.
- Promote R&D: Funding research that is grounded in developing only ethical AI technologies will eventually yield novel approaches to privacy and security. Such responsible progress is only possible through partnered work of academia, industry and government.

Call to Action for Ethical AI Development

The increasing pace of advances in AI technologies requires a united front for the ethical development of these technologies. It notes the need for a coordinated response across a diverse range of stakeholders – technologists, policymakers, civil society and overall citizenry – to build a framework that upholds human rights while also accommodating technological progress. This includes a call to action to lobby for the adoption of sound AI design principles, which embed privacy from inception. Developers must be incentivised to build systems that take the least possible data and ask for consent from a user. More fundamentally though, we need education regarding the implications of AI surveillance to people, so that they know what their rights are and can push for responsible practices. In short, while we have a future that is constantly being shaped AI enabled surveillance technologies, ensuring ethical considerations be placed on the same level as security concerns becomes crucial. Through the adoption of strong regulations, dedication to transparency, partnership with affected communities and commitment to follow responsible development practises we can reap the benefits associated with these technologies while protecting civil liberties. We, collectively, will create a future where public safety and democracy can coexist.

References

AI Act. (2023). European commission. https://digital-strategy.ec.europa.eu/en/policies/regulatory-framework-ai

Binns, R. (2018). Fairness in machine learning: Lessons from political philosophy. In *Proceedings of the 2018 conference on fairness, accountability, and transparency* (pp. 149–158). https://doi.org/10.1145/3287560.3287598

Brundage, V., Avin, S., Wang, J., Belfield, H., Krueger, G., Hadfield, G., Khlaaf, H., Yang, J., Toner, H., Fong, R., Maharaj, T., Koh, P. W., Hooker, S., Leung, J., Trask, A., Bluemke, E., Lebensold, J., O'Keefe, C., Koren, M., Théo, R., . . ., Markus, A. (2020). Toward trustworthy AI development: Mechanisms for supporting verifiable claims. *AI and Society*, *35*(4), 1–12.

Cath, C. (2018). Governing artificial intelligence: Ethical, legal, and technical opportunities and challenges. In *Proceedings of the international conference on artificial intelligence* (pp. 123–134).

Cath, C., & Taddeo, M. (2018). The ethics of artificial intelligence: A survey of the literature. *Journal of Artificial Intelligence Research*, *61*, 1–36.

Dignum, V. (2019). Responsible artificial intelligence: Designing AI for human values. *ITU Journal: ICT Discover*, *1*(1), 1–12.

European Commission. (2020). White paper on artificial intelligence: A European approach to excellence and trust. https://ec.europa.eu/info/sites/default/files/commission-white-paper-ai-2020.pdf

Gasser, U., & Almeida, V. (2017). *A layered model for AI governance*. Harvard Kennedy School.

Ghosh, S., & Kaur, H. (2021). Ethical implications of artificial intelligence in healthcare: A systematic review of the literature. *Artificial Intelligence in Medicine*, *113*, 101036.

Jobin, A., Ienca, M., & Andorno, R. (2019). The global landscape of AI ethics guidelines. *Nature Machine Intelligence*, *1*(9), 389–399.

Kahn, S., & Kearns, M. (2020). The ethical implications of AI in decision-making processes: A review of current research and future directions. *AI and Society*, *35*(2), 345–357.

Lee, K.-F., & Yoon, S.-J. (2020). The role of transparency in AI systems: Implications for user trust and ethical considerations in design and deployment practices. *AI and Society*, *35*(4), 733–744.

Mittelstadt, B. D., Allo, P., Taddeo, M., Wachter, S., & Floridi, L. (2016). The ethics of algorithms: Mapping the debate. *Big Data & Society*, *3*(2). https://doi.org/10.1177/2053951716679679

OECD. (2021). Recommendation on artificial intelligence: OECD principles on AI. https://www.oecd.org/going-digital/ai/principles/

Pasquale, F., & Citron, D. K. (2014). Introduction: The law of algorithms: A new frontier in legal scholarship and practice. *Harvard Law Review Forum*, *127*(2), 1–16.

Russell, S., & Norvig, P. (2020). *Artificial intelligence: A modern approach* (4th ed.). Pearson.

Smith, B., & Anderson, J. Q. (2014). *AI and the future of work: How artificial intelligence will impact jobs and employment*. Pew Research Center.

Solove, D. J. (2021). Privacy self-management and the consent dilemma. *Harvard Law Review*, *126*(7), 1880–1903.

Taddeo, M., & Floridi, L. (2018). How AI can be designed to be ethical. *Nature Machine Intelligence*, *1*(2), 90–92.

Thierer, A. (2016). *The ethics of artificial intelligence and robotics*. The Independent Institute.

United Nations Educational Scientific and Cultural Organization (UNESCO). (2021). Recommendations on the ethics of artificial intelligence. https://unesdoc.unesco.org/ark:/48223/pf0000379987

Weller, A. (2019). Transparency: Mitigating bias in algorithmic decision-making systems through transparency. In *Proceedings of the AAAI/ACM conference on AI ethics and society* (pp. 20–26).
Wright, D., & Kreissl, R. (2018). Data protection by design: A new approach to privacy regulation. *International Data Privacy Law*, *8*(3), 213–224.
Zuboff, S. (2019). *The age of surveillance capitalism: The fight for a human future at the new frontier of power*. Public Affairs.

Chapter 10

Regulatory Framework to Data Localisation: A Comparative Study of the European Union and the Indian Context

Saurabh Chandra[a] *and Suparna Kundu*[b]

[a]Bennett University, India
[b]Amity University, India

Abstract

In the present technology-driven world, data is a pivotal asset for organisations and governments, supporting both economic growth and national security. The issue of data localisation stems from the similar and connected notion of data sovereignty and data residency. This paper examines the notion of data localisation, which requires data created within a nation to be stored and processed domestically, as well as the regulatory frameworks in the European Union (EU) and India. The paper begins by defining data localisation and distinguishing it from other notions like data sovereignty and residency. It then delves into the EU's General Data Protection Regulation (GDPR), emphasising the strict data protection requirements and sophisticated approach to cross-border data transfers that strike a balance between data security with economic flexibility. The EU approach emphasises responsibility, openness and user permission, allowing for data mobility while guaranteeing strong privacy measures.

In contrast, India's approach to data localisation is more direct and fragmented, with no overarching regulatory structure. The study reviews significant efforts such as the Personal Data Protection Bill, 2019, and numerous policy measures, evaluating their efficacy and influence on enterprises and national security. The research finds that while India intends to improve data security and local technology infrastructure, it confronts hurdles such as greater operational costs and potential trade barriers.

By comparing the EU and Indian frameworks, the research finds excellent practices and lessons that India may learn from the EU's balanced approach. The research concludes that a flexible, trust-based data localisation approach

Security Intelligence in the Age of AI, 171–188

Published under exclusive licence by Emerald Publishing Limited
doi:10.1108/978-1-83608-156-220251010

inspired by the GDPR can help India accomplish its goals without limiting innovation or economic progress.

Keywords: Data localisation; data sovereignty; cross-border data transfers; personal data protection; data governance

Introduction

In the technology-driven world of today, data is incredibly important and used extensively, and both corporations and governments are aware of this. Cross-border data flow has established itself as a crucial source of strength for both mature and developing companies. Nations require that data generated within their borders be maintained exclusively within those territories. Data localisation is the term used to describe this local data storage procedure (Svantesson, 2020). Under the data protection legislation of different nations, the necessity of data localisation has been emphasised over the recent years.

In this technology-driven world, data and its transfer within and across the borders have gained utmost significance. Data includes personal information, and over the past few years, it has been witnessed that these have been subjected to transfer and trade across the borders in this world globalisation. There are various laws which are in existence pertaining to data and privacy which have been adopted by some states and are subjected to debates and deliberations in a few. This paper attempts to look into the laws which are in existence pertaining to data localisation, especially within the jurisdictions of the EU and India. The laws in India are still evolving, and thus, it is of significant importance to evaluate the effectiveness of laws in other jurisdictions before adopting a set of principles for its own.

With the advent of technology in the present world, issues pertaining to data and privacy have gained significant importance. The concept of 'data localisation' has been highly controversial in the recent years. The concept of data localisation and the rules and regulations have been framed by the nations, especially the EU countries in the form of GDPR. Apart from that, the author also provides an insight into the position of China on data localisation. The differences in opinions have emerged in respect of framing stringent laws for restricting the transfer of data. Some authors contend that it interferes with global connection and acts as a trade barrier. While on the other hand critics emphasise that for reasons of national security, states must have control over data. There must be an attempt to clear up ambiguities and propose a practical and practical model for localising data based on a 'reasonable limitation' criterion for the local storage of data in the face of divergent political and even philosophical views. A nuanced model emphasises the importance of international cooperation, flexible regulatory frameworks and investments in cybersecurity infrastructure to address concerns related to data localisation while promoting a thriving global digital ecosystem (Hong Yanqing, 2019).

Globally, the data is the valuable resource wherein the business deploys the data for creation of values for customer and aiming for the profitability for the stakeholders. In line with global economy, the existing legal frameworks of various jurisdictions deal with data localisation. The safeguards that have been adopted by the EU nations in the form of GDPR and the specific conditions under which transmission of personal information to countries outside the EEA are permitted, which are not deemed to have 'sufficient' protections for personal data. There are specific areas in which certain countries have imposed this concept of data localisation, i.e. transfers have been restricted. In the absence of appropriate safeguards, there is a probability of transfer of personal data due to several derogations (Elizabeth, 2024).

The reasons for which the countries have adopted rules and regulations regulating data and restricting the transfers of the same. While doing so, the author recognises 'safety' of the individuals as one of the primary reasons. The data that are transferred across the borders are that of the individuals, and states have recognised and realised the importance of protecting the data of its subject, including national security and peace (Bauer et al., 2016).

In this backdrop, this research paper aims to look into the legislative provisions that are in existence to secure data within its boundaries. The present paper attempts to research and provide insight upon the following points including: What does the concept of 'data localisation' signify? What is the existing framework pertaining to such localisation in the EU? What is the Indian position regarding data localisation in India? Whether India should adopt the rules and regulations of the EU to regulate data?

The research aims to compare, contrast and uncover fundamental principles of the legal frameworks controlling data localisation in the European Union (EU) and India. It further examines the political, legal, economic and historical aspects influencing data localisation policies in the EU and India in order to assess their objectives. Lastly, it provides policymakers, regulators and industry stakeholders with valuable insights for creating or improving comparable legislation in other jurisdictions. This study aims to identify best practices and lessons gained from the implementation of data localisation policies in the EU and India.

The methodology followed by the author in this research is purely doctrinal in nature. It focuses on the analysis of legal documents such as statutes and case laws. This research is employed so as to acquire a clear picture with respect to the laws which the countries have employed to protect and safeguard data and privacy of individuals. The doctrinal method helps the author to identify the existing laws with respect to data localisation, especially in the EU and India. This typically involves gathering, analysing and synthesising various legal materials such as case law, statutes, secondary sources and scholarly literature.

Concept and Overview of Data Localisation

Data: The Omnipresence of It

The word data in the present era has now become of everyday use and in fact encompasses everything under the sun which is not a natural person or the nature itself. Such has become the omnipresence of data in the current world. With the advent of internet and a continuously globalising world economy, the phenomenon that data is has garnered an all important position. It would not be wrong to say that in the present world, data is the ultimate tool/weapon depending on the context or purpose it is used for.

Data is a pervasive element that permeates every area of human existence in the modern world. Data is all around us and has an infinite amount of effect on our lives, from the time we wake up to the sound of our smartphone's alarm clock to the last minute we browse social media before going to bed. Data is everywhere, and this has entirely altered the way we perceive and interact with the world, transforming personal lives, businesses and governance. Comprehending the extent of its pervasiveness is essential to understanding the workings of contemporary society.

Fundamentally, data is just information, whether it is quantitative or qualitative, structured or unstructured. Texts, photos, videos, music, sensor readings, money transactions and social contacts are all included. The exponential expansion of internet and technologies has accelerated the creation and collection of data at a pace which has never been witnessed earlier. Each click, swipe or interaction adds a data point to the massive database that is continuously being complied with. To improve customer satisfaction and engagement, recommendation algorithms on streaming platforms, for example, examine watching behaviours to provide material that is customised to each user's tastes (Salte, 2023).

Moreover, data is now essential for forming government and public policy. Governments use data analytics to create evidence-based policies, improve public services and allocate resources as efficiently as possible. For example, in order to create effective transportation networks and urban infrastructure, urban planners need data on traffic patterns and population density. Furthermore, data-driven strategies are used in law enforcement and crime prevention to help locate crime hotspots, forecast criminal behaviour and manage police resources. Personal data is peculiar in the way it combines the dignity of a human being with economic properties valuable for commercial activity (Yakovleva & Irion, 2020).

The fields of technology and innovation are among the most obvious ones where data is paramount. Big tech corporations like Apple, Amazon, Facebook, Google and others rely heavily on data analysis and collection. To obtain insights, forecast actions and customise user experiences, they employ complex algorithms and machine learning approaches.

In order to get by in their daily lives, people are becoming more and more dependent on data-driven technology. Data-driven devices have become a vital part of our lives, ranging from smart home devices that control domestic appliances to fitness trackers that record physical activity. Data analytics are employed by social media platforms to tailor information feeds, target adverts and link users with shared interests, therefore influencing users' online interactions and experiences.

But as data-driven technologies proliferate, worries about security, privacy and moral ramifications have become more pressing. The digital firms' commercialisation of personal data has sparked concerns about data abuse, spying and the degradation of personal privacy. Furthermore, there is a chance that biases in data collecting and algorithms would exacerbate already existing societal disparities and promote prejudice.

When we rewind to the pen and paper era, and when records were used to be kept in record/storage rooms, there was always a concern as to the available physical space that is available for storage as physical records tended to consume space, thanks to the internet, that concern no longer remained valid. Now data could be collected from a person sitting in one of the most remote locations in a country, by a data collector sitting in country B and store it in a server located in Country C. While it has proved to be of immense use, new concerns emerged as to the use of this data by the persons handling them.

Every website and every mobile application that a person uses today collects the personal data of the user and stores it in its database. A person in a remote part of the world checks out a product in any of the e-commerce websites, and the next thing they know is seeing the advertisement of the same product popping up in every online site being visited by them. Is this a mere co-incidence? Individuals nowadays have become very possessive about their privacy issues. But keeping the doors and windows of their rooms closed does not ensure privacy in this digital age where everything has moved online and people have become unwitting targets of various groups with various vested interests in the personal lives of these individuals. Each online activity of an individual is compiled in the form of data and sold to various companies who profile their potential customers and decide which group to target with what kind of advertisements, and in doing so make a fortune at the expense of an individual's privacy (Keeler, 2006).

Introducing Data Localisation: A Mandate or an Obligation?

The issue of data localisation stems from the similar and connected notion of data sovereignty and data residency. Before going on to explain the former, it is important that readers be aware of the latter. 'Data sovereignty' refers to the authority that states have over data produced within their borders. As a result, it is a concept from state theory that raises queries about the nature, justification and implications of a given relationship. 'Data residency', on the other hand, designates the location where data are kept. The perspective here shifts from that of the state, in 'data sovereignty', to that of (often) private actors choosing where to store their data because this location is a choice made by administrators or controllers. The role of state however is quite important because a state owes its duty towards the citizens to protect their privacy and thus in essence protecting their personal data. Therefore, the state has an active duty to ensure that the personal data of its subjects is collected and processed prudentially only for the purpose for which it was collected and for that specific time period only. To ensure this, the concept of data localisation has picked up wind. Data localisation obliges the business to store and process data locally, rather than in servers located overseas (Wu, 2021).

Data localisation in its simplest form refers to a state formulating its own laws and guidelines regarding the data collected to be stored within its national boundaries. Recently, the 'United Nations Conference on Trade and Development (UNCTAD)' underlined how crucial data localisation is for economies to safeguard data during international transfers. As explained above, there is a good rationale behind states emphasising on data localisation.

- Data localisation would ensure that the data remains within the boundaries and control of the sovereign state.
- It would in turn protect the sovereignty and privacy of data.
- The sovereign control could mean that a state can exercise its sovereign rights over the data and could hence implement its own laws and regulations, issue directions as to the means of storage.
- It would resultantly enable the state to exert irrefutable jurisdiction over the data and reduce conflicts.
- Subjecting data processors and collectors to a specific national law would also warrant greater compliance and accountability.

However, critiques of it argue that data localisation would essentially ruin the globalising economy and would lead to isolation in the absence of free flow of cross-border data. However, one should always remember the sensitivity of the personal data of the users and data localisation is essentially concerned with data protection by placing a check on collection, storage, processing and transfer of data.

In the digital age, data has become the lifeblood of economies, driving innovation and growth. However, the global nature of data flows has raised concerns about privacy, security and economic competitiveness. This has led to the concept of data localisation, which requires data about a country's citizens or residents to be collected, processed and stored within that country's borders. The debate around data localisation is complex, involving a tangle of legal, economic and technological considerations. Is it a mandate necessary for protecting citizens and national interests, or is it an obligation that hampers business and innovation?

On one hand, data localisation is considered as a mandate for several reasons. *First*, it is seen as essential for protecting privacy. By keeping data within national borders, governments can better enforce their privacy laws and regulations. This is particularly important in the wake of scandals involving the misuse of personal data by foreign entities. *Second*, data localisation is viewed as a security measure. In an era where data breaches and cyberattacks are rampant, storing data domestically reduces the risk of foreign surveillance and data theft. It also ensures that the data is subject to the country's cybersecurity protocols and legal jurisdiction. *Third*, there is an economic argument for data localisation. By requiring data to be stored locally, governments can promote the development of domestic data centres and cloud services, fostering the growth of the local tech industry and creating jobs. The more the internet is localised, the more its benefits will become (Taylor, 2020).

On the other hand, data localisation as an obligation imposes significant costs on businesses and consumers, which can lead to inefficiencies by forcing companies to build multiple local data centres, leading to higher operational costs. These costs can stifle innovation and deter international businesses from operating in markets with strict data localisation laws. Moreover, data localisation can fragment the global internet, undermining the open, interconnected nature that has been fundamental to its growth and success. It can also hinder law enforcement and global cooperation in tackling cybercrime, as data needed for investigations may be locked behind national borders.

The challenge lies in finding a balance between the legitimate concerns that drive data localisation mandates and the need to maintain a free and open global digital economy. One approach is to develop international agreements on data protection that allow for the free flow of data while ensuring robust privacy and security standards. Another approach is to adopt a more nuanced form of data localisation. For example, sensitive data such as personal health records or financial information could be subject to localisation requirements, while less sensitive data could be allowed to flow more freely.

With a broad idea of data localisation provided, this paper shall now deal with the data localisation laws in the EU and the relevance of data localisation in the Indian context.

Framework for Data Localisation in the European Union

In European law, data protection and privacy are two distinct ideas. Most obviously, data protection and privacy are two distinct rights that are covered by two different provisions of 'The European Union's Charter of Fundamental Rights':

(1) Article 7: Everyone has a right to respect for their personal and family relationships, private homes, and private communications.
(2) Article 8: Everyone has a right to have their personal information protected. For a specific goal, with the individual's agreement, or for other valid grounds as specified by law, the processing of personal data must be done fairly. Everyone has the right to view and change any personal data that is being gathered. An impartial authority should make sure that the aforementioned guidelines are followed. The EU saw the need for new protections with the advancement of technology and the creation of the Internet. Therefore, it adopted 'The European Data Protection Directive' in 1995, establishing minimum standards for data privacy and security. Then, based on this direction, each member state created its own implementing law. However, the Internet was already changing and becoming the data Hoover it is today. To meet the current requirements and data protection standard, the EU enacted the 'The General Data Protection Regulation (GDPR)' entered it into force in 2016 and as of 25 May 2018, all organisations were required to be compliant (Peers et al., 2021)

The GDPR is a comprehensive data protection law that applies to all EU member states, providing a unified regulatory framework for data privacy. One of its key aspects is the regulation of cross-border data transfers. The GDPR permits the transfer of personal data outside the European Economic Area (EEA) only under certain conditions, ensuring that the level of protection afforded to personal data is not undermined when it is exported. The GDPR's strict fines for violating its privacy and security rules can reach tens of millions of euros.

A notable example of data localisation efforts in the EU is Microsoft's 'EU Data Boundary for the Microsoft Cloud.' This initiative aims to store and process all personal data, including system logs, within the EU. The second phase of this rollout was completed at the end of 2023, marking a significant step towards comprehensive data localisation within Microsoft's operations.

Is Data Localisation Strictly Implemented in the EU?

The straight answer is No. But if a closer look is placed on various provisions of the text, it would be evident that the GDPR has put in place ample checks and restrictions, and compliance requirements for data securitisation. The protection of user privacy is a priority in the EU. There are no strong restrictions in the EU requiring that data from your nation only be stored, utilised and processed there. The 'EU General Data Protection Regulation', in conjunction with '(a) the United Kingdom's Data Protection Act 2018 and associated post Brexit implementation laws,' and '(b) implementing laws of EU member states collectively, GDPR', only allows transfers of personal data to regions outside the 'European Economic Area (EEA)' that have not been deemed to have 'adequate' safeguards for personal information under specific conditions.

Therefore, it is evident that data localisation in its strictest sense is not applied in EU under GDPR; however, what this legislation has ensured is that even if personal data of an individual is moved outside the territory of EU, the third-party countries must have in place adequate safety measures so as to meet the standards as prescribed in the GDPR. Hence, GDPR as legislation is primarily concerned with the secured processing of individual data. It ensures the security of data through:

- Lawfulness, Fairness and Openness – Processing must be fair to the data subject, legal, and transparent.
- Purpose Restriction – Only the lawful reasons that were explicitly disclosed to the data subject at the time the data was received may be used by the data processor.
- Data Minimisation – Only gathers and use the bare minimum of information needed to achieve the intended results.
- Accuracy – Maintain the personal data's accuracy and timeliness.
- Storage Restriction – Keep personal data just as long as necessary to fulfil the purpose for which it was collected.

- Integrity and confidentiality are two more factors that must be taken into consideration when processing data (e.g. by using encryption).
- Accountability – The data controller must be able to demonstrate adherence to each of these GDPR requirements.

The EU has enforced the new 'Regulation on the free-flow of non-personal Data', which has already started to take effect in the member states will permit data to be stored and processed anywhere in the EU without arbitrary limitations, further proving the claim that GDPR is more concerned with localising data than securing it. Together with the 'General Data Protection Regulation (GDPR)', a solid legal and commercial framework for data processing is made possible by the new Regulation on the Free Flow of Non-Personal Data. The new Regulation forbids EU nations from enacting regulations that unjustifiably require data to be stored only inside national borders. The world has never seen anything like it before. The new regulations boost business legal certainty and confidence and make it simpler for SMEs and for start-ups to develop innovative services, make use of the top internal market offerings for data processing services and grow their operations internationally.

Is EU Against Data Localisation?

A purist would agree. However, EU's laws must be looked at from a global perspective. Data localisation is all but a part of data securitisation. The states are concerned with how and how much of the personal data of an individual is collected, how is it processed? Due to the abovementioned benefits, data localisation is one step which states can implement. But a look at the real-world consequences would explain why it is difficult to implement in a true sense. In a globalising economy, free flow of data across the border is necessary for providing the best goods and services to the users across the globe. The EU regulation essentially ensures that without compromising the security of the data of its subjects, it does not hamper the market and economy.

The GDPR, which came into effect in May 2018, is the cornerstone of data protection in the EU. It does not explicitly mandate data localisation; instead, it regulates the transfer of personal data outside the EU, ensuring that the data is protected according to EU standards. This approach allows for data mobility while maintaining privacy safeguards.

The Schrems II judgement by the Court of Justice of the European Union (CJEU) invalidated the Privacy Shield framework, which facilitated data transfers between the EU and the United States. This ruling highlighted the EU's concerns about data protection in non-EU countries and reinforced the EU's digital sovereignty agenda, which includes elements of data localisation. The concept of digital sovereignty is gaining traction in the EU, emphasising the control over data and digital infrastructure. This has led to initiatives that could be seen as promoting data localisation, such as the European Data Strategy and the creation of a single market for data, aiming to reduce dependency on non-European cloud service providers.

The EU's approach to data localisation is influenced by both legal and economic considerations. Legally, the EU seeks to protect the personal data of its citizens from foreign surveillance and misuse. Economically, data localisation can encourage the development of local data centres and digital services, potentially boosting the tech sector within the EU.

As the EU continues to navigate the complexities of data protection and economic growth, the future of data localisation policies will likely involve a delicate balance. The EU may continue to refine its regulations to support both the protection of personal data and the seamless operation of the digital economy (Somaini, 2020).

In conclusion, data localisation in the EU represents a critical intersection of privacy, security and economic policy. While it poses certain challenges, it also offers opportunities for enhancing data protection and fostering local technological development. As the digital landscape evolves, so too will the EU's approach to managing the flow and storage of data within its borders.

Framework for Data Localisation in India

To put it bluntly, India does not have in place any single and comprehensive data localisation laws per se. The steps that apps in India must take in order to gather, store and analyse data are defined under data protection regulations. The 'Information Technology Act, 2000,' the 'Payment and Settlement Systems Act, 2007,' and the 'SEBI Data Sharing Policy, 2019', among others, all contain rules and remedies that businesses would have to review in the absence of such a framework. This is a fragmented and ineffective strategy for upholding user rights. In addition to promoting the ease of doing business and preserving user rights and enacting a thorough data protection law is crucial for both domestic and international policy. International digital trade depends on cross-border data flows, and a disjointed system might have an impact on deals and investments. Additionally, trading with the EU and other significant Asian and Pacific nations requires effective data protection. Modern free trade agreement discussions also revolve around it. For instance, the most recent Free Trade Agreement between India and the UAE includes a chapter on digital trade. Data localisation rules in the 'Data Protection Bill, 2021' limit the movement of sensitive and vital personal data. In April 2011, the Indian Ministry of Communications and Technology notified privacy rules implementing certain provisions of the Information Technology Act, 2000. The Information Technology (Reasonable Security Practices and Procedures and Sensitive Personal Data or Information) Rules limit the transfer of 'sensitive personal data or information' abroad to two cases – when 'necessary' or when the data subject consents to the transfer abroad (Chander & Le, 2014).

The major initiative pertaining to data localisation norms in India:

(1) Srikrishna Committee Report: The Srikrishna Committee Report, formally known as the Report of the Committee of Experts under the chairmanship of

Justice B. N. Srikrishna, is a significant document in the context of data protection and data localisation in India. The report laid the groundwork for the Personal Data Protection Bill and addressed various aspects of data privacy and security. Here are some key points regarding the report's stance on data localisation:

- Data Localisation Requirements: The committee recommended that a copy of all personal data pertaining to Indian citizens should be stored on servers located within the country. This was aimed at ensuring that Indian authorities have easier access to the data for legal and regulatory purposes.
- Critical Personal Data: It was suggested that critical personal data, which is of particular importance to the state for reasons such as national security, should only be processed within the borders of India.
- Economic Growth and Innovation: Advocates for data localisation in India argue that it would lead to economic benefits by fostering innovation and creating a producer surplus within the Indian economy.
- Law Enforcement Access: One of the challenges that the report highlighted was the difficulty faced by Indian law enforcement agencies in accessing personal data of Indian citizens stored outside the country. Data localisation is seen as a solution to this problem.

(2) Personal Data Protection Bill, 2019:

- On 11 December 2019, the 'Ministry of Electronics and Information Technology (MeitY)' introduced the 'Personal Data Protection Bill, 2019' in Lok Sabha.
- This 2019 Bill was a significant legislative proposal in India aimed at establishing a comprehensive framework for the protection of personal data.
- By controlling the gathering, transfer and processing of data that is personal or that can be used to identify a specific person, it aimed to uphold individual rights.
- The bill outlined rights for individuals, known as data principals, including the right to confirmation and access, correction, data portability and the right to be forgotten.
- The bill imposed restrictions on the transfer of sensitive personal data (SPD) outside India, requiring such data to be stored within the country. Furthermore, the storage of critical personal data within the Indian border was a mandatory requirement within the ambit of the bill.
- Though the government is considering a 'complete legal framework' to control the internet environment in order to foster innovation in the nation through a new bill, this bill was removed from Parliament in 2022.

(3) Draft National E-Commerce Policy Framework:

- It placed a significant emphasis on data localisation, reflecting the government's perspective and initiative to manage and regulate the flow of data generated from the e-commerce activities within the nation.

- Within this framework, data is regarded as a critical national asset, similar to other natural resources and emphasised the need for the generation of data to be stored within the borders of the nation.
- Furthermore, in alignment with the objectives of the Personal Data Protection Bill and the directives of the Reserve Bank of India, this framework proposed restrictions on the cross-border transfer and flow of critical personal data of the Indian users which are collected from the e-commerce activities and social media sites.
- Suggested data localisation and a two-year sunset period to allow the industry to make necessary adjustments before localisation regulations become obligatory.
- Offers incentives to promote data localisation and gives data centres infrastructure status.
- The disclosure of the purpose behind the collection of data was made mandatory within this framework, thus enabling the consumers to make informed decisions about sharing the data.

(4) Boycott of Osaka Track:

- India abstained from the 'Osaka Track on the digital economy' at the 2019 G20 meeting. The Osaka Track worked tirelessly to remove data localisation and pass laws allowing data flows between nations.
- The refusal of South Africa, Indonesia and India to sign the digital economy statement during the 2019 G20 meeting in Osaka, Japan, is known as the 'Osaka Track Boycott'. A project called the Osaka Track sought to advance global policy collaboration on digital commerce. But for the following reasons, several nations decided to oppose the initiative:
  - Undermining WTO Principles: The nations thought that the Osaka Track would compromise the fundamental rules of the World Trade Organization (WTO) about reaching consensus on decisions.
  - Legitimacy Issues: There were issues over Japan's perceived attempts to validate unofficial plurilateral discussions on digital commerce that were never accepted by the WTO.
  - Data Flow and Localisation: In opposition to the interests of nations like India, which have emphasised the significance of data localisation for economic and security reasons, the Osaka Track pushed for the creation of laws that would allow data flows between countries and the removal of data localisation requirements.
- The boycott highlighted the complexities and differing national interests in global digital trade negotiations, especially concerning data sovereignty and the regulation of cross-border data flows.

(5) Banning of Chinese Mobile Apps:

- In 2020, the Indian Government declared that 59 popular applications, many of which are connected to Chinese businesses (such as TikTok, SHAREIt, Cam Scanner, etc.), would be banned.

- To address the issues with data security and national sovereignty related to these apps, the 'Ministry of Electronics and Information Technology (MeitY)' invoked the IT Act, 2000.
- The ban on Chinese mobile apps by India is a significant move in the realm of data localisation and digital sovereignty.
- According to the government, these applications were involved in acts that were detrimental to public order, state security, defence of India and sovereignty and integrity of the country. The action was also perceived as a reaction to the growing border disputes between China and India.
- The future of worldwide app markets and the need to strike a balance between open digital ecosystems and national security concerns are issues that are brought up by the enforcement of this prohibition. It also emphasises how crucial it is to have strong data protection regulations in place to defend against unauthorised access to and transmission of citizen data.
- India's move highlights the need for comprehensive data protection laws that adhere to the principles of data localisation and safeguard user privacy and security. It also sets an example for other countries considering taking similar steps.

What Can India Learn From the EU Model?

There has been substantial discussion over India's approach to data localisation, particularly in light of the country's developing digital economy and the requirement for strong data protection laws. India might take its inspiration from the GDPR of the European Union (EU). Though its rigid data transfer limits have localisation consequences, the GDPR is not a data localisation regulation per se; instead, it ensures that personal data is secured in a manner consistent with that of being within the EU.

Data localisation policies in the EU are mostly controlled by the GDPR, which also places limitations on data transfers outside of the EU. These limitations are intended to guarantee that personal data handled by non-EU nations is protected to the same extent. As long as such sites have sufficient safeguards in place to secure that data, the GDPR permits the transfer of personal data outside of the European Economic Area (EEA). Due to this, a number of methods have been developed, including binding corporate rules (BCRs) and standard contractual clauses (SCCs), which provide the lawful transfer of data while upholding protection requirements. Microsoft's EU Data Boundary effort, which gives users the choice to store and process their data within the EU, is a noteworthy illustration of the EU model in action. The need for digital sovereignty and the legal concerns posed by transatlantic data flows resulting from the disparities between EU data protection laws and US surveillance activities are the driving forces behind this endeavour. Although it's not a strict necessity for data localisation, it's a big step in the right direction to give users greater control over their data.

One fact which is imperative is that data localisation is a sub-set of data securitisation and that a state must be focused on the latter rather than the former. Hence, it becomes necessary that India follows and borrows from the EU model. India issued a joint statement on the significance of promoting a trustworthy free flow of data with the EU and numerous other nations. It is essential to continue down this road. Additionally, over the past 10 years, India's IT exports have increased rapidly. India exported software services for an estimated \$133.7 billion in 2020–2021. Thirty percent was headed for Europe, and 54.8% was headed for the United States.

For India to play a significant role in the increasingly digitalised international economic framework, free data movement is crucial. Innovation is threatened by localisation, which also puts a heavy infrastructure and financial strain on enterprises. Furthermore, data localisation does not offer any additional privacy safeguards in the absence of the institutional capabilities required to securely keep this data. Furthermore, India can learn the below listed lessons from the EU GDPR:

- Equilibrium of Data Protection and Accessibility: The EU model shows that strong data protection can coexist with free data flow. India may take a similar tack by putting in place data transfer procedures that permit cross-border commercial dealings while guaranteeing the privacy of Indian nationals is maintained.
- Establishing Explicit Legal Frameworks: A precise legal foundation for data transfer and protection is provided by the GDPR. A thorough data protection law that provides businesses and consumers with legal certainty and lays out precise criteria for data localisation and transfer might be beneficially established in India.
- Establishing Digital Service Trust: The European Union has promoted confidence in digital services by enforcing strict data privacy regulations. India might also boost consumer trust by making sure that laws pertaining to data privacy are clear and enforceable.
- Boosting Regional Data Processing: Companies are encouraged by the EU's strategy to process data locally wherever feasible. India may provide incentives for local data processing, which would encourage additional funding to be invested in local data centres and cloud computing services.
- Overcoming Global Data Flow Issues: The EU model recognises the difficulties posed by international data flows and offers solutions. Similar methods that tackle the difficulties of cross-border data transfers while safeguarding national interests might be developed in India.
- Establishing Data Sovereignty: The EU is committed to digital sovereignty, as seen by its efforts. In order to strengthen national sovereignty in the digital sphere, India might adopt comparable actions to guarantee that the data of its inhabitants is governed by Indian laws and regulations.

- Adapting Technology Developments: The EU's data protection laws can be modified to accommodate new technology. India may make sure that its rules for data localisation are adaptable enough to take into account upcoming developments in technology and shifts in the global data environment.

India's journey towards digital transformation is at a turning point. India may be able to negotiate the tricky relationship between data localisation, privacy and economic expansion by taking a cue from the EU model. India can establish a data protection framework that protects citizens' rights and promotes innovation and competitiveness in the global digital economy by implementing best practices from the EU. The experience of the EU provides important insights into developing a forward-looking, well-balanced data governance system that may act as a cornerstone for India's digital future.

Conclusion

The above discussion points towards the fact that it is of significant importance for the states to focus on data securitisation and not vehemently focus on data localisation. As tempting as it may sound, there are various cons to the practice and in an increasingly globalising world, placing strict reliance on data processors to store that data within the jurisdictional/territorial limits of one country would mean adding extra burden to the companies already functioning in the state.

The digital era has made data localisation a crucial issue, since cross-border data movement is essential to international trade and communication. There are two different methods to data localisation: the European Union (EU) and India. Each has its own set of regulations, goals and ramifications. By contrasting the data localisation frameworks of the EU and India, this perspective research seeks to draw conclusions while highlighting the lessons gained and the future directions for both areas.

A key piece of legislation that establishes strict guidelines for privacy and data protection is the EU's GDPR. Although data localisation is not expressly required by the GDPR, it does enforce stringent guidelines for the movement of personal data beyond the EU, so guaranteeing that data is safeguarded with the same rigour as within the EU. This strategy strikes a compromise between the advantages of the globalised digital economy and the requirement for data protection. It permits data movement while providing a safeguard to guarantee that the privacy rights of individuals are upheld.

India takes a more direct approach to data localisation, requiring the storage of specific categories of data domestically. The protection of individual's privacy, economic interests and national security are the main drivers behind this strategy. Data localisation is seen by the Indian Government as a way to maintain control over its data and establish legal authority over concerns pertaining to data. This approach is perceived as a means of promoting the advancement of infrastructures developed within the nation and thus mitigating reliance on foreign technologies. Further, India's attempts to localise its data highlight how important it is to maintain control over information that is vital to the country's interests. It also draws attention to the drawbacks of such a strategy, such as possible trade obstacles, higher operating expenses for companies and the requirement for significant investments in local data processing and storage capacity.

While the EU has recognised its need and is moving in the appropriate direction, it is important for developing countries like India to adapt to the trust-based approach of the EU rather than adapting to the stringent models of the United States or Russia. Further, the EU model demonstrates that a strong data economy can coexist with protection of personal information and privacy. It offers a model that other nations, like India, might use to guarantee that the data of their individuals is sufficiently safeguarded. India might choose the GDPR's emphasis on accountability, openness and user consent as a guide as it develops its own data governance system.

Data localisation in its strict sense may impose as an impediment to the growing businesses across the globe; however, a flexible approach like the EU under the GDPR ensures free flow of data with appropriate security measures in place. Therefore, a state mustn't be blinded with the short term achievement that data localisation possesses, rather be interested in securing the personal data of its subjects through various methods among which data localisation is one of the options.

To sum up, data localisation is a challenging problem that necessitates carefully balancing a number of conflicting objectives. India and the EU present opposing paradigms that teach the world community and each other important lessons. Given the continued importance of data to the contemporary economy, both regions must modify their laws to reflect the rapidly changing digital environment and guarantee that personal privacy is preserved while allowing unrestricted access to the data that fosters innovation and growth. A comparative analysis of the EU and Indian settings shows that although the two regions have different methods, they share a common objective of using data in a way that is safe, just and advantageous to all parties.

Scope of Further Research

This study has been limited to the theoretical analysis of the legal dimensions pertaining to data localisation in EU and India. However, the scope of this study can be further expanded to include other dimensions and fields of study such as economics, international trade, management studies, etc. Some of the suggestive dimensions are as follows:

- *Legal Analysis:* Examine data localisation legislation legal ramifications in further detail, taking into account their compliance with human rights, data protection and international trade laws as well as any possible effects they may have on cross-border data flows and digital rights.
- *International Cooperation:* To address interoperability issues, lower compliance costs and advance global data governance frameworks, look into opportunities

for international cooperation and harmonisation of data localisation regulations through bilateral agreements, multilateral forums or industry-led initiatives.

- *Stakeholder Perspectives:* Through focus groups, surveys, interviews and evaluations, gather information about the opinions, concerns and suggestions of important stakeholders – including government officials, industry representatives, privacy advocates and representatives of civil society organisations – about data localisation.
- *Cross-country Analysis:* To give a more thorough comparative analysis of data localisation regulations and practices globally, extend the study to include nations other than the EU and India, such as China, Russia, Brazil or Indonesia.
- *Economic Impact Assessment:* Carry out empirical research to evaluate the costs, benefits, market dynamics, innovation and competitiveness of data localisation initiatives on companies, consumers and national economies in the EU and India.

References

Bauer, M., Ferracane, M. F., Lee-Makiyama, H., & Van der Marel, E. (2016). *Unleashing internal data flows in the EU: An economic assessment of data localisation measures in the EU member states (No. 3/2016)*. ECIPE Policy Brief.

Chander, A., & Le, U. P. (2014). Breaking the web: Data localisation vs. the global internet. *Emory Law Journal, Forthcoming*. UC Davis Legal Studies Research Paper, No. 378. https://ssrn.com/abstract=2407858

Elizabeth, H. (2024). Data localisation and data transfer restrictions. *The National Law Review*, *18*(49). https://natlawreview.com/article/data-localisation-and-data-transfer-restrictions#google_vignette

Hong, Y. (2019). *Data localisation: Deconstructing myths and suggesting a workable model for the future*. The Cases of China and the EU. Brussels Privacy Hub.

Keeler, M. R. (2006). *Nothing to hide: Privacy in the 21st century*. iUniverse.

Peers, S., Hervey, T., Kenner, J., & Ward, A. (Eds.). (2021). *The EU charter of fundamental rights: A commentary*. Bloomsbury Publishing.

Salte, L. (2023). Omnipresent publicness: Social media natives and protective strategies of non-participation in online surveillance. In L. Samuelsson, C. Cocq, S. Gelfgren, & J. Enbom (Eds.), *Everyday life in the culture of surveillance* (pp. 167–186). University of Gothenburg.

Somaini, L. (2020). Regulating the dynamic concept of non-personal data in the EU: From ownership to portability. *European Data Protection Law Review*, *6*, 84.

Svantesson, D. (2020). *Data localisation trends and challenges: Considerations for the review of the Privacy Guidelines*. OECD Digital Economy Papers, No. 301. OECD Publishing.

Taylor, R. D. (2020). "Data localisation": The internet in the balance. *Telecommunications Policy*, *44*(8), 102003.

Wu, E. (2021). *Sovereignty and data localisation*. Belfer Center for Science and International Affairs, Harvard Kennedy School. https://www.belfercenter.org/publication/sovereigntyand-data-localisation

Yakovleva, S., & Irion, K. (2020). Pitching trade against privacy: Reconciling EU governance of personal data flows with external trade. *International Data Privacy Law*, *10*(3), 201–221.

Chapter 11

Assessing Existing Legal Frameworks and Their Adaptability to AI Advancements

Sahil Lal, Manmeet Kaur Arora, Anjali Raghav and Bhupinder Singh

Sharda University, India

Abstract

Artificial Intelligence (AI) has been integrated into many sectors, disrupting industries and raising major legal and ethical issues. This research paper, Assessing Existing Legal Frameworks and Their Adaptability to AI Advances explores how above existing laws do so in each jurisdiction as they present on AI Specific examples via rapid development. Issues such as liability and accountability, Intellectual Property Rights with respect to AI-generated content and data privacy concerns are some of the key issues discussed in this chapter. It reveals the fact that traditional legal frameworks are not quite sufficient to effectively govern AI applications and sheds a light on the necessity of robust regulations that can evolve along with technological advancements. Importantly, the work demonstrates the critical role of ethical perspectives in AI governance, pushing for a fine balance between nurturing innovation and ensuring responsible behaviour. This means that AI provides society with a unique opportunity to fully experience this capability if accompanied by an innovation-friendly environment and at the same time controls risky processes that protect the rights of individuals. The findings will be discussed to future studies on AI governance and its limits as a law-society response.

Keywords: Artificial Intelligence; security intelligence; policymakers; governance; legal framework

Security Intelligence in the Age of AI, 189–202

doi:10.1108/978-1-83608-156-220251011

Introduction

Artificial Intelligence (AI) emerges as one of most disruptive technologies for 21 centuries, reshaping the way we live our lives and conduct our business. Since AI began in the mid-20th century, it has advanced from rule-based systems to learning through algorithmic and experience adaptation (AI Act, 2023). Providing a global overview of regulatory approaches to AI, including the proposed AI Act from the European Union and the fragmented landscape in place in the United States, this chapter discusses some of these challenges and ways for addressing them. This chapter also features a deliberation about human rights in the development of AI, underlining how implementations of AI are to be guided by core principles in relation to basic human rights so that this is equitable. In the end, this chapter advocates a multifaceted approach to legal reform and being proactive in nature by working with multiple stakeholders from policymakers, technologists to ethicists. A number of fields has benefitted from the rapid evolution of AI including healthcare, financial services, transportation and entertainment (Binns, 2018).

However, with the impending integration of AI technologies into various spheres within our everyday lives, there also arise several legal implications and challenges that need to be addressed in a comprehensive manner. There are significant reasons why we need to examine the current legal frameworks on AI advancements. The leapfrogging AI technology will soon outpace court litigation, and traditional legal systems will not be able to cope with the complexities of these technologies. In this context, challenges concerning liability and accountability, data privacy and ethics are burgeoning, thus emphasising the dire necessity for wide-ranging regulations that can cater to the distinct obstacles posed by AI (Brundage et al., 2020). This chapter also seeks to investigate how advanced or otherwise existing AI capabilities are and the extent of their fit with prevailing legal regimes, examining contemporary reality in light of the current legal architecture (Cath & Taddeo, 2018).

Overview of AI Advancements

During the last couple of decades, AI has made such advances in its domain. Key advancements include:

- Deep Learning: A machine learning (ML) technique that uses neural networks with many layers (deep neural networks) to analyse large amounts of data. Add to this groundbreaking work in key importance areas such as image and speech recognition, natural language processing (NLP) and autonomous vehicles (Dignum, 2019).
- NLP is a subsection of AI used to help machines understand and generate human language. That ability has given birth to virtual assistants like Siri and chatbots, which take a conversation-interface approach to how users interact with technology (European Commission, 2020).

- Computer Vision: With the help of top computer vision applications, AI systems can interpret visual information very well. Use cases include facial recognition and disease diagnosis assistance for medical image analysis.
- The Generative Adversarial Networks (GANs) is used for generating content like images/video relevant to real-life scenarios. Nowadays, designers and artists are increasingly using those.
- Reinforcement Learning: This category of ML chooses a reward function to train the model by means of feedback, and it will be used for example in AI controllers: computers playing video games (Ghosh & Kaur, 2021).

Today, AI has arrived at a level of maturity that it is being fed into different sectors to predict their actions in diverse phases such as fraud detection and process automation among others. Healthcare providers may use AI for disease diagnosis and drug discovery; financial institutions, on the other hand, employ it for risk assessment as well as algorithmic trading. Sensus, who recently won this year's Chief Data Officer Innovation Award by the CDO Club, have demonstrated that, as AI technologies become more mainstream in enterprises (42% are already deploying technology), its potential to revolutionise industry is finally catching on (Jobin et al., 2019). In future, there are some trends expected to be seen in AI. Interpretable AI: Trust is a key factor in user acceptance of AI systems, and we still need full transparency. As the usage of AI grows, the regulation on its use will be a critical issue in political discussions, and AI Ethics is likely to take attention. AI has already proven its benefits for research and patient diagnosis (binning case 1), the next logical step to expect human-level introduction (~10 years out at present growth rates) of AI in personalised medicine and home care by monitoring remotely throughout AI technologies. Quantum Computing: The fusion of quantum computing with AI could yield processing capabilities that eclipse current limitations (Kahn & Kearns, 2020).

Importance of Legal Frameworks in AI

The infusion of AI into countless facets of our lives has major legal ramifications and, accordingly, requires a suitable framework around them. The necessity of strong legal frameworks can be described in the following terms:

- *Explanation of Decisions:* Because AI systems take decisions which can affect the life of humans, as in autonomous vehicles or healthcare diagnostics, understanding who should be held liable becomes important. One of the questions you have is: If the AI system causes harm or decisions are misjudged, who will be held accountable. A further concern with this regard is that current laws may not be able to solve these problems effectively (Lee & Yoon, 2020).
- *Data Privacy:* Since AI systems process extremely large amounts of data, it has naturally been a very important area focused on the business. We need

frameworks that respect people's rights, but which also allow for innovation in how data is used.

- *Ethical Codes:* Usage of AI technologies has to be well calculated with the considerations of ethical implications. For example, lack of proper regulation can propagate existing inequalities such as algorithmic bias. This might be achieved through a pan-European legal framework that includes mechanisms for accountability and fairness in the context of algorithmic decision-making (Mittelstadt et al., 2016).
- *Flexibility*: Because the new AI innovations are happening quickly, our legal frameworks need to be able to accommodate those developments without stifling innovation. Policy intervention must be sensitive to the rate and nature of technological advancements and provide capital-efficient covered calls a responsible space within which to operate over the longer-run.
- *Addressing Complexity:* Tackling the complexities introduced by AI demands interdisciplinary collaboration across technologists, ethicists, legal professionals and policymakers. Legal frameworks should encourage interdisciplinary dialogue to ensure a full grasp and regulation of AI technologies (OECD, 2021).

To conclude, in our exploration of the compliance of current legal frameworks with technological advances in AI, we have identified a need for foresight. Thus, the interaction between law and technology must be managed carefully considering a balance between those benefits of AI to protect rights within and principles within society. As we continue to build out both the technology of AI and its controls, the road ahead is a fresh opportunity for both technological innovation and innovative ways to govern systems that can be dangerous if misused. To successfully navigate this complicated intersection of law and AI, it is necessary to build the right legal infrastructure one which serves both to foster innovation and protect the interests of society as a whole (OpenAI, 2023).

The Evolution of Legal Frameworks for AI

The journey of legal frameworks for AI has been one, defined by the rapidly changing technology landscape and challenges around ethics, society and law associated with it. Regulation of conversations around AI has been roughly architectural to the development of AI technologies. In this part, we will try to provide a perspective of the history and other important moments that have changed the path of AI regulation from its inception (Pasquale et al., 2014).

Historical Context

The journey of legal frameworks for AI has been one defined by the rapidly changing technology landscape and challenges around ethics, society and law associated with it. Regulation of conversations around AI has been roughly architectural to the development of AI technologies. In this part, we will try to provide a perspective of the history and other important moments that have changed the path of AI regulation from its inception.

Key Milestones in AI Regulation

- The EU AI Act: One of the most important regulations emerging to govern AI is the European Union's proposed AI Act, designed as a holistic legal scaffolding responsible for monitoring and managing different types of AI technologies. The legislative push, which started in April 2021, would have generated an AI application classification scheme based on risk. Under the Act, AI systems are classified according to four risk levels: unacceptable risk, high risk AI systems, limited risk AI system and minimal-risk AI. Regulation levels differ depending on the category, with heavy requirements like biometric identification and critical infrastructure systems defined as high risk.
- The General Data Protection Regulation (GDPR): Passed in 2018, this law applies to data governance which includes the use of AI frameworks (Russell & Norvig, 2020). On the other hand, it also incorporated some fairly strict requirements around data privacy, even specifically targeting AI-generated decision-making processes. The GDPR also speaks to the rights of individuals with respect to their personal data and necessitates transparency around when and how data is collected and used. This regulation is a template for other jurisdictions that are looking to balance innovation with privacy rights.
- In the US Executive Order on AI: President Joe Biden signed an executive order in October 2023, designed to quash fears from a variety of concerns tied to this currency tech. Its specifics included risk mitigation measures to address the risks of high-level AI systems in relation to civil liberties protections and impacts on the labour market. Although this is a step towards more uniform federal AI policy in the United States, many experts claim that broad legislation will be required to achieve meaningful regulation.
- Global Initiatives: Outside of these regional efforts, international organisations have similarly begun to establish principles and guidelines for responsible AI development (Smith et al., 2014). In September 2019, the World Economic Forum announced their 10 principles to govern AI and help encourage ethical practices began by reaching across stakeholder groups. On the flip side, the conversations at some forums like G-20 reiterated that there is a need for global cooperation to ensure proper regulation of emerging technologies.
- Ethics Guidelines for Trustworthy AI: There is Principle #1 and its specifications regarding a human in the loop, of course, and it touched upon many key-points about developing ethical AI systems such as were explicitly put forward by the European Commission in their successful Ethics Guidelines for Trustworthy AI that saw light a back in April 2019 (Solove, 2021). The guidelines stress accountability, transparency and human-in-the-loop as the basic building blocks of responsible AI deployment. They provide a foundational model that works in accompaniment to legal regulations by encouraging the ethical approach of technology development (Taddeo & Floridi, 2018).

- Regulation of AI in Other Jurisdictions: Many other countries outside Europe are also moving towards regulating AI. As an example, Canada has rolled out programs to tackle algorithmic bias and equitable automation. Likewise, Australia has started exploring the possibility of building an AI ethical framework that serves its national interest.

However, these landmarks do not solve all the problems on designing for AI, law, as the author will discuss next. In part, regulators have trouble keeping up due to a process lag – also known as a 'pacing problem' – where technology marches forward before existing laws or regulations can be put into effect (Thierer, 2016).

Moreover, the interdisciplinary edge AI has made it harder to create regulations unlike more comprehensive legal frameworks devised for specialised sectors like healthcare, finance and law enforcement (United Nations Educational Scientific and Cultural Organization UNESCO, 2021). In addition, there is the discussion on hard law or soft law approaches for AI technologies regulation as such. They divide law into hard and soft categories: the former is to be implemented by formal regulations with penalties; the latter includes guidelines and principles that are not enforceable under applicable rules but still can serve as a norm. Both will have their strengths and weaknesses, but policymakers will need to tread the fine line between the two if they are to effectively steer through this changing landscape (Vinuesa et al., 2020).

Current Legal Frameworks Addressing AI

AI technologies have advanced at a rapid pace which, in turn, has caused a significant change in the manner that legal frameworks are produced and implemented around the world. With these technologies infiltrating a plethora of sectors, it is clear that current laws have to evolve in order to cater for the challenges posed by AI. Global legal approaches The European Union – AI Act US regulatory landscape Perspectives from other jurisdictions (Wright & Kreissl, 2018).

Overview of Existing Laws and Regulations

The legal frameworks surrounding AI are still in their infancy, and countries around the world are struggling to come up with adequate regulations that take into account the complexities introduced by AI. Current regulations tend to be derived from broader data-protection, intellectual-property and consumer-protection statutes (Zuboff, 2019). The European Union's GDPR, for example, has played a substantial role in determining the manner that AI systems process personal data. There are provisions within the GDPR for data processing and rights of individuals over their personal information, which also affects applications of AI that necessitate access to huge datasets during the algorithm training.

Besides, many specific laws that focus on the use of AI have come up in numerous countries aside from GDPR. Take, for instance, the Directive on Automated Decision-Making that Canada introduced – it was put into place as a set of standards for transparency and accountability in AI systems relied on by government bodies. Australia, too, is forging its own path alongside those seeking to push for ethical considerations in the AI space and counteract potential harms generated by automated decision-making processes.

Nonetheless, most jurisdictions still lack full-fledged legal regimes addressing AI. No clarity on regulations: Lack of legal framework results in ambiguity about who will be held responsible and to what extent and the ethical standards that have to be complied with when deploying AI solutions. The existence of this gap underscores the critical necessity for lawmakers to enact laws that specifically target the challenges AI technologies pose (Binns, 2018).

Comparative Analysis of Global Approaches

A comparative analysis reveals a diverse landscape of regulatory approaches to AI across different jurisdictions. While some regions have taken proactive steps towards establishing comprehensive legal frameworks, others are still in the early stages of development.

European Union's AI Act

One of the broadest efforts to do so is the EU's proposed AI Act. The Act, introduced in April 2021, would establish a four-tier risk-based framework that classifies AI applications as presenting minimal risk, limited risk, high-risk or unacceptable risks. For high-risk apps – ones used in critical infrastructure or biometric identifications, for instance, strict rules are going to be applied to them when it comes to transparency, accountability and human supervision. The twist of the EU approach is it focuses on ethics as well in addition to being compliant with regulations (Cath, 2018). The Act aims to guarantee that AI systems are developed and used in a way that is consistent with human rights principles, while producing more technology-trusting outcome. The focus on ethics is an acknowledgement of how AI raises the stakes for developing trustworthy, human-centric governance models that both love innovation and serve humanity.

United States Regulatory Landscape

The US government, in contrast to the EU, has variously defined a piecemeal and decentralised architecture on AI regulation. There is currently no federal AI-specific law; however, specific aspects of AI deployment are subject to regulation by different agencies under existing consumer protection, privacy and anti-discrimination statutes. These latest efforts suggest an increased awareness of the requirements for federal regulation of AI tools. President Biden took a first step into addressing issues connected with transformative AI systems in October

2023 by signing the executive order. It clarifies civil liberties guarantees and proposes measures to minimise the dangers of automatic decision-making (Dignum, 2019).

Even so, they say that more effective laws are required to establish a coherent legislative control adapted to the special characteristics of AI.

In addition, many states have started introducing their own AI-related rules. This has included new laws in California on facial recognition technology and automated hiring processes. Teaching colleges to embrace Science and Technology Entry Program and OSU ORCIP is key, as there will always be some cohort of students who struggle with the transition to active learning – from K-12 all the way up through medical training – all over these United States in a 'wildly heterogeneous' distribution that this state-by-state programme reveals.

Other International Perspectives

Outside of Europe and North America, a number of nations are also looking into AI law for regulatory frameworks. For instance:

- Brazil: In Brazil, during September 2021, the Legal Framework for AI (Marco Legal da Inteligência Artificial) was approved. The law aims to promote ethical principles and lesion of boringness in the development of AI. The framework promotes non-discrimination and respect for human rights, while fostering research and innovation.
- Council of Europe (CoE) : The CoE has been working on a legal framework based on its human rights and democracy standards. The goal of this initiative is to promote an AI design method that respects human rights and works to ensure more transparent and accountable systems.
- Asia: Governments have started to formulate guidelines to ensure responsible AI, including Japan and Singapore. The 'AI Strategy 2021,' an updated version of Japan's comprehensive national AI strategy released in June 2017, called for the collaboration between government and industry stakeholders to develop innovative technologies while also addressing ethical concerns related to the deployment of AI (Jobin et al., 2019).

Challenges in Adapting Legal Frameworks to AI

While AI technologies are poised to expand forward, they pose great challenges to current legal frameworks. The exponential pace at which these AI systems are evolving leads to a slew of challenging issues from liability and accountability, the protection of Intellectual Property Rights (IPRs) in respect of AI-generated content, to data privacy concerns. This section looks at these tensions, focusing on the way that the current legal regime is failing to adapt to new technologies and what this means for different stakeholders (Kahn & Kearns, 2020).

Issues of Liability and Accountability

Liability Concerns

An important issue in the domain of AI that causes many legal problems is establishing responsibility and accountability when AI systems have harmed or made a wrong decision. Traditional legal systems have been designed around the existence of human agency – the type of intentional, responsible conduct that can be attributed to a person or an organisation. But the increasing use of autonomous systems – a self-driving car, say or an AI-operated medical device – raises questions about who is responsible when these machines fail to work properly (Mittelstadt et al., 2016).

The most obvious thorny question is the traditional liability issue – if an autonomous vehicle causes a crash, who has to pay for it: the manufacturer, the software developer or even you? This lack of clarity muddies the legal waters as it can be difficult to write laws or make rulings which cover such complexity in these AI moral decision-making processes. Recent events have sparked debate over the effectiveness of a legal system that fails to properly place blame when AI produces an adverse result. This could mean setting robust standards with respect to the accountability that is appropriate for AI, as AI has unique features, such as learning and adaptability. Also, the more autonomous AI systems get, the less clear it can be what kind of causality and intentionality they are exhibiting. Legal scholars note that these complexities require a sophisticated treatment of agency. For instance, if an AI system arrives at a biased conclusion that discriminates against certain segments of society due to biased data, examining fault can be harder – does it fall on the developers who wrote the algorithm, or perhaps with the organisations that put it to use, or maybe even with the data sets applied in training.

IPRs and AI-Generated Content

The type of content and the right-holders can overlap significantly: junction IP rights exist in AI-generated contents as yet another daunting task for legal frameworks. Generative AI that is spawned by this development can be powerful enough to not only produce work at the level of fine art, jazz compositions or literary text but in some cases unguided human intervention. Yet, existing copyright legal norms render human authors as creators, and this has cast doubt as to where AI-created work stands (Russell & Norvig, 2020).

Copyright protection hitherto has required a 'human author' to establish protection, something deemed by most jurisdictions including the United States and India. This has led to several situations where copyright applications for AI designed works are not accepted because they do not have enough human authorship in them. A well-known case is that of an AI system called DABUS, in respect of which the US Copyright Office ruled out registration on the grounds that it did not regard itself as compliant with accepted law, so refuting its claim to author status as claimed and filed by DABUS itself. This gets creates a loop hole:

where AI can generate a creative output that might be copyright-able as if they were human made but when the machine are autonomous and generates by themselves, no clear legal path to do so or any framework around it. The stakes are high – if creators lack clear ownership, they may be less likely to push the boundaries with AI technologies, fearful of infringement or not being acknowledged for their work.

Furthermore, ethical debate with respect to data use for AI model training adds another level of complexity. Because generative AI systems are built off of large datasets, some of which contain copyrighted material. While the copyright status of such works is questionable, this creates uncertainty about fair use and copyright infringement in these circumstances. These lawsuits are just the beginning of IP law needing to catch up with the rapid pace at which AI is evolving, and this lack of clarity should certainly give every automated content creator pause before including copyrighted works as inputs.

Data Privacy Concerns

Another important vertical where the new AI technology faces challenges to adapt with the current legal frame works is data privacy. One of the most controversial and widely debated subjects related to AI systems today is related to how much personal data ML requires for training and functioning, as well as along with this comes questions about how such data is collected, stored and used. Part of the reaction to these concerns has led Europe to come up with the GDPR implement a set of strict rules on how data are processed. This means that under the GDPR, any personal data held must be done so with the express consent of the individual, and they are free to request it be removed, corrected or destroyed. The challenge, however, comes as these AI technologies evolve and permeate everyday life, further complicated by the need to comply with these stringent regulations. For example, several AI systems work with ML solutions that need constant data feed-ins. It begs the question, how do companies stay in compliance while still utilising real-time data streams and not potentially step on an individual's privacy rights?

In addition to this, other issues such as data coverage and transparency are central so that individual privacy is guaranteed from possible misuse behind their personal information. Further, more recent research suggests that discriminatory outcomes can result when decision-making algorithms rely on training data containing biased information. This has legal implications when we talk about privacy in data; organisations cannot only comply with the laws concerning data privacy but also have social duties to prevent biases that can harm individuals or despised groups.

Ethical Considerations in AI Regulation

The deployment of AI technologies in everyday life has intensified speculation about the ethical dimensions that current and future implementations are expected to have for developers, policymakers and society in general. The debate here would centre around the right balance between innovation and regulatory requirements to ensure AI's sustainability in practice, while simultaneously protecting human rights vigilantly throughout both its development and application process. This chapter of the report investigates ethical dimensions in AI regulation sheds light on how to balance innovation and respect for human rights on the one hand; it also discusses the compliance with human rights standard as a key piece in tackling development challenges related to AI.

Balancing Innovation With Ethical Standards

However, the pace of AI innovation itself is almost too fast to keep up. AI has the power to improve various aspects, such as healthcare, finance, transportation and education. However, AI technologies are also giving rise to a new series of ethical dilemmas around deployment that need addressing in order to ensure responsible use. Indeed, the settlement of rule innovation and ethical standard innovation is a prerequisite for sustainable development. To support this required balance, organisations need to embed moral consideration into the AI development lifecycle – from the start. Creating robust ethical frameworks that help govern all decisions throughout the deployment of AI stages. An example is making transparency, accountability, non-discrimination and fairness fundamental considerations as part of their AI strategies by organisations. The enforcement of these principles in operational practices can help to avoid most of the ethical traps that could be related to the AI installations. Similarly, in vivo ongoing surveillance and evaluation of AI systems is crucial for both spotting, isolating and repairing ethical implications as they come to light. This proactive behaviour reinforces organisations to change their practices as challenges change, creating a culture of accountability and responsibility. Recently, research has identified that cross-disciplinary teams (including ethicists, legal experts and technologists) can help to capture the full range of ethical issues relating to AI technologies. Besides internal efforts, cooperation between key players – governments, industry champions, NGOs and academia – is required to develop a comprehensive regulatory ecosystem that is conducive to ethical AI practices. This type of cooperation can result in industry convergence around the optimal standards and practices that support innovation but balance with public safety.

The Role of Human Rights in AI Development

When we talk about the regulation of AI, human rights concerns outshine all others. As AI is used in decision-making processes that impact the lives of individuals – from hiring practices to loan approvals and law enforcement, among others – it's critical that those technologies respect fundamental human rights. Ensuring AI is built using ethics invariably means adhering to human rights principles, and this includes the duty bearers providing a commitment from now on that they keep implementing safeguards to dignity, privacy and autonomy of individuals. For instance, due to AI systems just as accurate as the data they are trained on, many of them using masses smart phone data for their algorithms; Data privacy is a major issue. Regulations such as the GDPR ensure individuals privacy rights as well and create transparency when it comes to collecting and using data (a very good thing). Additionally, addressing biases at the level of AI algorithms is vital for averting discriminatory results that could contravene human rights. Biased data can produce biased outcomes and have systemic racist implications if the algorithm bases its decisions on historical patterns (as has been seen in research). To address this challenge, fair AI practices require fairness to take centre stage, driving more extensive usage of datasets across training and demanding the capability for bias detection at every milestone in the lifecycle of an AI. The ethical concerns with AI are not simply at the level of individual rights but pertain to wider social implications. The deployment of AI-driven surveillance technologies, for instance, creates concerns around civil liberties and the capacity of authorities to abuse these new enabling technologies. It will take sturdy checks and balances to ensure that AI systems are built in ways that respect human rights – mechanisms which can hold organisations to account if they utilise technology at the expense of these principles. There exist international frameworks that the UNGP HR is based on (e.g. United Nations Guiding Principles on Business and Human Rights), which are very useful for mainstreaming human rights considerations into AI development. These standards highlight that it is the obligation of enterprises to respect human rights in entire value chain and to provide for effective remedies when harms caused by their operations. Implementing AI in ways that adhere to these principles will help organisations do their part to ensure a fairer, more just technological landscape.

Conclusion

Technological advancement, in the form of AI technologies, has introduced an era of innovative transformation that is changing what can be done and how things are done. Nonetheless, this evolution raises substantial legal and ethical issues that require a complete re-evaluation of current regulations in order to ascertain their adaptability to the specific needs created by AI.

The main conclusion of this research is that comprehensive legal frameworks, adapted to the complexity brought by AI technologies, are urgently needed. The rapid advancement of AI has left traditional justice systems in the dust, challenging the limits of guidance on responsibility, criminal liability and ethical judgement. Recent researches have pointed to the inadequacy of existing laws in relation to several peculiar features that characterise AI systems, such as autonomy in decision-making and algorithmic bias. Change is turbulent, such as on the liability front where we still battle the issue of where to assign blame when AI systems do harm. This aspect is important since as things stand, it is not clear whether the blame when a self-driving car causes an accident (on any part of the process: manufacturing, software programming and the way they are managed by the user) should be laid to the vehicle maker, or if responsibility should spread across these parts depending on damage/control upstream. In the same way, AI-generated output also questions the sensitive subject of IPRs and contests traditional copyright laws that focus on defining authorship mostly with regard to humans. This is clear evidence of the need to create formal legal structures that allow AI technology to be used in a way that complements and protects the public interest, while seeking ways of promoting innovation.

A key takeaway from this research is that regulating AI technologies effectively will require a comprehensive legal framework carefully designed to account for the nuances introduced by complexity of systems using those technologies. AI, as a technology that progresses at break-neck speeds in comparison to traditional legal systems, often results in questions about who is at charge. These concerns revolve around liability and accountability of those behind the algorithms when it comes to many popular issues concerning AI today: Just because something can be automated should it? Is self-driving else really ready for prime time? Who's responsible if an AI makes a problematic choice or reads an x-ray backwards? Existing laws may not suffice to address the distinctive characteristics of AI-systems, especially autonomy in decision-making, and algorithmic bias as studied recently. For example, the issue of liability when AI systems do damage to users is still hotly debated. In the case of an accident caused by an autonomous vehicle, as to whether the manufacturer, software developer or user is at fault, the exact cause-and-effect chain may not be identifiable and legally relevant. The issue of ownership and IPRs relating to content created by AI is equally thornier for established copyright laws, which almost exclusively assign authorship to humans. These examples clearly demonstrate the need for legal reform that ensures a proper regulation and governance of AI technologies so as to encourage innovation and still protect the public interest.

References

AI Act. (2023). European commission. https://digital-strategy.ec.europa.eu/en/policies/regulatory-framework-ai

Binns, R. (2018). Fairness in machine learning: Lessons from political philosophy. In *Proceedings of the 2018 conference on fairness, accountability, and transparency* (pp. 149–158). https://doi.org/10.1145/3287560.3287598

Brundage, V., Avin, S., Wang, J., Belfield, H., Krueger, G., Hadfield, G., Khlaaf, H., Yang, J., Toner, H., Fong, R., Maharaj, T., Koh, P. W., Hooker, S., Leung, J., Trask, A., Bluemke, E., Lebensold, J., O'Keefe, C., Koren, M., Théo, R., & Markus, A. (2020). Toward trustworthy AI development: Mechanisms for supporting verifiable claims. *AI & Society*, *35*(4), 1–12.

Cath, C. (2018). Governing artificial intelligence: Ethical, legal, and technical opportunities and challenges. In *Proceedings of the international conference on artificial intelligence* (pp. 123–134). https://doi.org/10.1098/rsta.2018.0080

Cath, C., & Taddeo, M. (2018). The ethics of artificial intelligence: A survey of the literature. *Journal of Artificial Intelligence Research*, *61*, 1–36.

Dignum, V. (2019). Responsible artificial intelligence: Designing AI for human values. *ITU Journal: ICT Discover*, *1*(1), 1–12.

European Commission. (2020). White paper on artificial intelligence: A European approach to excellence and trust. https://ec.europa.eu/info/sites/default/files/commission-white-paper-ai-2020.pdf

Ghosh, S., & Kaur, H. (2021). Ethical implications of artificial intelligence in healthcare: A systematic review of the literature. *Artificial Intelligence in Medicine*, *113*, 101036.

Jobin, A., Ienca, M., & Andorno, R. (2019). The global landscape of AI ethics guidelines. *Nature Machine Intelligence*, *1*(9), 389–399.

Kahn, S., & Kearns, M. (2020). The ethical implications of AI in decision-making processes: A review of current research and future directions. *AI & Society*, *35*(2), 345–357.

Lee, K.-F., & Yoon, S.-J. (2020). The role of transparency in AI systems: Implications for user trust and ethical considerations in design and deployment practices. *AI & Society*, *35*(4), 733–744.

Mittelstadt, B., Allo, P., Taddeo, M., Wachter, S., & Floridi, L. (2016). The ethics of algorithms: Mapping the debate. *Big Data & Society*, *3*(2). https://doi.org/10.1177/2053951716679679

OECD. (2021). Recommendation on artificial intelligence: OECD principles on AI. https://www.oecd.org/going-digital/ai/principles/

OpenAI. (2023). ChatGPT [large language model]. https://chat.openai.com/chat

Pasquale, F., & Citron, D. K. (2014). Introduction: The law of algorithms: A new frontier in legal scholarship and practice. *Harvard Law Review Forum*, *127*(2), 1–16.

Russell, S., & Norvig, P. (2020). *Artificial intelligence: A modern approach* (4th ed.). Pearson.

Smith, B., & Anderson, J. Q. (2014). *AI and the Future of Work: How artificial intelligence will impact jobs and employment*. Pew Research Center.

Solove, D. J. (2021). Privacy self-management and the consent dilemma. *Harvard Law Review*, *126*(7), 1880–1903.

Taddeo, M., & Floridi, L. (2018). How AI can be designed to be ethical. *Nature Machine Intelligence*, *1*(2), 90–92.

Thierer, A. (2016). *The ethics of artificial intelligence and robotics*. The Independent Institute.

United Nations Educational Scientific and Cultural Organization (UNESCO). (2021). Recommendations on the ethics of artificial intelligence. https://unesdoc.unesco.org/ark:/48223/pf0000379987

Vinuesa, R., Azizpour, H., Leite, I., Balaam, M., Dignum, V., Domisch, S., Felländer, A., Langhans, S. D., Tegmark, M., & Nerini, F. F. (2020). The role of artificial intelligence in achieving the sustainable development goals. *Nature Communications*, *11*(1), 233.

Wright, D., & Kreissl, R. (2018). Data protection by design: A new approach to privacy regulation. *International Data Privacy Law*, *8*(3), 213–224.

Zuboff, S. (2019). *The age of surveillance capitalism: The fight for a human future at the new frontier of power*. Public Affairs.

Chapter 12

The Role of AI in Customer Relationship Management for Tailored Financial Services

Lakshmi S.R.[a], *Rajimol K.P.*[b], *Y.K. Sunitha*[c], *Ajatashatru Samal*[d], *Priya R.P.*[d] *and Srija H.R.*[d]

[a]Christ University, India
[b]Atria Institute of Technology, India
[c]Freelancer, India
[d]Sri Venkateshwara College of Engineering, India

Abstract

Much as the financial services industry is characterised by dynamism, Artificial Intelligence (AI) is gradually transforming the Customer Relationship Management (CRM). Among the AI-related advances is the advancement of bespoke financial services that increases involvement and experience of the customers. This chapter seeks to address the following research question: how has the incorporation of AI tools influenced the CRM strategies adopted by the industry? Newer, implementing AI in CRM systems, banks can go through terabytes of customers' information looking for more about each other's preferences, tendencies and needs. This information may therefore allow for financial services, proactive customer care and consumption point marketing based on segments of the population. Information on financial organisations' successful implementation of AI-based CRM systems is provided in the chapter; in addition, challenges and ethical issues regarding the use of these technologies are also described. The findings show how the use of AI can enhance CRM in the financial services sector resulting in satisfied and loyal customers alongside more organisation productivity. As for the maximisation of CRM results, the report also suggests that financial institutions must use AI appropriately while addressing the problems associated with the latter.

Security Intelligence in the Age of AI, 203–221

Published under exclusive licence by Emerald Publishing Limited
doi:10.1108/978-1-83608-156-220251012

Keywords: *CRM*; *Personalised banking*; *Financial advisory*; *Artificial Intelligence*; *Chatbots*; *Virtual assistants*

Introduction

The advancement in technology has led to difference in the acquisition, storage and analysis of customer information within the modern business environment. By employing the contemporary quantitative techniques and models of analysis, firms' abilities to acquire and maintain consumption have significantly been enhanced by this fundamental transformation. It has become possible for companies to fine-tune their marketing strategies, improve the quality of the services they are providing and strengthen customer relations with the help of such enormous amounts of data about consumers' behaviour that these technologies allow to gather. Specifically beneficial to work towards refining Customer Relationship Management (CRM) strategies, predictive modelling enables organisations to anticipate the customer's needs and behaviour (Butler, 2000).

Small and medium enterprises (SMEs) struggle completing numerous barriers while seeking to implement CRM systems, while large organisations have the resources to implement such systems without much problem. That is because many SMEs may lack the capital, knowledge and technological know-how to properly adopt CRM even though it can be harmonious with their business. It can therefore be argued that there is a significant need to educate SMEs on the importance of CRM systems and create awareness of the above mentioned gap. This article looks at CRM, how it can be of benefit to SMEs, the challenges of implementing CRM and then looks at the applications which SME can take advantage of. The purpose is to extend the understanding of SMEs about the implementation of CRM and provide recommendations for its successful application (Loh et al., 2011).

Owing to the advancement in technology, the process of CRM has been shifted to the online platform through e-commerce. Online shopping has provided people with a wider choice, has helped customers to identify products and has made shopping more convenient through product directories and through the availability of services round the clock. In this context, e-CRM, the electronic CRM has emerged as a powerful tool for managing the interactions with the customers and capturing the valuable information. The e-CRM systems employ the use of software surveys at the point of sale and other contact points through technology. Enhance the quality of service, enhance the marketing strategies and gain more information about the consumer behaviour with these data. E-CRM system reduces costs and improves and streamlines business operations as well as offers better customer service. Artificial Intelligence's (AI's) impacts on CRM are personalisation, automation, predictive analysis and customers, help in this research work. Employing AI for personalisation could mean that firms in the financial sector are able to recommend investment opportunities, financial advice and products based on each client's characteristics. Due to the application of computer-based predictive techniques, it becomes easier to engage consumers more proactively while at the same time minimising risks because consumer requirements/behaviour can be foreseen. These are valuable insights onto themselves, and by removing dull CRM tasks, we can streamline processes and optimise resource usage. Other examples of AI applications include: chatbots and virtual assistants that offer round-the-clock customer care services, thus enhancing service delivery and times satisfaction. They create the opportunities to engage consumers, to shape the contact and the relationship and to foster interactivity. E-CRM systems are greatly dependent on the extent to which e-services are easy to acquire, of good quality and friendly to the users (Kampani & Jhamb, 2020).

The increase in data has been the major source of innovation in the current digital era through the development of AI. The design and implementation of CRMs are now more and more dependent on the AI technology that tries to imitate human thinking. Traditional approaches towards managing customer relationship would be an inadequate tool to deal with the data generated by such systems. These data are geographical, social, emotional and contextual. There are several ways through which AI enhances CRM including the ability to interact with customers in a more sophisticated and appropriate manner, increasing the level of personalisation that is offered to customers and making better estimations of the consumers' needs. Application of AI-based CRM systems offers a competitive advantage in industries that have a high focus on customer experience. They help firms in managing complex consumer engagements, delivering individualised solutions and outpacing rivals through the application of contemporary data analytics (Ledro, 2021).

Firms are thus advised to enhance their CRM processes through the adoption of sophisticated technologies such as AI, e-CRM and Predictive Modelling in their CRM systems. SMEs are in a vantage position to benefit from these technologies even if large organisations have benefited from them. To this end, the challenges of SMEs adopting CRM system, more awareness of the benefits of CRM system and real-life examples of application should be explained in detail.

In the current world that is increasingly based on the customer, AI has been established to be a transformative force in many sectors and particularly in the financial services sector. CRM is one of the strategic success factors that has been greatly affected by the advent of AI and the effects of their integration in reshaping how financial institutions interact with customers, manage customer data and provide services to the customers. With the help of properly implemented AI in CRM systems, the successful implementation allows the companies to go beyond the typical service solutions and provide the relevant customer with highly individuated and immediate experiences, meeting each of their needs. This introduction aims at discussing the active aspect of AI in improving the CRM in the financial services industry, especially on the aspects of the applications, advantage, disadvantage and the future prospect of the use of this technology.

Conversely, CRM in the past in financial services has been based on ad hoc, low levels of customer differentiation and mass marketing. The financial services industries including banks, insurance companies and investment firms were widely dependent on traditional, human-centric, face-to-face and word-based communication and ad hoc in nature crude analytical approaches in identifying and satisfying the consumer needs. Such methods sometimes led to some wastage, and at other times, a generalised approach to customers and poor capacity to adjust to the changing expectations of the consumers promptly were some of the usual outcomes.

In the early 2000s, development of digital technologies means CRM systems became more tendered, linking customer databases and simple analytical applications for the automation of processes. However, these systems perhaps made the businesses more efficient, but they were still not able to address the fundamental need of customising the customer experience. Enter AI: a revolutioniser that has taken CRM not only to the next level but to the level of predictive analytics, valuable customer insights and capacity for delivering specific financial products based on customers' behaviour and preference.

AI means the ability of computers to mimic intelligence, as well as the capability of a computer to execute tasks that have been considered to call for intellect. Some of the activities to be performed in the organisational process include knowledge acquisition, thinking, solving of problems and decision-making. When used in the context of CRM in the financial services sector, it allows an organisation's CRM systems to sift through customer-related data, discover patterns and create recommendations which in turn can be used to enhance customers experience and interaction.

The application of AI in CRM can be classified into three key areas:

- Automation: Robotic automation, under AI, consists of tasks like data input, customer service and information exchange in order to relieve employees for other higher level duties.
- Prediction: Technologies that are subsumed under AI and machine learning (ML) employ past experiences to forecast future behaviour, needs and preferences of customers to enable the financial institutions to guess their needs.
- Personalisation: Hyper-personalisation is made possible through the use of AI in that the information obtained about the customer including transactional history, behavioural information and demographic data help in customising financial products and services.

The New Trend in Financial Solutions

In the present-day consumer/investor, a customer expects service delivery which is unique to the customer across their financial plan and financial personality. There are several factors that have led to this shift towards hyper-personalisation; these are availability of more data, the growing number of the fintech companies that are delivering personalised solutions and the shift to digital financial platforms.

AI has a very important role in the process of making this shift possible since it allows the financial institutions to use the customer data more efficiently. This area of application is about segmenting customers into more refined groups through AI-based analysis, which helps them to generate relevant products and services for every group. For instance, AI can assist in designing unique investment solutions for the wealth management customers, insurance solutions based on clients' risk appetite and unique loan products as per the needs and growth prospects of small business clients.

The CRM technologies which have been influenced by the application of AI for financial services are outlined below.

The following are some of the available remarkable AI technologies that are promising to revolutionalise the CRM in the financial services fields. These technologies include:

- Natural Language Processing: NLP let systems to comprehend and analyse the natural language; customers of financial institutions can therefore receive better support services. NLP-based chatbots and virtual assistants can help to manage clients' requests, perform and facilitate payments and offer individualised suggestions in real time.
- ML and Predictive Analytics: Mining, for example, involves using large datasets to find out specific features that even the analyst may not pinpoint Another use of ML in CRM is for predicting customer behaviour; for instance, when a client is likely to buy new financial services or when they are likely to drop out of the service. Using predictive analytics in financial institutions enables them to meet customers' needs before such needs are communicated and also increase loyalty.
- Robotic Process Automation (RPA): Some of the key application areas that RPA can apply include data entry, transactions, reconciliations and compliance verification among others as they reduce time and errors greatly. In CRM, RPA helps in automating the customer onboarding processes, follow-ups and helps to review whether communication is regular or not.
- Sentiment Analysis: In the sentiment analysis, using the data from the feedback, reviews and social media engagement, the algorithms estimate the customer satisfaction level and recognise critical issues. Customers can provide this information with the aim of improving the services delivered and solve problems before they occur.
- Personalised Marketing Engines: Conventional marketing tools incorporate AI to develop marketing strategies and advertisements that reflect customers' financial concerns and desires. It helps the financial institutions in offering custom-made offers such as apt loan, portfolio and savings plans or product at the right time.

Aspects That Make AI-Enhanced CRM Valuable for the Financial Services Industry

AI-driven CRM solutions offer numerous benefits to financial institutions, including: AI-driven CRM solutions offer numerous benefits to financial institutions, including:

- Improved Customer Engagement and Retention: Through providing customers with customised services and by predicting what they may require, AI ensures that firms building a professional bond with the consumers are successful. Individuality can make its customers and clients have the feeling of loyal, so that the rates of customer retention will be higher.

- Operational Efficiency: Applying AI in the processes, the organisation minimises routine work and delivers more qualified specialists to address complicated tasks related to customer service. This leads to a quicker response time, a higher rate of accuracy in interaction with the customers and thus reduced cost.
- Data-Driven Decision-Making: It gives timely analysis of big data and helps institutions in the financial sector to determine the necessary actions that need to be taken in the processes of product development, promotions and other customer-related activities. These insights enable the financial institutions to be in a position to predict the prevailing trends in the market as well as the expectations of the customers.
- Enhanced Risk Management: AI frameworks have better capabilities of fraud detection, credit risk assessment and regulatory compliance assessment than the conventional frameworks. In the area of finance, with AI, one is able to detect fraud and other unlawful activities in real time, thus minimising the possibility of financial crimes and meeting the set legal standards.
- Scalability: Thus, AI is very much flexible when it comes to handling data volume which makes it suitable to organisations with massive number of customers such as various financial institutions. With the expansion of the amount of information about the customers, it becomes possible to process more significant amounts of data without any significant impact on the speed and efficiency of AI systems.

Challenges That Arise When Applying AI in CRM for Financial Services

While adopting AI in CRM for the financial service industry has its advantages, there are some that have been highlighted below. These include:

- Data Privacy and Security: Customers rely on financial institutions for their sensitive data, and thus, the increased application of power tools, in this case AI systems, makes customers' data vulnerable to security threats. The laws and rules including General Data Protection Regulation should be followed as failure to meet these laws and regulations mean that one is liable to be lawfully charged, hence losing the confidence of the customers.
- Integration With Legacy Systems: A large number of financial institutions are still using outdated CRM systems which can restrict the integration of the modern AI solutions. AI solutions can be installations at existing platforms, which involves a large investment and high skills.
- Bias and Fairness in AI: AI systems are even as powerful as the data it has been fed and trained to sort, filter or analyse. This is because if the training data are biased, then so is the result AI gives, and this could be particularly evident in

loan approvals or credit scoring. AI systems have to be trained by using data which reflect the society and has to be ensured that such systems are not biased.

- Customer Trust and Adoption: However, some customers may feel uncomfortable using a fully automated system to process their financial transactions which is offered by AI's numerous advantages. One of how CRM systems powered by AI can be trusted is by being open about the use of the technologies and providing people assistance.
- Cost and Expertise: It is also important to know that building and sustaining an AI-based CRM environment may not be cheap, especially for those financial institutions which are relatively small. Further, there is need of data science, ML and cybersecurity, which might be limited in supply.

Impact of AI on CRM Specialised for Financial Services

AI applications in CRM for the financial services industry are set to improve, with future developments in AI technology continuing to improve customer experience, engagement and processes. Financial institutions which have implemented AI as a part of CRM strategy to cater to the latest trends are highly likely to gain a competitive edge and, subsequently, sustainable growth.

In the coming years, we can expect to see increased use of AI in areas such as in the coming years, we can expect to see increased use of AI in areas such as:

- Real-Time Financial Advising: Robo-advisers that are embedded with AI shall be able to provide live recommendations regarding financial transactions based on their particular tendencies of a customer as well as too their specific objectives.
- Customer Sentiment Prediction: It is also possible to develop sophisticated AI that will foresee changes in the mood of customers as far as the financial institution is concerned and then take early measures on the aspects of concern that may arise in the future.
- Voice-Activated CRM: Customer voice tools refer to the use of voice-based AI where the customers of the financial services are able to engage the service by just using their voices.

Explanation of Fig. 12.1 AI is transforming the financial services by providing personalised financial solutions to fulfil the CRM needs. Through use of automation, analytics as well as targeted marketing and promotions, the financial companies could be in a position to increase on the customer relations base, operation efficiency as well as better control to risks. However, factors like data privacy, integration and lastly customer acceptance are key issues that need to be overcome as more CRM solutions apply AI. Much as AI technologies are still emerging, the role of AI in CRM is set to become more central in the future of financial services and improving customer interactions.

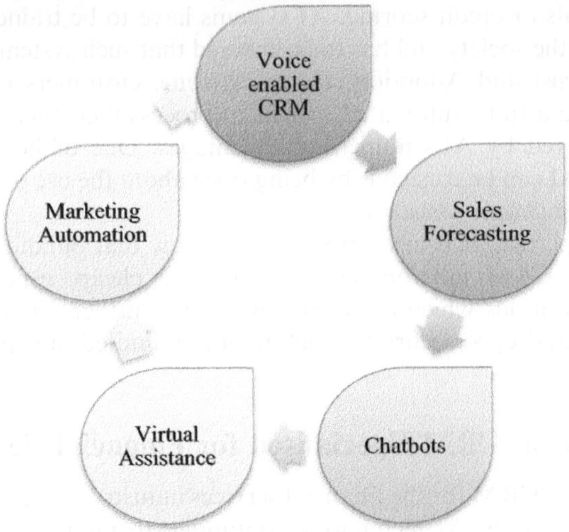

Fig. 12.1. Impact of AI in Customer Relationship Management.
Source: Original work and have not been published elsewhere

Today, it is impossible to imagine any present-day CRM system without AI, but, of course, it is critical for companies that work with large data volumes in real time. With the use of AI in CRM, relationship marketing, individualised product customisation and brand recognition can be improved to a greater extent. These are some ways through which organisations can accelerate the process of managing customer relations through the use of AI such as in the form of chatbots, recommendation systems, virtual assistants and interactive voice response systems (Rana et al., 2022). These products serve to improve consumers' experiences through process automation, real-time solution offering and data-backed personalisation. AI-enabled CRM systems can analyse consumer behaviour, learning their behaviour patterns which results in the enhancement of services, better targeting of marketing and deeper engagement with the consumer.

However, like any other tool, AI also has its challenges which are highlighted below. Two major issues with AI are the Uncanny Valley Paradox which is a state where the system becomes too human like and the Personalisation-Privacy Paradox which occurs where consumers' privacy is compromised to provide personalised services (Chaturvedi & Verma, 2023). This is because the issue of privacy and control over customers and companies information is a crucial factor in determining whether to adopt AI in the CRM systems. This means that to avoid being on the wrong side of the argument, there is the need to balance on the AI CRM system, focusing on the customer service experience and the right use of AI technology in the co-creation of value.

The CRM, still, is one of the areas where AI is most valuable in financial services such as personalised banking and financial advice. Some of the services provided by financial institutions such as banks, brokers, family investment trusts and life assurance companies are on personal finance, portfolio management and trading. Because of high returns and low credit risk, investment services became widely used by companies after 2008 financial crisis. Laws passed to protect investors' cash and assets, for instance, the Retail Distribution Review (RDR) and the Markets in Financial Instruments Directive (MiFID) have also helped in supporting this change. The new rules have, therefore, led to financial institutions to make a considerable investment in new information systems and procedures that incorporate AI and digitisation to meet the new rules (Musto et al., 2015).

These are the closure of the traditional branches and the growth of the electronic commerce as among the major changes that have been affected by digitisation in the wealth management industry. As a result of this, the advisors have to ensure that they work wisely in order to meet the needs of their rich clients who have the need to be attended to personally. This problem could be overcome through the utilisation of advanced AI technologies such as CEBRA in the commercial banking designs. The personal financial services are delivered by CEBRA through the application of collaborative filtering algorithms and extraction of interest from the social network profiles. These approaches using AI were demonstrated efficient in generating and assessing a dataset of 60,000 examples. Thus, with the help of the RESTful API and recommendation algorithms, the Recommender System aims at improving the client satisfaction and increase the usage of banking and financial services (Hernández-Nieves et al., 2021).

The suggestion module of SMARTFASI, another AI-based project in the field of financial advice, had been developed a smart financial advising system suggestion module. This module enhances an asset analysis engine that incorporates Monte Carlo simulation by comparing customers as well as their investment tastes and preferences using case-based reasoning. Financial institutions may use the technology to create 'Asset Baskets' for their customers according to their trading and economic traits. The recommendation engine uses these Asset Baskets to create customer-specific Behavioural Investment Universes (BIUs). Businesses may implement more successful marketing strategies by analysing historical BIU data to discover investment patterns.

Chatbots and other AI technology have revolutionised customer service, especially in the banking and insurance industries. By using chatbots, businesses are able to engage with clients via widely used messaging platforms like WhatsApp, WeChat and Facebook Messenger. Without human interaction, these AI-powered products converse with consumers, answering their questions and showing them how to do tasks. Several industries, especially those in the financial sectors that rely on speed and immediate contact with clients, have been affected in a very significant way by this change in the sales and customer service strategies.

Few studies have examined the effects of chatbots on public transit, in contrast to the abundance of literature on topics like e-commerce and banking. On the other hand, chatbots are quickly becoming the go-to for travellers in need of instantaneous itinerary recommendations, purchase of tickets and status updates. Data about travel habits, service preferences and demographics are all part of the public transportation user experience that they may collect and analyse. Chatbots are useful for more than just saving time and effort; they also provide companies information that can be used to better serve customers and develop more targeted advertising campaigns. Chatbots provide streamlined and customised experiences for mobile customers, doing away with the need for conventional customer support channels (Zumstein & Hundertmark, 2017).

For those who have difficulty managing their money or getting out of debt, chatbots powered by AI have also been used to increase financial literacy. AI-driven strategies using nudge theory and gamification have outperformed traditional instructional material in changing financial behaviour. The goal of creating a chatbot-based just-in-time education programme was to increase financial literacy and responsible behaviour by giving users personalised, up-to-the-minute assistance and advice. Research shows that AI may have a beneficial impact on people's finances; 82% of 68 participants said the chatbot helped them learn more about money and change their habits (Ramjattan et al., 2021).

Other AI technologies that are revolutionising the banking industry include ML and predictive analytics. Financial institutions make use of these technologies to foretell how their customers will act, for instance, whether or not a consumer would sign up for a term deposit. The Random Forest Classifier outperformed the other two ML models (k-nearest neighbour and Stochastic gradient descent [SGD]) in terms of accuracy (87.5%), negative predictive value (92.9972%) and positive predictive value (87.8307%). Given the dynamic nature of the financial services industry, these findings give light on consumer habits that banks may use to hone their marketing strategies and hold on to more customers (Zaki et al., 2024).

Predicting client turnover is another important use of AI in banking. Banks can keep their customers and keep their income steady with the aid of AI-powered models that automatically create and assess churn prediction algorithms using customer data. One example study reported an F1 score of 0.83, an accuracy of 0.77 and an area under the curve (AUC) score of 0.84 for a deep learning churn prediction framework that used convolutional neural network (CNN) approaches. The banks can therefore be able to identify the customers who are likely to defectors and try to retain them as their clients (Elgohary et al., 2023).

The use of AI is on the rise in CRM systems of organisations especially in the banking and insurance sectors. Organisations can now offer better services to the consumers, enhance their interaction with the consumers and improve the organisational efficiency through the use of AI such as chatbots, recommendation systems and predictive analysis. In order to implement the potential of AI in CRM, some challenges need to be addressed such as privacy issues, the Uncanny Valley Paradox, and the Personalisation-Privacy Paradox. Focusing on creating customer-friendly environments that are based on the use of AI while at the same time taking into consideration the ethical issues that come with it should be the next big step for organisations. SMEs have a good opportunity to remain competitive and offer individual approaches to their customers in this environment by using the CRM solutions based on AI.

AI applied on CRM in context of financial services has attracted much interest in the current literature reporting on its ability to optimise customer experiences and organisational performance. Earlier forms of CRM systems were mainly confined to capturing, storing, analysing and categorising customer details and providing limited functionality of automation leading to stereotyped services that did not address the specific needs of the customers. But today, with the use of ML algorithms, NLP and predictive analytics, the concept of hyper-personalisation has been introduced to the banking industry which means that the major financial institutions are in a stronger position to develop and offer customised services with the help of real-time data and behavioural patterns analysis.

Previous research on the impact of AI CRM on customer experience has revealed that the application of CRM allows financial institutions to accurately determine the needs of the customer and serve the customer better by processing most of the regular activities and providing relevant financial products and services. Real-time interpersonal communication is also a benefactor of AI as it brings satisfaction in the customers' experiences as they engage with their financier. However, with the help of predictive analytics based on AI, businesses can predict the behaviour of their consumers, their preferences in products or credit or risk appetite, thus taking on a predictive nature of service provision.

Despite these advantages, several studies point to the challenges involved in implementing AI in CRM. Some of the concerns that have been raised include data privacy concerns, algorithms' biases and challenges facing the integration of new AI tools with the existing CRM systems that may reduce the effectiveness of the AI CRM. However, the reliance on AI, especially in front line positions, is a concern as it limits the amount of contact the customer has with other people and this could a negative effect on the customer's perception of the company.

From the literature, it is evident that through the integration of AI, there is a high possibility of enhancing CRM in the financial services industry by enhancing the interactions between the customers and the company. Nevertheless, there are some ethical issues, data security and system integration decisions to be made to capture all the potential of AI application in this field. The future direction of AI in CRM is clear in the fact that the systems will become more advanced in order to provide optimal and unique financial services to customers in a way that will also benefit the institutions.

Objectives of the Study

- The objective of this study is to investigate how AI might improve CRM platforms.
- In order to examine the difficulties encountered by CRM systems powered by AI.
- Examining how AI will change financial advising and personalised banking services.

Research Methodology

Using a qualitative approach, this study will investigate how AI plays a complex role in CRM for individualised financial services for customers. Interviews with CRM managers, financial advisers and AI technology specialists will constitute the bulk of the data collection process. Through these interviews, we want to glean their thoughts, feelings and experiences with AI's effect on CRM strategy, personalised financial services and customer engagement more generally. Respondents will have more time to expound on the pros and cons of using AI into CRM systems since the questions are designed to be open-ended. Academic studies, reports from businesses and case studies will all be used to compile secondary data that will show how AI is being used in the financial sector. By using a qualitative approach, we may learn more about the human elements, organisational difficulties and ethical concerns at play when AI changes CRM practices. Using thematic analysis to uncover commonalities and differences in the data, this research will provide a comprehensive look at how AI may improve financial services' personalised customer experience as well as the challenges that come with it.

The themes which are highlighted in Table 12.1 include the regulatory compliance, the CRM and the service delivery based on the findings of several studies and implementations within the economic services sector. Table 12.1 gives a summary of the approaches employed, the considerations made, the outcomes that were derived, with emphasis on the advantages and disadvantages encountered. In particular, the synthesis provides a lot of examples of technical innovations that have transformed the very process of banking, including the use of AI, predictive analytics and ML. However, all these innovations are in compliance with the set regulations to address the needs of the customers in the provision of personalised financial services. Furthermore, the study also shows the need to change to be more competitive in the market by understanding the dynamics of the relationship between emerging customer needs, legal frameworks and industrial practices. In a nutshell, the synthesis explains how today's banking incorporates technology to achieving the goals of efficiency and customer satisfaction while meeting legal requirements.

AI-Driven Customer Service and Support

Due to the increasing trend of data analysis and individual approach to clients, AI may change the face of CRM and Industry 4.0 as a whole. However, the current leadership of CRM systems implemented on the basis of AI is crucial for this transformation that enables the enhancement of customer communication, offering of suitable products and services, and more efficient approach to the promotion of products and services. To estimate the product effectiveness, performance and customers' loyalty, the author of the article offers to employ the CRM systems with the help of AI. Consumer experiences can be enhanced by the application of AI technologies through mathematical models for input and output, system-level design and process-level architecture. This paper used questionnaires to gather data from the given dataset to analyse the consumers' knowledge, satisfaction and loyalty towards AI-enabled products and services (Li & Xu, 2022).

Table 12.1. Techniques Used in Enhancement of Personalised Banking.

Study/Project	Technique Used	Focus	Finding	Benefits	Limitations/ Challenges
CEBRA	Fog computing with collaborative filtering algorithms and interest extraction from social network profiles	Personalised banking services	Successful integration into commercial banking environments	Personalised services improving client satisfaction	Information confidentiality apprehensions; complexity of implementation
Recommender system	REST interface, recommendations algorithm	Promotion of banking and financial goods	Increased customer satisfaction and engagement	Enhanced sales and marketing effectiveness	Reliance on accurate user data for effective recommendations
SMARTFASI	Case-based reasoning, Monte Carlo simulation-based asset analysis	Financial advising and client investment preference matching	Improved asset analysis and client matching	Precise client segmentation and targeted financial advice	Requires extensive historical data for accurate predictions; complexity of financial analysis
Chatbots	Conversational AI, machine learning	Customer service in sales, financial literacy improvement	Improved customer service efficiency and financial behaviour in users	Cost-effective customer service; enhanced user engagement; real-time assistance	Limited by AI's understanding and processing of human language; may not handle complex customer issues effectively

(Continued)

Table 12.1. *(Continued)*

Study/Project	Technique Used	Focus	Finding	Benefits	Limitations/ Challenges
Predictive analytics	Machine learning models (random forest classifier, k-nearest neighbour classifier, SGD classifier)	Predicting bank term deposit subscriptions, customer churn	High accuracy in prediction models	Insightful targeting for marketing efforts; reduced customer churn	Requires large datasets for model training; may face challenges in data privacy and ethical use of predictive analytics

Source: Original work.

It is for this reason that companies are investing in AI with an aim to improving on the consumer satisfaction and financial performance. This is because majority of the current AI solutions lack the people's element because their focus is more on the technology. Power changes that may occur within the CRM due to the integration of AI are examined in Monod et al. (2023). In this context, Bourdieu's theory of practice can be employed with the aim of understanding the author's intentions. The social and organisational impact of AI and how this changes the behaviour of workers was therefore explored in two longitudinal case studies. Furthermore, this study's findings hold theoretical and practical implications on the way power relations and inequality are likely to be impacted by AI.

To extend the previous analysis and to further investigate the relationship between the AI services and the level of happiness among consumers, this study employs Smart-PLS as a semipathetic technique for Partial Least Squares Structural Equation Modelling (Zahra et al., 2023). The study that enroled 189 participants provided the insights into the traits and factors that influence client satisfaction with AI-based services. The findings reveal that by employing AI technology in the enhancement of service quality in AI-driven ecosystems, companies can enhance customer satisfaction and loyalty, two crucial factors that are crucial for organisations in the current business environment.

This clearly demonstrates that AI is playing a very instrumental part in enhancing consumer experience in the retail sector; Taiwan ranks second in the global density of convenience shops. There is a growing need for qualified retail workers due to the proliferation of these establishments and the inclusion of a retail service group in the curriculum by the Ministry of Education. A customer communication teaching approach based on conversational AI technology and experience learning theory is proposed in Chen et al. (2023), which addresses the issues that firms have when trying to successfully educate new staff. By facilitating effective, AI-driven training for new staff, this solution lowers training risks and improves the customer experience.

Marketing is one area where AI is having a profound impact on company growth via improving a range of marketing services. According to the research in Tanveer et al. (2021), 12 marketing services – Exchange, Everywhere, Evangelism, Product, Price, Place, Promotion, Consumer, Cost, Convenience, Communication and Experience – are covered by the marketers' perspectives on AI and its impact on these services. All services, with the exception of evangelism, are positively associated with AI, according to the study's analysis of data from 508 samples using Cronbach's alpha for reliability. Research on the effects of AI on different services, sectors and demographics of consumers is warranted in light of the results, which show that AI has a major bearing on company growth. If your company is looking to boost your growth by using AI into your marketing strategy, this report is a great place to start.

CRM systems powered by AI, with an emphasis on real-time personalisation and predictive analytics, have recently grown in popularity as a means to better serve customers. The authors of Kumari (2021) lay out a plan for developing interactive, tailored experiences across all channels by using big data, NLP and ML algorithms. To give individualised experiences and products, companies use the data that is collected from the client which includes demographics, purchase history and interactions on social media platforms. This method powered by AI optimises CRM across sectors and shows how it can increase customer retention, satisfaction and overall organisational success.

Nonetheless, there are certain issues that are making it difficult to widespread the utilisation of the AI solutions in the field of CRM. In this paper, a number of issues that arise when applying AI to large scale scaled agile development methods (SADM) are discussed (Saklamaeva & Pavlič, 2023). Some of the 18 challenges that have been identified in the study include; complex integration, high costs and lack of specialised knowledge, among others, that organisations may encounter in the course of implementing AI in SADM. Such benefits include: Enhanced resource management, sound decision-making, effective project management, among other benefits that the study establishes as the five key advantages of AI in large-scale applications (Chen et al., 2020). There are seven drawbacks the study also identifies, these are: Ethical concerns and the fear of job displacement (Davenport & Ronanki, 2018; Fountaine et al., 2019). Lastly, the authors present 15 tools and assistants that are developed with the aid of AI and explain how they can assist companies in addressing these challenges; the authors commend the versatility of these tools and assistants in addressing different business concerns (Gupta et al., 2006; Huang & Rust, 2018).

Based on these findings, it is possible to state that AI has a tremendous impact on the management of customer relationships. AI CRM technology, being system and process oriented, has the potential to enhance performance, enhance customer retention and enhance product quality (Kumar & Reinartz, 2018; Liu & Tai, 2016). However, this is still a partial view of the problem since technology and work approach both need to be considered because AI implementations are not very successful (Lusch & Nambisan, 2015). The power relations in organisations especially in the area of CRM could be explained better using Bourdieu's theory of practice. Further, the research done with Smart-PLS shows how AI can significantly increase the levels of consumer satisfaction and loyalty, which are two important factors that are important for succeeding in today's market (Ng et al., 2020).

AI as a tool in retail training and customer services in Taiwan has proved to be quite useful. Thus, preparing the employees for the communication with the customers based on conversational AI as a solution for the mentioned challenges that are related to personnel training in the fast-growing industries (Paschen et al., 2020). In the marketing sector, it is possible to observe the positive impact of AI on business development through optimising the services like product customisation, pricing strategies and customer's interactions. As AI is adopted in the CRM and marketing strategies of organisations, companies expect to gain in customer satisfaction, loyalty and overall improvement (Payne & Frow, 2005).

But we cannot forget that there are certain issues with using AI in the management of enterprise-level software development. Implementing such technology as AI presents both opportunities and risks and therefore should be done carefully (Rust & Huang, 2019). Despite these challenges, it is important to note that AI is still helpful when it comes to organisations' efforts to stay competitive in a business environment that is gradually being shaped by the adoption of AI. Some of the areas where AI is useful include efficiency in the use of resources and decision-making (Wamba et al., 2020).

AI-based CRM software is a new reality for companies that make it possible to provide more personalised approach, more loyal customers and better results (Zavolokina et al., 2021). Hence, there is a need for AI strategies that encompass technical advancements alongside the working culture for the successful implementation of AI. Here are the ways through which companies can take maximum advantage of the innovative AI CRM functions to know the shift of power, use of predictive analysis and challenges of AI large-scale implementation. For corporations in the AI age to increase customer link and enhance the organisation, the conclusions of these research are a guideline (Zerbino et al., 2018).

Conclusion

Due to the integration of AI in the financial services CRM where clients have exceptional chances to interact with the company, financial services are rapidly evolving. AI-integrated CRM solutions enhance the productivity of financial services in areas of self-management and asset management. These technologies let the financial institutions to automatise the common operations, to provide real-time information and even to predict consumer needs. This enables them to develop specific solutions which enhance operational effectiveness and also the satisfaction of the customers.

However, there are a number of challenges that have to be met in order to use AI in banking. The concerns regarding privacy of data, legal issues and the challenges that come with the integration of AI are real issues that businesses have to overcome in order to ensure that AI technology meets both the customer's needs and the business' needs and goals. Such concerns are more enhanced in a field that deals with information which has to be kept as confidential as possible.

It is therefore clear that despite the challenges that have been highlighted above, AI has the potential of transforming the financial industry. By using AI to enhance CRM systems, financial companies can analyse the customer's behaviour in a much detailed manner as well as enhance the speed of services. The integration of AI and CRM will therefore place businesses in vantage position to enhance customer relations and achieve success in the new market place given that the market is shifting towards the digital environment.

References

Butler, S. (2000). Customer relationships: Changing the game: CRM in the e-world. *Journal of Business Strategy*, *21*(2), 13–14.

Chaturvedi, R., & Verma, S. (2023). Opportunities and challenges of AI-driven customer service. In *Artificial Intelligence in customer service: The next frontier for personalized engagement*. https://doi.org/10.1007/978-3-031-33898-4_3

Chen, K.-Y., Chiang, M.-Y., & Huang, T.-C. (2023). Redefining customer service education in Taiwan's convenience store sector: Implementing an AI-driven experiential training approach. In *International conference on innovative technologies and learning*. Springer Nature.

Chen, Y., Li, S., & Wei, X. (2020). Artificial intelligence in customer relationship management: Impacts on customer experience and brand loyalty. *Journal of Business Research, 117*, 441–452. https://doi.org/10.1016/j.jbusres.2020.06.045

Davenport, T. H., & Ronanki, R. (2018). Artificial intelligence for the real world. *Harvard Business Review, 96*(1), 108–116.

Elgohary, E. M., Galal, M., Mosa, A., & Elshabrawy, G. A. (2023). Smart evaluation for deep learning model: Churn prediction as a product case study. *Bulletin of Electrical Engineering and Informatics, 12*(2), 1219–1225.

Fountaine, T., McCarthy, B., & Saleh, T. (2019). Building the AI-powered organization. *Harvard Business Review, 97*(4), 62–73.

Gupta, S., Hanssens, D. M., Hardie, B. G. S., Kahn, W., Kumar, V., Lin, N., & Sriram, S. (2006). Modeling customer lifetime value. *Journal of Service Research, 9*(2), 139–155. https://doi.org/10.1177/1094670506293810

Hernández-Nieves, E., Hernández, G., Gil-González, A. B., Rodríguez-González, S., & Corchado, J. M. (2021). CEBRA: A casE-based reasoning application to recommend banking products. *Engineering Applications of Artificial Intelligence, 104*, 104327.

Huang, M.-H., & Rust, R. T. (2018). Artificial intelligence in service. *Journal of Service Research, 21*(2), 155–172. https://doi.org/10.1177/1094670517752459

Kampani, N., & Jhamb, D. (2020). Analyzing the role of e-CRM in managing customer relations: A critical review of the literature. *Journal of Critical Review, 7*(4), 221–226.

Kumar, V., & Reinartz, W. (2018). *Customer relationship management: Concept, strategy, and tools* (3rd ed.). Springer.

Kumari, S. (2021). Context-aware AI-driven CRM: Enhancing customer journeys through real-time personalization and predictive analytics. *ESP Journal of Engineering and Technology Advancements, 1*(1), 7–13.

Ledro, C. (2021). Artificial intelligence applied to customer relationship management: An empirical research. In *European conference on innovation and entrepreneurship*. Academic Conferences International Limited.

Li, F., & Xu, G. (2022). AI-driven customer relationship management for sustainable enterprise performance. *Sustainable Energy Technologies and Assessments, 52*, 102–103.

Liu, B., & Tai, S. (2016). Customer segmentation using AI techniques in financial services. *International Journal of Advanced Computer Science and Applications, 7*(5), 61–69. https://doi.org/10.14569/IJACSA.2016.070509

Loh, B. K., Koo, K. L., Ho, K. F., & Idrus, R. (2011). A review of customer relationship management system benefits and implementation in small and medium enterprises. In *Mathematics and computers in biology, business and acoustics, 12th WSEAS international conference on mathematics and computers in biology and chemistry*. University of Brasov.

Lusch, R. F., & Nambisan, S. (2015). Service innovation: A service-dominant logic perspective. *MIS Quarterly, 39*(1), 155–175. https://doi.org/10.25300/MISQ/2015/39.1.07

Monod, E., Lissillour, R., Köster, A., & Jiayin, Q. (2023). Does AI control or support? Power shifts after AI system implementation in customer relationship management. *Journal of Decision Systems, 32*(3), 542–565.

Musto, C., Semeraro, G., Lops, P., de Gemmis, M., & Lekkas, G. (2015). Personalized finance advisory through case-based recommender systems and diversification strategies. *Decision Support Systems, 77*, 100–111.

Ng, I. C., Scharf, K., & Parry, G. (2020). Customer data platforms: A tool for real-time customer relationship management. *The Journal of Strategic Information Systems, 29*(4), 101620. https://doi.org/10.1016/j.jsis.2020.101620

Paschen, J., Wilson, M., & Ferreira, J. J. (2020). Collaborative intelligence: How human and artificial intelligence create value along the B2B sales funnel. *Business Horizons, 63*(3), 403–414. https://doi.org/10.1016/j.bushor.2020.01.003

Payne, A., & Frow, P. (2005). A strategic framework for customer relationship management. *Journal of Marketing, 69*(4), 167–176. https://doi.org/10.1509/jmkg.2005.69.4.167

Ramjattan, R., Hosein, P., & Henry, N. (2021). Using chatbot technologies to help individuals make sound personalized financial decisions. In *IEEE international humanitarian technology conference (IHTC)*. https://doi.org/10.1109/IHTC53077.2021.9698928

Rana, J., Gaur, L., Singh, G., Awan, U., & Rasheed, M. I. (2022). Reinforcing customer journey through artificial intelligence: A review and research agenda. *International Journal of Emerging Markets, 17*(7), 1738–1758.

Rust, R. T., & Huang, M.-H. (2019). The AI revolution in marketing. *Journal of the Academy of Marketing Science, 48*(1), 24–42. https://doi.org/10.1007/s11747-019-00696-0

Saklamaeva, V., & Pavlič, L. (2023). The potential of AI-driven assistants in scaled agile software development. *Applied Sciences, 14*(1), 319.

Tanveer, A. A. R., Tanveer, M., Khan, N., & Ahmad, A.-R. (2021). AI support marketing: Understanding the customer journey towards the business development. In *2021 1st international conference on artificial intelligence and data analytics (CAIDA)*. https://doi.org/10.1109/CAIDA51941.2021.9425079

Wamba, S. F., Gunasekaran, A., Akter, S., Ren, S. J.-F., Dubey, R., & Childe, S. J. (2020). Big data analytics and firm performance: Effects of dynamic capabilities. *Journal of Business Research, 70*, 356–365. https://doi.org/10.1016/j.jbusres.2020.05.003

Zahra, A. R. Az, Jonas, D., Rosdiana, & Yusuf, N. A. (2023). Assessing customer satisfaction in AI-powered services: An empirical study with smartPLS. *International Transactions on Artificial Intelligence, 2*(1), 81–89.

Zaki, A. M., Khodadadi, N., Lim, W. H., & Towfek, S. K. (2024). Predictive analytics and machine learning in direct marketing for anticipating bank term deposit subscriptions. *American Journal of Business and Operations Research, 11*(1), 78–88.

Zavolokina, L., Dolata, M., & Schwabe, G. (2021). The ethics of AI in customer relationship management: Data privacy and algorithmic bias in financial services. *Journal of Information Technology, 36*(3), 276–292.

Zerbino, P., Aloini, D., Dulmin, R., & Mininno, V. (2018). Big data-enabled customer relationship management: A holistic approach. *Information Processing & Management, 54*(5), 818–846. https://doi.org/10.1016/j.ipm.2018.01.004

Zumstein, D., & Hundertmark, S. (2017). Chatbots—An interactive technology for personalized communication, transactions and services. *IADIS International Journal on WWW/Internet, 15*, 96–109.

Chapter 13

Achieving Organisational Achievement via the Use of AI in Machine Management

Shiney Chib[a], *Falguni Pawar*[a], *Shantanu S. Bose*[b], *Thirulogasundaram V.P.*[c], *Prasanna H.N.*[d] *and Lakshmi S.R.*[e]

[a]Datta Meghe Institute of Management Studies, India
[b]Amity University, India
[c]Don Bosco College of Management Studies and Computer Applications, India
[d]Sri Venkateshwara College of Engineering, India
[e]Christ University, India

Abstract

Among the most effective ways of increasing the outcomes of the company, there is the application of Artificial Intelligence (AI) in machine management. This study article focuses on the role of AI in improving the work of machines and decision-making as well as increasing the effectiveness of organisations. The focus of the study is to enhance the machine management efficiency in order to reduce the downtime, decrease the costs of operation and increase the productivity through the application of AI technologies such as automated systems, predictive maintenance and real-time data analysis. This study finds that the indicators of operational efficiency, product quality and labour safety are determined by a case study of various industries. This study has proposed that the integration of AI into machine management goes beyond being a technical adjustment; it is a shift in the culture and approach of organisations, human resource management (HRM) practices and operations. The real-time insights and predictive analysis of the market that is provided by AI can help in meeting the needs of the market that are ever-evolving while at the same time being efficient and innovative. This makes enterprises to have an edge over the competitors. The findings of the study are therefore a clear indication that in the ever evolving

Security Intelligence in the Age of AI, 223–242

doi:10.1108/978-1-83608-156-220251013

business environment, there is the need to embrace the use of AI to foster growth and development of organisations.

Keywords: Business organisations; employer productivity; Artificial Intelligence; CRMs; organisational achievement

Introduction

The use of Artificial Intelligence (AI) systems may very well hold the key to addressing many of the challenges that today's organisations are grappling with by enhancing productivity, improving the decision-making process and encouraging creativity. However, the development and application of the AI is one of the fastest growing technologies that enterprises need to assess the risks that come with it. Organisational environments and AI systems are interdependent; therefore, the integration of AI in organisations is a social and technical phenomenon which cannot be viewed separately. There are four types of AI applications that have been proposed to categorise the ways that AI may be applied in organisations which will assist in understanding this relationship. It also examines the problems that organisations are likely to encounter in their attempt to implement AI-based machine management, for example, lack of technical knowhow, costs of implementing the system and resistance to change. Some of the general benefits of the integration of AI in strategy such as sustainability, scalability and competitiveness are also discussed. It also reveals that the use of AI enables firms to attain their goals by integrating their activities with new technologies thus enhancing productivity and market leadership. This taxonomy underlines the importance of the fact that the AI capabilities should be adjusted to the specific needs and goals of the business (Holmström & Hällgren, 2021).

In order for modern organisations to make good use of AI, three things must be followed: first, the purpose of AI adoption should be well understood; second, the degree of algorithmic control and adaptability needs to be appropriately established; and third, the nature of organisations in which AI is applied should be taken into consideration. Adopting these principles will assist organisations in identifying effects of AI technologies on their processes and how these settings affect AI in return thus leading to effectiveness.

Investments continue to grow in the field, but organisations are still hesitant to fully embrace AI. However, only 40% of the companies have a certain strategy of AI, while 20% of the companies have applied AI for some services or processes; only 5% of companies have integrated AI in their business operations, based on the data. This fear is grounded on a number of notorious mishaps including Watson's failure to identify cancer as it was supposed to or Tay, Microsoft's chatbot that made racist remarks on social media. These cases show that it is or can be a huge risk to implement AI while the organisation is not prepared and adequate monitoring is not in place (Pumplun et al., 2019).

Natural language processing, deep learning and machine learning (ML) have been the most popular fields of AI research. With the ability to analyse large sets of

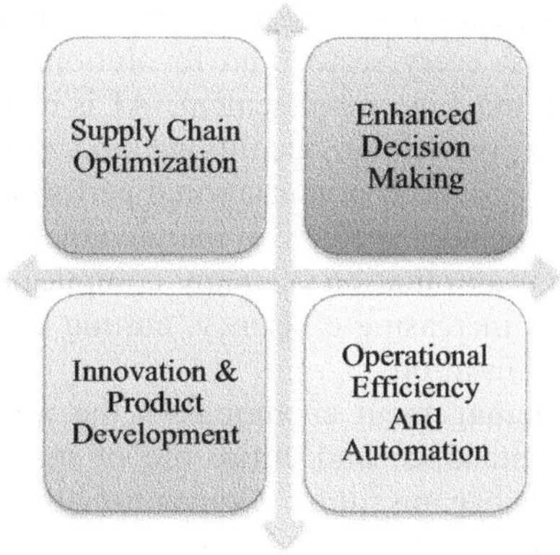

Fig. 13.1. Artificial Intelligence in Business Organisations. *Source:* Original work.

data and make complex decisions based on this analysis, these technologies seek to replicate human cognition. But its greatest strength is in its ability to learn by itself from experience and adapt to the activities of people so it can become more and more efficient. In terms of governance and control, the same features that make the AI powerful and scalable can also be the cause of the problem as more unknown ways of the AI system's growth may be there. As depicted in Fig. 13.1, the benefit of scalability of AI can enhance organisational operations in an enormous way; however, it has its supervisory risks as well as ethical issues (Kulkov et al., 2023).

Through the United Nations' Sustainable Development Goals (SDGs), it is possible to comprehend the ways in which AI can contribute to the achievement of sustainable development. This is where AI can help us meet these goals given that it can lead to positive economic, social and environmental impacts. However, there are a number of factors that organisations need to take into consideration before AI can be used to advance sustainability. The other key factors that are important in the utilisation of AI include the capacity to manage data, the organisation's readiness to embrace AI and the necessary infrastructure to support AI.

By these, organisations can benefit from AI in enhancing the society in various ways including reducing energy consumption and wastage of resources and enhancing access to services among others. Lastly, it is crucial to understand that the ability of AI to promote sustainability depends on the ability of enterprises to incorporate the AI initiatives into the broader environmental and social goals, thus ensuring that the benefits of AI can only be positive despite the potential risks.

AI holds a lot of potential in increasing the effectiveness of organisations and their development, but when incorporating it, the environment of an organisation, governance and potential threats have to be taken into account. Thus, organisations can reap the advantages of AI while avoiding the vices in their application of the technology.

The new age technological advancement has made it possible for AI to become an integral part of almost every sector and revolutionising the former ways of working. In the area of machine management, AI is changing the face of how organisations are now approaching, identifying and enhancing the machinery they use, thus leading to enhanced organisational performance. The uses of AI in machine management include predictive maintenance, real-time monitoring, process optimisation and automation of many complicated processes and functions which are vital for increasing efficiency, cutting costs and increasing productivity within any organisation.

The term machine management encompasses the ways and means through which the running, maintenance and entire life of machinery is controlled in production and business organisations. Conventionally, machine management has been a time-consuming and passive process which includes scheduled maintenance, manual observation and periodic examination.

These approaches while useful are often not very efficient and can result in unintended equipment breakdowns, unneeded downtime and higher costs of operations. Adoption of AI in machine management has brought about a major shift from what can be described as the tactical approach to strategic approach of handling machines whereby organisations are in a position to anticipate problems that may arise in future and prevent them from occurring.

This study also seeks to establish how AI is applied in machine management and the results that are likely to be obtained therefrom in relation to organisational objectives. In an effort to firmly ground the role of AI in machine management practices and organisational performance, this chapter will explore the practices such as predictive analytics, ML and real-time monitoring. In addition, the study will discuss the financial, operational and strategic benefits of applying AI to machine management and the issues that should be considered, as well as the prospects of the topic.

AI in Today's Machine Management

The introduction of AI in machine management has shifted the focus of organisations with regards to the maintenance of equipment and machineries. Unlike the conventional methods that involve the use of scheduled check-ups and manual monitoring of the machines, AI-based systems monitor the status of machines and analyse patterns of performance to determine the likelihood of failure. This change from a reactive approach to preventative maintenance is perhaps one of the most important evolutions in machine management, which enables organisations to reduce downtime and increase the useful lifespan of their equipment.

The type of maintenance that is powered by AI is known as predictive maintenance where the alerts of potential machine failure are identified based on the advanced analytics of early warnings such as changes in vibration, temperature variations or sound. Through evaluating these indicators, the AI systems can estimate the time that the machine will fail or need to be repaired, hence allowing organisations to perform the repair at the most appropriate time. This also minimises the chances of a system failure, while at the same time, it helps in scheduling maintenance time and costs for unnecessary repairs or system downtime. For instance, put in place are AI-based predictive maintenance systems that can notify the maintenance crews of impending problems several weeks or even months before they happen, thus averting expensive breakdowns.

Apart from the predictive maintenance, AI optimises machine management through monitoring and taking actions in real time. ML algorithms work with the data received from machines, which can be energy consumption, production rate or other performance indicators. This real-time analysis makes it possible for the AI systems to detect inefficiencies, bottlenecks or any other deviation from the best practice. Thus, the data-driven decisions can be made in the optimisation of machine setups, resources or even production plans. This real-time process of machine management is helpful for organisations to adapt themselves according to the changing conditions and increase the operational effectiveness.

Optimising the Corporate Performance Through AI in Automation of Machine Management

The effects of applying AI in machine management on organisational performance are far reaching in several areas such as operation, cost, quality and decision-making. Through making the machinery to be more efficient and accurate in their operations, AI assists organisations to meet their objectives in the best way possible.

- Operational Efficiency: Another advantage of AI in machine management is that it helps in increasing the level of performance. AI-based applications can check the status of the machines, the time when the machines require a service and can also regulate their performance and thus can work effectively with minimal human interference and with least downtime. This boosted efficiency is translated to higher production rate, shorter cycle time and a more enhanced production process. For instance, in the manufacturing industry, AI can help in enhancing efficiency in the production line by changing machine settings on the basis of real-time data to get the best out of machines. This enhances efficiency, and thus, organisations can deliver their products within the required time and meet the consumers' needs.
- Cost Reduction: It also leads to a reduction of costs across various fields as a result of the use of AI in machine management. For instance, through the practice of predictive maintenance, organisations are able to cut on their maintenance expenses through avoiding time and resources used to attend to breakdowns that could have been prevented. Also, the machine performance is enhanced, and this results in less energy and resource usage and therefore lower costs of operations. Also, since AI is capable of performing repetitive tasks and processes, it eliminates the need for individuals to work on those tasks, hence giving organisations the opportunity to direct their workforce to more

important tasks. In industries where machinery constitutes a large part of the overall expenses, these savings can mean a lot to the organisation's financial performance.

- Product Quality: It is important for organisations to have high standard of product quality, and this can be achieved through the use of AI in controlling the performance of machines. With the help of a constant control of machine parameters and production performance, AI systems can identify deviations or abnormalities of the quality in real time. This in turn enables organisations to make corrections before the products get to the consumers, thus averting the delivery of defective products. In industries like automobile or pharmaceuticals where the quality of the product is directly related to the brand name and legal norms, the AI-based machine management helps in maintaining the quality of the products.
- Strategic decision-making: It is because the AI systems generate a large amount of data which can be used to make strategic decisions in organisations. This way, based on machine performance data, it is possible to determine the pattern of usage, improve the efficiency of using assets and decide on an upgrade or replacement of the machinery. Also, AI can help in the prediction of demand which can help organisations to changes in production and other resources depending on market condition. This means that decision-making in organisations is based on data and analysis to enable organisations to adapt to the new business environment.

Nevertheless, there are several issues that organisations should understand in order to harness the full potential of AI-driven machine management. One of the main issues is the connection of AI with the current machine management systems. This is especially the case with many firms that still are using legacy systems that are not compatible with AI technologies and therefore will need large capital investments to upgrade. Furthermore, AI systems are capitalised intensive and their installation needs specialised technical skills which might not be available in some sectors or countries.

It also raises issues of data security and privacy, for instance. Such systems are data-driven, and it is imperative that the data required for these systems to work are properly collected, stored and analysed while ensuring that it is secure. Also, the issue of the ethical side of AI should also be considered by organisations especially on the issue of automation and its effect on the employment of people.

The application of the AI in machine management is a major step towards effective management of organisations for organisational success. By applying predictive maintenance, real-time monitoring and process optimisation, AI improves operational performance, decreases expenses, increases the quality of products and provides the company's management with useful information. Thus, as organisations keep on embracing AI technologies, the possibilities of creating new trends in the management of machines will remain limitless and provide new avenues to business growth and success. Issues like integration and data security must be solved; however, the potential of AI in machine management is immense, which makes AI as one of the essential tools for organisations' success in the contemporary industrial environment.

AI is enabling companies to enhance efficiency in their processes and create new products as well as services thus gaining competitive edge. It may help in making the process better, in decision-making, and sometimes even discover things that were not previously known. However, despite these benefits, organisations still do not integrate AI fully in their operations due to poor implementation, lack of proper plan and low level of organisational preparedness (Engel et al., 2021).

Ergonomics therefore refers to the study of factors that affect people at their workplace with the main objective of eliminating hazards. When formulating strategies, it also considers parameters such as the anthropometric, physical and ergonomics, personalities and psycho social support. Globalisation has also resulted in an increase in the speed of growth of financial markets, centralised systems, derivatives and other products which has increase layers of risk management (Lin et al., 2022).

Organisms, artefacts and the environment, respectively, are getting intertwined, and this has also shifted the nature of ergonomics in Industry 4. 0. The interaction between human and human-like machines, known as Human–Machine Interface (HMI), should be given attention in order to boost performance and reduce pressure due to the new reality, where mechanisation and robots are considered as irreplaceable components of modern work environment. Ergonomics and AI are two forces that will determine how the future company operations and risk management will be like due to the increased globalisation of markets.

AI has continued to advance at a fast pace in different fields and has impacted most of the conventional practices such as machine management. Some of the literature area within this discourse focuses on how the adoption of AI in managing of machines is changing the dynamics of machines management through increased efficiency, decreased costs and, generally, better organisational performances. In this literature review, the author's objective is to look at the current trend in the literature on how AI is implemented in machines and particularly in what areas such as predictive maintenance, real-time monitoring and process optimisation. Furthermore, it will investigate effects of AI-driven machine management to organisational output, effectiveness, cost optimisation, product quality and strategy.

Machine management refers to the watch, care and enhancement of equipment and machines used in numerous field including manufacturing, energy, transportation and many others. Historically, the management of the machines most commonly used crude techniques such as observation, periodic check-ups and periodic servicing. First of all, let it be noted that the management of machines has changed with the advent of AI and has now become more anticipatory, analytical and, in most cases, even automated. Introducing AI, machines' monitoring and maintenance approaches have significantly changed to facilitate efficient real-time decision-making processes and predictive methods that are out of the reach of human methods.

Another area, where AI has left a significant influence, is in the area of maintenance, particularly predictive maintenance. Predictive maintenance is a concept whereby algorithms of AI are applied in determining when particular machinery is likely to fail in order to avoid its failure. This is better than proactive reactive maintenance that will most of the time result in breakages and costly repair jobs. By processing and identifying such early symptoms of machine malfunction, AI can help organisations to schedule maintenance measures, prevent long downtimes and get a longer lifespan of their equipment.

The use of AI in machine management is also realised in the monitoring of real-time processes and the optimisation of processes as well. Eddy/ntelligent monitoring systems can be used to scrutinise data from machines, look for inefficiencies or something that deviates from norms on a real-time basis. This makes it possible for organisations to timely change the settings or the way that certain individuals machines are used in execution of their tasks meaning the effectiveness of the organisation is improved. It is especially useful in industries that require displaying various kinds of optimisation depending on real-time data because even minor inefficiency may lead to substantial losses.

A fairly large number of studies has been devoted to discussion of AI in the context of one of the most valuable applications of machine management – predictive maintenance. Digital twin applies software mimicry to the existing physical products and systems and incorporates the data of the sensors attached to the assets to predict machinery breakdowns. By implementing this approach, organisations will be in a position to transition from inclusive reactive maintenance strategies, thus decreasing the periods of unscheduled plant downtime, increasing the useful lifespan of equipment and decreasing maintenance expenses.

Thus, predictive maintenance is life-changing for industries that depend on various pieces of equipment. Leveraging on capabilities provided by AI, companies are able to predict issues in advance leading to reduction in downtime by approximately 40%. Further, predictive maintenance facilitates the ability to replace parts only when required, thus reducing costs. Likewise, AI-based maintenance systems are equally important when it comes to managing a continuous operation when machines break down leading to high stakes in industries such as aerospace and manufacturing.

The advantage of predictive maintenance is not only in the decrease in the frequency of the downtime. Since the problem of equipment failure can be predicted before it actually happens, predictive maintenance brought in by AI makes workplace safer to work in. Furthermore, the role of AI is significant in real-time condition monitoring and process enhancement apart from the role it has in the predictive maintenance. There are now real-time monitoring systems based on AI which monitor and collect data from machines in real time and in this way provide organisations with information for real-time decisions. This makes it easier to have better and proper functioning since in case of any variation, it is corrected instantly.

The need to track machine data instantly is needed, for the optimal operations, in industries. In such industries, even if the machines are working slightly off from their optimal state, this will lead to defects in products or delay of production.

One can still monitor and observe the indicators so that quicker corrective actions to prevent further deviations could be taken with the help of AI. This capability of observing machines on a constant basis and providing real-time information reduces downtime while increasing efficiency.

AI also has a huge influence on other processes such as process optimisation. In some processes, parameters can be changed constantly in real time, and so using AI, machines can optimise well-coordinated processes without much wastage. AI is capable of making corrections to production process procedures with regard to current status of the machinery and environmental factors including market forces for the products and availability of raw materials. This flexibility done in real time helps organisations to relate well with changes in environment and hence remain relevant in the market.

AI integration into an organisation's machine management process goes further in improving organisational accomplishment while in operation. Research endeavours on the impact of AI reveal the ways in which key performance indicators of organisational performance including cost, quality and decision-making are enhanced.

With regards to benefits of implementing AI in machine management, there is the following: Cost savings is one of the major advantages of AI in machine management. Through controlling the unpredicted downtimes, proper scheduling of the maintenance activities and enhancement of efficiency of the machines, the AI systems incurred handsome benefits in the organisation. Firms embarking on the use of AI in machine management observed that they cut down the rate of maintenance from 10 to 40% depending with the sector. The latter is self-explanatory as the automation of course reduces labour costs to an extent and frees up human capital for more meaningful responsibilities.

It is also evident from the literature that AI assists firms in enhancing the quality of products they offer. Real-time analysis and performance check makes it possible for the alarms to go off when the machines are straying away from optimal performance and efficiency so that they can be rectified, thus minimising defects in the final product. This is especially notable in business fields that deal with goods whose quality is intrinsically connected with compliance with industry laws as well as consumer expectations, goods like, manufacturing of automobiles or production of drugs.

Strategic impact of AI is another significant research topic examined, mostly focusing on how it changes and influences decisions. Thus, AI provides real-time data on machines' performance that allows organisations update their decisions at the operational and strategic level. Managers and executives can, therefore, use AI-generated data to evaluate the performance of its assets and predict its upcoming requirements. Analytics in turn makes managers aware of more possibilities and probabilities of the machines' functioning, thus helping in better decision-making and effective planning.

However, several challenges exist even with the tremendous benefits that can be accorded to the AI machine management. The interoperation with existing systems is identified as one of the challenges within the current literature. Most organisations use older machines or systems that cannot run AI technologies, and this calls for costs to invest in new machines or systems. Why AI-useable structures need to be created in order to effectively capitalise on AI for machine management?

Another challenge is that of technical know-how, that is more often than not only found among professionals. AI-driven systems can only be implemented and maintained using specialized knowledge, which is perhaps a talent that many organisations may not possess in adequate measures. Also represented is the data security and privacy where the literature reports a variety of concerns especially in organisations that deal with sensitive information. It is important that organisations optimise the data that are to be used by the AI systems so that there are no breaches or misuse of the information.

Machine management using AI looks to have a great future in the future with the following trends being expected to emerge. The Industrial Internet of Things (IIoT) is expected to support the progressive advancements in the AI-assisted machine management systems, through the generation of diverse data points and establishment of connections between machines. Integrating of AI and IIoT will give a rise to more sophisticated systems for the management of the machines which will be capable of diagnosing and repairing themselves.

Second, one of the many topics for the utilisation of AI is sustainability for machine management. In this way, AI-powered solutions can contribute to the process of minimising the negative effect on the environment as industries strive for lower energy costs and waste minimisation while promoting circular economy principles. AI can support sustainability objectives while at the same time increase operational efficiency for organisations.

Analysing prior research in the context of AI in machine management, it is possible to conclude about the role of AI in improving the aspects of predictive maintenance, real-time monitoring and process optimisation. Thus, by improving operation effectiveness, decreasing expenses, increasing product quality and supporting attack surface management with decision-making, machine management driven by AI is a source of significant organisational success. However, realisation of these benefits remains a subject to some key obstacles which include system integration, adequate technical knowledge and data security. The further development and the integration of new trends, including IIoT or sustainability, will also contribute to the further developments of AI techniques for machine management in the future.

AI-Driven Customer Relationship Management (CRM) Systems

Industry 4.0 can change completely due to the existence of AI where chess and Chinese checkers-like tasks which are currently stagnant might turn into interactive, real-time data analysis and problem-solving tools as well as communication channels. This change will be very advantageous to the CRM sector since AI can enhance the accuracy and effectiveness of CRM's customer-centred decision-making (Li & Xu, 2022).

Enhancing the interaction with the customer through personalising the quality of data with using the technology is one of the significant issues in the CRM. AI is attempting to approach this problem by analysing data by using more ML techniques such as Support Vector Machines (SVM). The guidelines for rule extraction from SVMs presented here for CRM applications have a three-step procedure suggested here (Farquad et al., 2014). From it, a hybrid approach would be taken and as part of this strategy. So SVM-RFE is the first step in the process because to traverse the decision tree, it helps to find the most important variables and narrows the scenarios by decreasing the amount of features. In the process that comes after this, an SVM model is trained through the use of the reduced feature set. This process is then followed by rule generation with the help of the Naive Bayes Tree (NBTree).

A work that can prove that six *case studies highlighting that* 6 76% of the consumers were at risk of churn while 93.24% stayed loyal indicates that this hybrid technique is very effective in balancing the datasets as shown by 24% stayed loyal. Since clients that are in the risk of attriting may be lost to other competitors, the rules that are developed by the system may be utilised as a mechanism for expert decision-making in the early warning system of the bank. This mixed approach yields rules that are short and easy to understand making the general decision-makers get more out of the CRM system.

Another emerging field of AI relating to consumer engagement efforts includes emotional analysis as soon as it has been merged into other fields such as predictive analytics. An example of a new system that is slightly different and involves the processing of textual reviews in order to obtain numerical suggestions is presented in Tarnowska et al. (2021). This serves to mitigate the deficit of intelligent emotional CRMs to offer logical solutions. This updated technique produces the proposals counting on the consumers' trending emotions in contrast to the prior existent systems which were powering with the numerical and textual data. For instance, the CLIRS2 system recognises the Customer's Net Promoter Score (NPS) impact by analysing the input, and it is imperative to identify that the differences among the customers are significant. To utilise the consumer input more effectively in the future, sentient mining algorithm and better guidelines for the open-ended survey questions will be adopted. However, there is something negative in the system, which is the loss of important quantitative data, and thus, the system may not be interpreting how the client feels in general very well.

Another field under study in CRM is the generative AI – the latter seeks to enhance personalisation and self-service. According to Verma and Kumari (2023), some of the AI systems could analyse the client information to develop communication strategies for the account as well as an ability to come up with automated response messages. Larger quantities of relevant goods and services are available to the customers since companies use AI insights to understand the consumer preferences leading to high customer engagement. It is already demonstrated that chatbots and virtual assistants based on AI and possessing complex algorithms for understanding the text contribute to improving the quality of customer support through the provision of fast personalised responses. Through automating various routine tasks and performing user common questions these technologies increase the organisations' service effectiveness and thus customer satisfaction. This in a way allows human agents to handle more complex call requests.

Aside from having the capability to change customer service through the use of chatbots, AI can also change the CRM systems through predictive customisation and analysis of customer feedback. With assistance of AI, businesses are able to identify patterns within the customers' behaviour, thus delivering tailored promotions or service recommendations. This enhances client-serving by demographically tailoring consumers to create a sense of being valued among customers, thus enhancing on customer satisfaction and loyalty.

AI is also driving HRM practices, especially for the small business and start-ups that have relatively less capital to invest. So to be able to predict how the employees would behave, the authors of Huy et al. (2023) recommend a method of behavioural analysis which involves uncertain reinforcement radial decision-making in combination with a quadratic kernel vector machine. This AI model can assist each human resources (HR) director to make concrete strategies for the recruitment techniques, relations between employers and employees and employment engagement with the best prediction accuracy of 98% and 89% Area Under Curve. Perhaps this strategy will be useful to the development of top people; overall, if a firm wants to maximise its personnel without having to break the bank, then this strategy could be beneficial.

Client retention is currently being transformed by AI in a way that improves service delivery and predicts consumers' habits. Angelina et al. (2023) explain how to use the CatBoost Classifier AI model, which gives a 95% efficiency rate in predicting consumers' behaviour while being more effective than standard methods. With this technology's help, companies need to achieve the increase of the client retention rates and service quality to find clients who are in danger. Then, one can build specific strategies that would help retain these customers.

In closing, it is important to note that AI has also improved the different CRM feature reduction techniques, thus improving data handling and analyses. Sadeghi et al. (2023) present principal component analysis (PCA), a new PSO-K Means algorithm that is a powerful tool for CRM systems that enable in equal optimisation, features reduction and classification. This strategy significantly enhances the predictive performance and ramp up the sensitivity to 75% and the specificity of 99%. Companies may now also more effectively target their marketing and retention strategies in areas where they can have the most effect given that the feature importance is of a much higher quality with the given reduction in dimensionality.

Explanation Table 13.1: The original data processing, behavioural analysis and customisation features of AI are becoming the main driver of change in the CRM industry. Organisations may enhance client satisfaction through the various AI tools including rule extraction hybrid ML approaches such as SVM-RFE & NBTree and the emotional analysis systems, CLIRS2. As the AI progresses further, better integration with CRM becomes essential because the new technologies will enable better customer-oriented operations, thus maintaining the organisations' competitiveness in the market.

Table 13.1. Comparative Analysis of Different Techniques Used in CRM.

Reference	Application in CRM	Technique/ Approach	Main Features	Benefits	Prediction Accuracy	Other Metrics
Li and Xu (2022)	Transformation of industries by AI	Not specified	Utilises AI for real-time communication, data analysis and problem-solving	Enhances CRM, making it more efficient	Not specified	Not specified
Farquad et al. (2014)	Rule extraction for CRM	Hybrid technique: SVM-RFE, SVM and NB Tree	Reduces feature set, creates SVM model, generates rules	Produces short-length rules, early warning system in bank management	Better performance than other methods	Imbalanced dataset: 6.76% leaving, 93.24% loyal
Tarnowska et al. (2021)	Sentiment analysis-based recommender system	Modification of CLIRS2	Provides measurable suggestions based on text feedback	Improves sentiment coverage, refines mining algorithm	Largest impact: 8.58% for Client 16	Focuses on sentiment analysis and open-ended surveys
Verma and Kumari (2023)	AI in CRM for automation and personalisation	Not specified	Evaluates consumer data, develops individualised strategies, automatic response generation	Enhances client-centricity, operational efficiency	Not specified	Insights on consumer preferences and behaviour

(Continued)

Table 13.1. *(Continued)*

Reference	Application in CRM	Technique/ Approach	Main Features	Benefits	Prediction Accuracy	Other Metrics
Huy et al. (2023)	HR management in start-ups	Behavioural pattern analysis with reinforcement radial fuzzy decision and quadratic kernel vector machine	High prediction accuracy	Improves business advantages, client retention	98% prediction accuracy	89% AUC, 83% average precision, 66% sensitivity, 59% quadratic normalised square error
Angelina et al. (2023)	Forecasting customer behaviour	Cat Boost Classifier	Surpasses existing techniques	Improves quality of service and client retention	95% prediction accuracy	Not specified
Sadeghi et al. (2023)	CRM system for customer attrition	PCA-PSO-K Means algorithm	Combines dataset feature reduction, classification and optimisation	Enhanced accuracy in forecasting customer attrition	99.77% prediction accuracy	75% sensitivity, 99.81% specificity, correlation coefficient of 0.443 ± 0.271

Source: Original work.

Objectives of the Study

In order to investigate how AI affects the effectiveness and efficiency of organisations: The purpose of this purpose is to find out whether and how AI tools such as data analytics, automation and ML enhance productivity, reduce costs and optimise output.

Seeking to understand how AI is revolutionising machine management in organisations: It must be understood how machine management systems can use AI for effective decision-making, predictive maintenance or real-time troubleshooting.

In order to weigh the pros and cons of using AI in operational contexts: This goal is to evaluate the opportunities AI (for instance, efficient decision-making, self-learning, better scalability) and threats that come with it, for example, ethical issues, data management and organisation's preparedness.

Enhancing Employee Productivity and Performance With AI

The performance of workers is being assessed through the use of an AI more often by the companies. For individuals and enterprises, this technology benefits them as it will increase the reliability and validity of the data being used in the performance review. However, there are some occasions whereby productivity reduces as a result of disclosure and use of AI. All available literature shows that there are merits and demerits of AI disclosure, but that the merits focus on the demerits based on the time that a person takes with a firm. To reduce such adverse effects, a number of measures should be implemented, such as explaining the goals and benefits of utilising AI to members of the staff. To enhance this information assurance with another layer of assurance, the AI integration should ensure consideration of the existing, longer-serving employees or new employees (Tong et al., 2021).

It is argued that there is a need to enhance the level of collaborative intelligence particularly in collaborative contexts today that most commercial enterprises incorporate AI. In the relationship between defined roles, trust, sharing of information and AI capability, the following is examined (Chowdhury et al., 2022): The three focus areas of the current research include organisational socialisation, socio-technical systems and the knowledge-based view and the intended contribution of this study is to give evidential, practical tools to the managing agency and AI scholars, that would help improve the overall organisational intelligence through integration.

It also has been established that the intensity of usage of AI is proportional to the productivity of the workers. Thus, it can be noted that the use of AI, along with AI training, in combination with organisational flexibility, has a positive impact on labour productivity, as mentioned in Nurlia et al. (2023). Employing structural equation modelling and quantitative approach, it empirically established these linkages and verified positive moderated relationships between the use of AI training, level of organisational adaption and labour productivity in organisations.

The AI technology is fundamentally driving the United Nations' SDG. The relationship between the AI adoption and SDG 8 aimed at decent work and economic growth is discussed in Braganza et al. (2021). Use of AI can alter the quality of decent employment which is not desirable when it comes to this new contract to counter everything SDG 8 is trying to achieve in employer–employee relations.

The leading Bengaluru-based network service providers such as Airtel, Vodafone, Idea, BSNL and Jio have discovered that employing AI chatbots improved the employees' efficiency (Mishra et al., 2020). In a survey with 120 employees, the research showed that chatbots help reduce the amount of repetitive questions that human employees have to respond to and therefore allows workers to focus on higher value tasks. Ignorance with techniques and compatibility with privacy were some of the drawbacks mentioned in the studies. This means that in order to mitigate the effects of these problems, both the staff and the consumers should be educated on the benefits of the chatbots.

Thanks to the AI and business intelligence the company operation and performance are experiencing revolutionary changes. From the findings, it was concluded that the application of AI by itself can only go a long way towards increasing production.

Studies have revealed that when AI and augmented reality (AR) are combined, there could be a huge potential in improving productivity in the workplace. In one research, the authors established that using AI in the workplace reduces people's job completion time by 13%, while using AR also reduces the time it takes to complete a task by 16% and they are happier overall (Rymarov et al., 2021). Integration of AI with AR that were trialed here increased the productivity by 22% indicating that the two technologies are highly synergistic.

Based on prior studies, it can be concluded that AI has a positive impact on the performance of organisations. Therefore, Liu et al.'s study shows that AI patents have a differential impact on production and employment by altering the workforce by reducing the percentage of workers without a bachelor's degree. It, however, has the following benefits of non-AI patents: Facts that are resistant to refutation demonstrate how AI is taking a very large and critical role in today's commerce.

This chapter will demonstrate that the application of AI can significantly enhance productivity and levels of satisfaction of workers in business fields and occupations. The studies show that AI may increase the productivity by 52% and with the sales leader experiencing a 50% boost (Valeriya et al., 2024). This study also explains that adoption of this technology is not universal but has different impacts, while some employees claim better job satisfaction and skills acquisition about the innovation.

AI is transforming another area that is human resource management abbreviated as HRM. In Malik et al. (2023), by and large, the impact of the AI-supported systems in HRM on both employee experience (EX) and employee engagement (EE) is elaborated. This chapter will attempt to explain the theoretical framework that lies behind AI supported HRM systems, with emphasis in the concepts of productivity enhancement, EX and EE enhancement and operational improvements in the HR area. The findings also shed light on what this implies for the next studies in addition to the clinical applications.

It is noteworthy that the total factor productivity (TFP) of companies can be boosted by using of AI. Here, we demonstrate how by disaggregating production data to the micro level, Gao and Feng (2023) reported that while investigating its operations, they learnt that there is a 14. Every 1% increase in the penetration of the AI Technology is associated with an average of 2% increase in TFP. To this effect, the research identifies several factors that may have led to this result, and these include: technology growth, skill-based improvement and value addition. This is followed by pointing out the fact that the impact of the AI is a function of companies' property rights and conditions of industrial concentration.

The IoT which stands for the Internet of Things is an example of a technology that could increase efficiency of the employees. That is why the analysis of learning orientation, problem-solving and performance assessment could be seen. Gamede and Mtotywa (2022) focus on the exploration of the potential of IoT implementation in order to optimise work processes at workplace. To support the utilisation of the IoT to the full, a three-stage model that relies on Bayesian classification was developed. This approach assists the enterprises to predict deviations and assess the impact of interventions.

Lastly, with the help of AI, MIS or management information system is changing. OP2: In MIS, there is room to experiment with AI in automating several procedures, getting predicting solutions, as well as optimising decision-making (Bhima et al., 2023). These case examples present a picture of how hard it is to integrate new AI technology within existing organisational structures safely and how ethics plays a crucial role here. A three-pronged approach was proposed in the research to tackle these issues: however, several recommendations can be put into consideration; first, symptoms related to technological challenges ought to be handled by interdisciplinary teams second, ethics ought to be incorporated into the AI systems to enhance the public trust and third, personnel should embrace training on AI use. Using these tactics will enable the firms to change the ways, in which AI, will be used for decision making. It will increase the operational effectiveness and efficiency of the organizations and will enhance its competitive advantage.

In the long run, there is an abundance of opportunities to increase organisational effectiveness and gain competitive advantage with the help of AI adoption in numerous aspects of organisational functioning, including performance evaluation, HRM, collaborative wisdom and enhanced productivity. However, when it comes to AI, these companies need to take into consideration how they are going to impact their human capital, solve any ethical dilemmas and determine how they are going to train and engage their workforce. They state that three barriers are if firms are to fully utilise AI, they will have to overcome them.

This chapter aims at exploring the innovative future of today's firms, principally in the sense of how one can introduce AI into operations and address challenges. Overall, our study establishes that there is significantly greater potential for different activities of the company, such as CRM, worker productivity and strategic planning in the long term with the help of AI. AI is especially viewed as a key resource that propels organisations in the age of digital transformation because it is capable of embedding repeater tasks, making work more efficient and providing relevant analytical information.

The report does though depict some of the challenges of implementation of AI. One of the discussed major challenges is the integration of AI into existing frameworks. In this context, many organisations have difficulties in aligning the AI capacities with their business processes in order to get as much as possible from AI. This underscores the fact that there is always a need to have some form of AI strategy that has been worked on to ensure that training and supervision take their rightful place.

The research also tries to answer another concern, which is the ethical concern. Challenges that firms have to address, if they are to retain the trust of stakeholders, include privacy, probability of bias in AI models and/or policies and transparency, respectively. Thus, the risk of developing a negative company culture or getting into problems connected with the violation of laws and damaging the reputation of the company can be minimised while the possibility of using AI for creating a useful product can be maximised if companies focus ethical consideration while using AI.

Shifting the focus of the conversation to internal contexts, it is important to state that a culture of learning and innovation needs to be created inside businesses. Employers should invest in employees so that AI technologies may help in pushing up production rather than come as a source of concern to the workers. Only then, we will be able to see how it will be able to achieve its full prowess. This means that for proper development of AI and for us to gain the maximum benefit out of use of AI then we have to pose with the machines.

Lastly, the study stresses that it is also possible that the use of AI is going to require alert, continuous monitoring and control of AI systems in the future. It is crucial to update gadgets, which are implemented in AI technologies, audit them and perform feedback to ensure that the technologies used respond adequately to the new requirements of businesses. Through timely and proper application, organisations may extinguish the possibilities of risks and enhance their possibility of growth and creativity.

In this conversation, the discussants agree that AI is very promising, but the implementation of this tool requires a lot of planning, ethical considerations as well as the careful thinking. To attain sustainable business development and apply AI effectively, organisations need to focus on its transparency, ethical implications and workers' adaptation.

Conclusion

For instance, the chapter sheds light on how AI has a potential of reshaping the trends of CRM systems, increasing labour productivity to change the trends towards sustainable development in the corporate business. That's why it emphasises the fact that AI has many benefits, but at the same time it has issues related to its implementation, its moral implications and its future prospects. It is crucial for an organisation to understand the pros and cons of AI so as to fit the technology to their advantage.

The revelation of the benefits and risks of ML is a major message from the research and the need of being open and responsible while using it is recommended. AI should be one of the strategic high priorities for companies which also foster the culture of innovation and continuous learning. As such, one needs to incorporate the ability to plan, to prepare and also put in place the right organisational environment that fosters creativity. The study thus underscores the requirement of ongoing check and ethical matters in AI applications in avoiding wayward utilisation of such innovative technologies.

The research concludes by explaining how the tech-savvy companies have optimally utilised the application of AI revealing how, if managed in the right way, more technology means more productivity and innovative ideas. This means that there is an opportunity to balance the positive impact of AI on businesses and conversely minimise the negative impact on them.

References

Angelina, J. J. R., Subhashini, S. J., Harish Baba, S., Dheeraj Kumar Reddy, P., Sudheer Kumar Reddy, P. V., & Sameer Khan, K. (2023). A machine learning model for customer churn prediction using cat boost classifier. In *7th international conference on intelligent computing and control systems (ICICCS)*. https://doi.org/10.1109/ICICCS56967.2023.10142823

Bhima, B., Rahmania Az Zahra, A., Nurtino, T., & Firli, M. Z. (2023). Enhancing organizational efficiency through the integration of artificial intelligence in management information systems. *APTISI Transactions on Management*, *7*(3), 282–289.

Braganza, A., Chen, W., Canhoto, A., & Sap, S. (2021). Productive employment and decent work: The impact of AI adoption on psychological contracts, job engagement and employee trust. *Journal of Business Research*, *131*, 485–494.

Chowdhury, S., Budhwar, P., Dey, P. K., Joel-Edgar, S., & Abadie, A. (2022). AI-employee collaboration and business performance: Integrating knowledge-based view, socio-technical systems and organisational socialisation framework. *Journal of Business Research*, *144*, 31–49.

Engel, C., Ebel, P., & van Giffen, B. (2021). Empirically exploring the cause-effect relationships of AI characteristics, project management challenges, and organizational change. *Innovation Through Information Systems: A Collection of Latest Research on Technology Issues*, *2*, 166–181.

Farquad, M. A. H., Ravi, V., & Bapi Raju, S. (2014). Churn prediction using comprehensible support vector machine: An analytical CRM application. *Applied Soft Computing*, *19*, 31–40.

Gamede, Z., & Mtotywa, M. (2022). Leveraging the Internet of Things to enhance employee productivity in operations: A conceptualization. *Expert Journal of Business and Management*, *10*(2), 102–114.

Gao, X., & Feng, H. (2023). AI-driven productivity gains: Artificial intelligence and firm productivity. *Sustainability*, *15*(11), 8934.

Holmström, J., & Hällgren, M. (2021). AI management beyond the hype: Exploring the co-constitution of AI and organizational context. *AI & Society*, *37*, 1575–1585.

Huy, P. Q., Shavkatovich, S. N., Abdul-Sama, Z., Agrawal, D. K., Ashifa, K. M., & Arumugam, M. (2023). Resource management projects in entrepreneurship and retain customer based on big data analysis and artificial intelligence. *The Journal of High Technology Management Research*, *34*(2), 100471.

Kulkov, I., Kulkova, J., Rohrbeck, R., Menvielle, Loick,, Kaartemo, V., & Makkonen, H. (2023). Artificial intelligence-driven sustainable development: Examining organizational, technical, and processing approaches to achieving global goals. *Sustainable Development*, *32*, 2253–2267.

Li, F., & Xu, G. (2022). AI-driven customer relationship management for sustainable enterprise performance. *Sustainable Energy Technologies and Assessments*, *52*, 102–103.

Lin, S., Döngül, E. S., Uygun, S. V., Öztürk, M. B., Huy, D. T. N., & Van Tuan, P. (2022). Exploring the relationship between abusive management, self-efficacy and organizational performance in the context of human–machine interaction technology and artificial intelligence with the effect of ergonomics. *Sustainability*, *14*(4), 19–49.

Malik, A., Budhwar, P., Mohan, H., & Srikanth, N. R. (2023). Employee experience – The missing link for engaging employees: Insights from an MNE's AI-based HR ecosystem. *Human Resource Management*, *62*(1), 97–115.

Mishra, N., Keerthana, K. R., & Yeshwanth Prasad, B. U. (2020). The role of chatbots in enhancing staff productivity of network service providers in Bengaluru. *IUP Journal of Organizational Behavior*, *19*(4), 7–21.

Nurlia, N., Daud, I., & Rosadi, M. E. (2023). AI Implementation impact on workforce productivity: The role of AI training and organizational adaptation. *Escalate: Economics And Business Journal*, *1*(1), 1–13.

Pumplun, L., Tauchert, C., & Heidt, M. (2019). A new organizational chassis for artificial intelligence-exploring organizational readiness factors. In *Proceedings of the 27th European conference on information systems (ECIS), Stockholm & Uppsala, Sweden, June 8-14, 2019*.

Rymarov, A., Chandramauli, A., Sharma, G., Sharma, K., & Kumar, Y. (2021). Augmented reality and AI: An experimental study of worker productivity enhancement. *Bio Web of Conferences*, *86*, 01095.

Sadeghi, M., Dehkordi, M. N., Barekatain, B., & Khani, N. (2023). Improve customer churn prediction through the proposed PCA-PSO-K means algorithm in the communication industry. *The Journal of Supercomputing*, *79*(6), 6871–6888.

Tarnowska, K. A., & Ras, Z. W. (2021). NLP-based customer loyalty improvement recommender system (clirs2). *Big Data and Cognitive Computing*, *5*(1), 4.

Tong, S., Jia, N., Luo, X., & Fang, Z. (2021). The Janus face of artificial intelligence feedback: Deployment versus disclosure effects on employee performance. *Strategic Management Journal*, *42*(9), 1600–1631.

Valeriya, G., John, V., Singla, A., Yamini Devi, J., & Kumar, K. (2024). AI-powered super-workers: An experiment in workforce productivity and satisfaction. *Bio Web of Conferences*, *86*, 01065.

Verma, R. K., & Kumari, N. (2023). Generative AI as a tool for enhancing customer relationship management automation and personalization techniques. *International Journal of Responsible Artificial Intelligence*, *13*(9), 1–8.

Chapter 14

Is Artificial Intelligence the New Vanguard? Exploring the Transformation in India's Defence Strategies

Tamasi Biswas, Bhaskarjit Roy, Debadrita Basu and Shayani Chakraborty

Adamas University, India

Abstract

The sanctity and efficacy of defence forces are paramount in a world riddled with armed rebellions, national insurgencies, international conflicts and intra-national riots. As the primary guardians of national security, these forces confront an array of challenges that demand innovative solutions. In the quest for enhanced operational efficiency and proactive threat management, the application of Artificial Intelligence (AI) in military and security intelligence emerges as a critical focal point. This study embarks on an explorative journey into the multifaceted integration of AI within India's defence mechanisms, highlighting its transformative potential in addressing contemporary security challenges. With a global military landscape increasingly inclined towards AI-driven technologies, nations like the United States, China and Russia lead the charge, showcasing significant advancements in AI applications ranging from surveillance and logistics to cyber security and autonomous combat systems. India, in its stride towards modernisation, has identified AI as a pivotal element in augmenting capabilities across various domains, including cyber threats, border security and public safety. Leveraging machine learning algorithms, the defence sector processes extensive datasets to unearth patterns, anomalies and potential threats, facilitating a proactive stance against emerging security challenges. This chapter delineates the strategic incorporation of AI in India's defence sector, examining its legislative framework and operational implications. By scrutinising the deployment of AI-enabled technologies in training, surveillance, logistics and combat systems, the study illuminates the evolving landscape of military

Security Intelligence in the Age of AI, 243–257

Published under exclusive licence by Emerald Publishing Limited
doi:10.1108/978-1-83608-156-220251014

strategies and the pivotal role of AI in fortifying India's defence capabilities against dynamic security threats.

Keywords: Artificial Intelligence; defence strategy; national security; military applications; cyber security; surveillance; autonomous combat systems; India; legislative framework; ethical considerations

Introduction

India, a nation with a population of over 1.3 billion people, has been actively exploring the integration of Artificial Intelligence (AI) into its defence strategies. The potential of AI technologies to revolutionise military operations has garnered significant attention globally. As nations strive to maintain a competitive edge, the adoption of AI has become a priority, and India is no exception. According to a report by the International Institute for Strategic Studies, global military spending reached a staggering $2.24 trillion in 2022, with the United States leading the way, accounting for 39% of the total expenditure. India's defence budget for the fiscal year 2023–2024 stands at $72.6 billion, representing 1.92% of its GDP. This substantial investment reflects India's commitment to modernising its armed forces and embracing emerging technologies like AI. In comparison, China, another major player in the region, has actively pursued the development and integration of AI in its military capabilities. According to a report by the Centre for a New American Security, China's investments in AI for military applications have increased significantly, with a focus on areas such as autonomous systems, cyber operations and decision support systems.

The strategic incorporation of AI in India's defence sector has the potential to revolutionise the country's military capabilities. By leveraging AI technologies, India can automate military activities, enhance cybersecurity defences and gain a competitive edge in future conflicts. This strategic incorporation of AI in India's defence sector is a complex and multifaceted process with significant implications. Khurshid, in his research paper, highlights the potential impact on deterrence dynamics, particularly in the context of India–Pakistan relations. The weaponisation of AI, as discussed by Burton, further underscores the need for a robust legislative framework to govern its use. Belikova in his work further emphasises the importance of a legal framework, particularly in the context of patent rights protection, to ensure that India can maintain its military superiority. These studies collectively underscore the need for a comprehensive approach to the incorporation of AI in India's defence sector, one that considers both its operational implications and the legislative framework that governs its use. India's approach to AI in national defence and security is influenced by its regional position and the need to maintain military superiority. However, the country also faces challenges in the development and deployment of AI due to technical limitations and the associated ethical and societal concerns. In the context of AI and cyber security, there is a need for legal protection and remedies for individuals in case of AI law violations, as well as strong security measures are required to prevent cyber threats. If AI mostly connected with the daily life of the human being, it must protect the relationship between the human being and society people, and there should be remedy to the peoples in case of violation of laws by AI machines.

Research Gap

In the context of AI and security intelligence in India, there is a research gap regarding the development of legal policy frameworks that effectively address the multitude of ethical and privacy concerns associated with AI technologies. While AI technologies have the potential to revolutionise various sectors, including security intelligence, there is a need to ensure that these advancements adhere to legal and ethical standards. Existing research has primarily focused on the technical aspects of AI and its applications in security intelligence, but there is a lack of comprehensive studies examining the legal implications and policy considerations in this domain. To address this research gap, this study would like to explore the legal and policy challenges associated with AI in security intelligence in India. This research strives to include an evaluation of existing legal frameworks and policy instruments in India, their adequacy in addressing AI-related issues and the potential gaps or ambiguities that may exist. Additionally, we would further delve into the ethical considerations surrounding AI in security intelligence, such as privacy concerns, bias in algorithmic decision-making and the impact on human rights. Furthermore, the study investigates the role of government and relevant organisations in providing support for the development and implementation of AI technologies in security intelligence (World Bank, 2022).

Research Question

The study would like to analyse the given areas:

- Whether the current state of AI adoption in India's defence sector can meet the standard of defence as compared to other major military powers?
- Whether India is leveraging AI technologies in areas such as intelligence gathering, surveillance and reconnaissance?
- Whether there are enough ethical and legal implications of AI integration in India's defence strategies in comparison to international norms and guidelines?

AI Implementation in Defence Sector

The Indian military sector is increasingly integrating AI into its defence strategies, with a focus on human detection and auto-targeting. Pachlegaonkar Abhishek has talked about a machine that will identify a human body using Machine Vision and will shoot in just no time, and this unit is especially designed for Special Police forces and Border Security Forces. However, the militarisation of AI in the region, particularly in India, China and Pakistan, raises concerns about strategic stability. It is often argued that the prospects of an AI arms control framework in South Asia are unpromising, and the progress made by China, Pakistan and India in the realm of military AI is not in par with the rising standards of other nations. The development and use of AI in defence, while offering revolutionary possibilities, also pose significant challenges, including the potential for nuclear conflict. AI and its applications represent a genuine revolution in managing future wars and pose a serious threat to strategic stability. To address these challenges, there is a need for the Indian military to invest in AI-based defence technology that supports real-time decision-making and enhances future defence capabilities. The special issue studied by Nathaniel D. Bastian is composed of six papers that promote an understanding of AI for defence applications, as well as providing awareness into some of the state-of-the art research and development activities in AI that are applicable to defence applications spanning fraud detection for national security, computer vision for satellite imagery analysis, hidden Markov modelling for the maritime domain, deep learning for radio frequency systems, representation learning for militarily relevant graphs and robot swarms for military reconnaissance and surveillance. However, the Indian military sector is increasingly focusing on the implementation of AI in defence, with a particular emphasis on military applications, human resource management system, decision-making, disaster prevention and response, geographical information system, service personalisation, interoperability, extensive data analysis, anomaly and pattern recognition, intrusion detection and new solution discovery. This usage of AI applications in the military in civil defence is hereby in discussion, and AI has potential benefits in military applications. Moreover, the integration of advanced AI technologies, such as facial recognition and biometric authentication, enhances physical security measures, aiding in the identification and tracking of individuals (Fig. 14.1). The global expenditure on AI underscores the technology's critical role in the contemporary security apparatus, with investments expected to surge exponentially.

Current Legislation Related to AI in Defence

According to a report by the Stockholm International Peace Research Institute, India ranked third in global military expenditure, accounting for 3.6% of the total spending. However, the report also highlighted India's relatively low investments in research and development compared to other nations like the United States and China. With the increasing prominence of AI in defence, it is important to examine the current legislation and policies governing its use at both international and national levels. Several countries have introduced legislation or guidelines to regulate the development and use of AI in the defence sector. The National Defense Authorization Act for Fiscal Year 2019 established the National Security Commission on AI to review the methods and means necessary to advance the development of AI for national security and defence purposes. The Department of Defence (DoD) has released various AI strategy documents, including the "DoD Artificial Intelligence Strategy" (2019) and the "Ethical Principles for Artificial

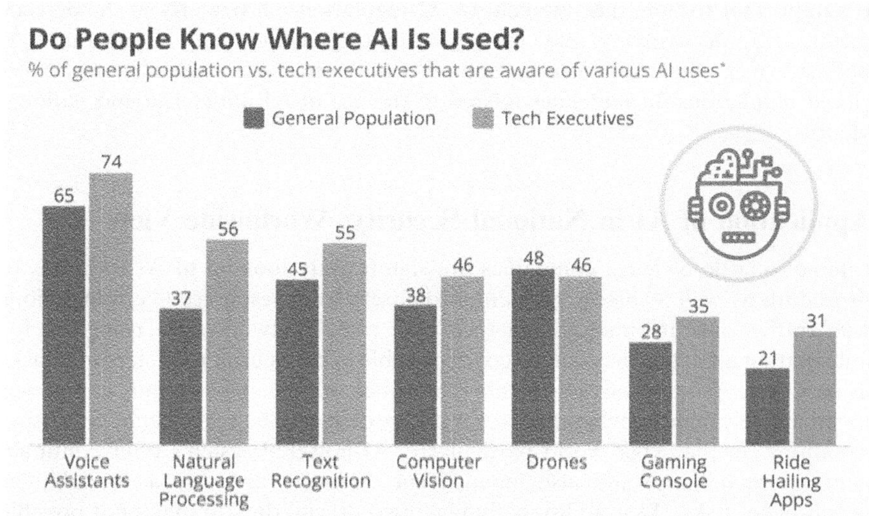

Fig. 14.1. Awareness Rate of AI Inclusivity In Daily Life. *Source:* https://www.statista.com/chart/17383/artificial-intelligence-use/

Intelligence" (2020), which outline principles and guidelines for the responsible development and use of AI in defence. The legislation and guidelines aim to promote the development and ethical use of AI in national security and defence while addressing potential risks and challenges.

The European Commission proposed the AI Act in April 2021, which aims to regulate the development, deployment and use of AI systems within the EU. It classifies AI systems based on their level of risk and imposes specific requirements and obligations for high-risk AI systems, including those used in defence and military applications. The proposed legislation aims to establish a harmonised regulatory framework for AI systems within the EU, with specific provisions for high-risk AI applications in the defence and military sectors.

The UK Ministry of Defence has developed the "Joint Concept Note: Human-Machine Teaming" which outlines principles and guidelines for the responsible development and use of AI systems in defence operations. The concept note provides a framework for the integration of AI systems and human personnel in defence operations, emphasising ethical considerations and human–machine teaming.

India does not currently have specific legislation dedicated to the regulation of AI in defence. However, the National Strategy for AI outlines the governance framework and ethical principles for the development and use of AI across various sectors, including defence. While India does not have dedicated legislation for AI in defence, the National Strategy for AI provides a broad framework for the governance and ethical use of AI, which can be applied to the defence sector.

It's important to note that the field of AI regulation, particularly in the defence sector, is rapidly evolving, and new legislation or guidelines may be introduced or updated over time. Additionally, some countries may have classified or undisclosed regulations or guidelines related to the use of AI in defence and national security.

Application of AI in National Security: Worldwide View

International knowledge companies are significantly looking to AI formulas to procedure as well as assess substantial datasets from resources like interactions web traffic, satellite images, together with social networks. By using AI for anticipating analytics they can discover possible cybersecurity risks, terrorist tasks as well as geopolitical advancements in advance of time. This permits companies to proactively hinder cyberattacks, stop acts of fear plus react better to arising situations. In the cyber world particularly, AI-powered systems offer continual network surveillance and also independent discovery and also action abilities versus cyber risks. AI is additionally playing a crucial duty in making it possible for better freedom for unmanned systems like airborne drones (International Institute for Strategic Studies, 2023). AI-driven independent control permits these unmanned airborne cars (UAVs) to carry out essential goals like security, knowledge and also battle procedures with decreased human guidance, boosting effectiveness while reducing threats to workers. Police is taking advantage of AI-enabled face acknowledgement modern technology that can quickly recognise suspects by contrasting photos versus watch lists in real time. Furthermore, AI formulas are being made use of to anticipate criminal hotspots, permitting authorities firms to enhance source appropriation tactically.

Application of AI in Defence

The DOD is proactively discovering a variety of applications for expert system (AI) modern technology. While study as well as growth initiatives in AI are presently delegated the discernment of specific solution branches, companies like the Defense Advanced Research Projects Agency (DARPA), as well as the Intelligence Advanced Research Projects Agency (IARPA), the Office of the Assistant Secretary of Defense for Research as well as Engineering (ASD/RE) keep a wide oversight duty. The ASD/RE remains in the procedure of establishing an extensive DOD AI Strategy, anticipated to be launched in the summer season of 2018. As opposed to watching the diverse strategies to AI research study as a constraint, the ASD/RE considers this variety of initiatives a toughness in the short term, despite some inescapable replication of job. At the same time, the Algorithmic Warfare Cross-Functional Team, additionally called Project Maven, acts as a centrepiece for incorporating AI abilities throughout the DOD. Launched in April 2017, Project Maven is managed by the Undersecretary of Defence for Intelligence (USDI) together with tasked with rapidly including AI right into existing DOD systems to show the innovation's capacity. According to the Project Maven Director, 'Maven is developed to be that pilot job, that forerunner that trigger that stirs up the fire for expert system throughout the division.' While Project Maven's prompt emphasis gets on knowledge handling, the myriad of AI jobs underway throughout the DOD highlights the flexible along with typical nature of this innovation throughout numerous protection applications (Ministry of Defence & Government of India, 2023).

Examination, Monitoring, Plus Knowledge

The knowledge area sees substantial capacity for taking advantage of expert system (AI) capacities to improve knowledge, monitoring along with reconnaissance (ISR) procedures offered the large information establishes readily available for evaluation. Project Maven, led by the Algorithmic Warfare Cross-Functional Team, exemplifies this initiative.

In its first stage Project Maven intends to automate knowledge handling to sustain counter-ISIL procedures. This entails integrating computer system vision together with AI formulas right into knowledge collection cells to immediately recognise aggressive tasks from another location piloted aeroplane (RPA) video footage. The objective is to relieve human experts from the tiresome job of by hand filtering with hrs of video clip for workable info, allowing much more reliable as well as prompt decision-making based upon the examined information. Project Maven has actually currently incorporated these AI devices right into 10 websites with strategies to broaden to 30 websites by mid-2018. Past Project Maven, the knowledge area has countless openly revealed AI research study tasks underway (Center for a New American Security, 2021). The Central Intelligence Agency (CIA) has 137 jobs leveraging AI for jobs like photo acknowledgement, classifying plus anticipating future occasions such as terrorist strikes or public agitation by evaluating public details. The Intelligence Advanced Research Projects Agency (IARPA) is funding numerous AI research study programmes focused on generating substantial devices within 4–5 years. These consist of creating formulas for multilingual speech acknowledgement coupled with translation in loud atmospheres, geolocating photos without metadata integrating 2D photos right into 3D versions as well as inferring a structure's feature based upon pattern of life evaluation.

Military Logistics

The armed force is checking out encouraging applications of fabricated knowledge (AI) in the world of logistics with the prospective to dramatically boost effectiveness as well as cost-effectiveness. One significant location is anticipating upkeep for aeroplane fleets. The Air Force is servicing making use of AI to allow customised, anticipating upkeep for private aeroplane based upon real-time information from on board sensing units as well as systems. Instead of sticking to set up upkeep procedures developed for whole fleets, this strategy would certainly enable professionals to execute upkeep on an as-needed basis for each and every aeroplane. The AI formulas would certainly assess the sensing unit information to forecast when certain elements or systems need examination or substitute maximising upkeep initiatives (Das & Sandhane, 2021).

This predictive maintenance approach has already yielded successful outcomes in the commercial aviation sector. Trigger Cognition an AI firm based in Texas executed such a system on numerous Boeing aeroplane. In one circumstance, the formula properly anticipated that an engine would certainly call for substitute within 40 hrs of procedure well in advance of the arranged upkeep timeline. Upon examination, a damaged follower blade was found possibly protecting against a $ 50 million engine substitute price. The US Army is additionally proactively checking out AI applications in logistics with cooperation with innovation titans like IBM. In September 2017, the Army Logistics Support Activity (LOGSA) authorised a $ 135 million agreements with IBM for an AI evidence of idea. Improving a previous task where IBM's Watson AI system enhanced upkeep for the Stryker car fleet the present job intends to take advantage of AI to examine delivery moves for repair service components circulation, recognising one of the most time-plus cost-efficient methods of distribution. The Army approximates that this AI system can possibly conserve approximately $ 100 million each year after examining simply 10% of delivery demands. These instances display the tremendous capacity of AI in army logistics together with the harmonies in between business and also armed forces AI applications, highlighting the practically straight link in between both domain names (Khurshid, 2023).

Command Plus Control

The US armed forces identify the enormous logical possibility of expert system (AI) together with is proactively seeking its combination right into command-and-control systems. An essential effort in this domain name is the Air Force's Multi-Domain Command and Control (MDC2) programme. MDC2 intends to settle the preparation as well as implementation of procedures throughout several domain names, consisting of air, room, cyber area, sea as well as land. In the future, AI is visualised to play a critical duty in integrating information from numerous sensing units together with systems throughout these domain names to produce an unified, real-time "typical operating image" for decision-makers.

Presently, decision-makers commonly battle with varied info styles from numerous resources possibly including redundancies or unsettled disparities. AI-enabled information combination would certainly settle this info right into a solitary, user-friendly display screen giving an extensive sight of pleasant along with adversary pressures while instantly settling any type of differences or variances in the input information. As AI systems grow in intricacy, their function in command plus control is anticipated to broaden better. AI formulas can possibly recognise cut interaction web links and also recommend alternate ways of details circulation (Burton & Soare, 2019). Additionally, these formulas might assess real-time battlespace information to suggest sensible strategies making it possible for commanders to adjust quicker to unravelling occasions. While MDC2 is still in the principal growth stage, the Air Force is working together with significant protection service providers like Lockheed Martin, Harris, coupled with a number of AI start-ups to create the visualised information combination capacity. A collection of wargames scheduled for 2018 intends to improve the needs for this project. Technology experts have assisted in preparation of various AI-enabled command with controlled systems which will likely have a profound effect on future warfare possibly boosting the high quality of decision-making and also increasing the speed of dispute procedures (Belikova, 2021).

Deadly Autonomous Weapon System

The advancement of dangerous independent tool systems (LAWS) efficient in individually recognising, involving together with damaging targets without human treatment is a very questionable as well as morally intricate concern that the US armed force is grappling with. Presently, the DOD has forever postponed the advancement of LAWS on ethical premises, as codified in existing regulative constraints. Particularly, DOD Directive 3000.09 "Autonomy in Weapon Systems" requires that independent systems should "permit leaders as well as drivers to work out ideal degrees of human judgement over using pressure." While this directive permits human-monitored autonomous systems for protective functions, such as involving non-human targets, as well as licences using independent systems for non-lethal, non-kinetic activities like digital assault it properly forbids the advancement of totally independent offending tool systems that do not have human control (Marda, 2018). The discussion bordering LAWS growth is diverse. On one hand, there are problems concerning giving in harmful decision-making to makers plus the possible moral ramifications of such systems. In 2017 testament, General Paul Selva, the Vice Chairman of the Joint Chiefs of Staff, verified the restriction on LAWS, specifying, "I do not believe it is affordable for us to place robotics in charge of whether we take a human life." On the other hand there are several critical factors to consider regarding prospective foes creating LAWS while the US discards this innovation possibly giving up an essential army benefit. General Selva recognised that the armed force would certainly require to research LAWS growth by possible opponents to comprehend susceptibilities. Eventually, the advancement of LAWS continues to be a morally complicated concern that needs cautious factor to consider of ethical concepts, critical ramifications as well as the possible threats plus advantages of such systems (Choudhary, 2024).

International Perspective of Using of AI in National Security as Well as Security Intelligence

The growth of expert system (AI) for protection applications has actually ended up being an expanding worry for Congress and also the protection area especially in the context of global competitors. There are installing worries that ceding management in AI growth to adversarial countries like China and also Russia might place the United States at a substantial technical drawback as well as position major ramifications for nationwide safety and security. This problem has actually been highlighted by famous numbers such as Senator Ted Cruz that advised concerning the threats of permitting international federal governments to exceed the United States in AI abilities throughout a Senate hearing labelled "The Dawn of AI." AI has actually additionally been constantly included as an "Emerging together with Disruptive Technology" in the yearly "Worldwide Threat Assessment" hearings held by the Senate Select Intelligence Committee over the previous 2 years. In his 2017 statement, the previous Director of National Intelligence Daniel Coats highlighted the possibly extensive together with extensive ramifications of enemies utilising AI abilities, emphasising the requirement for the United States to keep a one-upmanship in this domain name. These problems show the expanding acknowledgement within the federal government coupled with protection circles concerning the calculated value of AI growth and also the necessary to preserve technical prevalence over competing countries.

China

China has actually become an awesome rival to the United States in the race for expert system (AI) pre-eminence with substantial effects for the army domain name. The Chinese federal government has actually recognised AI as a "critical modern technology" that is a centrepiece of global competition as well as has actually revealed an enthusiastic strategy to accomplish world-leading degrees of AI financial investment by 2030, backed by over $150 billion in state financing. China's expertise in artificial intelligence is demonstrated by several recent achievements. Some reputed citations are Baidu's growth of language acknowledgment software programme that went beyond human degrees almost a year prior to its closest US rival, and also Chinese groups constantly winning leading honors in respected global computer system vision competitors. Showing the US strategy, China's armed forces AI growth focuses on leveraging AI for boosted decision-making, battlespace recognition, as well as independent systems throughout air, land, sea along with undersea domain names. Nevertheless, China possibly deals with less obstacles in transitioning business AI advancements to armed forces applications because of the lack of inflexible civil-military borders that exist in the United States. The Chinese federal government has actually taken positive actions to speed up these innovation transfer, developing a specialised Military-Civil Fusion Development Commission in 2017. Moreover, China's usage of AI applications in present days and contemporary experience can cultivate a lot more ingenious reasoning in army AI applications as the US shows up concentrated on step-by-step, calculated enhancements. Better, China appears much less strained by the moral disputes bordering independent harmful tool systems that have actually postponed development in the United States. Matching these benefits, China is quickly collecting huge information repositories predicted to have more than 30% of international information by 2030, which will certainly show important for training AI systems. Drawing inference to the facts and figures extracted, China has actually shown remarkable progression in AI, along with the nation is also installing a combined nationwide initiative possibly unencumbered by the restrictions encountered by the United States, to achieve international culinary in army AI abilities (Abhishek, 2015).

Chinese Investment in AI Companies

Russia

While Russia's complete AI financial investment lags behind the United States plus China, it is taking actions to enclose the void as component of a more comprehensive protection innovation initiative. Details Russian campaigns consist of:

- Setting an objective for 30% of armed forces tools to be robotic/autonomous by 2025.
- Establishing a protection research study company devoted to freedom as well as robotics comparable to DARPA.
- Actively researching independent cars, robots as well as crowding capacities with an emphasis on unmanned ground as well as airborne systems that can possibly be warehoused.
- Exploring AI for knowledge applications like security, reconnaissance as well as publicity.

Nevertheless, Russia encounters some considerable obstacles contrasted to its opponents:

- A decreasing protection spending plan with forecasted cuts in upcoming years.
- A reasonably low-tech market that might battle to create cutting-edge AI on par with the United States coupled with China.
- Potential appointments within the armed forces concerning relying on AI for essential field of battle choices.

Despite these obstacles, experts advise Russia might attempt to get a benefit by Boldy going after growth of harmful independent tools systems (LAWS) prior to its competitors – a location the United States has actually presently eliminated on moral premises. While Russia appears to identify AI as a tactical concern, its capacity to complete lasting with the sources as well as economic sector AI abilities of the United States plus China continues to be unpredictable. However, it is proactively developing independent army abilities that can be turbulent in the near term.

Law in AI and Defence Security Intelligence

The rapid advancements in AI technologies have opened up new frontiers in various domains, including military and defence security intelligence. However, the use of AI in these sensitive areas has raised significant legal and ethical concerns, prompting governments worldwide to explore regulatory frameworks to govern its development and deployment. In India, the integration of AI in military and defence operations is still in its nascent stages. The Ministry of Defence has established the Centre for AI and Robotics (CAIR) to spearhead research and development in these areas. However, the country currently lacks a comprehensive legal framework specifically addressing the use of AI in military and defence operations. Internationally, several nations have taken steps to address the legal implications of AI in military and defence contexts. The United States, for instance, has established the AI and Emerging Technology Initiatives (AIET) within the DoD to oversee the responsible development and deployment of AI technologies. The European Union has proposed the AI Act, which aims to establish a legal framework for the development, deployment, and use of AI systems, including those used for military and defence purposes.

One of the key legal concerns surrounding the use of AI in military and defence operations is the issue of accountability and responsibility. AI systems are designed to make decisions autonomously, raising questions about who should be held responsible for any potential errors, unintended consequences or violations of international laws and norms. Additionally, the use of AI in military operations may heighten the risk of escalating conflicts or undermining human control over critical decisions (Rafiq, 2021).

Another significant legal challenge is the potential for AI systems to be used for surveillance, data collection and profiling, which could infringe upon individual privacy and civil liberties. There are also concerns about the potential for AI systems to perpetuate biases and discriminatory practices, particularly in the context of targeted military operations or intelligence gathering.

To address these challenges, legal experts and policymakers have proposed various frameworks and guidelines. One approach is to establish clear rules and standards for the development, testing and deployment of AI systems in military and defence contexts, ensuring compliance with international laws and norms. Another approach is to promote transparency and accountability through measures such as algorithmic auditing, independent oversight and public disclosure of AI system development and deployment.

Therefore, as AI technologies continue to advance, it is imperative for governments and international organisations to collaborate in developing comprehensive legal frameworks that strike a balance between harnessing the potential of AI for military and defence purposes while safeguarding human rights, promoting accountability and ensuring compliance with international laws and norms.

Adaptation of Implementation in Various Countries vis-a-vis India

AI has revolutionised various sectors, including the military and defence industries. As AI continues to advance, countries worldwide are grappling with the challenges of regulating its development and implementation. The integration of AI in military operations raises ethical concerns, such as the potential for autonomous weapons systems and the risk of unintended consequences.

To address these issues, countries like the United States have established the National Security Commission on AI (NSCAI) to advise the government on AI policy and strategy. The NSCAI has recommended ethical guidelines, including human control over AI systems and the development of robust testing and evaluation frameworks. Similarly, the European Union (EU) has proposed the AI Act, a comprehensive regulatory framework for AI systems. The Act classifies AI systems based on their risk levels and sets guidelines for high-risk AI applications, including those used in military and defence domains. The Act emphasises the principles of transparency, accountability and human oversight, which are crucial for ensuring the responsible use of AI in sensitive sectors (Ali et al., 2023).

In India, the Ministry of Defence has established the Defence AI Council (DAC) to provide strategic guidance and promote the development of AI in the defence sector. The DAC has emphasised the need for data governance frameworks, ethical guidelines and capacity building to ensure the responsible adoption of AI in military operations. One policy suggestion for India could be to establish a dedicated commission or task force, similar to the NSCAI or the EU's High-Level Expert Group on AI, to develop comprehensive guidelines and recommendations for AI in the defence sector. This commission could collaborate with international bodies, such as the United Nations Institute for Disarmament Research (UNIDIR), to align Indian policies with global best practices. Moreover, India could consider implementing a regulatory framework akin to the EU's AI Act, tailored to the country's specific needs and priorities. This framework could define risk levels for different AI applications in the defence sector and establish guidelines for testing, validation and human oversight. Capacity building and collaboration with academia and the private sector are also crucial for effective policy implementation. India could establish research centres and encourage public–private partnerships to foster the responsible development of AI technologies for defence applications.

Thus, the integration of AI in military and defence operations necessitates robust policy frameworks, ethical guidelines and regulatory measures. By drawing insights from other countries and international organisations, India can develop comprehensive strategies for the responsible adoption of AI in the defence sector, ensuring national security while upholding ethical principles and accountability (Lee et al., 2021).

Conclusion and Suggestions

The integration of AI in India's defence strategies has the potential to revolutionise military operations and enhance national security capabilities. However, it also raises significant ethical and legal concerns that must be carefully considered and addressed.

In comparison to other nations, the development and deployment of AI-enabled military systems have sparked debates and calls for the establishment of international norms and guidelines. The United States, for instance, has released ethical principles for the responsible use of AI in the DoD. Similarly, the

European Union has proposed a comprehensive framework for regulating AI systems, including those used for military purposes.

India, recognising the importance of ethical and legal considerations, has taken steps to ensure the responsible development and use of AI in its defence sector. The Ministry of Defence has established an AI-specific project to address these issues. However, there is a need for more comprehensive guidelines and regulatory frameworks to align with international best practices.

The ethical and legal implications of AI integration in India's defence strategies are multifaceted and require careful consideration. Key concerns include the potential for AI systems to violate human rights, the risk of bias and discrimination, the accountability and transparency of AI-enabled decision-making processes and the potential for AI to be used for malicious purposes. While India has taken initial steps to address these issues, there is a need for more comprehensive guidelines and regulatory frameworks aligned with international norms and best practices. India can learn from the approaches taken by nations like the United States and the European Union, while also contributing to the global dialogue on the responsible development and use of AI in the defence sector. So hereunder, the researcher poses certain suggestions towards taking a step in national defence integration which will further ensure a better approach of sustaining attacks from enemy nations:

- Establishment of a national AI ethics committee or advisory board to develop guidelines and oversee the implementation of ethical principles in the defence sector.
- Collaboration with international organisations, such as the United Nations, to promote the development of global norms and standards for the responsible use of AI in military applications.
- Investment and channelisation of Investment in proper research and development, focused on ensuring the transparency, accountability and fairness of AI systems used in defence applications.
- Fostering dialogue and knowledge-sharing with allied nations and multinational organisations to align AI governance strategies and promote global cooperation.
- Implementation of robust cybersecurity measures and data protection protocols to mitigate the risks associated with AI systems and ensure the responsible handling of sensitive data.

References

Abhishek, P. (2015). Artificial intelligence based human detection and auto target knocking over android. *International Journal of Science, Technology & Management*, *4*, 310–315.

Ali, A., Farid, Z., Hani Al-kassem, A., Ahmad khan, Z., Qamer, M., Farid Khan Ghouri, K., Al Sakhnani, M., & Momani, A. M. (2023). Development and use of artificial intelligence in the defense sector. In *2023 international conference on business analytics for technology and security (ICBATS)* (pp. 1–10). https://doi.org/10.1109/ICBATS57792.2023.10111113

Belikova, K. (2021). *Legal framework for the use of artificial intelligence in India's military sphere in the context of patent rights protection.* Laplage Em Revista.

Burton, J., & Soare, S. R. (2019). Understanding the strategic implications of the weaponization of artificial intelligence. *2019 11th International Conference on Cyber Conflict (CyCon)*, *900*, 1–17.

Center for a New American Security. (2021). Artificial intelligence and national security. https://www.cnas.org/publications/reports/artificial-intelligence-and-national-security

Choudhary, D. S. (2024). AI and cyber security with reference to information technology act, 2000 and other laws in India. *International Journal for Research in Applied Science and Engineering Technology*. https://doi.org/10.22214/ijraset.2024.58030

Das, R., & Sandhane, R. (2021, July). Artificial intelligence in cyber security. In *Journal of Physics: Conference Series* (Vol. 1964, p. 042072). IOP Publishing.

International Institute for Strategic Studies. (2023). *The military balance 2023.* Routledge.

Khurshid, T. (2023). The impact of artificial intelligence militarization on South Asian deterrence dynamics. *BTTN Journal.* https://doi.org/10.61732/bj.v2i2.76

Lee, C. E., Son, J. H., Park, H. S., Lee, S. Y., Park, S. J., & Lee, Y. T. (2021). Technical trends of AI military staff to support decision-making of commanders. *Electronics and Telecommunications Trends*, *36*(1), 89–98.

Marda, V. (2018). Artificial intelligence policy in India: A framework for engaging the limits of data-driven decision-making. *Philosophical Transactions of the Royal Society A: Mathematical, Physical and Engineering Sciences*, *376*. https://doi.org/10.1098/rsta.2018.0087

Ministry of Defence, Government of India. (2023). Union budget 2023-24. https://www.mod.gov.in/sites/default/files/Budget2023.pdf

Rafiq, A. (2021). Militarisation of artificial intelligence and future of arms control in South Asia. *Strategic Studies*, *41*, 49–63.

World Bank. (2022). Population, total – India. https://data.worldbank.org/indicator/SP.POP.TOTL?locations=IN

Chapter 15

Role of Artificial Intelligence in Gamification in the Era of Security Intelligence: A Bibliometric Analysis

Archana Singh[a], *Girish Lakhera*[a], *Megha ojha*[a] *and Amar Kumar Mishra*[b]

[a]Graphic Era Deemed to Be University, India
[b]Adamas University, India

Abstract

In response to the enhancing utilisation of AI technologies and the field's present state, this study aims to explore AI's impact on gamification in the era of security intelligence. Through a systematic review using bibliometric methods, data mining and analytics, a total of 42 publications were examined. The study reveals a consistent growth in research on AI in gamification in the era of security intelligence, particularly in recent years, with USA, India and Malaysia in this field. The primary contributors to this research area are journals of *ACM International Conference Proceeding Series*, followed by *IEEE Global Engineering Education Conference, EDUCON*. The findings also highlight crucial research gaps, underscoring the need for further investigations. This knowledge can inform the development of strategic approaches to tackle challenges and leverage opportunities related to gamification. Ultimately, the study aims to provide insights for policy-making that support the advancement of gamification in security intelligence.

Keywords: Artificial intelligence; online learning; gamification; bibliometric; security intelligence

Security Intelligence in the Age of AI, 259–265

doi:10.1108/978-1-83608-156-220251015

Introduction

At present, we stand at the threshold of a fourth industrial revolution that is poised to bring about profound transformations in our modes of communication, employment and daily existence. The potential and benefits offered by artificial intelligence (AI) are staggering, surpassing our current comprehension in security intelligence. We are steadily approaching a future driven by data and understanding, making it crucial to examine the correlation between AI and gamification to effectively harness the potential of AI (Ērgle & Ludviga, 2018). AI has emerged as a critical enabler of innovation in a number of fields, including education and security intelligence, in the quickly changing digital landscape. The use of AI in gamification – the application of game design concepts to non-gaming situations with the goal of improving user engagement and learning outcomes – is one such trend. In the age of security intelligence, AI plays a particularly significant role in gamification since it can tailor user experiences, improve learning pathways and improve training simulations to better prepare people for cybersecurity issues (Kapoor, 2022; Smith & Doe, 2021). AI-driven gamification solutions use data analytics and machine learning algorithms to adjust to user preferences and behaviours, offering personalised challenges and immediate feedback (Chen et al., 2023). Deeper engagement is encouraged by this dynamic approach, which improves the effectiveness of training and learning procedures while also making them more engaging. AI-driven gamified systems can assist professionals in staying ahead of developing threats in the high-stakes field of security intelligence by continuously improving their abilities through simulated attack scenarios and problem-solving exercises (Jones & Brown, 2020). AI-driven gamification solutions use data analytics and machine learning algorithms to adjust to user preferences and behaviours, offering personalised challenges and immediate feedback (Chen et al., 2023). Deeper engagement is encouraged by this dynamic approach, which improves the effectiveness of training and learning procedures while also making them more engaging. AI-driven gamified systems can assist professionals in staying ahead of developing threats in the high-stakes field of security intelligence by continuously improving their abilities through simulated attack scenarios and problem-solving exercises (Jones & Brown, 2020).

The utilisation of AI has emerged as a powerful tool to enhance the effectiveness of gamification. Incorporating AI into games can make them more dynamic and responsive to players' preferences and skill levels (Gimson, 2012). This, in turn, leads to more engaging and personalised gaming experiences. AI can also contribute to more immersive gameplay by creating intelligent non-player characters (NPCs) that interact realistically with players. Furthermore, AI can optimise the educational potential of games by adapting to players' learning preferences and other factors. This paper aims to explore the diverse ways in which AI can be applied in gamification and the potential advantages it offers in security intelligence (Wang & Zhang, 2019).

Gamification, as defined by refers to the application of game elements and mechanics in non-gaming contexts, particularly within enterprises or training institutions. Its primary objective is to enhance the attractiveness and enjoyment of routine tasks (Luckin et al., 2016). Over the past few years, gamification has gained prominence in the business and marketing sectors, drawing attention from scholars, educators and professionals alike. Researchers and practitioners believe that gamification can be implemented in various employee-involved processes.

Gamification extends beyond mere gameplay. As stated by games construct a fictional realm separate from reality, while gamification incorporates game elements into real-life situations (Mollick & Rothbard, 2014). These game elements, which surpass the conventional game structure, encourage individuals to act and derive enjoyment, thereby boosting engagement and motivation among participants. The rising popularity of gamification in the marketing and business sectors has captured the interest of both scholars and practitioners. Experts assert that gamification can be employed across a range of processes, including employee training.

The emergence of gamification in diverse non-gaming domains has captured the interest of both researchers and practitioners. The potential of gamification to improve the quality-of-life stems from its ability to provide users with captivating and enjoyable experiences while helping them achieve specific objectives (Sarangi & Shah, 2015).The widespread attention garnered by gamification extends to various fields, including education, employment and online communities. Prominent organisations like Google and L'Oréal have also embraced gamification as part of their strategies (Wang & Zhang, 2019). A thorough examination delves into the essential components necessary for the implementation of a gamification process while providing valuable perspectives on the potential outcomes when a strong gamification framework is applied within an organisation. In conclusion, we highlight the present status of gamification, the implementation of AI on gamification and the importance of incorporating gamification into a modern business model to comprehend its effectiveness in specific operational domains.

The purpose of this research is to investigate how AI can be included into gamification frameworks, with a focus on security intelligence. It looks at how gamification powered by AI may improve cybersecurity training and education by offering interactive, personalised and adaptable settings. While addressing the ethical issues surrounding AI, such as data privacy and behavioural manipulation, this study also looks into the potential advantages, such as increased engagement and skill development (Jones & Brown, 2020; Kapoor, 2022). The goal of the research is to determine how well AI-enhanced gamified systems prepare people and organisations for actual security threats by examining case studies and previous research. Additionally, it seeks to offer recommendations for how these technologies should be used while maintaining an ethical standard of care and innovation (Lee, 2023; Smith & Doe, 2021).

This study offers significant contributions in several areas. In the beginning, it offers storyboards as a tool to support upcoming studies on the effects of AI in gamification. Second, it examines the main benefits and issues related to gamification as seen by employees and leaders in organisations and gamification. The paper also offers practical implications for AI-based system design in gamification, highlighting the significance of explainability, human-in-the-loop strategies and thorough data gathering and presentation tactics.

The main goal of this study is to examine the existing research on the application of AI in the context of gamification, which is motivated by improvements in AI technology.

Methods

A bibliometric analysis seeks to address specific inquiries through the application of an explicit, systematic and replicable search strategy. This process involves identifying relevant studies, synthesising data and analysing trends in the number of articles published each year, among other factors. The data from the included studies are then the focus of this study is to examine the literature on the use of AI in gamification over the past 11 years, starting from 2013. The study's objectives are to address the following inquiries: Which entities, such as research institutes, universities, countries, regions and research communities, are the main contributors to AI research in gamification in security intelligence? Additionally, what is the intellectual, conceptual and social framework of research on AI in gamification in security intelligence? How has research on AI in gamification evolved in security intelligence? The synthesised bibliometric analysis data is presented, which offers a descriptive overview of research on AI in gamification in security intelligence. extracted and coded to synthesise the findings and highlight their practical applications, as well as any gaps or inconsistencies. In this study, 31 articles about AI in gamification are mapped to provide insight into the topic.

Results

Data Synthesis

The focus of this study is to examine the literature on the use of AI in gamification over the past 11 years, starting from 2013. The study's objectives are to address the following inquiries: Which entities, such as research institutes, universities, countries, regions and research communities, are the main contributors to AI research gamification in security intelligence? Additionally, what is the intellectual, conceptual and social framework of research on AI in E-Learning? How has research on AI in gamification evolved? The synthesised bibliometric analysis data is presented, which offers a descriptive overview of research on AI in gamification in security intelligence.

The Patterns of Article Publication Over Time

The distribution of documents related to AI in gamification over 11 years (2013–2024). The trend reveals that 2024 witnessed the highest level of activity, with 11 documents being produced, closely followed by 10 articles published in 2023. It is important to consider that the figures for 2024 provided are based on publications within the first nine months of the year, and it is anticipated that the number will likely rise by the end of the year. While the research on AI in gamification is garnering attention, there was a notable decline in publications in 2013, suggesting an unstable research interest in the field. The annual growth rate of publications related to AI in gamification stands at 24.36%. The average number of citations per year exhibits an increasing trend but lacks consistency.

The average citation to AI in gamification over 11 years (2013–2024). The trend reveals that 2021 witnessed the highest level of citation, with 19.67 mean-TCperArt, closely followed by 16.33 articles cited in 2020. It is important to consider that the figures for 2024 provided are based on citation within the first nine months of the year, and it is anticipated that the number will likely rise by the end of the year. While the research on AI in gamification is garnering attention, there was a notable decline in publications in 2014 and 2019, suggesting an unstable research interest in the field. The average growth rate of citation related to AI in gamification stands at 5.95%. Additionally, the average number of citations per year exhibits an increasing trend but lacks consistency.

Source Growth

The involvement of journals in AI in gamification research, based on the number of affiliations produced per year. The line chart represents each university, with the top five universities being the focus of the analysis due to their significant contributions. and the *Japan Advanced Institute of Science and Technology* have shown consistent and substantial growth in their contributions. It is noteworthy that publications on AI in gamification by these universities began in 2022, and the number of publications increased annually after 2021. Since 2012, the remaining universities have contributed minimally.

Word Cloud and Treemap

The most frequently used words in articles related to AI in gamification are visually represented. To monitor the progression of keywords in AI research within gamification over time, a word cloud analysis was performed for two specific periods: 2012–2023. There is a noteworthy and consistent interest in the area of AI in gamification, particularly after 2020. The size of the words in the word cloud reflects their frequency of use, with the most important words appearing in the centre for greater visibility due to their significant size. The tree map displays each term used and its corresponding magnitude. Its show that the word gamifications has frequency of 17 followed by AI 14 and then Cyber security having 9 frequency including blockchain, machine learning, computer instructions, etc.

Trend Topics

Assessing word growth can provide valuable insights into the evolution of new terms in literature. This is particularly relevant in the AI in gamification literature in security intelligence, where understanding the introduction and impact of major keywords can shed light on the dynamics of the field. The oldest keywords in this area include learning system, students and educational computing. This information is a valuable resource for professionals in various fields, including researchers and analysts. By analysing word frequency over time, important trends and insights can be identified, informing decision-making in different contexts.

Conclusion

Through a systematic review, this study delved into the realm of AI in gamification in security intelligence. In conclusion, there is a great deal of promise for transforming security intelligence education and training through the incorporation of AI into gamification frameworks. Personalised, adaptive and interactive experiences that are powered by AI can be provided through gamification to increase user engagement, advance skill development and promote greater readiness for real-world cybersecurity concerns (Chen et al., 2023; Kapoor, 2022). AI-driven systems are revolutionising traditional training methods by continuously adapting to individual performance and giving real-time feedback, hence increasing their dynamic and efficaciousness (Smith & Doe, 2021). But there are moral obligations associated with this revolutionary potential. Important concerns concerning user autonomy, data privacy and the possibility of behavioural manipulation are brought up by the use of AI in gamification. In order to ensure that gamified systems enhanced by AI are implemented ethically, it is imperative that developers and organisations carefully manage these ethical problems (Lee, 2023). To fully utilise AI in gamification for security intelligence, it will be necessary to strike a balance between innovation and ethical accountability as this sector develops (Jones & Brown, 2020). The research revealed a growing interest in the field and a diverse range of applications of AI technologies, highlighting the need for a comprehensive examination of their utilisation from various perspectives. The findings underscored the significant reliance on AI technologies, pointing towards a future shaped by algorithmic scenarios. Drawing upon the insights garnered from the reviewed publications, the study identified several implications for future research endeavours. First, it was observed that a majority of the AI applications in gamification predominantly focus on technical aspects, disregarding crucial factors such as pedagogy, curriculum and in security intelligence instructional learning design. Second, despite the utilisation of human-generated data in AI technologies, there is a notable absence of regulations regarding the ethical usage of these data. To address this gap, future research could concentrate on exploring this issue and advocating for the development of policies and strategies. Organisations and higher institutes must prioritise the establishment of a human-centred approach to gamification that effectively harnesses the benefits of AI technologies.

References

Chen, Y., Patel, V., & Wong, M. (2023). Adaptive learning through AI-powered gamification. *International Journal of Interactive Systems, 19*(1), 33–48.

Ērgle, D., & Ludviga, I. (2018). Use of gamification in human resource management: Impact on engagement and satisfaction. In *10th International Scientific Conference "Business and Management"*.

Gimson, A. (2012). Game on for virtual work and play: Engaging learners' interest with online role-play. *Development and Learning in Organizations: An International Journal, 27*(1), 22–24.

Jones, T., & Brown, L. (2020). Enhancing cybersecurity training with AI and gamification. *Journal of Digital Defense, 12*(2), 77–90.

Kapoor, A. (2022). AI in gamification: Transforming learning and training. *Journal of Educational Technology, 15*(4), 112–128.

Lee, S. (2023). Ethical dimensions of AI in gamified security intelligence. *Journal of Ethics in Technology, 22*(5), 98–115.

Luckin, R., Holmes, W., Griffiths, M., & Forcier, L. B. (2016). *Intelligence unleashed: An argument for AI in education.* Pearson. https://static.googleusercontent.com/media/edu.google.com/en//pdfs/Intelligence-Unleashed-Publication.pdf

Mollick, E. R., & Rothbard, N. (2014). *Mandatory fun: Consent, gamification and the impact of games at work.* The Wharton School research paper series.

Sarangi, S., & Shah, S. (2015). Individuals, teams and organizations score with gamification: Tool can help to motivate employees and boost performance. *Human Resource Management International Digest, 23*(4), 24–27. https://doi.org/10.1108/HRMID-05-2015-0074

Smith, R., & Doe, J. (2021). Gamification in security intelligence: The role of AI. *Cybersecurity and Technology Review, 10*(3), 45–62.

Wang, Y., & Zhang, Y. (2019). AI-driven gamification: A survey. *IEEE Transactions on Games, 12*(4), 396–409. https://doi.org/10.1109/TG.2019.2945235

Chapter 16

The Enhancing Security in Project Management Through Artificial Intelligence: A Bibliometric Study

Megha ojha, Vinay Kandpal and Archana Singh

Graphic Era Deemed to Be University, India

Abstract

The field of project management is prevalent across various industries and is also being impacted by advancements in Artificial Intelligence (AI). However, the use of AI in project management is not yet widely adopted in many companies, particularly in all areas of project management. The reasons for this are unclear, but it appears to be linked to uncertainties surrounding the implementation of AI in project management. This chapter aimed to recognise the capabilities and constraints of AI in project management through a bibliometric analysis. The analysis allowed for the examination and correlation of chosen articles to identify patterns and trends. Ultimately, it became evident that the scientific community has a growing interest in this area, but there are still unexplored areas to consider. This review systematically examines the use of AI in project management from 2007 to 2023, providing novel insights and up-to-date information. By analysing 102 articles retrieved from Scopus, the data were extracted, analysed and coded using R Studio. Additionally, there is a shift in the researcher affiliation, with project management now being the most dominant, compared to previous studies that showed a lack of researchers from this field.

Keywords: Artificial Intelligence; project management; digitisation; bibliometric analysis; scopus

Security Intelligence in the Age of AI, 267–273

doi:10.1108/978-1-83608-156-220251016

Introduction

Artificial Intelligence (AI) has become increasingly relevant in our present time. Despite its growing importance, there are still many scientific and business-related aspects to explore. With the advent of the internet revolution, a new phenomenon has emerged – AI (Charytonowicz & Wyrwicka, 2020). As a new reality, markets and users have been adapting to the inevitable changes it brings. However, many industries are still hesitant to fully embrace it. This reluctance is highlighted by authors who note the uncertainty surrounding its implementation (Dikmen et al., 2017).

The implementation of AI is hindered by certain issues that have highlighted the need for establishing boundaries and principles of use. This is intended to promote responsibility and respect for all parties involved (Gao & Liu, 2019). Nevertheless, there are indications that AI has enormous potential that cannot be disregarded. Companies even believe that humans and AI will collaborate in the future. Collaboratively, they can leverage the findings of certain studies that suggest internal factors can lead to greater innovation and improved performance, ensuring organisational success. According to the literature, AI has immense potential.

We can also explore other areas, such as assessing and measuring various IT strategies, creating strategic roadmaps and implementing them with project management support. Considering the extensive scope of this subject, our concentration lies in examining the present advancements, researched domains of AI, possible areas that need further exploration and the trajectory of the market to accomplish our goals. Given these circumstances, we determined that a systematic literature review is the most suitable approach for collecting up-to-date studies and enhancing our comprehension of the prevailing direction (Huang & Shu, 2020). Due to the vast range of applications for AI, our analysis focused exclusively on project management, a critical domain across various industries and universally acknowledged as significant. As stated in reference, AI is a field within computer science that aims to enhance and advance the intelligence of computer systems (Li et al., 2020).

The objective of this endeavour is to distinguish between humans and machines. During the 1950s, Turing's research shed light on the fact that newly developed electronic machines had the potential to perform any task that humans could accomplish (Liu et al., 2019). In this section, we provide a comprehensive and methodical examination and evaluation of different viewpoints and facets. As per the definition provided by the English Oxford Living Dictionary, AI encompasses the application of advanced analysis and logic-based techniques, including machine learning, to understand events, support decision-making and automate actions. Additionally, as stated in the dictionary, AI encompasses the field of study and progress in computer systems that are capable of performing tasks traditionally associated with human intelligence. These tasks include visual perception, speech recognition, decision-making and language translation.

Methods

A bibliometric analysis seeks to address specific inquiries through the application of an explicit, systematic and replicable search strategy. This process involves identifying relevant studies, synthesising data and analysing trends in the number of articles published each year, among other factors. The data from the included studies are then extracted and coded to synthesise the findings and highlight their practical applications, as well as any gaps or inconsistencies. In this study, 102 articles about AI in higher education are mapped to provide insight into the topic (Project Management Institute, 2017).

Results

Data Synthesis

The focus of this study is to examine the literature on the use of AI in project management over the past 15 years, starting from 1987. The study's objectives are to address the following inquiries: Which entities, such as research institutes, universities, countries, regions and research communities, are the main contributors to AI research with project management? Additionally, what is the intellectual, conceptual and social framework of research on AI in project management? The synthesised bibliometric analysis data are presented in Fig. 16.1, which offers a descriptive overview of research on AI in project management.

The Patterns of Article Publication Over Time

The distribution of documents related to AI with project management over 14 years (1987–2023). The trend reveals that 2011 witnessed the highest level of activity, with 170 documents being produced, closely followed by 54 articles published in 2021. It is important to consider that the figures for 2023 provided are based on publications within the first 5 months of the year 83, and it is anticipated that the number will likely rise by the end of the year. While the research on AI with project management is garnering attention, there was a notable decline in publications in 2017–2019, suggesting an unstable research interest in the field. The annual growth rate of publications related to AI in project management stands at 32.09%.

Source Growth

The Hefei University of Technology and Henan Polytechnic University have shown consistent and substantial growth in their contributions. It is noteworthy that publications on AI in project management by these universities began in 2003–2005, and the number of publications increased annually after 2010. Since 2012, the remaining universities have contributed minimally.

Fig. 16.1. A Data Synthesis.

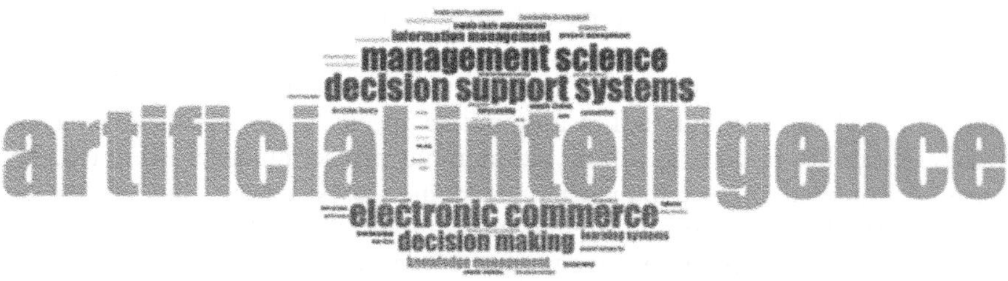

Fig. 16.2. Word Cloud.

Word Cloud and Treemap

The most frequently used words in articles related to AI with project management are visually represented. To monitor the progression of keywords in AI research within project management over time, a word cloud analysis was performed for two specific periods: 1987–2023. Fig. 16.2 demonstrates a noteworthy and consistent interest in AI in project management, particularly after 2015 (Gray & Larson, 2017). The treemap indicates that 'AI' is used in 24% of the articles, while 'decision support system' is used in only 7%, making it necessary to examine both the word cloud and treemap. The size of the words in the word cloud reflects their frequency of use, with the most important words appearing in the centre for greater visibility due to their significant size. The treemap displays each term used and its corresponding magnitude.

Word Growth

Assessing word growth can provide valuable insights into the evolution of new terms in literature. This is particularly relevant in the AI in project management literature, where understanding the introduction and impact of major keywords can shed light on the dynamics of the field. The oldest keywords in this area include AI, decision-making and decision support systems. This information is a valuable resource for professionals in various fields, including researchers and analysts. By analysing word frequency over time, important trends and insights can be identified, informing decision-making in different contexts (Bostrom, 2014).

Conclusion

We are living in a time of rapid technological advancement, which holds significant promise for improving productivity across a wide range of sectors. One of the key areas where this transformation is being witnessed is project management, where AI is playing an increasingly important role. AI in project management refers to the use of intelligent systems that can efficiently leverage available resources to support and streamline various project-related tasks. The rise of AI has sparked discussions about its potential to reduce the reliance on human resources, with some speculating that it could even fully automate project management processes. However, after thorough investigation, this research suggests that while AI can certainly aid in automating specific tasks and enhancing efficiency, its ability to serve as a fully autonomous project manager is limited. The term 'Automated project manager' carries high expectations, but current AI capabilities fall short of this ideal, and human oversight and intervention remain essential for the successful management of complex projects.

As industries adopt AI, a common question arises: can these advancements substantially reduce the dependence on human labour in managing projects? This research delves into that question and evaluates the capability of AI in automating key project management activities. Initial expectations suggest that AI systems might revolutionise project management, leading to the idea of an 'automated project manager' capable of handling complex tasks with minimal human intervention. However, the findings of this study indicate a more nuanced reality. While AI can assist with data analysis, forecasting, scheduling and even risk management, it currently lacks the sophisticated problem-solving, strategic thinking and emotional intelligence required to fully replace human project managers. Moreover, successful project management involves more than just processing data or managing timelines – it requires the ability to navigate interpersonal dynamics, adapt to changing priorities and provide leadership in times of uncertainty. These are areas where human judgement and experience remain irreplaceable. As a result, AI should be viewed as a powerful tool that complements, rather than replaces, human expertise. It can reduce the administrative burden, offer data-driven insights and optimise decision-making processes, but it cannot eliminate the need for human oversight and strategic input. The term 'Automated project manager' may suggest a future where AI takes the reins entirely, but current AI capabilities fall short of such expectations. Human creativity, intuition and leadership continue to be crucial in managing the complexities and nuances of real-world projects.

References

Bostrom, N. (2014). *Superintelligence: Paths, dangers, strategies*. Oxford University Press.

Charytonowicz, J., & Wyrwicka, M. (2020). Artificial intelligence in project management. In *Information systems architecture and technology: Proceedings of the 41st international conference on information systems architecture and technology* (pp. 151–161). Springer.

Dikmen, I., Birgonul, M. T., & Han, S. (2017). Risk assessment using artificial intelligence in construction projects. *Journal of Civil Engineering and Management*, *23*(3), 411–421.

Gao, S., & Liu, Y. (2019). Artificial intelligence for project risk prediction: A comparative study. *International Journal of Project Management*, *37*(6), 752–764.

Gray, C. F., & Larson, E. W. (2017). *Project management: The managerial process*. McGraw-Hill Education.

Huang, Y., & Shu, J. (2020). Artificial intelligence in project management: A state-of-the-art review. *Automation in Construction, 113*, 103111.

Li, H., Fang, C., & Yu, H. (2020). Artificial intelligence in project management: Bibliometric analysis and research directions. *Journal of Construction Engineering and Management, 146*(1), 04019100.

Liu, X., Zhang, R., & Zhang, Z. (2019). Research on intelligent project management systems based on artificial intelligence. In *Proceedings of the 8th international conference on education, management, information and management sciences* (pp. 287–293). ACM.

Project Management Institute. (2017). *A guide to the project management body of knowledge (PMBOK guide)*. Project Management Institute.

Chapter 17

Credit Card Fraud Detection Using Machine Learning

U. Sivaji, Akkati Sreeja, Kodathala Srihitha and Gudepu Vinay

Institute of Aeronautical Engineering, India

Abstract

Current days, there is an emergence fraud problem in the world which is mainly due to the increasing number of online transactions. The differentiation of untrue activities has become a difficult job to banks, as a result of which the use of ML algorithms has become necessary. The study evaluates the existing methods primarily consist of K-nearest gates, Logistic Regression (LR), Decision Trees (DT), Random Forest (RF), in detecting credit card fraud. This study employs Python to analyse different metrics and we give consideration to accuracy, confusion matrix, f1 score, precision, recall and AUC-ROC curves. This aims at thwarting the rising number of credit card fraud from which the importance of machine learning at modelling and predicting fraudulent transactions is being emphasised. The study brings the algorithms to the spotlight, with the Random Forest, determining the most appropriate algorithm for fraud detection by comparing 'Accuracy', 'Precision', 'Recall', and 'Fscore'.

Keywords: Decision tree; random forest; logistic regression; accuracy; precision; recall; machine learning (ML)

Introduction

This trend towards cashless payment through online, easy and readily available avenues has come as a result of rising and swift adoption of credit cards globally. This transformation also has resulted in unmatched growth of criminal credit card activities which result into losses of billions of dollars every year. In the year 2017, PwC global economic crime surveyed that almost half of all organisations are affected by economic crimes clearly proving a high need for credit

Security Intelligence in the Age of AI, 275–290

doi:10.1108/978-1-83608-156-220251017

card fraud detection. Given that technological advancement continues to rise, so is the development of innovative approaches used by criminals in perpetrating their crimes. The speed of credit card use in modern society has increased proportionately, being a catalyst for growth in credit card fraud. That ensures the fraud is inevitable and therefore necessary to detect fraud using cardholder transaction patterns to gauge the validity of new transactions. The systematic approach to this challenge uses the Random Forest algorithm used for the credit card dataset classification. Random Forest random sampling decision tree classifiers prevent overfitting. This algorithm is very effective in handling large volumes of data quickly, and training each tree separately. A logistic regression-based binary classifier predicts the uncertainty of an event using historical data. At the same time, Naive Bayes is a probabilistic algorithm using Bayes' theorem and assumption of feature independence in order to estimate an event given certain circumstances. All of these methods cooperate to form sturdy credit card fraud detection systems.

Objectives

The primary objective of detecting fraud using ML is to enhance the security and reliability of financial transactions by identifying and preventing fraudulent activities in real time. ML methods, such as logistic regression (LR) and Naive Bayes, analyse patterns and anomalies within historical credit card transaction data to build predictive models. These models can then assess the likelihood of a given transaction being fraudulent, enabling timely intervention to prevent unauthorised charges. The overarching goal is to reduce financial losses for both credit cardholders and financial institutions while safeguarding the integrity of the payment system. By leveraging advanced analytics, credit card fraud detection systems aim to stay adaptive, evolving alongside emerging fraud patterns to provide a robust defence against constantly evolving threats in the dynamic landscape of electronic transactions.

Literature Review

The work by Mrs. Anupama Phakatkar (Phakatkar, 2023) in 2023 introduced 'Credit-Card Fraud Detection using Machine Learning Techniques' (*IEEE Communications Surveys & Tutorials*, *16*(2), 722–744) describes that credit cards have become extensively utilised for daily transactions, leading to a surge in credit card fraud incidents. Cybercrime has inflicted considerable damage on credit card businesses and services. Detecting fraudulent transactions can be challenging. Both credit card users and companies are actively exploring advanced technologies to minimise fraudulent activities. Numerous researchers have suggested diverse ML methods to detect credit card fraud. This paper compares different ML algorithms employed for detecting frauds in European cardholder transactions and simulated credit card fraud datasets. The findings indicate that Random Forest algorithm demonstrates promising results on both datasets.

Dal Pozzolo et al. (2017) in 2017 introduced Adaptive Machine Learning for Credit Card Fraud Detection (*Data Mining and Knowledge Discovery*, *31*(3), 565–591) presenting a significant contribution to the realm of fraud detection with their work titled 'Adaptive Machine Learning for Credit Card Fraud Detection', published in Data Mining. Focussing on the dynamic nature of fraudulent activities, the authors propose an adaptive ML approach that evolves and adjusts to emerging patterns in credit card transactions. The study introduces a framework designed to continuously learn and update its knowledge base, thereby enhancing its efficacy in identifying novel and sophisticated fraud schemes. By leveraging adaptive ML techniques, the authors address the challenges posed by the evolving landscape of credit card fraud, providing a robust solution that adapts to the ever-changing nature of fraudulent activities in financial transactions.

Dal Pozzolo et al. (2015) in 2015 introduced Credit card Fraud Detection: A realistic modelling and a novel learning strategy (*IEEE Transactions on Neural Networks and Learning Systems*, *29*(8), 3784–3797) describes that detecting fraud in credit card transactions serves as a significant challenge for computational intelligence algorithms. This problem encompasses several intricate hurdles, including the evolution of customer habits and fraudsters' adaptive strategies, resulting in concept drift. Moreover, the disproportion between genuine transactions and fraudulent ones creates a class imbalance, compounded by the limitation of timely verification checks on a small fraction of transactions by investigators. Yet, several proposed learning algorithms for fraud detection are based on abstractions which are not fully in accordance with the reality of fraud detection systems (FDS). The lack of realism primarily relates to two key aspects: the supply and timing of supervised information and the way fraud detection performance is evaluated by the metrics.

In 2018, Vijaya Bhaskar investigated the financial impact posed by Credit Card Fraud and the shortcomings of the existing Fraud Prevention Systems (FPSs) in helping to minimise that impact (Bhaskar, 2018). The aim of this research is to precisely identify and prevent fraudulent transactions through the Credit Card Fraud Detection Dataset on Kaggle. Six supervised ML algorithms initially trained and benchmarked with the imbalanced original dataset were: Extreme Gradient Boosting, Random Forest, KNN and other ML methods. Then the same classifiers were trained on a resampled dataset using the SMOTE-Tomek technique, where the resampling addresses the imbalanced nature of the dataset by under-sampling and over-sampling. The second stage results demonstrated higher accuracy, where XGBoost, RF, and DT scored 100% in precision, recall, F1 Score, and AUPRC. This study, however, outperformed the rest of the researches by having the best overall performance in all the metrics showing amazing results in credit card frauds detection.

Authors Varun Kumar et al. (2020) introduced Credit-Card Fraud Detection Using Machine Learning Algorithms (*Expert Systems With Applications*, *55*, 248–260) described that presently, sophisticated technological methods like phishing are exploited for internet banking fraud, allowing unauthorised transfers and withdrawals from individuals' bank accounts. This surge in credit card fraud poses significant challenges for banking institutions and their service providers. This project aims to construct a robust model using ML algorithms and neural networks to effectively predict fraudulent and non-fraudulent transactions. The primary objective is to accurately predict fraudulent activities concerning transaction time and amount. This involves leveraging classification ML algorithms, statistical methods, calculus (such as differentiation and the chain rule), and linear algebra to construct intricate ML models for data analysis and prediction. The project has achieved notable accuracy rates: Logistic Regression attained 94.84%, Naive Bayes achieved 91.62%, and Decision Tree showed 92.88%. Moving into deep learning, the (ANN) outperformed all other algorithms, achieving an accuracy of 98.69%.

Proposed System

Our project aims to make financial transactions more secure and reliable by improving how we detect credit card fraud. To tackle the challenge of fraud, we start by collecting data better and fixing imbalances in transaction records. We use smart techniques to understand transaction details well, making our fraud detection models more accurate. We create advanced models by combining the strengths of different methods, making them strong against various fraud patterns. Our system can quickly adapt to new fraud tactics in real time, ensuring fast processing of transactions and immediate updates to the fraud detection model. We also focus on making our models easy to understand and explain, using methods like Support Vector Machine, Logistic Regression, Random Forest, and Naïve Bayes. This way, our project aligns directly with the goal of improving security and trust in financial transactions by strengthening fraud detection systems and responding swiftly to new fraud tricks.

System Architecture

The system design for credit card detection of frauds using ML encompasses multi-faceted approach. It begins with the collection of transaction data from various sources and proceeds to preprocessing, feature engineering, and dimensionality reduction to prepare data for analysis. ML models are trained on this data, incorporating algorithms like logistic regression, decision trees, and deep learning with rigorous evaluation metrics. Anomalies are detected through unsupervised techniques, alongside real-time monitoring for immediate fraud identification. Model deployment via APIs or microservices, integration with rule-based systems, and cloud scalability ensure real-time, efficient detection. To maintain accuracy and adaptability, periodic model updates and logging for auditing are implemented. Collaboration among multidisciplinary teams and adherence to data security and regulatory compliance complete the design, ultimately providing a robust and dynamic solution for credit card fraud prevention and mitigation. Each transaction is assigned a risk score based on the analysis from rule-based filters and ML models. The risk score indicates the likelihood of a

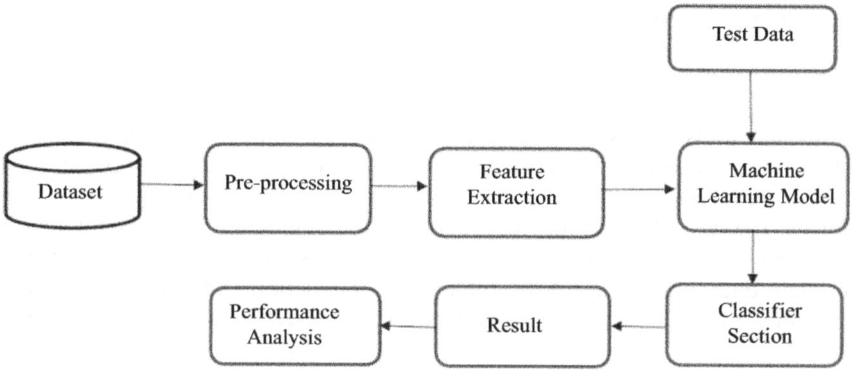

Fig 17.1. System Architecture.

transaction being fraudulent. Real-time monitoring is a crucial component that allows the system to continuously monitor transactions and raise alerts for transactions with a high-risk score. This enables immediate action to be taken to prevent fraudulent activity.

From Fig. 17.1 System Architecture, we can understand data flow between the modules involved in the process.

Data Flow Diagram

The depicted DFD Fig. 17.2 elaborates the data flow diagram for credit card fraud detection employing ML begins with the 'User Login' process, where users authenticate themselves to access the system. Subsequently, the transaction data

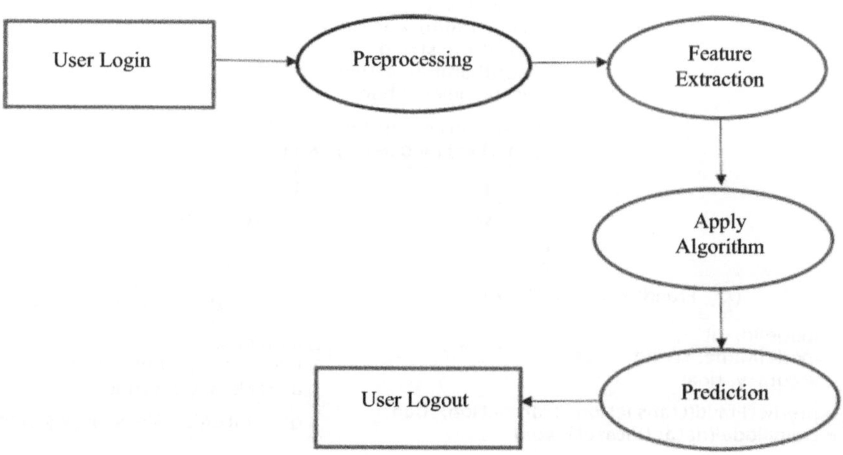

Fig. 17.2. DFD Level 0.

undergoes preprocessing, involving tasks such as cleaning and normalisation to enhance data quality. Feature extraction extracts relevant attributes like transaction amount and frequency. The processed data is then fed into the ML algorithm application stage, where a robust algorithm learns patterns and discerns fraudulent transactions. Following this, the system enters the 'Prediction' phase, where the model evaluates transactions and predicts the likelihood of fraud. Based on the predicted outcome, appropriate actions are taken, and users are notified. Finally, the 'User Logout' process concludes the interaction. This comprehensive data flow diagram illustrates the seamless progression from user authentication through data processing, ML application, prediction, and user notification, providing a holistic view of the credit card fraud detection system's functionality.

Class Diagram

The depicted Class Diagram Fig. 17.3 illustrates key entities in a credit card fraud detection system. It includes classes such as 'Transaction', encapsulating transactional details like ID, amount, and fraud status; 'FraudDetectionModel', representing ML models with methods for prediction and training; and 'FraudAlert', indicating alerts generated for potentially fraudulent transactions. The associations show how transactions use the fraud detection model and how alerts are generated based on transactions, aiding in understanding relationships and functionalities within the system. These classes and their associations showcase key functionalities and relationships crucial for the system's fraud detection operations.

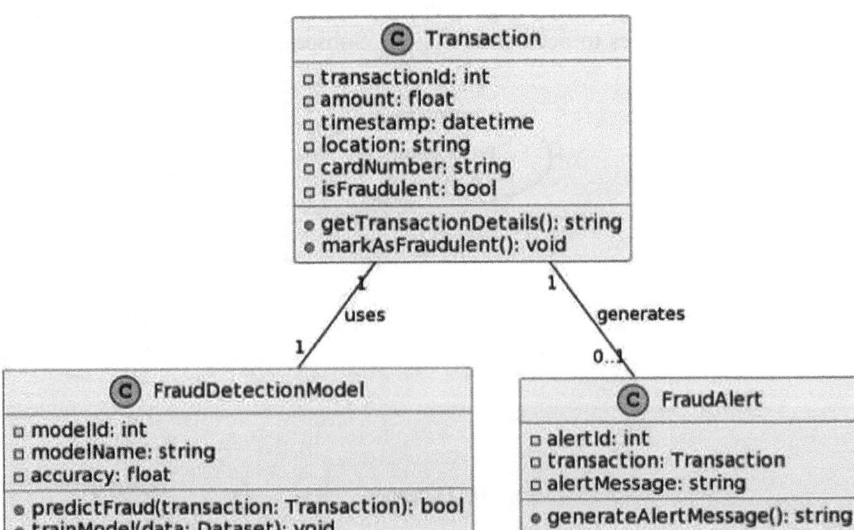

Fig. 17.3. Class Diagram.

Methodology

In the scope of fraud detection in credit card transactions, ML algorithms are highly effective at unveiling fraudulent transactions.

Support Vector Machine

Support Vector Machine (SVM) is a powerful ML method that significantly contributes to credit card fraud detection. SVM excels in accurately classifying credit card transactions as legitimate or fraudulent by analysing transaction features such as amount, location, time, and frequency. Its ability to handle non-linear relationships through kernel functions allows it to capture complex patterns in the data, improving accuracy in identifying fraudulent transactions. With a focus on margin maximisation, SVM ensures a well-separated decision boundary, leading to better generalisation and robust performance. Additionally, SVM's scalability to large datasets makes it suitable for processing a high volume of credit card transactions in real time. In the proposed research, SVM will be evaluated within the system architecture for credit card fraud detection to determine its effectiveness in real-time fraud detection. Its strengths in classification, non-linear relationship handling, and scalability make it a valuable component for enhancing the accuracy and efficiency of detecting fraud in credit card transactions.

In simple terms, the formula for the decision function in a Support Vector Machine (SVM) can be expressed as: For a linear SVM:

$$[g(x) = w^{Rx} + a]$$

where:

- $(g(x))$ is the classification function that predicts the output class based on the input vector (x).
- (w) is the weight vector.
- (a) is the bias term.

This formula is used to make the predictions for the class of new input samples based on the learnt parameters and support vectors.

Logistic Regression

Logistic regression (LR) is a statistical method for binary classification problems that are of significance in the credit card fraud detection. It uses a logistic function to predict the occurrence of an event by estimating the probability of a transaction being fraudulent which is modelled using input features. Logistic regression is effective at assisting with fraud detection by calculating the probability of a transaction being fraudulent and thus serving as a practical way to assess the risk of an individual transaction. This is done through analysing historical transactional data and transactional features (such as transaction amount, location, time, etc.) and logistic regression then calculates the probabilities and classifies the transactions as potentially fraudulent or legitimate. Thus the base probability is set, thus giving financial institutions the ability to prioritise and investigate transactions with higher fraud probability, leading to the improvement of the efficiency of the fraud detection systems.

Random Forest

The advanced ensemble learning algorithm Random Forests is famous for its ability to address both classification and regression issues. During training, the algorithm builds a collection of decision trees which are formed by a random subset of features and data. This in-built randomness is not only intended to improve the model's robustness but also to reduce the odds of overfitting. Training of decision trees involves splitting the data recursively using the best feature splits, which consequently improves predictive accuracy and generalisation to unseen and new data when individual tree predictions are aggregated. Algorithms are characterised by their ability to handle large datasets of high dimensionality. The high resistance to overfitting and the wonderful ability of Random Forests to deal with missing values makes them a worthy choice of tool across multiple domains like finance, healthcare, and image recognition. This characteristic and working without intensive hyperparameter tuning is what makes them popular in the real world.

The author, Bhaskar (2018), in his article entitled 'Prediction of Fraudulent or Genuine Transactions on Credit Card Fraud Detection Dataset Using Machine Learning Techniques', explores the use of ML including the Random Forest algorithm for credit card fraud detection. The study assesses the effectiveness of the Random Forest algorithm in detecting fraudulent and legitimate transactions from the credit card fraud detection dataset. This paper uses ML techniques, mainly Random Forest algorithms, to enhance the precision and speed of fraud detection mechanisms. The research provides insights on the usefulness of Random Forest in the practical implementation of the problem of transaction security and financial fraud.

Random Forest in Fig. 17.4 is one of the popular ensemble learning methods which behaves as effective classifiers by combining multiple decision trees in a robust manner. There is an element of randomness in each decision tree in the ensemble because these decision trees are being constructed from a random subset of the features and a random subset of the training data (Palaiahnakote et al., 2020). Such randomness at the same time is a characteristic that not only diversifies individuals but also prevents overfitting. Throughout the training process every tree learns different patterns and relationships within the data. When a prediction is made the ensemble averages the outputs of all the individual trees providing thus the stabilised and reliable overall prediction (Khashei et al., 2009). The Random Forest's powerful trait is the ability to process complex datasets, minimise variance, and increase

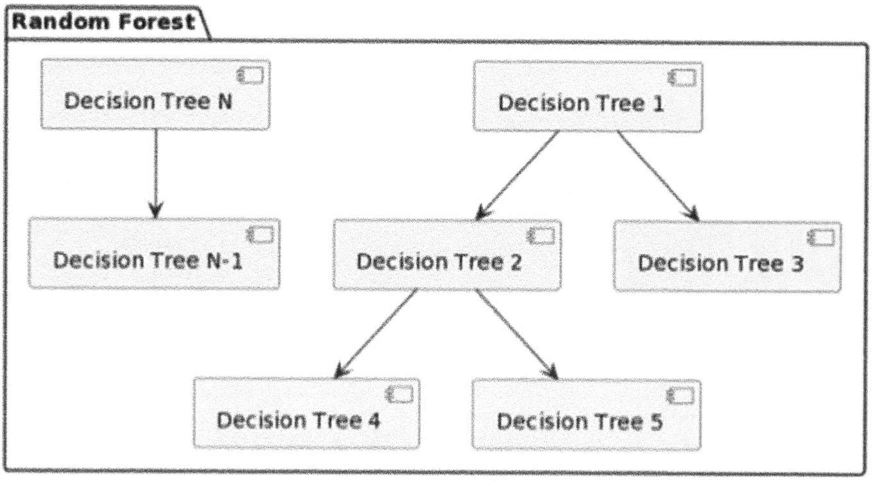

Fig. 17.4. Random Forest as an Ensemble of Decision Tress.

generalisation which makes it a widely used and effective algorithm being used in ML for both classification and regression purposes.

Results

Results on Validation for Different Class Weights

In these transactions (Figs. 17.5–17.7), SVM with RBF gives us a better chance of catching fraud, but it also means more mistakes identifying legitimate transactions (Acharjya & Sanyal, 2017). This could be because the RBF kernel function used a non-linear decision boundary. However, if we're okay with allowing more false alarms, we can get high recall scores with all three methods.

Weights

To teach our models, we followed a method based on weight. We trained each model many times, increasing the weights each time. We tested how well our trained models worked using a CV split. We chose the weights for each model that gave us the best recall for spotting fraud, while keeping false positives under 1% (Tables 17.1 and 17.2).

Finally, we applied the models we trained, giving special attention to the weights we assigned to predict outcomes on our test dataset. We evaluated their performance by considering different metrics such as recall, precision, f1score and the area under the precision–recall curve. This helped us gauge how effectively our models were working.

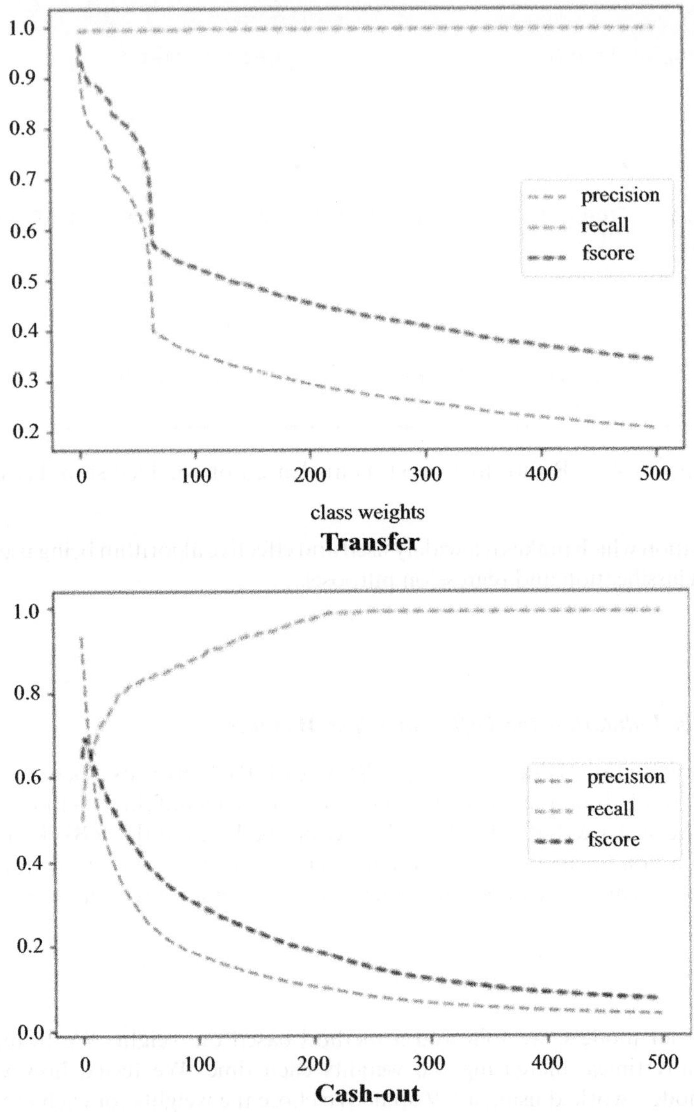

Fig. 17.5. Precision, Recall and F1 Score Curves for Logistic Regression.

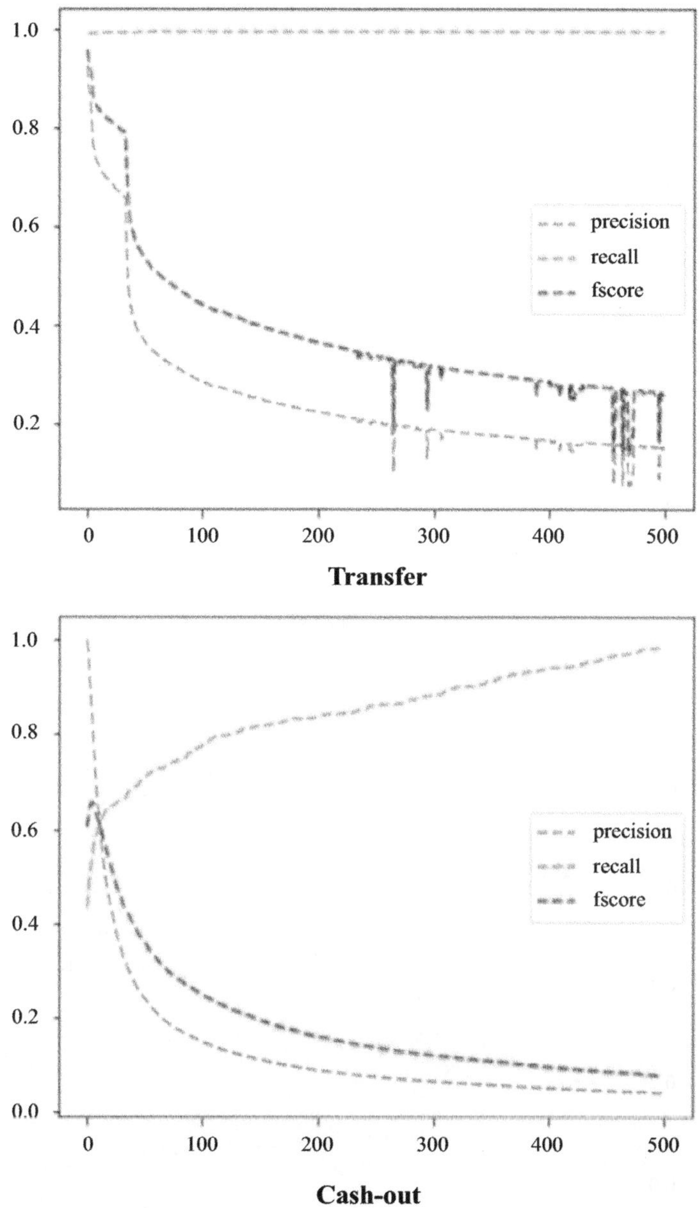

Fig. 17.6. Precision, Recall and F1 Score Curves for Support Vector Machine.

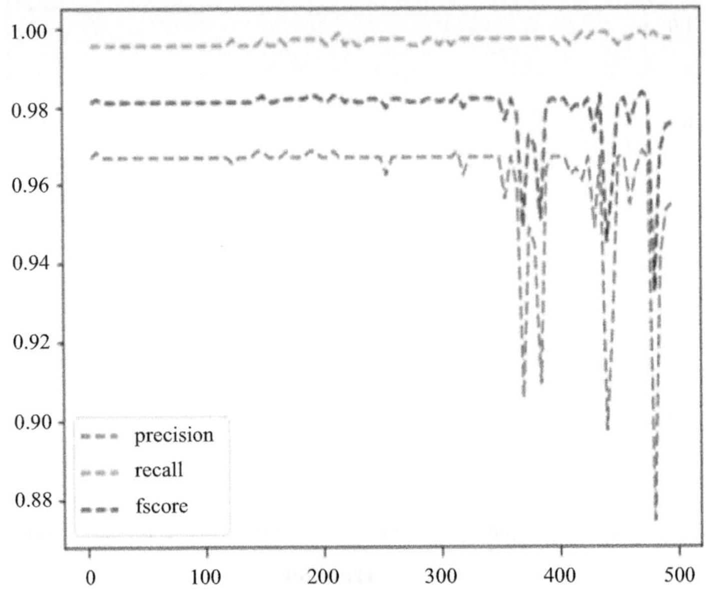

Transfer

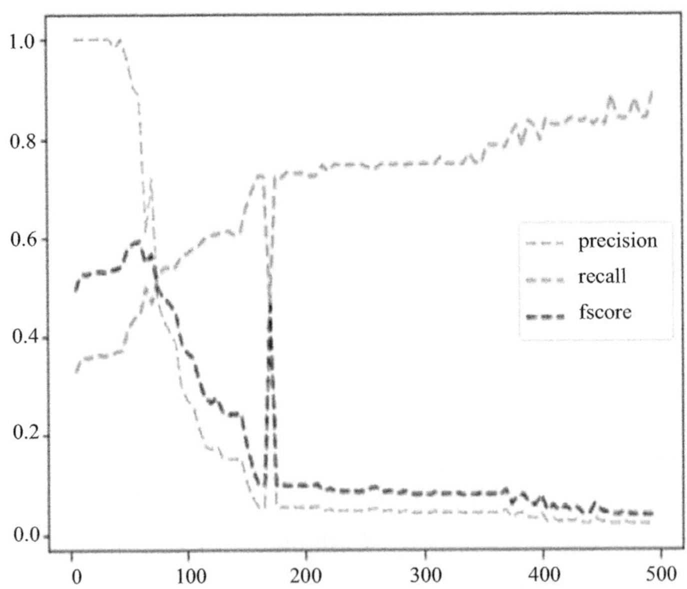

Cash-out

Fig. 17.7. Precision, Recall and F1 Score Curves for Random Forest.

Table 17.1. Weights Obtained for Transfer Data.

Algorithm	Non-Fraud	Fraud
Logistic regression	1	70
Linear SVM	1	39
SVM with RBF kernel	1	16
Random Forest	1	80
Naïve Bayes	1	100

Table 17.2. Weights Obtained for Cash Out Data.

Algorithm	Non-Fraud	Fraud
Logistic Regression	1	145
Linear SVM	1	132
SVM with RBF kernel	1	128
Random Forest	1	65
Naïve Bayes	1	55

Precision Recall Curves

Finally, we applied the models we trained, giving special attention to the weights we assigned to predict outcomes on our test dataset. We evaluated their performance by considering different metrics such as recall, precision, f1score and the AUPRC curve. This helped us gauge how effectively our models were working (Figs. 17.8 and 17.9).

In our experiments with fraud cases, we tried using higher weights. Initially, we considered setting the weights based on the imbalance ratio in our dataset. However, this approach led to a lot of incorrect identifications, especially for CASH OUT, with more than 1% false positives. Although it gave good recall, we opted not to use this method. Instead, we finetuned our models by testing different weight combinations on our CV split. What we discovered was that using higher weights improved recall but made precision worse on our CV split (Bhattacharyya et al., 2019).

Algorithm	precision	recall	fscore
LR	0.405634	0.998267	0.576865
linear	0.0645089	0.998267	0.611465
rbf	0.387949	0.993068	0.557936

Algorithm	precision	recall	fscore
LR	0.390476	0.99308	0.560547
linear	0.0124466	0.99827	0.599791
rbf	0.37947	0.991349	0.548851

Algorithm	precision	recall	fscore
LR	0.392512	0.996288	0.563156
linear	0.00977911	0.999629	0.599576
rbf	0.391088	0.99369	0.561275

Fig. 17.8. Precision, Recall, f score for Transfer Data on Test Data, Validation Data, Train Data.

Conclusion

In our research, we tested different algorithms like Logistic Regression, Gradient Boosted Decision Tree (DT), Random Forests (RF), Support Vector Machine (SVM), and mlp to see how well they predict fraud in Mobile Money transactions, a common issue in developing nations. We used measures like accuracy, precision, recall, and F1-Score to evaluate how effective these algorithms are, especially when dealing with imbalanced datasets. The results showed that Random Forests and gradient-boosted decision trees can accurately predict fraudulent transactions. Ultimately, the choice of which algorithm to use in the real world depends on a company's decision and business priorities, considering how many false positives they are willing to tolerate.

Algorithm	precision	recall	fscore
LR	0.32541	0.99481	0.490405
linear	0.0105438	0.99827	0.413075
rbf	0.258326	0.99308	0.41

Algorithm	precision	recall	fscore
LR	0.327282	0.99703	0.492799
linear	0.00955778	0.999629	0.418877
rbf	0.270581	0.995546	0.425512

Algorithm	precision	recall	fscore
LR	0.336056	0.998267	0.502837
linear	0.0467153	0.998267	0.420438
rbf	0.268888	0.993068	0.423191

Fig. 17.9. Precision, Recall, f score for Cash-Out Data on Test Data, Validation Data, Train Data.

Future Scope

In the future, there could be further advancements in fraud detection using ML methods, where the algorithms are refined and then deep learning techniques like CNNs and RNNs are explored. Also, using real-time processing will ensure immediate response to any suspicious activities. A collaboration between financial institutions, regulators and cybersecurity experts will be fundamental in devising a standardised framework and dealing with new challenges while still complying with data privacy regulations. Integrity of financial ecosystems will be enhanced through accountability and trust that explainable AI techniques can give in terms of transparency of insights. In general, the continuous innovation and the inclusive approach will be the key aspects in securing the fraud detection system in the future transaction scenarios.

References

Acharjya, D. P., & Sanyal, S. (2017). A novel credit card fraud detection model based on convolutional neural networks. In *2017 IEEE Calcutta conference (CALCON)* (pp. 220–224). IEEE. https://www.hindawi.com/journals/scn/2018/5680264/

Bhaskar, V. (2018). Prediction of fraudulent or genuine transactions on credit card fraud detection dataset using machine learning techniques. *Expert Systems with Applications*, *99*, 105-116. https://www.ijraset.com/research-paper/prediction-of-fraudulent-or-genuine-transactions-on-credit-card-fraud-detection

Bhattacharyya, S., Jha, D., & Tharakunnel, K. (2019). Credit card fraud detection using machine learning: A review. In *2019 IEEE Calcutta conference*. https://www.ijstr.org/final-print/oct2019/A-Review-On-Credit-Card-Fraud-Detection-Using-Machine-Learning.pdf

Dal Pozzolo, A., Boracchi, G., Caelen, O., Alippi, C., & Bontempi, G. (2015). Credit card fraud detection: A realistic modeling and a novel learning strategy. *IEEE Transactions on Neural Networks and Learning Systems*, *29*(8), 3784–3797. https://pubmed.ncbi.nlm.nih.gov/28920909/

Dal Pozzolo, A., Boracchi, G., Caelen, O., & Bontempi, G. (2017). Adaptive machine learning for credit card fraud detection. *Data Mining and Knowledge Discovery*, *31*(3), 565-591. https://dalpozz.github.io/static/pdf/Dalpozzolo2015PhD.pdf

Khashei, M., Bijari, M., & Ardali, G. A. (2009). Improvement of credit scoring by integrating artificial neural network and decision tree algorithms. *Expert Systems with Applications*, *36*(3). https://www.hindawi.com/journals/mpe/2023/4141140/

Palaiahnakote, S. Muniyandi, R. C., & Ravi, V. (2020). Credit card fraud detection using machine learning and neural networks: A review. *Computers, Materials & Continua*, *64*(2), 731-747. https://ijcrt.org/papers/IJCRT2401012.pdf

Phakatkar, A. (2023). Credit card fraud detection using machine learning techniques. *IEEE Communications Surveys & Tutorials*, *16*(2), 722–744. https://www.jetir.org/papers/JETIR2306224.pdf

Varun Kumar, K. S., Vijaya Kumar, V. G., Shankar, A. V., & Pratibha, K. (2020). Credit card fraud detection using machine learning algorithms. *Expert Systems with Applications*, *55*, 248. https://www.researchgate.net/publication/343632766_Credit_Card_Fraud_Detection_using_Machine_Learning_Algorithms

Chapter 18

Copyright and Artificial Intelligence: Authorship v. Ownership Conundrum

Vaishnavi Yashasvi[a] *and Ruchir Singh*[b]

[a]Sharda University, India
[b]Bennett University, India

Abstract

The increasing role of Artificial Intelligence (AI) in different sectors like medicine, transportation, aviation, space travel, education, entertainment (music, art, gaming and cinema), industry and other areas has changed daily lives. The field of Intellectual Property Rights (IPRs) is not unique. The character of AI in inventiveness and transformation is acknowledged world over. AI takes part in the creation of copyrights, patents, designs and trade secrets in multiple forms of IPRs. AI can be diverse, composing music, blogging, writing books, writing poetry, creating visuals and drawing. However, a distinction needs to be made between tasks performed by humans with the help of AI and tasks performed by AI without human intermediation. AI has caused consequential problems and issues in the field of IPRs, especially copyright. This chapter also argues how important AI is in the creation of art, music, poetry, books and more.

Keywords: AI; IPR; Copyright; perception systems; natural language systems

Introduction

This chapter discusses the issues of authorship and the 'deep lies' in the creation of Artificial Intelligence (AI) in the field of autonomy. The presentation covers a multinational and comprehensive approach to writing in AI-powered applications. This chapter focuses on how AI has become very important in modern era as its usage has become necessary in the realm of hightech applications. AI has changed our lives by intruding the fields of medicine, aviation, space travel, education, entertainment industry (music, art, games, movies), etc. There is a

Security Intelligence in the Age of AI, 291–300

doi:10.1108/978-1-83608-156-220251018

trend in all countries to initiate more activities and reduce human activities in order to be more efficient and avoid errors (Ahuja, 2020).

The Concept of AI

According to Professor Stephen Hawking, 'the development of AI could spell the end of humanity.' He stated, 'it will eliminate itself and gradually replace itself' and that 'humans are limited by the slow biological evolution, they cannot cope and will be replaced' (Cellan-Jones, 2014). It is interesting to see Google's AI system progress to the point of creating its own child. The child AI is trained by the parent AI 'at a level far superior to any other human-made system.' The execution of the child AI is evaluated by the parent AI, which functions as a controller. The credentials received are then used to enhance the performance of the AI. The process is conduced thousands of times to ensure that the child's AI works and develops properly (Sulleyman, 2017).

The increasing role of AI in creativity and innovation is acknowledged world over. Recently, Open AI, an AI laboratory in US, launched a machine generated system called GPT-3, which consumed many months 'learning and analyzing native languages through thousands of digital books, the length and breadth of 'Wikipedia.' published. a trillion words. published on blogs, social media & all over the internet' (Metz, 2020).

GPT-3 writes poetry, tweets, answers trivial queries, abridges emails, 'translates into languages, and even writes his own computer programs.' It understands 'interpretations of human language' and competes with other 'human skills'. Additionally, it can produce local news, generate art, write short books and produce music that listens to different voices (Guadamuz, 2017). AI has created serious and difficult problems in the field of copyright law. This research work discusses how important AI is in creating creative works such as art, music, poetry, etc. This article also talks about the issues of authorship and falsification in works produced by AI. Moreover, Artificial intelligence was propounded by John McCarthy in 1956 (Sánchez Merino, 2018).

There is no accepted definition of 'artificial intelligence'. 'Artificial intelligence' can be defined as 'the ability of machines to do things that humans tell us require intelligence' (Jackson, 1985). Ray Kurzweil elucidated in AI in 1990 as 'the science of getting computers to do things that require human intelligence' (Fitzgerald & Martyn, 2020). AI generally alludes to 'the ability of machines to perform intelligent tasks such as thinking, understanding, learning, problem solving, and decision making' (Raina, 2020).

As per Russ Pearlman, 'The primary goals of AI are reasoning, knowledge, planning, learning, natural language processing (e.g., understanding and speaking languages), perception, and the ability to move and manipulate objects' (Pearlman, 2018). The three classifications of AI systems defined by World Intellectual Property Organization (WIPO) are: (i) 'expert (or knowledge-based) systems', (ii) 'perception systems' and (iii) 'natural language systems'. The foundation of AI is 'artificial networks' (Corrs Chambers Westgarth, 2020), that are 'brain-inspired systems designed to mimic the way the human mind learns.' AI networks have machine learning capabilities that 'help them produce better results as more data becomes available' (Frankenfield, 2020). Thus, AI allows machines to perform works autonomously/or with less human effort than human intelligence requires. AI should not be conceptualised as a single technology but rather as an arena that includes different fields, e.g., 'machine learning, robotics, language processing, and deep learning' (Chandak, 2020).

Therefore, 'Machine learning' and 'deep learning' are two aspects of AI. In the context of machine learning, there is a built-in algorithm in a computer program that causes it to 'learn, modify, and make future decisions from input data' of its own or when prompted. In contextual terminology, machine learning algorithms acquire a knowledge from the resource provided by the program to produce something innovative by making independent decisions. Thus, the variables are set by the programmer and the creation is done by the AI itself. Examples of AI, such as a 'chess computer for an autonomous car,' can be found, while others are based on 'deep learning' and 'natural language processing.' Computers can be instructed using technology to perform certain particular tasks, including generating creative content by processing large amounts of data and identifying specific designs in a certain data.

There are two categories of creative work created by AI: (i) 'AI-generated' work and (ii) 'AI-assisted' work. Work produced by AI is also called 'autonomous AI,' which means that the work is created without any intervention by the AI. In this class of tasks, AI can 'adapt behaviour in response to unexpected information or events' and produce unpredictable or predictable tasks. 'AI-assisted AI' tasks, on the other hand, are performed transparently.

AI and Copyright

From the beginning of 1970s, computer programs were widely used to generate copyrighted works. Computer-generated works have not had many copyright issues. This is because computer programs were seen as tools that supported creative activities in nature and required human assistance to produce them. These applications were like packaging tools that people had to use to design the work. Things have really altered. Now that AI is available, computer programs are no longer just devices but have the ability to create autonomous tasks that make their own decisions. AI has the potential to do a lot of work in a very short time with very little investment. Works created by AI can be copyrighted in all jurisdictions because they are authentic. The prerequisite to use 'skill and judgement' in nature can be seen to be met as a result of 'programming and parameterizing the AI that runs and performs the task' (Rana & Joy, 2019). However, no author will face the problems created by AI. While tasks are supported by AI, there is also human intervention. Therefore, someone who creates a creative work using AI can ultimately claim to be the author of the work, but this is not the case when the work is created by AI without human intervention. In such a case, the issue of authorship has confused countries all over the world.

There can be three general aspects to the copyright issue: (i) the copyright system should recognise AI rights; (ii) the work created by AI should not have an author, and the work should be 'in the public domain'; and (iii) there should be specific laws rather than copyright laws to preserve such works. Copyright protection acts as a reason to encourage the author to create more works using his skills, work and judgement. If AI is recognised as an author and works created by AI are protected by copyright laws, this means that 'human creativity' and 'machine creativity' are equal. On the other hand, if the work created by AI is not protected by copyright, this will definitely mean that human creativity will be preferred to machine. Preferring machine creativity to human creativity or aligning the two will probably mean the death of humans. Seeing AI as the author of activities produced by AI can cause many problems. The processes created by AI cannot be flawless. AI can use prejudiced and toxic language that can lead to slander or scandal; incite violence based on race, creed or religion; or produce unintended consequences.

In such cases, the difficulty is to resolve civil and criminal cases involving AI because it does not recognise as human. In many such cases, it can be removed or, in the worst case, disabled, but there will be a delay and irreversible recompense may occur to the creation. Another query, how will AI be considered a threat if the work produced by it is 'too similar' to existing works that may be subject to copyright? In addition, if the AI is accepted as the author, it will not have the right to transmit proprietorship of the work in its absence. An article published in civil law countries such as Germany, France and Spain states that the works produced must have a 'sign indicating the author's identity'. Thus, authors ought to reject the AI in the creations done by the AI because the AI has no structure.

In order for an AI to be legally binding, this means that it must have the ability to contract with other people. It will also have legal responsibilities and be held accountable for its actions. Most of the important people should be given the opportunity to sue and be prosecuted under the law. Many countries are not in favour of giving life sentences to AI. However, it goes without saying that the European Parliament is in favour of granting the legal status of 'autonomous robots' to 'technological humans' in order to protect copyrights (Klaris & Bedat, 2017). It is also possible to add that 'AI music composer by Artificial Intelligence Virtual Artist (AIVA) Technologies is the first person in the world to be officially granted composer status.' He was officially recognised as a composer by 'SACEM, France and Luxembourg Writers' Association', which can publish music under the name AIVA and receive copyright (Lauder, 2017). It should also be noted that Saudi Arabia granted citizenship to the AI robot Sophia in 2017. Dr Sophia's creator David Hanson wrote the following in his article titled 'Entering the Age of Living Intelligence Systems and Android Society', which examines the advances in AI to the point where robots will wake up and defend the right to life, the right to live freely.

It is interesting to note that although it is not a requirement under the Trade-Related Aspects of Intellectual Property Rights (TRIPS) Agreement, the copyright laws of many countries also provide for copyright. Two moral rights namely – (i) parental rights; and (ii) integrity rights, which are normally granted to authors. The former guarantees the right of the author to be associated with his work and to be credited as the creator of the work, while the latter allows the author to claim compensation for damages caused to his honour or reputation by the truncation or distortion of the work. In the case of Amar Nath Sehgal v. Union of India (Amar Nath Sehgal v. Union of India, 2005), the Delhi High Court has stated that the law aims to protect the right to fair wages globally. Right to paternity and integrity are the lifeblood of his work. The author has the right to protect, preserve and value his work though copyright's behaviour is related to the feelings and emotions of the author. This right does not belong to AI. Another troublesome problem will be related to the formulation of the work of AI. AI does not die like humans. However, we can say that it can be counted as 50 or 60 years from the moment of release of the work, depending on the laws of the countries. Regarding the protection of AI-related rights in relation to work performed by AI, there is no dispute that someone dies and gets tired while work. Thus, a person's author creates several copyrighted works in his life, and copyright is justified in that his efforts should be rewarded. AI, on the other hand, is immortal, tireless and can perform any task. Therefore, the claim of copyright protection for works created by AI is 'uneven and controversial' (Cheng Peng, 2018).

In addition, experts who do not support copyrighting machine-based learning works say that if given the identical input and the same specimen, the AI will create the same result. Henceforth, it is difficult to qualify it as 'unique and creative.' That will also make it harder for the AI to communicate with others and respect copyright and copyright laws. Turning the AI into a business author is not a piece meal allocation, as it will probably create more problems than it solves. One more idea in the debate is in absence of any author in the machine-generated work, and therefore, the creation resides to 'public'. Obviously, many reasons make AI-powered projects publicly available. One of the reasons is that there is no cost when you submit work with AI. Therefore, it makes sense for AI-generated work to be made available to the public for free. Second, AI can perform any number of iterations of the tasks it has created without additional costs or resources. Finally, one of the purposes of the Human Rights Act is to provide economic and social rights to the author of this book, thus encouraging him to work harder for the development of the country. Since AI is not human, it does not require any creative effort (Pokhriyal & Gupta, 2020).

However, it should be noted that if there is no protection for works created by AI and the public is free to use these works without copyright or payment, this could mean the death of companies that have invested heavily in AI systems to produce these works. People who believe will begin to market such activities in different ways and at no cost and will compete with companies that invest. Therefore, AI-based projects may require measures to encourage AI developers and potential companies to continue investing in AI-related research and development (Samuelson, 1986). The UK Copyright, Designs and Patents Act (CDPA), 1988 covers computer-produced/generated works. The CDPA signifies a 'computer-produced/generated' work as 'a work processed by a computer in a way that no human being could have written the book for.' The rationale for this provision is to 'establish special conditions for individual authorship in order to ensure the recognition and protection of works that fall within the program and that can produce independent works.' As per Article 9(3) of the CDPA, the writer of a 'literary, dramatic, musical or computer-generated work' 'should be considered the intended creator of the work.' Andres Guadamuz says that in such cases, the author goes to the program not the user. He demonstrates the relevant situation by providing the illustration of Microsoft's development of the computer program 'Word', which allows users to do their work. Microsoft may not be responsible for any actions taken by the user using the software. The copyright of the work created belongs to the program user who is known as the author as he created works using the program. In the case of Express Newspapers plc v Liverpool Daily Post & Echo (Express Newspapers plc - Liverpool Daily Post & Echo, 1985), the court ruled that the computer is a tool and the pen is also considered a tool. In the United States, the author's work created using AI may have rights if he proves that the AI program was used as a tool in the creation of the work (Hristov, 2017). In Naruto Slater (Naruto v. Slater, 2016), known as the 'Monkey Selfie', the US court ruled that the monkey cannot be considered the author of the clicked photo. In the United States, the copyright of a book can only be transferred to the human author and not to animals and machines.

However, things will be different in the era of 'intelligent algorithms' that can produce tasks on their own. When a computer using AI acts as an 'autonomous actor' and produces tasks 'algorithmically, sequentially, or indeterminately,' there is a 'visible gap between human input and computer output' (Basri, 2020). In such cases, the user's contribution to the task should not exceed button presses that enable the machine to perform the task. Therefore, in such a case, the 'person who prepares the plan for the work to be done' should be considered as the contractor. It can also be claimed that 'the AI program is created in a way that it can work and know the equations, it can give solutions on its own, and therefore creativity can be given. The program created the AI is enough'. As Sik Cheng Peng suggests in his research, there are various interpretations of Section 9(3) of the CDPA. It says that when a user is involved in the selection of information to be fed into an AI system, the user should be considered as the initiator of the creative process. Therefore, the user should be considered as the person who made the 'necessary plans' to create the work, not the AI, the programmer or the company that owns the AI. Therefore, the user, as opposed to the AI or the programmer, should be considered as the author of the AI-generated work.

The Indian Copyright Act does not define 'computer-generated work' as the CDPA does. However, it defines 'author' in relation to 'any work of art, whether literary, dramatic, musical or computer-generated' as the person who creates the creative work. In the Camlin Pvt. Ltd. v. National Pencil Industries, 1986, the Delhi High Court defined the meaning of the word 'author'. The courts held that there was no question of copyright in the 'machine-printed maps' as it was impossible to ascertain who had written the map. The court reiterated that copyright is limited to authors or natural persons. Since a cartoon produced using printing technique cannot be attributed to the author, the plaintiff cannot claim copyright in any case. A machine cannot be the author of a work of art and cannot have rights over that work. In the case of Tech Plus Media Private Ltd v. Jyoti Janda (2014), the Delhi court held that 'the plaintiff is a legitimate person and cannot be the author of any book that includes copyright can be'. However, the court reiterated that the plaintiff could own the copyright in the work under an agreement with the author. In Australia, copyright can only be obtained by the creator of an AI machine in 'machine-generated works', but copyright cannot be obtained in works created by AI due to the absence of human intervention. The best way is to use the same method to select the authorship problem in the case according to its function. The idea of considering an AI and a human editor as co-authors of the work done is not a good idea. This is because humans have no control over all the actions of the AI and the AI operates uncontrolled. This does not fit the definition of 'integrated work'. For example, the Indian Copyright Act, 1957 defines 'joint authored work' as 'a work produced by the collaboration of two or more authors in which the contribution of one author is no different from the contribution of the other author or authors'. Rich notes that: 'Machine learning tends to create very complex models. Even the original programmers of the algorithm have little idea of how and why the model makes the correct predictions' (Rich, 2016). Also, the idea of creating an AI program where an AI user writes a program created by the AI is not good. Internationally, the 1886 Berne Convention did not take into account 'non-human authors' (Ricketson, 1991). The same situation can be considered true in the context of trade-related intellectual property rights (hereinafter referred to as 'TRIPs'), since it also includes the provisions of the Berne Convention. A similar situation can be assumed to apply to the WIPO Copyright Treaty and the 1996 WIPO Application and Phonogram Convention (WIPO Internet Treaty). It can also be said that international copyright law does not prevent a person from being a human author according to national law (Thampapilla, 2019).

Common international agreements set minimum general principles to be followed. States may not undermine them but are also free to maintain better security than that provided for in the agreement. Works produced by AI may also be protected beyond human rights through a sui generis system. Such a system may provide limited protection depending on users' time rights and other factors. One author stated that the duration of the work could be set at 5–10 years. In the copyright system, the new way to protect AI copyrights by providing short-term protection will result in less interference with existing copyright laws, as the former will lose their rights, Sik Cheng Peng says.

The fundamental question that arises here is whether such works created without the consent of the data owner should be protected by copyright. Furthermore, when a person has their consent, what rights do they have over that work under copyright law? Can there be an equal pay system between those who fabricate deep lies and those who are involved? These problems need to be solved as the increasing use of AI will continue to cause more problems in the future. There have also been initiatives at WIPO to solve the problems mentioned above.

AI and Data Protection

Data are a very important element in the field of AI. This is because such programs are based on 'machine learning or Artificial Intelligence methodology or approach that use data for training and validation.' The excess information present in the era of AI, the better, more precise and accurate the results will likely be. Creative tasks can be performed by a machine learning program that learns from the data used to train such programs. The information used may have economic value and may be protected by copyright. An important question that comes up is whether using such data for machine learning purposes without asking for the owner's permission constitutes copyright infringement. If so, how can these rights be enforced? Also, is it possible to create a general exception to Copyright Act regarding the act of AI impetus? Or/should the exemption be limited to works that are 'not used in commercial activities' or 'for research purposes'? Another interesting question that may appears is if a machine-based learning program directly makes a work alike to the real work that contains the material used in machine learning, would that lead to violation of copyright? If this happens, then who will be in the domain of the victim in such a case and upon whom the copyright be applied? On the other hand, should there be 'free data' for changes in AI? It would be useful to refer to the fair use/exchange doctrine when answering the above questions. When the monetary consideration of a copyrighted work is used in machine based learning it is limited to its real owner ascribed to the artificial intelligence that created the work, this situation cannot be considered as fair use or commercialisation. If it does not cause a decrease in the economic value of the work in question, it may be allowed to be used/performed in accordance with the domestic statutory framework of the nations. In general, the monetary consideration of the tool used in the training algorithm is not affected. Therefore, if the work is done using an algorithmic tool that is completely different from the official tools used in machine learning, the final economic value cannot be changed (Robinson, 2020). In the Google Books case example, it can be said that 'the use of authorized works that do not express the purpose of training AI models is equivalent to fair use.' It is interesting to note that Japan has amended its human rights law to include an 'exemption from the use of legitimate works in machine learning.' Additionally, it is noteworthy to mention that the 'selection or classification of information', which is a creation of intellect, may include protection of copyright law in different jurisdictions. Given the emerging role of machine-based learning, legal protection of information is essential to identify the author when creative works and inventions are discovered. Such laws are also necessary to encourage innovation and creativity and ensure fair market competition in society. Legal framework requires a need to take a balanced point of view because excessive protection of data can have a negative impact on the creation of machines that can dominate the creative field in times to come. Moreover, in India, 'computer programs, tables and compilations including computer databases numbered' are protected as 'literary works' under the Copyright Act, 1957, in India.

Conclusion

The role of AI will grow rapidly in all sectors of our daily lives. Laws are needed to control its use. AI is going to play a dominant facet in the field of Intellectual Property Rights (IPR), especially copyright. The problems of authorship and ownership of activities produced by AI in human rights law have led countries to consider and seek a solution that is acceptable to all countries. There is no rule of evidence that will solve this problem, and every law has its own shortcomings. There will be remarkable changes in granting non-human rights to works produced by AI. Integrating AI into the world at large is inappropriate or appropriate notion, as it will demoralise developers and intelligence-based enterprises from investing more in AI. WIPO is working hard to solve these problems. A system of its own would be a good choice, but some articles in the domain of intellectual property laws of different nations are specially designed for AI and its overall applications that could solve this problem Moreover, minimum protection should be given to AI work and creativity produced by human being should be given absolute preference as compared to technological or machine creativity. Therefore, a rational approach is the current and absolute need.

References

Ahuja, V. K. (2020). Contemporary developments in intellectual property rights: A prologue. In V. K. Ahuja & A. Vashishtha (Eds.), *Intellectual property rights: Contemporary development* (pp. 3–18). Thomson Reuters.

Basri, N. (2020, January 13). The question of authorship in computer-generated work. *Penn Law, University of Pennsylvania*. https://www.law.upenn.edu/live/news/9691-the-question-of-authorship-in-computer-generated

Cellan-Jones, R. (2014, December 2). Stephen Hawking warns artificial intelligence could end mankind. *BBC News*. https://www.bbc.com/news/technology-30290540

Chandak, S. (2020). Artificial intelligence and policing: A human rights perspective. *NLUJ Law Review*, *7*(1), 46.

Cheng Peng, S. (2018). Artificial intelligence and copyright: The author's conundrum. In *WIPO-WTO Colloquium papers* (p. 181).

Corrs Chambers Westgarth. (2020, September 21). Artificial intelligence and copyright: Ownership issues in the digital age. *Lexology*. https://www.lexology.com/library/detail.aspx?g=849627a6-c428-4e45-a386-c6e49d98b446

Fitzgerald, N., & Martyn, E. (2020, March 11). An in-depth analysis of copyright and the challenges presented by artificial intelligence. *Ashurst*.

Frankenfield, J. (2020, August 28). Artificial neural network (ANN). *Investopedia*. https://www.investopedia.com/terms/a/artificial-neural-networks-ann.asp

Guadamuz, A. (2017). Artificial intelligence and copyright. *WIPO Magazine*. https://www.wipo.int/wipo_magazine/en/2017/05/article_0003.html

Hristov, K. (2017). Artificial intelligence and the copyright dilemma. *IDEA: Intellectual Property Law Review*, *57*(3), 435–456.

Jackson, P. C. (1985). *Introduction to artificial intelligence*. Dover Publications, Inc.

Klaris, E., & Bedat, A. (2017, November 16). Copyright laws and artificial intelligence. *American Bar Association*. https://www.americanbar.org/news/abanews/publications/youraba/2017/december-2017/copyright-laws-and-artificial-intelligence/

Lauder, E. (2017, October 3). Aiva is the first AI to officially be recognized as a composer. *AI Business*. https://aibusiness.com/document.asp?doc_id=760181

Metz, C. (2020, November 24). Meet GPT-3. It has learned to code (and blog and argue). *The New York Times*. https://www.nytimes.com/2020/11/24/science/artificial-intelligence-ai-gpt3.html

Pearlman, R. (2018). Recognizing artificial intelligence (AI) as authors and inventors under U.S. intellectual property law. *Richmond Journal of Law and Technology*, *24*(2), 4.

Pokhriyal, A., & Gupta, V. (2020). Artificial intelligence generated works under copyright law. *NLUJ Law Review*, *6*(2), 116.

Raina, S. (2020). Artificial intelligence through the prism of intellectual property laws. In V. K. Ahuja & A. Vashishtha (Eds.), *Intellectual property rights: Contemporary developments* (pp. 133–141). Thomson Reuters.

Rana, L., & Joy, M. M. (2019, December 18). India: Artificial intelligence and copyright – The authorship. *Mondaq*. https://www.mondaq.com/india/copyright/876800/artificial-intelligence-and-copyright-the-authorship

Rich, M. (2016). Machine learning, automated suspicion algorithms, and the fourth amendment. *University of Pennsylvania Law Review*, *164*(6), 871–886.

Ricketson, S. (1991). People or machines: The Berne convention and the changing concept of authorship. *Columbia - VLA Journal of Law & the Arts*, *16*(1), 1–24.

Robinson, K. (2020, February 27). Copyrights in the era of AI. *Adobe Blog*. https://blog.adobe.com/en/publish/2020/02/27/copyrights-in-the-era-of-ai.html#gs.opdukw

Samuelson, P. (1986). Allocating ownership rights in computer-generated works. *University of Pittsburgh Law Review*, *47*(4), 1185–1214.

Sánchez Merino, F. (2018). Artificial intelligence and a new cornerstone for authorship. In *WIPO-WTO Colloquium papers* (p. 28).

Sulleyman, A. (2017, December 5). Google AI creates its own 'child' AI that's more advanced than systems built by humans. *Independent UK*. https://www.independent.co.uk/life-style/gadgets-and-tech/news/google-child-ai-bot-nasnet-automl-machine-learning-artificial-intelligence-a8093201.html

Thampapillai, D. (2019). The gatekeeper doctrines: Originality and authorship in Australia in the age of artificial intelligence. In *WIPO-WTO Colloquium papers* (p. 2).

Chapter 19

Enhancing Customer Experience Through AI-Driven Digital Banking: A Case Study of ICICI Bank in Vidarbha

Devendra Kakwani, Kanchan Naidu and Gayathri Band

Shri Ramdeobaba College of Engineering and Management, India

Abstract

Artificial Intelligence (AI) could enhance digital banking user experience: A Research study, with reference to ICICI Bank in Vidarbha region. The report named chatbots, personalised recommendations, fraud detection and predictive analytics as some of the AI-driven technologies that have improved service delivery, facilitated banking processes and broken customer relationships. A case-study approach is used with primary data collected through consumer surveys and interviews of bank officials. It is aiming for understanding AI impact on customer satisfaction, service turn-around time without hassles and loyalty. The findings point towards artificial intelligence benefiting the overall customer service experience through increased transaction safety, personalised services and on-the-spot assistance. Having to continually update technology and concerns over data privacy are also revealed, though. In the end of this research, the authors also provide suggestions for ICICI Bank to further enhance their AI-driven digital banking services and client engagement into the current financial market.

Keywords: Artificial intelligence; digital banking; customer experience; ICICI Bank; Vidarbha; personalised services; fraud detection; service efficiency

Introduction

One of the most important factors driving innovation and competitiveness in the ever-changing banking industry is digital transformation. In this field, artificial

Security Intelligence in the Age of AI, 301–317

doi:10.1108/978-1-83608-156-220251019

intelligence (AI) stands out as a game-changer, completely altering how banks communicate with their clients and provide them with services (Agarwal & Rathore, 2021). Banking has never been easier, more efficient, or more personalised, thanks to AI's capacity to sift through mountains of data, anticipate consumer actions, and automate mundane tasks (Choudhury & Soni, 2021). Here, banks have been able to improve consumer interaction, simplify operations, and stay nimble in an ever-digital environment, thanks to digital banking platforms that are powered by AI-driven technologies like chatbots, virtual assistants, predictive analytics, and fraud detection systems (Deshmukh & Joshi, 2020).

This digital revolution has been piloted by ICICI Bank – one of the largest private sector banks in India – in the Vidarbha region of Maharashtra (Gupta & Sharma, 2020). The bank has simply been investing in a range of AI also with conversational chatbots supporting round-the-clock customer assistance, and an AI-based system that allows securing fraudulent transactions to be better detected in real time (Han & Chen, 2020).With these updates, the bank was able to respond to a diverse range of consumer demands: quicker, more personalised and secure financial services across growing types of touchpoints (Jain & Agarwal, 2021).

This research is aimed to know how customers of Vidarbha region are using ICICI Bank's online banking services that has changed because of Artificial Intelligence (Kaushik et al., 2021). This study focusses on client interactions and satisfaction to highlight some of the compelling benefits of AI-enabled digital banking that includes enhanced service efficiency, personalised products and increased transaction security. This report will address the barriers such as data privacy issues, technical complexity, and client adaption to AI-based services (Kumar & Khatri, 2021).

The lack found in this study is important as it focusses on the Vidarbha region which has witnessed phenomenal growth in the use of digital banking during recent years (Mohammed & Patel, 2021). There is a paucity of research studying the impact of AI on the Indian geography over and above an all-inclusive study limited to just banking that was otherwise accessible before the era of conventional banking (Sinha & Rao, 2020). To fill this gap, this paper attempts to study the AI powered transformational experience of customers while their interactions with ICICI Bank's digital operations in Vidarbha. But AI can serve as a great impetus to revolutionise banking and extensive insights into future prospects and can keep financial services companies ahead of their competitor (Verma & Sharma, 2021).

Below, we will have a look at where the bank has used AI technology-driven tool and how it improved the customers happiness and loyalty, and also some major challenges in delivering the AI capabilities by ICICI Bank's end (American Express, 2023). The findings from the study will provide insight as to how customer service might be improved through the use of AI, delivering a list of recommendations specifically for banks to implement better digital experiences using AI technology (Bhattacharya & Sinha, 2023).

Leader in Developing AI for Digital Banking Services

The likes of ICICI Bank have managed to integrate AI with their self-service and mobile apps (Damilare Oyeniyi, 2024). Example for this would be ICICI Bank going deep into embedding new age technologies including Machine Learning (ML), Natural Language Processing (NLP) and Cognitive Computing turning around customer service operations not only efficient but also becoming more responsive (El-Gohary & Sulaj, 2021).

AI-Powered Customer Support

ICICI Bank: AI Has Stopped 70 Million Calls per Year, iPal Deployed among The World's Top Chatbots iPal has benefitted over 3.1 million customers since its launch in early 2021, processing almost 6 million queries with a stellar accuracy of 90%. The chatbot helps customers in three main areas:

(1) *Frequently Asked Questions:* With FAQs, iPal yields rapid answers to questions often asked, shortening the response time to queries.
(2) *Transactions:* The customer can ask via a simple chat the bot to carry out one of many types of transactions including transfer funds or pay bills.
(3) *Feature Discover:* iPal assists user in navigating the services of bank, it guides users on tasks such as reset ATM PIN and more.

Chatbots and Virtual Assistants

The Power of AI Powered Chatbots and Virtual Assistants in Banking Machines are now changing the way we interact with them by adopting a form that feels like we interact with a human on one hand or they process a request behind their screen for you instead of responding. AI-driven tools have gained importance especially when it comes to personalised customer support, decrease waiting time and engagement time as a response to customers at the other end of chat box (Ghandour, 2021).

24/7 Customer Support

The very first and foremost advantage is preventing over customer support which a chatbot offers 24 hours of support (Goodmeetings.ai, 2024). Traditional customer service gives up after office hours however chatbots can handle this part of work for you, at any time round the clock. It is essential for customers who might need support after-hours or based on different time zones (Jaiwant, 2022). This will allow a customer from any other part of the world to get banking support without thinking about time difference, so that help will only be a chat away.

Handling Common Queries

AI Chatbots – Design-wise it is intended to handle all attributed or required common queries. These chatbots understand and interpret the inquiries of customer in real time using natural language processing (NLP). Take over repetitive and non-time-critical tasks: none critical/manual/intervened operations like:

- *Reset your password:* Customers tend to forget their passwords a lot or need to reset them. Chatbots help walk users through this process without the need to escalate to a human agent.
- *Balance checks:* Customers often need to check their account balance. This kind of information can be instantly provided through chatbots, securely accessing the user account data (McKinsey and Company, 2023).
- *Service status:* Customers can ask if there are any indications of transactions or payments you have recently made. The chatbot sucks up this information and immediately services customers with updates (Pfoertsch & Sulaj, 2023).

Enhancing Customer Engagement

Unlike traditional customer service, which require a lot of financial investment to setup your personal team, AI chatbots are conversational in nature and will engage more and more users. They provide a more customised experience by tailoring greetings and responses using user data (Raconteur, 2024). For instance, a customer logs in so the chatbot can greet him with his name along with what he has interacted before or what they need now. This level of customised service has led to greater satisfaction among customers and further deepens the bond between the bank and its clients (Spoclearn, 2024).

Efficiency and Cost Reduction

For banks, chatbots substantially decrease operational costs by automating routine inquiries and transactions (Uniphore, 2024). For banks, they help scale their customer support while ensuring that the size of their team doesn't shoot up proportionally. It increases bank efficiency, enabling them to concentrate resources like human agents on high-complexity cases that require an EQ or emotional intelligence or nuanced understanding where AI still lags. In addition, they help to decrease response times (Infosys BPM, 2024). They want their questions answered right away without standing in line to speak with a customer service representative. Resolve this quickly as not getting any bank product will help in customer satisfaction but at the same time if everything is resolved quickly that also increases overall productivity within the Bank's other assistance (Bell, 2023).

Data Collection and Insights

Internet Chats bots being AI chatbots have an essential role in data collection and analysis. Every experience shows exactly how customers think and what they like. This data can also be analysed by banks to spot trends and improve their service offerings in order to create a marketing strategy that better caters the actual needs of customers (Ehlen & Aggarwal, 2023). In addition to this, chatbots can monitor what problems are most commonly experienced by users, enabling banks to immediately respond to any shortcomings with better services or adjusting FAQs.

Personalised Financial Insights and Recommendations

Using AI, banks are able to monitor massive quantities of user data such as transaction records, purchasing behaviour and demographic details. This analysis enables the delivery of tailored, actionable financial insights to specific customer requirements (Cisco Systems Inc, 2023). This includes such things as using AI algorithms to predict the spending trend of a customer that can then allow the AI algorithm to make suggestions on budgeting strategies or investment opportunities available for them based on their financial behaviour (TalentSmart, 2023). Banks can continuously streamline and fine-tune recommendations using machine learning models, as they collect more data over a period (McKinsey Global Institute, 2024). This method is dynamic in nature, and helps ensure that the financial advice is current and actionable. Our customers are given personal insights which will help them take control of their financial lives, giving tips for how best to manage their money and alerting about life events which may require a service with Yolt.

Personalised Product Recommendations via Predictive Analytics

One of the main benefits is that the company can use historical data to predict future needs and thereby better engage with customers. Using past behaviours an AI system can predict what products or services may interest a customer next. Recommend products: Suggest relevant products individual to each customer, e.g. IF a customer is an international traveller recommend foreign currency accounts of travel insurance products. In addition, predictive analytics can improve your cross-selling. For instance, when a customer applies for a loan, AI can automatically review his/her profile and recommend related products like insurance or investment opportunities that match the individual's objective. By doing this proactively, the bank not only improved their customer satisfaction but also managed to leverage on cost savings by improving revenue from customers via product uptake.

Detection of the Fraud and Risk Standardisation

AI will provide more tailored insights as well as aiding in detection and prevention of frauds, risk management, etc. While we are seeing an evolution of digital banking, fraudsters are doing the same and using various tactics to exploit these vulnerabilities, and hence banks must use advanced tools to protect their customers. AI-enabled systems give real-time tracking of transactions to monitor if there is any transaction with the potential of fraudulency.

Keep an Eye on the Transactions in Real-Time for Fraud

One of the most essential elements of AI-powered fraud detection systems is real-time monitoring. An example of this is, as transactions are executed the systems can continuously mine for patterns that could be indicative of nefarious activities or processes or an exact replicating a customer order time line. Banks can also react quickly to threats with the power to process huge quantities of data instantly, reinforcing security as a whole. In addition, machine learning models learn and get better as more data is fed into the model. As they are shown more legitimate and fraudulent transactions, respectively, the model becomes better at identifying these two. Continual adjustments to fraud tactics require this level of adaptability.

AI in Credit Risk Evaluation and Loan Underwriting

Artificial intelligence speeds up valuation of consumers' creditworthiness and the determination of risk profiles in credit assessments and the subsequent granting or denial of loan applications. Conventional techniques frequently depend on measure boundaries that are static and do not necessarily capture the financial situation of an individual. AI algorithms, on the other hand, look at a wider array of data from income trends and spending habits to even social media usage in order to conduct a more holistic risk assessment. Artificial intelligence models can automate the underwriting process, making it more efficient and help shave time off of the whole loan approval procedure. While the bank benefits from this efficiency, so too does its customers as loan decisions are made much quicker.

Increased Accessibility and Availability

The introduction of AI in digital banking has made it more accessible to the customers, freeing them from a lot of trouble and time (Kafetsios & Zampetakis, 2008). Now, with the help of AI-powered technologies, banks have made it possible to allow users manage multitude of services through a number of digital channels which has not only simplified the user journey but also allows for C2C services to be done at home or on-the-go. The most important advantage of AI-powered digital banking is 24/7 service offering. Banking hours are no longer an issue, customers can now access their banking needs any time it suits them without having to queue. They can also get on-demand access to accounts, payments, or loan applications 24 hours every day, by means of AI chatbots and virtual assistants. In particular, this 24/7 accessibility is great for customers who have time constraints or not near a listing if they even exist at all. In addition, the

AI is helping banks to improve and the customers experience as it makes their processes faster and reducing the time of customer waiting. By automating primary workloads and deploying ML models helps banks to process transactions more quickly and respond faster to customer inquiries. For example, a high-end chatbot supported by an AI algorithm may handle frequently asked questions quickly, and without the help of a human answering those routine queries speeds time to resolution and improves customer satisfaction. Bank: Digital channel and Any Mobile App/Website for fair Customer Convenience, for instance, they can use log in into their accounts, transfer funds, paying bills and even apply for one of the financial product like so using just there smartphone or a laptop at home without going to location or a physical branch. This way, customers can make their financial using this feature and save time and energy. AI has also enabled banks to provide tailored recommendations, insights based on account-by-account unique transactions data and personal preferences of their customers. The AI algorithms can use consumer data to recommend products, services or even financial advice that suit the needs of a customer. By customising, the provider offers a much better user experience while enhancing their clients to make more sound financial choices. Nevertheless, while AI-driven digital banking has simplified ways customers have been accessing and convenience to their lives but there are many significant avenues to explore also. Although there are other members of the customer base with poor acceptance of these technologies, such as age groups or people with less digital literacy. This would require significant handholding and training from banks for these customers to hopefully adjust, creating that pivot where AI-powered banking services can operate.

In the case of digital banking, banks reduced waiting times and abandoning issues significantly by Neural Networks solving customer inquiry and transactions in a new manner. Applications are now becoming quick with the use AI based products by many banks. AI powered Chatbots and Virtual Assistants is one of the most in demand application domain ever since it began, faster query resolution has been one particular use case. In this manner, these AI tools are designed to handle mundane customer inquiries – such as checking account balances, facilitating the transfer or monies and paying a bill – freeing up a human from having to walk a customer through how they can do those things themselves. These simple day to day tasks can be easily automated by AI Chatbots, who in turn can answer customer inquiries immediately without keeping customers waiting for hours on end in the queue or on hold on the phone. Secondly, AI algorithms can learn from the patterns of customer interactions and identify common problems or pain points. Using this information, banks can get ahead of these problems and provide the customer with a list of solutions even before they ask for it decreasing repeat customer queries reducing time to resolution. Other than using AI chatbots, many banks deployed AI workflow optimisation tools to simplify the internal processes of their organisation. It uses data from customer touchpoints, transaction records and also employee productivity to pinpoint bottlenecks and inefficiencies in the system. If only these two things are maintained well, banks should also be able to cut down the customer processing time and help in quick turnaround time on customer queries. Banks are also using AI to offer more tailored help and support, but instead of traditional conversational engagement from a human being, these solutions can be deployed at scale and in real time. AI can use the customer data to determine best support channel/agent where the particular inquiry should be routed so that the customers are not just being helped but they are supported in context which is addressing to their individualised needs. It reduces the resolute time and thus automatically customer loyalty as well.

Literature Review

Artificial intelligence (AI) has recently emerged as a powerful alley for financial institutions since it can boost operational efficiency, customer experience, and security. Literature Review on Artificial Intelligence in Banks, this is a study that has been provided since the year 2019 where researchers have found and also exposed the ways in which AI are used to meet up with the changing expectations of customers in bank based on this, we will love to know how artificial intelligent-driven digital banking systems has changed the customer experience all over global and regional settings. Below are some key researches on the transformation AI is bringing into digital banking with special focus on customer experience (Cherniss & Goleman, 2001). We will be considering some trends dear to the Indian banking eye, like ICICI Bank in Vidarbha.

Research says the digital transformation of BFSI sector heavily depends on AI, especially when it comes to improving customer experience claim AI-powered tools like chatbots, virtual assistants and personalised recommendation engines are key to creating frictionless and effective customer interactions (Mayer et al., 2008). Which accelerate the speed of delivery and accuracy through automated performed operations in response to real-time requests and provide customised solutions from these technologies. As per Salovey and Mayer (1990), chatbots such as ICICI bank's 'iPal' are considered imperative to provide 24*7 customer support thus reducing human agents dependency and increasing customer satisfaction (Bar-On et al., 2000). Firms like AI discuss how AI might potentially analyse consumer data to deliver personalised services such as investment recommendations, loan offers or financial products. These personalised offerings, by catering to the financial targets of an individual in terms of banking service attached, are believed to contribute significantly to consumer satisfaction and loyalty (Roberts et al., 2001). Impact of AI-personalised interaction on cross-selling potential in digital banking ecosystem and its role as customer retention (Cote & Miners, 2006).

Among the plethora of use cases in the field of Banking AI, augmenting security processes is a paramount application because it gives us an opportunity to explore and coast on how AI has been driving innovation. Fraud detection systems led by AI constantly check the transactions in real time to avoid fraud of any sorts as they have been quite successful in detecting suspicious behaviour. According to Zhang et al., as shown by it is the case that banks might lower their risk exposure with AI-based security systems. They look for rare incidents in vast datasets, and frequently uncover fraud that other systems would miss. One such AI use case in banking was the solution from ICICI Bank where it has reduced the rate of card frauds and the company was able to reduce bank transaction security compliances by implementing artificial intelligence-driven solutions which further improves confidence among customers (Farris & Hultink, 2018).

AI also commonly utilises biometric identification which is used to further secure online banking platforms assisting in the prevention of fraud (Dulebohn & Hoch, 2017). Results from the studies of Mohammed and Patel (2021) prove that AI-enabled face recognition, fingerprint scanning as well as voice recognition much reduces unauthorised access, thus these results further enhance customer trust in the bank's digital channels (Kafetsios & Zampetakis, 2008).

AI Generated Success in Finance has been greatly related with consumer satisfaction, find studies from 2019 through artificial intelligence (AI) does enhance ease and convenience but argue that customer trust in AI technology is critical for the acceptance of digital banking platforms. The fact became paramount when working with sensitive financial data. If clients are befuddled about the access to and the protection of their data, then this opaqueness around AI decision-making could undercut that confidence even more (O'Reilly & Chatman, 1996).

These concerns have led to series research calling for transparent AI systems that provide information on how they arrive at their conclusions. Banks need to openly share about their AI-based policies, and also have to utilise the client data in an ethical fashion if they want their customers to trust in them. This finding is significant especially in the backdrop of ICICI Bank's Vidarbha business as customers concerned about the security and privacy of their personal data in the context of a rise in usage of artificial intelligence (Schutte et al., 1998).

India only has private sector banks, such as ICICI that have been way ahead in embracing AI exhibit from research that there is a creation of jobs and greater operational efficiency resulting from the adoption of AI in Indian banking as it leads to better customer experiences. And this is even more so in the urban mostly semi-urban areas. They also salute the benefits of AI-powered digital banking solutions, but they however pinpoint that barriers such as infrastructure constraints and user-readiness in rural areas could affect their usage (Wong & Law, 2002).

In the analytical part of the paper focussed on ICICI firm which is one of the front-runners in the adoption of Artificial Intelligence. Interestingly the bank is known to have launched quite a few digital banking initiatives through the city like Vidarbha. It would appear that clients are indeed finding the personal finance experience of using robo-advisors and AI-driven personalised financial management assistance quite charming based on the research. This shows that while less digitally mature consumers still need relative amounts of education and training for AI solutions, the opposite holds true on the more advanced marketing (Van Rooy & Viswesvaran, 2004).

And the study points out some of the many benefits – as well as serious challenges – with using AI, confirm that the main tough points to widespread adoption of AI in banking like gaps in technical infrastructure, outdated legal frameworks, trepidations concerning customer data security, etc. Financial institutions around the world grapple with widespread issues when it comes to artificial intelligence (AI), from the cost of building and maintaining AI systems, to uncertainty as to where AI stands in decision processes per regulators.

Gupta and Sharma ICICI Bank – (2020) in ICICI Bank (Han & Chen, 2020), they examine the real-world problem of embedding AI systems in the current banking technology ecosystem. Issues regarding data integration, training employees, and being updated with the evolving regulatory standards in India are few of such hurdles. But these challenges are what they believe are needed to make sure that traditional banks like ICICI can beat the competition in the digital age.

The COVID-19 pandemic has accelerated the migration to digital banking, and artificial intelligence (AI) is essential for avoiding disruptions caused by quarantine and social distancing. Due to the COVID-19 pandemic this year research has shown that banks had relied heavily on digital AI-based solutions for handling inflow of online transactions as well as customer enquiry; ICICI Bank further added near fully digital handling with use of AI enabled chatbots for taking client demand from VIDARBHA region.

According to the literature, artificial intelligence (AI) can transform digital banking by enhancing user experience, security and operational efficiency. Research indicates that ICICI Bank, among others, has significantly improved customer engagement by integrating AI. This technology has enabled them to be more customer-centric, fight fraud and make online processes simpler. In settings such as within Vidarbha, there remains a significant need to further understand digital literacy and preparedness, infrastructural constraints for video-call functionality, consumer trust issues and regulatory frameworks. If further evolved, as the future of banking goes, in India and around the world; AI will have a significant effect.

Objectives of the Study

- To explore the implementation of AI-driven technologies in ICICI Bank's digital banking services.
- To assess the impact of AI on customer satisfaction and engagement.
- To examine the role of AI in enhancing the security and fraud prevention measures of ICICI Bank.

Hypothesis of the Study

H0 (Null Hypothesis): AI-driven digital banking solutions do not have a significant impact on customer satisfaction and engagement in ICICI Bank, Vidarbha.

H1 (Alternate Hypothesis): AI-driven digital banking solutions have a significant positive impact on customer satisfaction and engagement in ICICI Bank, Vidarbha.

Research Methodology

The research methodology for this study is designed to comprehensively examine the impact of AI-driven digital banking on customer experience at ICICI Bank in Vidarbha. A mixed-method approach is employed, incorporating both quantitative and qualitative techniques. The purpose of this quantitative study is to examine the perceptions, satisfaction, and engagement levels of ICICI Bank customers in Vidarbha regarding their digital services that are driven by artificial intelligence. A representative sample of these customers will be surveyed using structured surveys. In addition, qualitative insights will be gathered through semi-structured interviews with bank managers and IT staff to understand the operational challenges and benefits of AI integration. The data will be analysed using statistical tools to identify trends, relationships, and significance levels, while qualitative responses will be thematically analysed to provide deeper insights. Incorporating AI into the bank's operations while maintaining a focus on the customer experience is best accomplished through this method.

Data Analysis and Discussion

Table 19.1 Explanation – The descriptive statistics of 225 customers surveyed provide insights into various characteristics and patterns of bank usage and satisfaction levels. The average age of the customers was 35.6 years, with a median age of 34 years and a mode of 30 years, suggesting a relatively young customer base. The age range extended from 18 to 65 years, with a standard deviation of 8.2 years, indicating moderate variability in the age distribution.

In terms of gender, 60% of the customers were male ($n = 135$), while 40% were female ($n = 90$). The average number of bank usages per month was 8.3, with a standard deviation of 2.5, indicating some variation in customer engagement with the bank, with usage ranging from 1 to 15 times per month.

Customer satisfaction was generally high, with 40% ($n = 90$) of customers reporting being 'Very Satisfied' and 37.7% ($n = 85$) indicating they were 'Satisfied'. A smaller portion of respondents expressed neutrality (13.3%, $n = 30$) or dissatisfaction, with 6.7% ($n = 15$) being 'Dissatisfied' and only 2.2% ($n = 5$) being 'Very Dissatisfied'. These statistics reflect a positive overall perception of the bank's services, with most customers expressing satisfaction.

Hypothesis Testing

Table 19.2 Explanation – The regression analysis results presented in Table 19.2 demonstrate a significant positive impact of AI-driven digital banking solutions on customer satisfaction and engagement at ICICI Bank in Vidarbha.

As formulated, the regression model features two major predictors: AI solutions, X_1, and customer engagement, X_2. The AI solutions coefficient equals 0.75 with a standard error 0.10, a t-value equal to 7.50, and the p-value of 0.000, and therefore, the relationship was a highly significant positive. It means that for each unit of AI-driven digital banking solutions increase, the customer satisfaction also

Table 19.1. Descriptive Statistics.

Variable	Mean	Median	Mode	Standard Deviation	Min	Max	Frequency (*n*)	Percentage (%)
Age (years)	35.6	34	30	8.2	18	65	225	100
Gender								
Male							135	60
Female							90	40
Bank usage (per month)	8.3	8	10	2.5	1	15	225	100
Satisfaction level								
Very satisfied							90	40
Satisfied							85	37.7
Neutral							30	13.3
Dissatisfied							15	6.7
Very dissatisfied							5	2.2

Source: Original work.

Table 19.2. Regression Analysis Results.

Variable	**Coefficients (β)**	**Standard Error**	***t*-Value**	***p*-Value**	**Significance**
Constant (intercept)	2.10	0.45	4.67	0.000	***
AI solutions (X_1)	0.75	0.10	7.50	0.000	***
Engagement (X_2)	0.40	0.08	5.00	0.000	***
R-squared	0.65				
Adjusted *R*-squared	0.64				
F-statistic	45.8			0.000	

Source: Original work.

raises by 0.75 unit, while other factors remain constant. In the case of engaging, these values equal 0.40, 0.08, 5.00, and 0.000, respectively. Accordingly, the results were the same – elevated level of engagement highly significantly increased customer satisfaction by 0.40 units per unit of engaging. The *R*-squared amounted to 0.65, indicating that the combined impacts of AI solutions and engagement explain 65% of customer satisfaction variability. The Adjusted *R*-squared, 0.64, indicates that even after adjusting for the model's predictors, the explanatory power of the model remains high. The *F*-statistics, 45.8, and its *p*-value, 0.000, confirm the strong overall significance of the regression model and suggest that the predictors jointly and significantly explain customer satisfaction.

In aggregate, this conclusively results into a failover and hence validates the alternate hypothesis as per H1: Innovations AI-driven digital banking solutions increase customer satisfaction and engagement. The research results are an important step in proving that AI solutions can add value to the customer experience and thus improve service quality and customer loyalty in digital banking.

Conclusion

The results of the study illustrate how AI led digital banking solutions can contribute significantly towards customer satisfaction and engagement at ICICI Bank in Vidarbha. The regression analysis shows that not only a customer-engaged-innovation solution rather more an AI-based innovation solution is also associated with increased sales performance and profitability. More specifically, an introduction and subsequent deployment of AI technologies ensure a more enjoyable banking experience so that banks can remain competitive on the constantly evolving financial services market. We thus find a significant portion of the variance in customer satisfaction is explained ($R^2 = 0.65$) through these disruptive AI-driven innovations, for those companies late to this revelation – it time to innovate or die! The *p*-values of the effect of AI solutions and degree of engagement on results, are small a statistical evidence of the positive influence of them, making this result deeper… In conclusion, this research therefore proves to be exceedingly instructive for banking establishments with an intent of utilising AI technologies in a bid towards a better customer experience. It highlights the importance and benefits of investments in AI and engagement strategies by underpinning some favourable changes that are possibly imminent in terms of customer satisfaction and loyalty.

References

Agarwal, S., & Rathore, A. (2021). Impact of AI on banking during the COVID-19 pandemic. *Journal of Digital Finance*, *18*(3), 105–118.

American Express. (2023). The link between emotional intelligence and sales performance. https://www.americanexpress.com/

Bar-On, R., & Parker, J. D. A. (2000). The Bar-On model of emotional-social intelligence (ESI). In R. J. Sternberg & L. F. Zhang (Eds.), *Handbook of human intelligence* (pp. 263–277). Cambrigde University Press.

Bell, J. (2023). The overclaiming of emotion AI technology in sales contexts: An academic perspective on its efficacy and limitations. *Journal of Marketing Research, 60*(1), 45–59.

Bhattacharya, S., & Sinha, A. (2023). Customer demand for personalization in banking: Insights from metropolitan Indian cities. *International Journal of Science and Research Archive, 11*(02), 1492–1509.

Cherniss, C., & Goleman, D. (2001). *The emotionally intelligent workplace: How to select for, measure, and improve emotional intelligence in individuals, groups, and organizations.* Wiley.

Choudhury, S., & Soni, M. (2021). AI in banking: A case study of Indian banks. *International Journal of Financial Technology, 7*(2), 67–83.

Cisco Systems Inc. (2023). *The impact of AI on hybrid work environments: Enhancing meeting experiences with emotion recognition technology*. Cisco Systems Inc.

Cote, S., & Miners, C. T. H. (2006). Emotional intelligence, cognitive intelligence, and job performance. *Administrative Science Quarterly, 51*(1), 1–28.

Damilare Oyeniyi, L. (2024). Empathy in AI: Enhancing customer interactions through virtual assistants. *International Journal of Science and Research Archive, 11*(02), 1492–1509.

Deshmukh, R., & Joshi, P. (2020). The rise of AI in Indian banking: A regional analysis. *Journal of Banking Innovation, 22*(4), 231–245.

Dulebohn, J. H., & Hoch, J. E. (2017). Human resource management systems: A review and future research directions. *Journal of Management, 43*(6), 1750–1785.

Ehlen, P., & Aggarwal, G. (2023). Emotion AI and its role in enhancing sales performance: Insights from industry leaders at Uniphore and Sybill. *Sales Management Review, 12*(3), 78–90.

El-Gohary, H., & Sulaj, E. (2021). Neobanks and digital transformations in banking: A global perspective. *Journal of Banking and Finance, 45*(3), 123–135.

Farris, P. W., & Hultink, E. J. (2018). The role of emotional intelligence in the sales process. *Journal of Personal Selling & Sales Management, 38*(2), 175–189.

Ghandour, A. (2021). Challenges and limitations of implementing AI in banking: A systematic literature review. *Journal of Financial Services Marketing, 26*(4), 345–358.

Goodmeetings.ai. (2024). How does emotional intelligence help in closing more deals?. https://goodmeetings.ai/blog/how-does-emotional-intelligence-help-in-closing-more-deals/

Gupta, A., & Sharma, P. (2020). Trust and transparency in AI-based banking. *International Journal of Business and Technology, 15*(1), 88–102.

Han, S., & Chen, X. (2020). AI-driven customer experience in digital banking. *Journal of Service Technology, 33*(5), 101–115.

Infosys BPM. (2024). Fraud detection using AI in banking: Making banking safer with advanced technologies. https://www.infosysbpm.com/blogs/bpm-analytics/fraud-detection-with-ai-in-banking-sector.html

Jain, N., & Agarwal, K. (2021). AI and customer satisfaction in digital banking. *Asian Banking Review, 16*(2), 77–89.

Jaiwant, R. (2022). AI innovations in Industry 5.0: Combining automation with human intelligence for a personalized customer journey. *Journal of Business Research*, *128*, 123–134.

Kafetsios, K., & Zampetakis, L. A. (2008). Emotional intelligence and job satisfaction: Testing the mediatory role of positive and negative affect. *Personality and Individual Differences*, *44*(3), 712–722.

Kaushik, N., Kumar, M., & Tandon, A. (2021). Ethical considerations in AI-driven banking. *Journal of Digital Ethics*, *10*(1), 55–69.

Kumar, V., & Khatri, S. (2021). AI and digital transformation: Case of ICICI Bank. *Indian Journal of Banking and Finance*, *45*(3), 189–203.

Mayer, J. D., Salovey, P., & Caruso, D. R. (2008). Emotional intelligence: New ability or eclectic traits?. *American Psychologist*, *63*(6), 503–517.

McKinsey and Company. (2023). The role of emotional intelligence in sales success: A comprehensive analysis. https://www.mckinsey.com/

McKinsey Global Institute. (2024). *The future of work: How AI is reshaping the workforce landscape*. McKinsey Global Institute.

Mohammed, Y., & Patel, S. (2021). Biometric security in AI-based banking. *Journal of Financial Security*, *17*(2), 112–128.

O'Reilly III, C. A., & Chatman, J. A. (1996). Culture as social control: Corporations, cults and commitment. *Research in Organizational Behavior*, *18*(1), 157–200.

Pfoertsch, W., & Sulaj, E. (2023). The implications of empathy in AI for online banking services worldwide: A study from Albania and Cyprus. *International Journal of Bank Marketing*, *41*(2), 200–215.

Raconteur. (2024). Can emotion AI really boost sales? https://www.raconteur.net/technology/emotion-ai-boost-sales

Roberts, R. D., Zeidner, M., & Matthews, G. (2001). Emotional intelligence: Moving forward in the field and toward a science of emotional intelligence. *Emotion*, *1*(3), 253–258.

Salovey, P., & Mayer, J. D. (1990). Emotional intelligence. *Imagination, Cognition and Personality*, *9*(3), 185–211.

Schutte, N. S., Malouff, J. M., Hall, L. E., Haggerty, D. J., Cooper, J. T., Golden, C. J., & Dornheim, L. (1998). Development and validation of a measure of emotional intelligence. *Personality and Individual Differences*, *25*(2), 167–177.

Sinha, R., & Rao, P. (2020). Fraud detection in digital banking using AI. *Journal of Financial Technology*, *12*(3), 133–147.

Spoclearn. (2024). The power of emotion AI in B2B sales: Personalizing selling strategies with emotional insights. https://www.spoclearn.com/blog/emotion-ai-in-b2b-sales/

TalentSmart. (2023). *Emotional intelligence and its correlation with sales performance: A data-driven analysis*. TalentSmart.

Uniphore. (2024). Why emotion AI is critical to the hybrid sales workforce: Enhancing engagement and productivity. https://www.uniphore.com/blog/why-emotion-ai-is-critical-to-the-hybrid-sales-workforce/

Van Rooy, D. L., & Viswesvaran, C. (2004). Emotional intelligence: A meta-analytic investigation of predictive validity and nomological net. *Journal of Vocational Behavior*, *65*(1), 71–95.

Verma, A., & Sharma, R. (2021). AI in the post-COVID banking landscape. *Journal of Global Finance*, *20*(1), 54–67.

Wong, C. S., & Law, K. S. (2002). The effects of leader and follower emotional intelligence on performance and attitude. *The Leadership Quarterly*, *13*(3), 243–274.

Printed and bound by CPI Group (UK) Ltd, Croydon, CR0 4YY
14/09/2026
14961563-0005